EAGLE'S WINGS

Eagle's Wings

Hajo Herrmann

Translated from German by Peter Hinchliffe OBE

Airlife
England

Copyright © Hajo Herrmann, 1991

First published in 1991 by
Airlife Publishing Ltd.

British Library Cataloguing in Publication Data
Herrmann, Hajo
    Eagle's Wings
    1.   Germany, Luftwaffe — Biographies
    I. Title
    358.41332092
    ISBN 1-85310-161-3

Printed by Butler and Tanner Ltd., Frome.

Airlife Publishing Ltd.

101 Longden Road, Shrewsbury SY3 9EB, England.

Contents

Translator's Notes

I have, as far as seems to me to be reasonable, used the original German designations for ranks and for units. For those unfamiliar with them, I have listed below the nearest equivalent ranks in both the Royal Air Force and the United States Air Force. Any possible slight misunderstandings between ranks and functions (a *Kapitaen*, for example, is not a Captain but a leader of a *Staffel*) should be clarified readily by the context. I believe that to try to anglicise robs works such as this of much of their atmosphere.

The case for keeping to the original designations of units is very strong, in that there were no direct equivalents between those of the *Luftwaffe* and those of the Allied Air Forces. In the explanation that I now give, I am speaking in general terms, and the reader should bear in mind that there were variations to the general rule.

The basic flying unit of the *Luftwaffe* was the *Staffel*, which usually comprised nine aircraft: it was commanded by a junior officer, normally an *Oberleutnant* or a *Hauptmann*. He was the *Kapitaen*, or, to give him his full title, the *Staffelkapitaen*. The number of aircrew in a *Staffel* varied according to the type of aircraft it operated: clearly more flying personnel were needed for a *Staffel* of He 111 bombers than for a *Staffel* of Bf 109 fighters. A *Gruppe*, the next higher unit, originally contained thirty aircraft, made up of three *Staffeln* (I will speak of German plurals below) plus a Staff or Headquarters Flight (*Stabsschwarm*) of three machines. The commanding officer of a *Gruppe* was usually a *Major*, sometimes a *Hauptmann*, and he was the *Kommandeur* or *Gruppenkommandeur*.

Moving yet higher — to the largest flying unit — we come to the *Geschwader*, usually made up of three *Gruppen* — ninety aircraft — plus a *Stabsschwarm* of four, making ninety-four machines in all. It was commanded by an *Oberst*, an *Oberstleutnant* or a *Major*, who was the *Geschwaderkommodore*, or simply *Kommodore*.

Geschwader of all functions — bombers, fighters, dive bombers, reconnaissance aircraft and so on — were incorporated in *Luftflotten* (*Luftflotte* = Air Fleet). Each *Luftflotte* was in practice an independent air force and was deployed geographically. In 1943, for example, *Luftflotte 3* covered the Low Countries and Southern Germany, and *Luftflotte 2* covered Northern Germany.

In overall control of the *Luftwaffe* was the *Reichsluftfahrtministerium* (RLM), or Reich Ministry of Aviation [the Germans tend to string their individual words together to make up longer words — the RLM contains the words *Reich*, *Luft* (Air), *Fahrt* (Travel), and *Ministerium* (Ministry)]. The RLM was responsible for both military and civil flying matters. Its Head, Hermann Goering, had the dual responsibility of Commander-in-Chief of the Air Force *(Oberbefehlshaber der Luftwaffe)* and *Reich* Minister of Aviation *(Reichsminister der Luftfahrt)*.

Other elements of the military aviation organisation in the Third Reich were the *Luftgau* (a 'Gau' being an administrative district) and the *Fliegerkorps*. The geographical area covered by each *Luftflotte* was divided into a number of *Luftgaue*, which were responsible for administration, supply, airfield personnel and some aircraft servicing for the airfields within their area. The *Fliegerkorps* was the parallel organization responsible for all organizational matters.

Unit designations within the *Luftwaffe* were abbreviated: K = *Kampf* (Bomber); J = *Jagd* (Fighter); NJ = *Nachtjagd* (Night Fighter); and so on. To translate *Jagd* as 'Fighter', as I have done above, is inaccurate. Correctly, *Jagd* translates as 'hunting' or 'the hunt', and what we would call a fighter, a *Jaeger*, as a 'hunter' or 'huntsman'. The hunting ethic was very strong in Germany, and Goering was a passionate hunter: *Wilde Sau* fits nicely into this concept. More about *Wilde Sau* below. To revert to the naming of units: KG was a *Kampfgeschwader*, JG a *Jagdgeschwader*, NJG a *Nachtjagdgeschwader*, and so on. Each *Geschwader* had a number, for instance KG 4. The number of the *Gruppe*, in Roman numerals, preceded the *Geschwader* number, so IV./KG 3 was the Fourth *Gruppe* of *Kampfgeschwader* No 3. Individual *Staffeln* had their own numbers, and these, in contrast to those of *Gruppen*, were shown in Arabic numerals. *5./KG 4*, for example, was the 5th *Staffel* of *Kampfgeschwader* No 4. As there were three *Staffeln* to a *Gruppe*, it can readily be seen that the 5th *Staffel* belonged to the 2nd *Gruppe* (*II./KG 4*).

German plurals are not as simple as English ones. For instance, *Staffel — Staffeln, Gruppe — Gruppen, Geschwader — Geschwader, Kapitaen — Kapitaene, Hauptmann — Hauptleute* (believe it or not). I hope that when I use plurals in the original German they will be identifiable readily as such from the text.

Finally, *Wilde Sau*, which I have translated as 'Wild Boar', although I would have preferred to use 'Wild Sow', the literal translation. In German, to 'behave like a wild sow' is to act madly, unheedingly, crazily. The expression has its origins in the behaviour of the female wild pig when her young are threatened, and that fits rather nicely, I think, with the concept of Goering's night-fighter pilots defending their country and their people. But 'Wild Boar' has, by now, become an accepted item of vocabulary in the history of air warfare, and I have bowed to usage.

Approximate Equivalent Ranks

Luftwaffe	Royal Air Force	US Air Force
Flieger	Aircraftman	Private
Obergefreiter	LAC	Corporal
Unteroffizier	Corporal	Staff Sergeant
Feldwebel	Sergeant	Tech Sergeant
Oberfeldwebel	Flight Sergeant	Master Sergeant
Hauptfeldwebel	Warrant Officer	Warrant Officer
Faehnrich	Officer Cadet	Officer Cadet
Leutnant	Pilot Officer	Second Lieutenant
Oberleutnant	Flying Officer	First Lieutenant
Hauptmann	Flight Lieutenant	Captain
Major	Squadron Leader	Major
Oberstleutnant	Wing Commander	Lieutenant Colonel
Oberst	Group Captain	Colonel
Generalmajor	Air Commodore	Brigadier General
Generalleutnant	Air Vice Marshal	Major General
General	Air Marshal	Lieutenant General
Generaloberst	Air Chief Marshal	Four Star General
Generalfeldmarschall	Marshal of the RAF	Five Star General

When a senior German officer was appointed to a Staff job, the letters 'i.G' were added to his rank, 'i.G' being short for *'im Generalstab'* — 'On the General Staff'. So we have, for example, *Oberst i.G.* I have translated such ranks as *Staff Oberst*, etc.

Foreword

Letters, words and sentences did not come easily when I began to write down happenings about forty years after they began. The long lapse of time was primarily a result of inhibitions and a reluctance to commit myself to work over and above my professional responsibilities. I had therefore confined myself to supplying historians, writers, journalists and other interested parties with information, sometimes on tape, sometimes in writing, but more often in the evening hours over wine and a haze of pipe-smoke, drawing on my own experiences and those of my comrades, from notes I had made during the war and from many photographs and films.

For a long time I was satisfied with seeing fragments of the story of my life retailed here and there: but I was always aware that justice was not done to the detail and the dramatic content of some of the events. I was accused of being know-all and morose, and the accusation struck a sore spot, as did an exhortation to do better. Encouragement impelled me to completeness and truth. From then on, words came easily. Tight-lipped indifference permitted me to ignore praise and criticism that had been my lot in the past, or which I might now look forward to. What we once did, saw and heard on good authority was our own. What we didn't do, didn't see, and didn't have on good authority was not ours. That is the way a judge reaches his judgement when he has to pass sentence, to acquit, or sometimes, even, to eulogise. The guide line of the narrative historian, if he wishes to draw valid lessons, must be to immerse himself in the place, time and circumstances of events, in the boundaries of knowledge and experience and in the inner awareness of his subject-matter.

At the Frankfurt Book Fair in 1983 the British author Mailer said that history had to stand on its own feet. That was how I wanted to go about it: to present historical truth and the way my life took me through a dramatic decade of German history in order to portray vividly to younger generations what men went through, the great challenge — life or death. The reader will try to distance himself from horror and sympathy, to question the point of it all and, if possible, to find an answer. A poet puts these words into the mouth of 'Young, dead soldiers': *'Our death is not ours. It is yours, and it will mean whatever you make of it.'*

Hajo Herrmann
Dusseldorf

Chapter One
Peacetime, 1934–1936

After the First World War Great Britain and France, restored by means of German billions, richer by the former German colonies and territories, allow us a defence force of 100,000 men. We are not allowed an Air Force, nor even a defensive fighter force. In the East the Soviet Union, relying on an army millions strong, lays exclusive claim to historical truth — and seeks world revolution and world domination.

I was Number One Gunner. It was a pleasant morning in May 1935, and I was crawling up a hill on my elbows holding my light machine-gun in front of my nose. The hill was in the Doeberitz military exercise area in the Mark Brandenburg, west of Berlin, and I was more in Brandenburg sand than in Brandenburg heather.[1] On my head, my steel helmet swayed ahead of those of my comrades, the other members of my Section: we were all cadets, each with a Field Marshal's baton in his knapsack. Our Course Leader at Potsdam-Eiche had impressed upon us that when the visiting VIPs appeared we were to move like lizards.

The cavalcade emerged over the crest of the hill, came slowly towards us and halted to one side. I was neither deterred nor overawed, and without increasing my speed — being set for endurance — I crawled on, if only because I didn't want the others to be able to call me a rotten crawler afterwards. 'Halt!' shouted one of the gentlemen. I lay as ordered, at combat readiness, heels flat on the sand, looking straight ahead, alert for further orders. 'You with the light machine-gun! Do you find it uncomfortable down there?' I turned on my side and looked up, first catching the angry eyes of the Course Leader, who was a major. Our supervising officer, a lieutenant, who had been wandering around on foot in our attack sector, arrived on the scene at that very moment. With a piercing look straight at me he aligned himself with the major. Let them get on with it, I thought obstinately. I've got nothing to hide.

The fat gentleman in the uniform of a General of Infantry, perched high on his horse, showed that he at least had a human side. 'If this sort of thing doesn't suit you, you can come to me.' And he directed a quick glance at the sky. What does he mean, I thought. Haven't I seen him before? Isn't that Hermann Goering, the Air Minister I've seen on the newsreels? I was quite sure I recognised him. Quite certain. I'd often found difficulty in recognising people I'd met before — ladies with new hats, a change of coiffure, dyed hair. But this was something special. This was a man who sometimes appeared in brown, sometimes in blue-grey, sometimes even in hunting green.

Now that I understood the connection, I also understood the question.[2]

'*Jawohl, Herr General*,' I replied. 'I'd like that very much. I've got my "A" Gliding Certificate. I've flown 31.5 seconds!' I attached some importance to the 1.5 seconds I had done over and above the minimum qualifying time. Goering laughed out loud, and the other gentlemen joined in dutifully, my Course Leader and the Lieutenant following suit after a slight delay. 'Good,' said the General. 'Let's agree on that, then!' Nodding his approval, he let his gaze travel along the row on the ground to the very last man, and murmured something to the Course Leader and his party. Someone began to write something down, and then the order rang out: 'Carry on!'

The thought that eight years later I would sometimes sit for hours at a desk in intimate discussion with this man, at the end of which he would say, 'Let's do that then' was as far from my mind as the Andromeda Nebula is from earth.

For the moment, however — carry on! Carry on, then! 'The Brandenburg heath, the Brandenburg sand, are the Brandenburger's joy', as the song has it. So, crawl on! Crawl on!

From then on the Lieutenant had it in for me. Whenever he saw me his mood changed for the worse. It became even blacker one day when we were practising on the light mortar. According to the manual of drill there were about ten operations that had to be carried out between unlimbering and firing. When our mortar team had carried out the drill successfully about half-a-dozen times, I thought it was time to suggest a simplification, a way in which the procedure could be cut to about half the number of steps. Very calmly, the Lieutenant took a different view. I persisted, however, and said I would like to try out the new ideas right away. As he stiffened up, I offered him my most recently acquired item of Military History: General von Steuben wanted to teach the Americans Frederick the Great's combat drills, but General Washington pointed out to him that his independence fighters were farmers and trappers basically and that things would have to be made much less complicated for them.

A horse snorted behind me. It was our Course Leader's and was called Stern. Since I had been selected to ride at the head of the column, I had been allowed occasionally to have him as my mount, which, compared with the high throw of my own horse, Sirius, was a real delight. Stern had come close up to me and, ignoring the gulf between master and servant, was snuffling at the pocket of my tunic. I always used to bring along something nice and sweet for him. Reining him in, the gentleman astride his steed spoke. 'You've only been doing mortar drill a week, and you imagine that you know better already. But we aren't trappers here. One day you just might get a company of your own. If so, and then only after you've done three winter manoeuvres, you may put in your suggestions in writing. There's no way you are going to be allowed to drive the men crazy with your first bright idea!' He turned his horse, but then he reined him back and added something that clearly came from the heart: 'The men who made these regulations have got four years of war experience behind them. Don't you forget that!'

Having said his piece, he tickled Stern's flanks and left at a trot. I couldn't think that officer cadets, soon to be senior cadets, were men who could be driven crazy by a simple suggestion. However, in all honesty, I was not surprised when my final assessment from the Military Academy included the words

> . . . *tends to find fault and to think that he knows better than anyone else, for which he must be watched and kept on a tight rein.*

I was very depressed. My intentions had always been the best. Perhaps it would be better if I kept my mouth shut more often. In no circumstances did I want to disappoint the Hamburg State Police, who had sent me to the Academy. It was a strict military body, outstandingly commanded after the First World War by 'Red' *Oberst* Danner, and was equipped with heavy machine-guns and light mortars. At the selection board I had come second after Officer Cadet von Boch und Pullach, scion of an old military family, and the thought of failure was abhorrent to me.

Such was my depressed state of mind when, out of the blue, an order came for me to report, together with a large number of my fellow cadets, to the *Charité* in Berlin for an aircrew medical examination. I went on the Magdeburg train from the Wildpark station via Potsdam and Zehlendorf to the *Anhalter Bahnhof*. When the doctor asked me 'How many a day?', I was proud to be able to reply that I was a non-smoker. Then I had to report to a specialist in Savigny-Platz. He strapped me into an electrically-operated chair and made it — and me — spin dizzily round and round. It stopped abruptly. Then I had to be able to read a newspaper. 'Can't you make it out, yet? You must be able to!' I stared at black and white, all intermingled into grey. At last, more by guess than by judgement, I said '*Lokalanzeiger*!' 'Thank you,' said the Doctor, filling in my form without letting me see it. The questions I put to him fell on deaf ears. So I discovered nothing at all about my inherent abilities or inabilities.

I prepared for my finals at the Military Academy, correctly directed the main attack by the reinforced battalion on the left flank in the Tactics Examination and didn't end up on the casualty list. We brand-new Senior Cadets could never quite understand where we got our epaulettes and ceremonial swords from so rapidly. In the Mess we celebrated the battles we had fought in the lecture-room and on the sand-tray beneath the huge painting entitled 'The Germans to the Front', a battle honour brought back by our fathers from the Boxer Rebellion.

In June or July 1935 I took the train to Hamburg again, and went to the barracks of the old, pre-War 76th Infantry Regiment on *Bundesstrasse*, where we were shortly to become Infantry Regiments 46 and 47. By this time I had been promoted to lieutenant. I went proudly with my Heavy Machine-gun Platoon to the Fischbecker Heide training area. At the end of July I went to Kiel for two weeks' leave.

With two auspicious eyes — to misquote Shakespeare — I read the telegram that reached me in Kiel which was to cut short my leave. It called me to the flag that bore the eagle and was endowed and dedicated to the air and the winds. It was short and to the point: 'Posted to the *Luftwaffe*. Report for duty 1 August 1935, Pilots' School Kitzingen.' So, my mother gave me a box of Kiel sprats for my birthday, and, with a medium-sized suitcase and in high spirits, I wound my way by train through the German hills towards the River Main.

It was there that I first discovered which of our gang in Potsdam had passed the medical. There were thirty-four upright lieutenants in all, seven of us from Hamburg, in field-grey riding breeches, grey-green tunics and carrying long sabres — all costly items that would very soon have to be abandoned. We had to buy Air Force-grey uniforms. Life was getting expensive.

My sprats fell victim to the four lieutenants who were in my room, and in return bought me a glass of *Boxbeutel*,[3] which could hardly be expected to please a confirmed North German.

On 2 August we airmen were divided up into six groups and introduced to the

He 72 Kadett for familiarisation flying. On 3 August, as the first of my group, I found myself seated in the little biplane D-EZOP behind my Swabian flying instructor, Ernst Hetzel from Hechingen in Hohenzollern. The aircraft scurried briskly over the runway, rose into the air and swept away, gathering height, over the shining red apples in the meadow gardens, eastwards towards the *Steigerwald*. The air was fresh that August morning. My God! Could anything be more splendid? Carefully, I followed Hetzel through on the throttle and the rudder bar. He flew very low, following the curves of the River Main, and once he zoomed right down on the ground through a row of poplars, so that I felt sure that the branches were going to touch us. Then he asked me, thoroughly disorientated as I was, to point out the way back to the airfield.

On 13 August *Feldwebel* Hetzel got out of the aircraft and said 'Off you go!' It came like lightning out of a clear sky. I had expected that I would be able to enjoy a further period of easy irresponsibility. My comrades were no less impressed by the event. Was it possible that one of us was ready so soon? I opened the throttle, hesitantly. The aircraft moved forward, gathering speed. Lift off! I was airborne. It worked! A curve, then another curve, turn round Iphofen, to the starboard of the Schwanberg, for my approach. Sideslip properly, I thought, or you'll frighten them down there on the ground. I had done all of three minutes solo. I felt fine. I levelled out. My landing was good. The next day it was Karl Huelshoff's turn. Karl later became a long-range night-fighter pilot. He said he'd catch up with me: 'Just wait till we start aerobatics!'

Soon, thirty-four lieutenant-pilots were whizzing about in all directions, under strict orders to fly separately so that we would learn to navigate. Sometimes, however, out of view of the airfields, we would join up together and roam about in gaggles. When you're trying to find your way about there's strength in numbers, because a dozen eyes see more than two do. There was fun in numbers, also, because, now and then, a rapid dogfight developed — provided none of the aeroplanes were carrying that cursed, tell-tale altitude recorder.

The fact that training aircraft were equipped with turn-and-bank indicators was a temptation — a dangerous and illegal one — for us to practise blind flying, which it was forbidden to do before having completed the appropriate part of the training course, and even then it could be practised only if the aircraft was equipped with a radio. When I was about to start my next cross-country flight, I noticed that the turn-and-bank indicator had been removed from my aircraft, D-EZOP. Hetzel said that it had been removed for my own good and my own safety, because the altitude recorder and the weather map had both shown, beyond argument, that I had been flying above the clouds again. I had lied to him, he said, because there had been no gaps in the cloud and, therefore, no visual contact with the ground.

The next cross-country exercise was to Berlin. We reached the Thueringer Wald on time. The clouds had come in more rapidly than had been forecast. The picture was one I was not unused to: a swarm of biplanes buzzing about over the southern slopes like flies on a windscreen. No way through. I bet that no-one will try to go via the Werra Valley, I thought, because even lower clouds were forecast to the west. I saw one aircraft after another climbing upwards to clear the Rennsteig, the old highroad along the crest of the Thueringer Wald. Later, they would all report that the Thueringer Wald was just clear of cloud and that they had overflown it in visual contact with the ground. There would be no possibility of flying back to Kitzingen from Berlin the same way, of course — later, the Thueringer Wald would be closed in. The boys would want to stop overnight in Berlin where the *Zigeunerkeller*[4] beckoned. Am I to be the only one who is coward enough to turn back for Kitzingen? I asked myself.

Soon I was in the clouds, heading north-east towards Berlin. The airspeed indicator and the altimeter were both working. So far, so good. And my flying attitude? I had got my floating pilot's compass, and that was almost as good as the turn-and-bank indicator or an artificial horizon for showing you how your aircraft was sitting in the air. It also showed me what help I could expect from the wind, which was from my port quarter; it told me that if I kept steering left, I could even write myself off! I turned the control column smartly to the right. I was flying at 2000 metres. The breeze blew on my face from the right, so I turned the stick to the left. Ah, there's the sun, but where am I? I looked at the compass, which had settled down by then. I was heading west, and I should have been heading north-east. I supposed that it just could have been possible to fly a course more inaccurately!

If I wanted to get to the Reich capital, I would have to find the hole in the clouds that was on stand-by today! There were dark cloud-valleys embedded in the sea of white clouds, but fields, forests and rivers remained hidden from view. At last, through the wispy veil of a dip in the clouds, I first glimpsed then made out more clearly, angles and lines, traces of man's handiwork, still faint, obscure, moving past below me. I let them rise up towards me, because ahead of me it was getting greener and lighter. I throttled back and let down, humming a snatch of song, over the Elbe, its breakwaters a welcome feast for the hungry eyes of a navigator.

On the Kurfuerstendamm there was a really wonderful feeling of being at home. The breakfast I had with my dear relatives was substantial. When I got back to base, Ernst Hetzel's reprimand was redolent of despair. The altitude recorder, he said, had almost blown a fuse. However, when I had explained my free-style blind-flying to him, my instructor was understanding and mild. The words 'Hopeless . . . . . Lunacy . . . . Won't take any further responsibility for you', fell tonelessly from his lips. But he spared me the worst. That's good, my dear Ernst, because I'm not a performing horse! Remember that! He looked mad when I answered him in his own Swabian dialect.

The turn-and-bank indicator was put back into the aeroplane. To my great surprise, I had made my instructor do something I hadn't set out to make him do.

Aerobatics! Karl Huelshoff still hadn't caught up with me. It was a few days later that he came down from his first attempt, and he was pale and evil-smelling. He hadn't been able to prevent himself from throwing up during the twisting and turning manoeuvres. 'But don't think I won't make it. You think it's funny, don't you?' he said. I replied, 'I'd rather come first than second, for sure. Wouldn't you, Karl?'

Day after day he got airborne and, gradually, he got the better of his stomach and his nerves. He was as stubborn as only someone from the Rhine and Ruhr could be. His victory spurred me on to do something that Trenkle, the flying instructor of another group of six, used to do: a forward loop — not using an inverted-flight carburettor, as he did, but without one. The rush of blood to my head, the feeling of my Adam's apple being forced into my throat — these were unpleasant sensations; but my motto was: 'You started it, so you'll have to finish it.' In contrast, the rolls I did in the short, stocky runabout, the Arado 64, between Iphofen and Schweinfurt and back, were much sweeter. One roll after another, three to the left, three to the right. It must be possible, I thought, to do it — to be as confident to the right as I was to the left. I didn't want to have a side I favoured. The idea of having a weak side annoyed me. I was naturally right-handed, but when I had played football I used to concentrate stubbornly on my left foot, and it was as outside-left that I got into the Holstein-Kiel youth team. When I was doing Voluntary Labour service, in 1932 on the North Sea mud-flats, I handled my spade alternately with my left and my right hand. So, a roll to the right, a steep bank to the right, a turn to the right — all had to be performed as well as the other way round. In mock aerial combat exercises I was pleased to find that my flying to the right was progressing quite well.

As Christmas approached, our B2 training was coming to a close. We had flown the W 33, the W 34, the He 46, the He-45, the Albatros, the L 101 and the L 102. We had to make up our minds where we wanted to go — to fighters, bombers, transport, or reconnaissance aircraft. Hetzel, little dictator that he was, had told me 'You'll be a fighter pilot.' The aerobatics man, Trenkle, who was a member on my passing-out board, agreed with him. Then I saw Udet at a flying display in Bamberg. His aerobatics fired me with enthusiasm!

We were coming to the end of our time at Kitzingen, and our Group Leader, Herr Puetz, who in 1917/18 had flown as an infantry pilot with Ritter von Greim and had experienced hard tack and a lot of hot lead, spoke with a small number of us. He said that being on fighters was all well and good when the sun was shining, but if you were a fighter pilot you were helpless when the weather clamped down. If you set out on a cross-country flight on a weekend in a He 51 biplane (which the operational units were equipped with at that time), or if you took some other similar plane out, it was possible that, because of the weather, you wouldn't get back home on schedule, even supposing you made it to your destination at all. On bombers it was quite different. We would be trained properly in blind flying. We could set off for a weekend whenever we wanted and be back on duty in good time. We could take a suitcase containing our civilian clothes and a bathing kit, a coat and a hat. We would get there punctually and our girlfriends wouldn't have to wait for us or go home disappointed.

In my mind's eye I saw a lady-love, slim, blonde, her hair braided up in a figure of eight behind her head, longingly waiting for me. Just in case one day some sweet creature should be prepared to put up with me, it would indeed be no bad thing to be independent of the weather, able to fly on instruments and experienced on big aircraft. So daydreams, rather than mature deliberation, tilted the balance. Fate in the form of a vain, jovial goblin.

As the first soft flakes of snow were drifting down on Franconia and our course was coming to its end the *Kommandeur* of the Pilots' School surprised us raw pilots with the exciting announcement that two of us could fly to the Opera Ball in Berlin. I was the lucky bastard who climbed into a W 34, piloted by the School Adjutant. Karl Huelshoff, ever conscientious, remained behind, so Georg Reiss flew with me. It was exciting to call for a taxi and to tell the driver to take us (dressed for the first time in the newly introduced Luftwaffe Mess uniform of a big tail-coat and trousers with stripes on) the 200 metres from the Brandenburg Gate to the Opera House on Unter den Linden. The invitation cards had stated: 'Arrive by carriage'. At Pariser Platz the taxi driver eyed us suspiciously — in the unfamiliar outfit we looked confusingly like hotel porters. 'To the Opera? It's only a few steps! What do the likes of you want there?' It's impossible to do justice to his Berlin accent in an English translation.

Our Adjutant was there already, but he kept his distance. Quite clearly, he didn't want to be seen with us. He was with friends from his training course, each and every one of them wearing a flying badge, to our considerable envy. Then Clemens Krauss raised his baton for the overture to *Die Fledermaus* and, to the rapture of even the most senior dignitaries, the Opera Ballet in white surged over the stage, which had been combined with the stalls area to make a large dancing surface.

To the left, seated in one of the boxes, was Goering, the patron of the performance, with Emmy, whose beauty and charm seemed to overcome everyone. With him were the French Ambassador, Monsieur François-Poncet, and the Polish Ambassador, Herr Lipski, together with all the accredited military attachés from distant lands, resplendent in their uniforms. I looked particularly closely at the French Ambassador. France interested me. I had a high opinion of the strategic arts of the French, having read Clausewitz's commentary on Napoleon and other army commanders. I knew, by heart, Napoleon's speech to his soldiers when he was in sight of the Egyptian pyramids. My respect was mixed with curiosity. Since Military Academy I had been determined to take the military interpreter's examination in French. My French teacher had thought that an impossibility.

The dance was opened up to the guests and immediately Georg Reiss was rotating in a waltz with a beautiful girl, the Princess Wied (afterwards, he actually exchanged letters with her). I plucked up my courage and approached a pretty little ballet dancer, who seemed somewhat surprised by me and my formal bow, but who then floated happily away with me — or I with her! After the dance I was looking around for Reiss when an elderly Luftwaffe officer, in a Mess uniform on which were two rows of war medals, took me by the arm. I had, he said, just been dancing with a *Ballet-Ratte* which was not done as long as there were invited ladies still seated, waiting to be asked to dance. After midnight, he added benevolently, it would be a different matter. 'Ballet-rat' didn't sound nice, I thought; and she was very sweet, my little rat with a Berlin accent!

Having, in this way, been indoctrinated into the dictates of protocol, I conformed. There she sat, the famous Maria Hoppe, whose face I had seen many times in the cinema — sat and remained seated, even as far as the tenth and twentieth bar, and still none of the gentlemen at her table, among them Viktor de Kowa, asked her to dance. I conducted myself as I had been taught; rigidly to attention but inclined slightly from the waist. From the gentlemen I received astonished looks, from her perhaps a hint of embarrassment, but she rose from her seat. How slim she was; and how she could dance! Whatever I said she found amusing. She laughed from time to time, and looked at me so intimately that I began to hope that I might dare to suggest that we could meet again later. Then it occurred to me that, with an actress, there were certain, special factors one should take into account when considering the genuineness of her feelings and her way of expressing them. So I blurted out the question: How was it that joy and sorrow came across so convincingly in all her films? Surely they could only be, and be seen to be, genuine once — particularly love. She laughed heartily and said that that was the compliment of the evening.

I had made a great hit, I thought. I would have to write to my parents and tell them about it. It is a great comfort to remain in blissful ignorance when friendly, well-mannered people are just being nice to you. The evening at the ball passed by, as if on wings. As we had, wisely, not taken a table or had to order wine it was an inexpensive experience, in the truest sense of the word.

From that hall of luxury and splendour we returned to the Main, where, after our final flight, we had to pack our kit. My next stop was to be a *C-Schule* — a multi-engined training school. So, we band of brothers whose morale was high, who, of necessity, had to eat cheaply (but were not entirely inexperienced in the subject of wine nevertheless) went our separate ways. Our number had been reduced to thirty-three lieutenants; we had lost a fine comrade, *Leutnant* Luebke in a mock dogfight near Herzogenaurach. We had taken turns to stand guard over his coffin, and for the first time we had felt the hand of Fate as if it had been on our own shoulders.

There was a large number of big Junkers aircraft on Gablingen airfield, just north of Augsburg, ready for those of us who were to train to fly bombers. Huelshoff was there. Despite the cold and the snow, we did our circuits and bumps. We waited, our hands buried deep in fur muffs, for our turn to take off — not like *Leutnant* Horten[5], who had met up here with those few of us who had been at Kitzingen, and who used to spend all his time working a slide-rule, his fingers blue with cold. Soon afterwards, he took his first flying-wing aircraft into the air.

After a few weeks we were posted to Ludwigslust in Mecklenburg to complete our multi-engined training at the flying school there. We still hadn't completed our course when, to our great surprise, we were told that we were to be posted to operational units. *Major* Fruhner, the *Kommandant* (to whom somebody, either malicious or humorous, had given a nickname that can't be repeated here), asked us to say where we would like to be posted. I decided that it would be strategically sound to select a central point in the Reich from which, in accordance with Clausewitz's principles, I could approach the most attractive spots on the periphery by means of forays from the centre. So, I selected the airfield at Merseburg.

Major Fruhner said that my calculations were fundamentally sound, but that there was an unpleasant smell at Merseburg that came from the nearby Leuna Chemical Works. However, he added that close to my chosen centrepoint he could see the beautiful old town of Nordhausen in the Harz Mountains, the *Goldene Aue*, Kyffhaeuser, and Barbarossa.[6] There, he could hear the call of the deer in the Harz Mountains and the bickering of the witches on the *Brocken*.[7] I saw all that and smelt the pine forests. For the next few years, Nordhausen provided most of my food. Fruhner spared my sensitive nose from the chemicals and placed me in the green heart of Germany.

Once more, the wheels of the *Reichsbahn* carried me to a new domain, through Halle on the River Saale, where Karl Huelshoff left me and went off towards Erfurt-Bindersleben. We were both posted to the same *Geschwader* which was later to be christened *Kampfgeschwader 'General Wever'* in honour of the Chief of Staff of that name who was killed in a flying accident. Via Eisleben and Sangerhausen, I rode into the *Goldene Aue*, through to Nordhausen, near to which the local Schnapps, *'Nordhauser Korn'*, and the world-famous chewing tobacco *'Hanewacker'*, were both made.

The airfield was largely bare and empty; but on closer inspection it promised to become habitable within a few months. Initially, therefore, we were billeted privately in Nordhausen. I was told to report to the Binder family who lived at 1a Toepferstrasse, a crooked alley, close to the *Kornmarkt* in the centre of which, quite appropriately, a statue of Martin Luther stood among mediaeval half-timbered and early industrial stuccoed buildings, the venerable *Rathaus* and the Hotel *Roemischer Kaiser*. The only thing seemingly out of period and progressive was the tram, which squeaked its way, at frequent intervals, from the Market Place round into the main street.

I hope it's not in the oppressive narrowness of the alley, I thought, as I looked for No 1a in the stone-cobbled, gently rising, pavementless ravine of houses. Thankfully, my quarters turned out to be a very fortunate — and above all nourishing — piece of luck. The Binder family ran a delicatessen shop around the corner, in which could be found everything that luxury shops in the big towns could offer. For breakfast and supper I only had to go into the shop and point with my finger and, a short time later, I would be sitting at the table, feasting on my selection in a most civilised manner. In addition, my hosts expressly gave me permission to bring to supper one or two needy comrades whose meagre existences I had been at pains to mention.

Master watchmaker Gentzel, who lived next door and who had fought in the trenches until 1918 as a Senior NCO, attributed this agreeable atmosphere of friendliness towards servicemen to the bad conscience of the inhabitants of Nordhausen. In the 1920s they had refused to receive the *Reichspraesident, Generalfeldmarschall* von Hindenburg, within their walls, on the occasion (if I remember it correctly) of the 1000th Anniversary of the Imperial Free Town. Now they wanted to make amends — after all, having a garrison was good for business. Whatever the reason, I enjoyed good food and drink, with the sole exception of the whisky: it was an indigenous German product that saved foreign exchange but tasted awful.

On the airfield, fat sheep grazed between our huts, heavy lorries smeared the concrete roads with mud and clay, and the flying field itself, with its sparsely established grass, was in need of care and maintenance. Out of the blue, the order came to load our Ju 52s with practice bombs — load; unload. Load; unload.

A grave situation loomed. Military sovereignty had been re-established over the demilitarised zone in the West. *Wehrmacht* units had been ordered to go there. My *Staffelkapitaen, Major Graf* Luckner, a veteran of the First World War, didn't let it affect him unduly; he issued his orders in a calm, matter-of-fact way. I hoped that he didn't know that I hadn't got my multi-engined certificate, the *C-Schein*, and was not qualified, therefore, to fly a Ju 52 solo; to say nothing of my lack of a blind-flying licence, the *B-Schein*. I wanted to be in on the act when things started in earnest.

What would have happened if the French had marched into Germany? Later, in 1938, *General* von Kuehlenthal, our Military Attaché in Paris, told me that the French had judged that they could be in Mainz within seven days, and that, in his opinion, they would have done just that if their Government had given them the go-ahead. But they didn't, and we were able to stop loading and unloading practice bombs and being on stand-by. Instead, we set about tending the turf, tucking into the Binders' delicacies and, when on duty, swallowing more and more theory. The situation was awful, because there was nothing at all sensible to do.

Major Graf Luckner, the *Kapitaen* of the 8th *Staffel*, could find nothing better for the officers to do than to practise ceremonial drills with our *Luftwaffe* swords, in the attic of a barrack hut. There was, it is true, a lot of difference between the sword and the dagger we were used to, but the ritual did not inspire us as much as did the life of the sea-devil, the cousin of our chief.[8] Nevertheless, we had to prepare and practise for the ceremonial entry into Nordhausen.

My posting to Berlin-Templehof for three months of intensive training in blind flying and cross-country work swept into this monotony like a breath of fresh air. Karl Huelshoff, carried by the same wind, came too, threatening darkly that this time he really would catch up with me. In Nuernbergerstrasse, not far from the U-Bahn station of the same name, we rented a double room in the home of an emigré retired Colonel of the Tsarist Army. Karl pinned the photo of an Upper Sixth-former, his sweetheart from Oberhausen, on the wall. I, in popular opinion (which was shared by Karl), a non-starter in the matter of population policy, still couldn't look forward to being able to follow his example.

We travelled by U-Bahn to Tempelhof. There, we were pitchforked into flying night after night to Hamburg, Cologne, Stuttgart, Munich, Oberwiesenfeld, Nuremberg, Leipzig, Danzig and Koenigsberg in East Prussia. We were put through the mill in the most inadequate airfield lighting conditions, staring at our instruments so that we would, as the *Kapitaen* said, be able to operate in a real emergency. We looked neat and slim in our blue, double-breasted suits, which would not attract the attention of the Polish immigration controls in Danzig. (I seem to recall that my confirmation suit saw daylight again.)

The operation that we were part of at Tempelhof, where it was run from one of the many hangars, was code-named *RB-Strecke* — the *Reichsbahn*, or State Railways, Route — and was under the command of *Hauptmann* Pohle, who was taken prisoner shortly after the outbreak of war in the course of an attack on the Firth of Forth. He set up a flight operation of extreme accuracy and reliability, an organisation comparable with the *Reichsbahn* or the *Reichspost*, a treadmill for the students whom he had the job of training and bringing up to scratch. By night, Rudi Kiel, who also came from *Geschwader 'General Wever'*, Huelshoff and I took it in turns to sit at the controls, monitored by *Flugkapitaen* Boehner, formerly a gallant NCO-pilot in the First World War, who had found his way into Lufthansa and later into the *RB-Strecke*. Whoever wasn't at the controls turned the D/F loop, did navigational calculations, plotted, tried to make out the lights of some small town through the window — despite it being frowned upon — or got the fat radio-operator, Suppa, to get extra bearings for him.

Even that wasn't sufficient. Whenever we landed at Koenigsberg-Devau we took off again after a short rest and flew for practice, behind the blind-flying curtain, at low level and no matter how adverse the weather conditions, over the East Prussian lakes and forests, returning to Berlin after sunset across the endless, dark area of Pomerania, where scarcely a single light was to be seen. It was hard work, both physically and mentally — no less so, indeed, than crawling in battle order through sand and heather. We slept like the dead.

From April to June there were no cancellations because of the weather. In QBI (bad weather conditions) we landed using the ZZ blind approach procedure, and at some airfields, particularly Berlin, by the VHF-Lorenz system. For us it was a tense, exciting experience, and also an intoxicating one, to fly in over Neukoelln on the beam, losing height, gradually becoming aware of the lights of the great city emerging through the cloud haze around us. Brighter. Brighter. Throttle back at 50 metres altitude, when the main approach indicator shimmered green and bleeped — then we were out of the flickering light. Ahead of us were runway markers, perimeter lights, red obstacle lights; chimneys and church towers to the right and the left — close to us. Above us, even. And then the runway. A wonderful feeling after hours in the clag, or in the *Washkueche* — the wash-house, as we used to say. Slowly, we became real fliers.

After four to six weeks, *Oberleutnant* Giseke took over as our instructor. On the one hand he doled out yet more theory papers and gave us mathematical problems to solve while we were flying the aircraft, but on the other hand he rewarded us for good blind flying by taking us out after work to the Savarin Bar on the Budapesterstrasse, where he sat down at the piano and, as he put it, demonstrated to us the decline of culture from Mozart to Peter Igelhoff in a *pot pourri* of time and music. We immortalised ourselves on the lampshade at the Savarin; it is still to be seen today in a popular nightspot in Bad Godesberg, somewhat yellowed and overwritten by two subsequent generations.

It was during the day when I went solo on the huge aircraft, the Ju 52. I was due to take off between 0900 and 1000 hrs. I walked proudly out to the gleaming silver machine, a prime specimen of a Ju 52 (registration D-ADYL). I observed, with some surprise, the bound parcels of newspapers, the *Berliner Zeitung*, that were being put on board from a van. Fat Suppa was on board already. He wished me a cheery '*Guten Morgen*!', as if there was nothing special about the day. As I took my seat and looked back at him through the door, as I thought about his children, as the Flight Mechanic turned the trimmer-wheel, I suddenly realised what was meant by the serious side of life.

I taxied out to take off towards the west. Ahead of me, in the haze, I saw the Schoeneberg gasometer. The sky was completely covered, a sheet of stratus extending from 100 to 500 metres. Ideal conditions for a beginner! I opened the throttle, gathered speed and took off. The engineer wound the flaps in slowly. I throttled back, gently, and was in cloud.

Then — a series of thumps. Vertical currents hammered on the left wing, then on the right; then from above, then from below. In spite of the damping liquid the compass ball swung from corner to corner, the artificial horizon see-sawed and the turn-and-bank indicator shook like a lamb's tail from one stop to the other. That's the sun from above bringing the soup to the boil. I worked both the control column and the rudder bar for my, for our, very life. I thought: if only he were sitting there on my right, my old *Kapitaen*, relaxed, smiling; or the dapper Giseke, his hands adjusting the knot of his tie. But there was no-one there, and I felt very much alone. I won't make it, I thought. I just can't believe my instruments any more. I feel certain I'm going to crash. No! You mustn't think that! Push your thoughts to one side, like you've learned to. Do it mechanically — ball to the left, correct to the right; altimeter drops, pull back! It's agony to have to do what you've been taught: it goes against the grain. It's bloody hard to overcome your instincts. If only I could be out of this clag, up through it into the blue sky and the sun.

This situation persisted a little longer, then the nightmare was over. There was a strange, wonderful calm inside me. Everything flows from the unknown. I settled the compass ball, levelled the horizon, and corrected the turn-and-bank indicator. I did all that without losing sight of both the rate of climb dial and the airspeed indicator. What on earth was the matter with me? I didn't know. I altered course calmly from west to southwest, in the direction of Schkeuditz, the airport for Halle and Leipzig, where the first part of the cargo was to be off-loaded. I climbed higher. My eye caught the engineer's face. Was it possible that he didn't notice anything of the chaos that had taken possession of me?

I was in no hurry to get to altitude. I climbed gently, enjoying my safety, whether hard-earned or God-given. As I had been taught, I approached Schkeuditz directly on the VHF beam. I landed and off-loaded the cargo. I took off for Dresden, then flew on to Breslau and back to Berlin, empty.

Later, at Wesendorf on the Lueneburger Heide, I passed my blind-flying instructor's examination. When I did, I swore that I would indoctrinate each and every one of my students in every trick, difficulty and fear that accompanied this first major, mortal crisis, the mental loose connections that went with it, so that they would be prepared for the feeling you have when you realise that you are on your own and there is no-one else to take over and save you. Whenever it happened, I would leave the dual controls and go into the rear of the fuselage and pretend to doze. The mental burden of individual responsibility in human life is not a problem that is confined to flying, but it is one that occurs frequently in aviation, and when it does so, it is in a drastic form. That primitive fear of standing alone is part and parcel of it. In many individuals a calm current flows through their nerve fibres, isolated from external currents by a thick skin, but I didn't have that thick skin. I was inadequately prepared for myself. I was not going to let that happen to my students. I increased my demands upon them to the point at which they had only one wish: to be able to get away from this awful man and to fly alone.

After a three-month neck-and-neck race with Karl Huelshoff in the air and on the U-Bahn between Tempelhof and Nuernberger Platz we returned to our *Geschwader*, and I to the fleshpots of the Binders' *Delikatessen*, also. Gradually, the Officers' Hostels 'Scharnhorst' and 'Gneisenau' were made habitable, and I had to adjust to my lieutenant's pay of 200 Reichsmark, from which approximately 100 Reichsmark went on food and paying off the cost of my uniform. Despite having flown actively for about eleven months, I still hadn't completed my training, so I was not drawing my flying pay supplement.

To my disappointment, the flying time on our makeshift bomber, the Ju 52, was very restricted. Swearing didn't help. I found consolation and pleasure in the company of my new comrades in the *Staffel*. It was a splendid summer and the countryside around was rich in beauty. Sometimes there was a small biplane to be had to satisfy a pilot's cravings.

In July I flew the Ju 52 for the first time in *Staffel* and *Gruppe* formations. We were doing a diversion exercise. The last *Staffel* to take off was ours, the 9th, led by *Major* Dr. Wolff, with me as one of the two last wing-men. Our destination was the wartime operational airfield at Wenigenlupnitz, a small village near to Eisenach. The airfield was only partially equipped and would have been very difficult to recognise from the air, had a landing cross not been set out. The landing manoeuvre the lead aircraft performed resulted in a breach of regulations on my part that proved to be my undoing, but which, at the same time, led me on to a new, unforeseen road.

After our Commanding Officer, *Major* Maass, who was flying as an observer in the lead aircraft, had overflown the airfield he continued on, going further and further away. With frustration, I watched him travel a long distance towards Gotha, and making no move to turn in on his approach. How could that be a wartime landing manoeuvre when everything then would have depended on getting aircraft down quickly and in rapid succession, possibly in an emergency and with the last drop of fuel? You're not going to be part of such a nonsense, I told myself when I had the landing-cross on my beam. I lowered my flaps, throttled back, did a sideslip diving turn, touched down, taxied and switched off at the spot to which a mechanic waved me. I was already standing by my machine when the *Kommandeur*, followed by a loose gaggle of aeroplanes, appeared in the distance and slowly crept towards the airfield. Proudly aware that I had in no way delayed the landing of the *Gruppe*, but that I had in fact shortened it (because there had been no possible need for me to prolong matters still further) I waited for the stragglers, enjoying every moment as further confirmation that I had combined obedience with good thinking.

The aircraft touched down slowly in dribs and drabs, went to their dispersal points, switched off, and, the job being finished, silence took over. Time passed. I looked around, looked up at the nearby Wartburg.[9] Then *Oberleutnant* Diekoetter, also a flying instructor at Nordhausen, came chugging up on a motorcycle and told me I was to report to the *Kommandeur*; who was, he said, probably going to bawl me out. It was with some apprehension that I set out. I had perhaps acted a little high-handedly, but I'd be able to explain myself easily enough. I went to the farmhouse at the edge of the airfield that was fitted out as a workshop and store. Beneath a fine old tree near the house I saw a table with my *Kommandeur* sitting at one of the longer sides and my *Staffelkapitaen* at one of the shorter ones. I was requested to be seated at the side of the table.

The *Kommandeur* began by saying that I had recently incurred his displeasure by doing a racing take-off in a *Stieglitz*[10] at Nordhausen. I didn't reply, even though I knew better. (There was a strong wind blowing that day, which could have given the impression of a steep pull-up on take-off. The Air Traffic Controller had seen it and, as I was a young pilot, he had reported me for it.) In a measured tone the *Kommandeur* continued by saying that my indiscipline today unfortunately compelled him to take action. He paused, and the pause seemed, to me, to be endless. He wrinkled his forehead in a frown and then opened a file. He took out a sheet of paper, wider than it was long, on which I could see a few lines of writing. He took it in both hands, looked at me and announced that what I was about to hear, and whatever I myself might wish to say in reply, were to be kept secret under pain of the provisions of the military legal code. My God! What are they going to do to me? I felt slightly weak at the knees.

'Sign that!'

I read the paper, and signed it. The *Kommandeur* put the paper back in his briefcase, then he said, 'General Franco has approached the Government of the Reich and has asked for assistance.' I don't understand, I thought. Who is General Franco? After a short but clear summary of the situation in Spain the *Kommandeur* asked, 'Do you want to go, or don't you?' It sounded very much a threat of punishment for the 'flying offence' I had just committed. This Spain must be a rotten business; they want to get rid of you, I thought. My fears became even darker when the CO added that if I went there I would have to be discharged from the *Luftwaffe*.

Help! How did I get into this situation, and how am I to get out of it?

Tentatively, I mentioned that I ought to take my blind-flying instructor's exam first. I said I'd rather go on the course at Wesendorf. *Major* Dr. Wolff cut in and said that I could always go there later. The affair in Spain would last six weeks at the most; leaving the *Luftwaffe* was simply a matter of form, and I would be able to carry on in my *Staffel* afterwards, as if nothing had happened — but I would have to keep the whole matter strictly secret, of course. Anyone would jump at the chance of joining such a command. I was more ready to believe Wolff, my *Staffelkapitaen*, but I hummed and hawed a little longer, and then, without really thinking the thing through, I said, *'Jawohl!'*.

'*Na endlich,*' sighed my *Kommandeur* — 'At last!'

I was allowed to choose a crew for the venture. I chose *Feldwebel* Hillebrand (Radio Operator), *Unteroffizier* Eibisch (Flight Engineer) and *Unteroffizier* Wutkowski (Leading Mechanic). We would not have an observer. All I would have to do would be to fly Franco troops across the Straits of Gibraltar from Morocco to Spain.

The CO then wrote out a note, and I tried as hard as I could to read it. When he had completed it, he leaned back, raised the note and read out from it that *Leutnant* Hajo Herrmann was punished for a breach of flying discipline by loss of flying pay to the value of 50 *Reichsmark*. Although my flying supplement, the first of my military career, was already spoken for in my budget, the decision pleased me. Of course, I didn't show it; instead, I tried to simulate a modest degree of remorse because, by now, I could see that Spain was not going to be at all like the hell of Cayenne, where the French roasted their military sinners, but, if not exactly heaven, at least it was going to be an honourable enterprise. I had no complaints at all against this on-the-spot punishment, despite the fact that the *Kommandeur* had broken the rule, which was drummed constantly into us, that we should sleep on decisions before taking action.

Thank God! At least that was over and done with.

There was some urgency in the matter. I had to collect my flying suit and my kit from the aircraft and go back to Nordhausen with my CO by car. I looked, once more, at the surroundings I had hardly had time to get to know, gazed up at the Wartburg and the darkening sky, where only the gracious evening star[11] was lacking. Yet twilight covered the land[12] as we drove away, because behind me I could feel the puzzled gazes of my comrades. They had put up with me for many long months. My crew, confused and still not knowing just what was going on, followed us in a second car.

The next morning we all had to report to the *Kommandeur*, who briefed us again and collected the remaining written declarations of secrecy. My crew, who had no qualms of conscience, beamed with joy. In his best General-Staff manner, the *Kommandeur* explained all the details to us. As part of our cover in Spain, where there were spies all over the place, we would wear local-style clothes, snow-white trousers and shirts, and a peaked cap of the same colour, because it was essential that Germany's intervention should not become public. (*Major* Maass was a very serious man, but I cannot help thinking that even he would have laughed if he could have seen us when we appeared for the first time in front of the Hotel Christina in Seville, the crowd jubilantly welcoming us with cries of 'Viva Alemana' — the Spanish were all clad in black!)

It fell to me to bring up the embarrassing question as to what the arrangements were for money to live on, because we had been sacked from the *Luftwaffe*, hadn't we? The *Kommandeur* reassured us that we would continue to receive our pay; and then, prefacing his remarks with 'I'd almost forgotten', he added that there would be an additional 800 — eight hundred! — *Reichsmark* a month. A pilot would draw a little more. There was a show of general elation (as far as that was still possible) and it was Wutkowski, a Berliner, who expressed it in the vernacular, which caused the *Kommandeur* to pull a face.

That very same day we went by train to Berlin, clad as Central Europeans, to the *Geschwader Richthofen* at Doeberitz, where the Adjutant, *Oberleutnant* von Rettberg, booked us in and told us that we were members of the *Reisegesellschaft Union* (the Union Tour Group) and would be embarking by ship from Hamburg.

The other members of the 'tour group' inspired confidence. There were about ten transport crews, all trained on bombers, the same number of fighter crews and some ground personnel. From my *Geschwader* in Gotha there were *Graf* Hoyos, *Oberleutnant* von Moreau and *Leutnant* Oskar Schmidt, all observers. Among the fighter men were *Oberleutnant* Eberhard, Trautloft, Struempell, Henrici, von Houwald, Hefter, Knueppel and others. The leader of the group was *Major* von Scheele who was an old Gran Chaco campaigner and settler out there in the Southern Hemisphere and an expert in Spanish; he was an obvious choice for service in Iberia. Like myself, he came from the Nordhausen *Gruppe*, where, re-employed on the Staff, he had tried his damnedest to conform to the rigid bureaucracy of our *Kommandeur*. All too frequently, when asked about written orders that he should have issued, he was forced to reply 'All orders were given orally, Herr Maass', raising his hand (more a fist than an open hand) to his forage cap while bringing his feet awkwardly together. He made a point of not addressing Maass, his equal in rank, as '*Herr Major*' in the way that the Majors who were *Staffelkapitaene* did. The *Kommandeur* put up with this, but nevertheless disregard of regulations at the office desk and on the Staff was as hard for him to stomach as the peccadillos of pilots in the air.

Before von Scheele and I met at Doeberitz we knew nothing of each other. The necessity for complete secrecy had meant that each of us had gone his own way. Now, when we discovered each other in the Union Tour Group, one *persona non grata* found joy in the other, because nothing binds people together as much as common membership of the Unholy Band. We confirmed what we had suspected — that we had been got out of the way; but there was a consolation — 1000 *Reichsmark*!

Notes

1 'More in Brandenburg sand than in Brandenburg heather' a reference to the traditional Brandenburg song 'Märkische Heide, märkische Sand, sind des Märkers Freude, sind mein Heimatland' — 'The Brandenburg heath, the Brandenburg sand are the Brandenburger's joy, are my homeland'. The soil of the Mark Brandenburg is sandy and agriculturally poor.

2 '. . . I also understand the question'. It was not until March 1935 that the existence of the *Luftwaffe* as an independent element of the *Reichswehr* (Armed Forces) was acknowledged, and Hermann Goering appointed Commander-in-Chief.

3 Boxbeutel: a very dry, white wine from the Franconia region.

4 Zigeunerkeller: a popular Hungarian nightspot on the Kurfuerstendamm in Berlin.

5 Walter Horten. He and his elder brother, Reimar, conceived the idea of flying-wing aircraft, later developed by the Gotha Company.

6 'Golden Aue', Kyffhaeuser, Barbarossa: The Golden Aue — the Golden Lea — is a fertile region in Thuringia, between Nordhausen to the west and Sangerhausen to the east, the Lower Harz Mountains to the north and the Kyffhaeuser ridge to the south. Barbarossa's Cave is in the Kyffhaeuser Hills.
7 Brocken: the highest of the Harz Mountains.
8 Sea Devil: Felix Graf Luckner, born 1881, was Commander of the auxiliary cruiser and commerce raider *Seeadler* (Sea Eagle) during the First World War. Under the pseudonym 'Seeteufel' (Sea Devil) he also wrote adventure books.
9 Wartburg: a mountain southwest of Eisenach in the Thuringian Forest. The setting for Richard Wagner's 'Tannhaeuser'.
10 Stieglitz: the Stieglitz (Goldfinch) was the Focke-Wulf Fw 44 two-seat biplane trainer.
11 'The gracious evening star': quotation from 'Tannhaeuser'.
12 'Twilight covered the land': quotation from 'Tannhaeuser'.

Chapter Two
Spain, 1936–1937

Soviet Communism threatens to take hold in Spain and to spread. It is supported by the Government of the People's Front in France and communist volunteers from many lands. General Franco calls upon the Germans for help, and also on the Italians, who land in Spain fresh from their conquest of Abyssinia. The European powers agree a policy of non-intervention, but to no effect. The Civil War in Spain rages from 1936 until the beginning of 1939.

In the early hours of the morning of 1 August 1936 the *Usaramo* cast off from Hamburg South, and the Union Tour Group took its first breakfast aboard ship during the journey down the Elbe. The porridge was my birthday cake. We left Heligoland astern, sailed through the English Channel, passed Cape Finisterre, and, when we reached the latitude of Lisbon, a German destroyer sent a secret order to us by line. Up to that point the Captain had not known what his destination was to be. He had cast a suspicious eye on the heavy crates and on the spare parts that were indicative of aeroplanes, and he had guessed that we were on our way to the Cameroons, or to Togo to mount a coup. Now his orders were to sail to Cadiz. As if in a fairy tale the town emerged, softly gleaming, from the morning twilight. Then it spread out before our eyes, broad and dazzling white beneath the sun's rays. We entered harbour.

Once we were tied up at the quay the unloading of the *Usaramo* began without delay. The Hamburg-Sued ships, which usually plied to poorly equipped ports in Africa, were fitted fore and aft with derricks, and these were used to off-load the suspiciously heavy packing cases — one of them in a particularly down-to-earth manner: the case slipped from its ropes and burst open as it struck the ground. In the middle of the debris there lay, in all its glory, round-bellied and painted matt grey, a 250-kilogram bomb! The crowd of hundreds of inquisitive spectators scattered as if in a gale while I, stationed on the gangway with a Walther pistol to keep order, remained bravely at my post, confident that nothing could happen because I knew that, in accordance with standard practice when in transit, the fuse was not screwed in.

My crew, who were doing duty with me on the quay, rapidly covered up the political nakedness that the German Reich had just displayed. I had, however, to do without the assistance of my Wireless Operator, Hillebrand, who had been jostled into the water by one of the excited Spaniards. In his headlong career his nose had come into contact with a floating splinter just less than ten centimetres long. His good looks were marred for several days and his view of the world about him impeded. He was accident prone. Near Eisleben, when we had just begun our journey by rail, he had gone bottom-first through the toilet window, and it was only by accepting personal responsibility for him that I had been able to prevent the guard from discovering our secret.

So, we were to carry bombs, not just freight as the *Kommandeur* had said. Either he hadn't told me everything or someone hadn't told him everything. Bombs! That intrigued me. How did that fit with the speech that Hitler had made at the opening of the Olympic Games in Berlin in 1936? There were no German soldiers in Spain, he had said, and none would be going there. Oskar Schmidt, an observer from our *Thueringer Geschwader*, said that was crazy; but hadn't we been discharged from the *Wehrmacht*? Wasn't I described in my passport as a 'Salesman'? We didn't let double standards worry us unduly: we had an eventful future to look forward to.

Oskar Schmidt and I looked out on that future the following morning through the porthole of our cabin. One fountain of water after another was rising from the harbour basin, and we could feel explosions hammering against the ship's side. Outside! Let's have a look! A single Breguet biplane was dropping bomb after bomb, obviously trying to hit our ship. Our fighter pilots became impatient. If they could have done so they would have opened up the big packing cases, assembled their aircraft and then taken off from the quay! Heat fuels impatience.

The next day the explosions that rattled our cabin did not do so to the accompaniment of the noise of an aeroplane, but to the thunder of guns. The Red Spaniards, who had possession of the fleet, had brought an armoured cruiser into action, and it was firing broadside over the town at our quay. It was predicted fire, and therefore very inaccurate. 'No doubt about it,' said Schmidt. 'They're gunning for us.' It was my first contact with war. How simply, how adventurously it all began; with what high ideals was it pursued, and how bitterly was it to end.

We rolled further onward towards the future in a long goods train heading for Seville, the hot spot of Europe in those first August days of 1936. One or two Pullman cars with dusty plush were coupled on to the train, and we melted in them until the axle of one of the goods wagons melted as well, and we had to come to a full stop. The wait in the treeless plain of Guadalquivir, with its expanses of arid pastureland, was merciless. It was then that one word became fixed in my brain, a word that would be repeated again and again whenever we asked a question — '*Mañana*' — a word that in the not-too-distant future was destined to make me lose my self-control.

In Seville I moved into Room 125 in the Hotel Christina — '*ciento veinte cinquo*', I learned very soon to trot out fluently when I wanted my key. I kept the bath permanently full of cold water, and during the night I would immerse myself in it several times to escape from the heat.

Then it started in earnest: every day across to Tetuan and from there backwards and forwards to Jerez la Frontera, a flying-time of 40-45 minutes. It was exhausting work. I increased my load gradually from twenty to forty armed troops. When I was taxiing out for take-off the 'Moros' would chant their prayers in chorus which, at first, caused me no little concern. The gusty orographic winds from the Atlas Mountains helped me to lift my heavy cargoes rapidly to height. I soared to altitude at 20 to 30 metres a second, my wing-tips fluttering. I needed height. Red Spanish warships were patrolling in the Straits of Gibraltar, and they would frequently open fire on us. They were successful on one occasion. A direct hit! Several soldiers were seriously injured. There was a mighty yelling behind me. After that I had lumps of stone, iron bars and other such rubbish put on board and stored at readiness by the door, and over the Straits the Spanish platoon commander, when I gave him the signal, would shove them out with his foot. The non-aerodynamic objects didn't cause any damage — they were far too inaccurate — but they did cause considerable alarm by reason of the deafening shriek they made. That helped us on our way.

After each first flight in the morning, the landing and off-loading at Jerez la Frontera, Herr Gonzalez, a true *Grande* and the owner of a magnificent, castle-like home, would invite us to breakfast, and with breakfast he passed around his own excellent, world-famous sherry. His wife was English, and she often had relatives from home out on a visit. Without leaving his deck chair, their young son used to watch our landings and the numerous 'Moros' that poured out of the Ju 52, to be packed straight away into buses for transport to the Front, north of Seville. There could be no question of secrecy any longer.

That was confirmed beyond doubt when one day, at the request of the Spanish commanding officer of the airport at Tetuan, I had to take a Frenchman on board with me, a certain Comte de Pierrefeu. I suggested politely that he might like to sit beside me at the right-hand side of the cockpit during the flight, as it was quite clear that he wasn't happy about the crush in the cabin. So, as usual, I began the last flight of the day to Seville. It was dark already. My radio operator was not on board. I could do without him, and his presence was more necessary in the radio station in Seville. It was an easy flight to Seville, about 60 minutes. The wind was always the same.

After we had passed Gibraltar, all lit up, the Count asked me if he might take over the dual controls. I let him do so. He flew the machine smoothly, understood the compass errors, swung swiftly on to course. He knew what he was doing. In answer to my question, he said he had been a pilot in the World War. Ah! I see. Then it occurred to me that this form of flying had not existed in the war. Could it be that he was a traveller under cover, just as I was? In Seville the Count invited me to dinner at the Hotel de Paris, and during the various courses we circled around the central question — was he, or wasn't he? Good: you're a salesman. I see! Each of us told his own fairy tale, and each pretended that he believed the other's story; but the whole world knew the truth.

A Spanish naval officer was attached to me as second pilot so that he could learn instrument flying. He turned out to be a quick and able pupil. I also had high-ranking passengers — Generals from the Foreign Legion and other military outfits, Ministers and even their wives. This resulted in my meeting General Franco. *Major* von Scheele introduced me. *Major* von Scheele, at whose side or in front of whom the business manager of HISMA (Spanish Moroccan Transport Company), Herr Bernhardt, was always to be found, gave me, out of the blue, a new supplementary job. Both had noticed that I could communicate with my Spanish co-pilot in French, a language that was looked upon at that time as a standard part of one's general education. Both, therefore, nominated me as training officer in the subject of anti-aircraft gunnery. From the belly of the *Usaramo* had been raised to the light of day twenty 2-cm flak guns that were to be handed over to the Spaniards. The Spaniards, however, were not familiar with the weapon — just as little, in fact, as I was. In Berlin, forward planning had resulted in a flak corporal, in the guise of a mechanic, accompanying us on the ship but, although he was technically knowledgeable, he could only speak German.

Initially, I was trained. After my last flight in the evening I would practise, with my corporal, stripping down and reassembling the guns and studying the sighting mechanism. Early one morning, I began sighting on a lump of rock on the steep bank of the Rio Guadalquivir, on the far side of the river. I soon felt confident enough to begin to instruct the Spanish, again at night, inside a hangar in the oppressive heat. There were probably forty to fifty officers from the army and the navy, stripping down, reassembling, until, after several days, every single man had had his turn. It was with some longing that I thought of my bath tub of cold water. When I asked what forty to fifty officers could do with twenty guns, von Scheele and Bernhardt told me that more weapons were on their way.

Lacking motorised vehicles on to which the guns could be hitched or loaded, I whetted the appetite of my pupils for horses, which, together with limbers, could be commandeered from the artillery. Admittedly, the enterprise came up against opposition from the Commander of Artillery, but with the assistance of *General* Kindelan, the Chief of the General Staff of the Spanish Air Force, things moved in the right direction.

For firing practice, I obtained a number of paper, hot-air balloons, which I let drift out over the river. For the Spanish, live firing was great fun, particularly when they scored a direct hit. No-one gave any thought to the risk involved.

When I had been through the whole gamut of drills with the Spanish to my satisfaction; when setting up a battery of four guns, raising dust and delimbering had all been sufficiently practised; when I had indulged the Spanish liking for spectacular performances — I scarcely even dared mention that the guns were in fact German ones — the final whistle sounded. Training over. Guns to the battle front!

Two guns each were despatched to Cordoba, Granada, Toledo and Burgos, and I was made into a sort of minor inspector, flying around to each location to see that things were being done correctly. My very existence developed into sweaty labour, in that I still had 1000 soldiers to convey over the Channel, and ever more sons of the desert were turning up eager to go to Spain. That very evening as I, dusty and perspiring, was about to go and say goodbye to my flak pupils, a driver sped up to me and handed me a note on which was written 'Tonight Fiesta de la Raza, Alkazar in Seville. Have no time. Herrmann and Dr. Fischbach will represent me. Wash and shave first. Best suit. Signed, Von Scheele.' My leave-taking from the fliers and the sailors wasn't a proper one. We knew we would see each other again somewhere or other.

So, I rushed off. During my last stop at Tetuan I had eaten, as usual, had a sherry and taken one of the anti-malaria quinine tablets that were always available there in the Officers' Mess. I strode through the portal, together with our doctor. He was displaying his sabre-scars, I my smooth-shaven baby face. Both of us were dressed in lightweight, summer clothes. We discovered straight away that the gentlemen were in tails and the ladies in enchanting evening gowns (more traditional than modern European in style) and with high combs in their hair covered with expensive head scarves. The picture of the guests strolling in the palm garden past cool-spraying, Bengal-lit fountains, beneath a huge golden-yellow moon low on the horizon, was purely and simply a fairy tale from 'A Thousand and One Nights'.

A further tasteful and moving piece of theatre took place at midnight. In the centre of the *Salle de Ambajadores* the Grand Vizir of Morocco had taken his place in his white burnous, together with Minister Queipo de Llano, on a throne couch beneath a cupola of magnificent reflecting mosaics, while the senior guests, standing in a half-circle, awaited the dancers. While watching all this, I became aware of a light-coloured blot on the landscape in the circle of proud grandees and noble ladies. It was Dr. Fischbach's summer suit, but it didn't seem to worry the Spanish. I, no less a nonconformist, had moved into the back row and, quite suddenly, I found myself next to a delicate figure, a most attractive young girl in Andalusian costume, a girl who stood apart from the crowd in every sense of the word. But that was quite inconceivable here! Only wives and daughters were present, and they were firmly attached to their Senors. So, she must be a dancer.

When I had become a little more accustomed to the shade, I noticed that the beauty was moving her lips while lowering and then closing her long-lashed eyelids. As God is my witness, she was praying. When the guitars struck up, she looked up beseechingly to heaven and crossed herself. Then, with a light clicking of her castanets, she sprang forward, light-footedly, wound her way through the rows of guests and hastened towards the golden couch. At the same instant her partner appeared, as if from Heaven, coolly posing, and sank on to his knees beside her. A picture, at once humble and proud. Then passion, wildness, fire erupted and effervesced as the guitars took up the central theme. The girl, at first a true Carmen, full of hate and cruelty, radiating contempt, changed suddenly, seemingly effortlessly but without any great display of emotion, into a gentle lover.

So that I should not miss any of this experience, I had pushed my way already to the front, forgetting the unsuitability of my dress, which had in any case been accepted by our hosts. My applause was noticeably more enthusiastic than the measured acknowledgment on the part of the gentlemen and their ladies. In truth, it was not just wonderful — it was a miracle; and it was still in my mind as I strolled back to my hotel after midnight through rows of houses still radiating their heat.

Early next morning I reported to the *Major* how the evening had gone. What the doctor had told me was confirmed. Von Scheele made no bones about it: he hadn't wanted to go himself. He didn't like formality. After the First World War he had had to struggle for an existence in South America. I should take a look at his hands, he said. He stretched them out for me to see. I was moved, and I felt myself honoured by the comradely frankness of the old man. I liked the old campaigner. I saw what he meant. It was simply not possible for the hard, burly, stocky, rather thick-set planter to bring himself to identify with Spanish etiquette. I, on the other hand, approved of these non-productive yet beautiful traditions. They were also interesting: they existed, whereas there was nothing, or virtually nothing, of that nature to be seen or experienced in our society. If Fate had left her mark on me as she had done on the Major, perhaps I would have felt as he did.

My varied work, filling as it did every working hour, had one big disadvantage: I was not taken into the *'Pedros y Pablos' Staffel*, led by *Oberleutnant* von Moreau. This *Staffel*, renowned by and beloved of the Spanish, relieved the siege of Toledo and dropped urgently needed supplies and munitions into The Alkazar. When I touched down one evening in Seville with the final cargo of the day, von Scheele ordered the aircraft to be fitted out at once for dropping bombs. I was to stand by for a special job the following day.

Next morning I learned a little more from the German radio station, which was operated by undercover German naval officers from the top storey of the Hotel Christina. From there, shipping and fleet movements in both seas were monitored closely. The most recent report said that a large part of the Red Spanish fleet was about to enter the Mediterranean from the Atlantic and would pass through the Straits of Gibraltar at midnight. A twin-engined He 29 seaplane with a German crew was despatched at once, together with a flying boat, of a type unknown to me, that was piloted by a Norwegian who had also volunteered for service for Franco. While both aircraft were searching the Atlantic in a southerly direction I went on standby with my re-equipped Ju 52. A naval pilot, *Oberleutnant* Storp, had been sent to me as a stand-in observer. He came from a single-engined He 60 seaplane, which we had christened a '*Pantinenflieger*' — a flying clog — and he was flying in a Ju 52 for the first time in his life.

Storp had reported to our little 'Naval Warfare Staff' in the Hotel Christina that he was looking for a job, having the previous day incurred a direct hit in the course of a low-level attack on the airfield at Malaga. He had intended the attack to be a surprise, but in that he had failed. One of the Red Spaniards had jerked himself out of his siesta and had sent several lead bullets through the float of Storp's seaplane which had, most irregularly, left its proper area of action — over the sea — and ventured impertinently over land. The way the aircraft had listed on landing had made Storp make for the sandy beach very rapidly. He was a wild man, and I was now about to embark upon a great sea battle with him.

So, at the beginning of October, in considerable heat, I took off at 1430 hr in the Ju 52 which had six 250-kg bombs in its belly. We were under orders to be back by thirty minutes after sunset at the latest. We were heading southwest. One hour had passed, and the second was nearing its end. Storp was busy with his naval chart and pestering me with grid references and nautical miles (at that time units of measurement were not even standardised throughout the whole of the *Wehrmacht*).

'What's going on, Hillebrand?' He pressed the earpieces close to his ears, gave a meaningful, then a worried, then, finally, a hopelessly embarrassed look. It was always the same with this fellow.

We were approaching the point at which we would have to turn back when Hillebrand rushed triumphantly into the cockpit, beaming with joy, and showed me a few lines of writing on his notepad: a map reference, course of the fleet northerly, travelling at cruising speed. Having thought matters over very carefully, Storp said that we would need to fly a considerable distance past our point of no return. It would then be out of the question for us to return to Seville: indeed we would scarcely be able to reach the Spanish coast. Perhaps we could get to Spanish Morocco with our last drop of fuel? But where we were, we had French Morocco on our beam. It was from there that the ships were coming, having been overhauled in the dockyards at Casablanca by the supposedly neutral French.

We discussed the situation. Perhaps the ships were travelling faster. Perhaps their position was further north than had been reported. The sun was already low in the sky, so we had to get a move on. Perhaps the maritime reconnaissance people would send a more accurate report. Storp was raring to go. He ran down the ladder into the under-turret of the Ju 52, swiftly measured the drift with the bomb sight, then rushed back up again and wound the turret up (in its 'down' position it caused wind resistance, which slowed the aircraft down; 10 km an hour could have made all the difference between landing safely or having to ditch in the sea). I fiddled about with the throttles; we had to be economical.

The reconnaissance people gave another position and then they signed off. OK for some! They could spend the night on the surface of the water and have supplies brought to them the following day. At last, grey shapes emerged from the deep blue of the sea and the pale blue of the horizon. Our cruising altitude of 1000 metres seemed to me to make an attack too risky. Storp wanted to make a low-level approach at right-angles to the side of the ship, the so-called *Verfahren Steckrube* (Turnip Method). He wanted to copy *Oberleutnant* von Moreau and *Graf* Hoyos. These two had, in the course of a dawn attack, put the battle cruiser *Jaime I* out of action with a single 250-kg bomb. We, however, had six bombs. That meant six ships . . .

This man, I thought, is going to make mincemeat of me! There'll be no surprise attack here. He wants us to approach an opponent, long-since alerted by reconnaissance aircraft, in the open sea, in good visibility, over the wave tops in a ponderous '*Tante Ju*'. They'd annihilate us with their first broadside! Finally, Storp settled for 1500 metres. I was right with him as I approached the ships, which were sailing in line-ahead, from the front. Storp let the turret down and then let himself down into it, promising to get one ship with each bomb.

And so, into action! The ships disappeared behind and below the centre motor of the Ju 52, and I had to rely on the observer to steer the aircraft, which he did by means of a handle that was coupled to the rudder. I didn't like this intervention from below at all, because my rudder bar seemed to develop a will of its own suddenly. In all my life as a pilot I had, so far, not dropped a single live bomb, not to speak of doing so in collaboration with an expert observer, which I considered Storp to be. Of course, I accepted that this type of co-operation was the correct way.

Soon, the first fat tracers were streaking up in front of my nose, but Storp steered the aircraft along its course as if nothing was happening. The aircraft gave a little lurch. The first bomb was gone. After the third bomb there was such fierce flak around me — we were right in the middle of the flotilla — that I kicked the rudder bar to the left in order to take evasive action, but Storp steered in the opposite direction with the strength of a bear. He wanted to keep me on course. This is madness! Let's see whether my infantryman's thighs, toughened in hard route marches, can't crack his biceps. I used the ailerons to help. Good! Now we're in a steep turn. Let's get out of here!

The score so far — three bombs, three near misses. We held another council of war. I said that I would not do the same again. Next time we attacked, I wanted to be at 3000 m at least. We hadn't got either parachutes or life jackets with us; we had always flown like that on transport work. The shirt I was wearing was white and short sleeved, and my shorts were white also. The sharks could have got straight at the naked flesh! Storp said that he would not be able to hit anything from 3000 m. We settled for 2500.

Shortly before we dropped the first bomb, Hillebrand had received clearance to transmit. That put Seville in the picture and, of course, they knew that we had acted against direct orders. If things went wrong, we'd get into trouble: if things went well, they wouldn't have to commend us even. 'Ah, well. That went OK.' It's certainly hard to be a boss.

The second approach was worse than the first. By now the heavy flak was joining in with full salvos, every ship firing simultaneously. I saw the flashes and the thick smoke from the exploding shells. Then only Storp could see what was happening. I steered on instruments, and when Storp made a correction, my legs were sympathetic and understanding. My extremities had begun to think for themselves. Bump. Bump. Bump. Our three fat bombs were away. Let's get out of here!

Right at the end there was a bang, and a good-sized piece of shrapnel lodged between the cooling blades of the Hornet engine directly in front of me, and until nightfall I had to look out on to this piece of metal, fashioned and sent aloft by human hand. It only needs a very small step to take a man out of this world. We didn't hit any of the ships, even though the Red Spaniards steered stubbornly dead ahead. It was a bit pathetic, our 'Battle of the Atlantic'.

For the time being I suppressed my anger against the bombing-strategists who had so unexpectedly crossed my path. Our immediate task was to work together to reach land on board the long-suffering *Tante Ju* which, in the course of her peaceable life, had carried so many loads in the service of impatient men. Auntie, forgive me for having to take you into the tumultuous affairs of men.

Going down low, we tried to fly beneath the gentle wind that had helped us southwards. We adjusted the sensitive altimeter so that we would have clearance when it was dark. We flew to the Straits of Gibraltar, close by Ceuta, and to the airfield at Tetuan, with Eibisch standing by at the handle of the gravity tank pump, ready to inject the last drop of life blood. We made it. Our command post radioed from Seville: the Red Spaniards had cut the telephone cables. To help us in, there was a car headlamp standing by on the edge of the field at right-angles to the direction of approach. In the Hotel Nacional in Tetuan another message reached us post haste: we were to track the ships, which had passed through the Straits during the night, and above all to put submarines out of action.

There is not much to report: six bombs dropped, all at once, from low level on a submarine that was diving away into the cover of darkness, and wreckage and oil were its end. It was an easy success and so not a real one. It was a sad success. Had the lookout only been more alert, had he looked our way only five seconds earlier, the joke would have been on us. All this occurred at about midday, between Malaga and Almeria. I withstood successfully Storp's request that we should head for the aerodrome at Malaga, which he knew very well, and pay it a visit with our two machine-guns, him in the turret and Eibisch at the rear.

That same afternoon, a Sunday, the whole crew went to the bullfight in the Arena de Sevilla at the invitation of the Spaniards. I sat near to Franco's Chief of Propaganda, Queipo de Llano, who could be heard every evening on the loudspeakers. Nine bulls appeared, three in honour of Germany, three in honour of Italy, and three in honour of Spain. What interested me most was the faces of the beautiful, charming young girls and women in their Andalusian costumes. They radiated enthusiasm, and they became even more beautiful when they saw the *torero* skilfully plunge his spear or his dagger into the bull's neck.

More transports. I was approaching a total of 2000 soldiers, not counting guns and ammunition. In between there were Flak inspections in Cordoba, where I didn't miss the opportunity of gazing with wonderment at the mosque with its 800 different columns. On another occasion I took off for Burgos, together with *Oberleutnant* Eberhardt, the fighter pilot. He took over the controls: as I was his junior in rank I couldn't prevent him. He was on an inspection trip similar to my own. In Burgos, I paid a visit to the Commander of the Artillery Regiment to which the guns had been allocated. I spent a few days taking part in various exercises. In the course of this, a distressing event occurred.

Apparently Spaniards found it difficult to observe times and appointments or to keep promises. That was the subject of a discussion one midday in the Hotel de Paris (even here there was one of that name); I complained about the matter and one or two strong words passed my lips. A Spaniard in civilian clothes, who understood German (which was most unusual), heard what I said and felt that his national pride was injured. He sent a report to the responsible authorities. I first heard about this when I was summoned to *Major* von Scheele a few days later, in the course of further transport and inspection duties. He informed me that the Chief of the General Staff of the Spanish Air Force, *General* Kindelan, had demanded that I should leave Spain at once. As I was unable to deny the charge, I did my best to conceal my bewilderment. It seemed that I would have to crawl back to my colleagues and senior officers in Nordhausen like a dog that had been whipped. When von Scheele told me that my replacement had already been requested in Germany, I could have wept. It was a blow that hurt me more than a bullet in the guts. I obeyed orders and avoided all contact with Spanish officers and other ranks. When my replacement arrived I was to disappear.

When he arrived, *Freiherr* von Beust depressed me even more with his beaming high spirits. I had to brief him. We were now one too many; but he thought that there was room for both of us. So, he made it his job to plead my case with the Staff of the big up-and-coming German contingent, the *Legion Condor*. In ascending order of rank the people to whom he spoke were *Major* Balke, *Oberstleutnant von* Richthofen, and finally *General* Sperrle. Consideration of the request dragged on for weeks, during which I kept my head down. As the gentlemen concerned had had one or two similar experiences themselves, they pronounced that I had, in fact, described that state of affairs in Burgos accurately, but had expressed myself infelicitously. I was to go to *General* Mola, who was in command of the Northern Front, and apologise in a proper manner. They told me that my case had been put forward already and that they had said that I was indispensable in my function as an inspector of flak. They had also given me a very good write-up, they said — which was, of course, not deserved, so I shouldn't start getting ideas about myself. Further, they had informed *General* Mola that I had been selected to be attached to Staff Colonel Warlimont, who had arrived from Berlin to visit the Front. That was, in fact, the case. Immediately I got back from seeing the General I was to travel to the Front.

The senior officers were not unkind in the way they spoke to me. So, encouraged, I decided straight away to write down what I would say to *General* Mola and to learn it by heart. (Unfortunately the text, which I wrote in French, was later burnt during an air raid on Nordhausen.) Almost all the German officers spoke French with the Spaniards, and *General* Mola was said to speak it fluently. I worked on the text until it was just right. There were many flowery turns of phrase in it, such as delighted the ears of the Spaniards.

The General's headquarters must have been somewhere between Valladolid and the River Tajo. I was received there with full ceremony and ushered in to see the General. He stood up — Oh, my God! The man was nearly two metres tall —

about six foot six! Why didn't somebody tell me? He was wearing large spectacles. '*Bonjour, Monsieur le Général*,' I ventured.

'*Buenas tardes*,' he replied.

As I was trying to remember the first three words of my speech, he started to speak in French, quite loudly and in a deep basso profundo. Perhaps I could inform him how, with the few guns that I (I!) had supplied him with, he was supposed to shoot down all those Russian fighters. It made life difficult for the fighting men at the Front. 'Get me 100 guns!' Everybody said that the guns were first class, easy to use. 'You have my thanks!'

Keep your face straight, was all I could think. If that isn't a pardon, then my name's Meier! He's not interested in apologies. I said that I would take the necessary steps immediately with the General and the Staff in Salamanca. Von Beust had been correct. There was room for both of us in Spain.

Together with *Oberst i.G* (Staff Colonel) Warlimont and other officers from Berlin I drove from Salamanca (at that time Franco's headquarters) along badly damaged roads through and across the Sierra de Gredos towards Toledo which had, by then, been taken. The splendid, steadfast campaigners of the Alkazar had been relieved, at last. There were still corpses beneath the ruins, and everywhere along the road on which Franco's troops had advanced and the Red Spaniards had retreated I saw human beings in distress, exhausted; blood on church steps.

Madrid lay before us. We had moved forward as far as Carabanchel Bajo into a gun position before a village. The Reds were attacking with armour. It was the first time I had seen Soviet tanks. They rolled towards us, thumping up and down, stopping now and again to fire their guns. They advanced still further. Another halt; more firing. The shells were falling in the village behind us. The officers from the Army took cover. I found the whole business strange, almost unreal. Could this be War, about which our fathers had told us so much? *Oberst* Warlimont shouted to me, 'Be good enough to take cover. War's not a game. And take your light-coloured dust coat off!'

The tanks were coming alarmingly nearer. I looked at the Spanish gunners, and I asked myself whether they would be able to cope. I had my doubts. I felt helpless. There's nothing you can do, I thought; you haven't even got a weapon. For better or worse, you're dependent on what action foreigners take — or don't take! It was an idiotic feeling. So: 'To the rear, Don Rodrigo!'

The officers from Berlin were of the same opinion. After all, they hadn't come there to fight, but simply to gather impressions and to report back to Germany. We moved into a quieter sector of the Front, where we knew that we would enjoy the protection of an 8.8 cm Flak Battery, commanded by *Oberleutnant* Aldinger. The battery's guns were often used in ground fighting. I was pleased to renew the acquaintance of two young Germans whom I had been able to help to desert from the Spanish Foreign Legion, where there had been too much physical brutality. *Oberleutnant* Aldinger had absorbed them swiftly but discreetly into two newly invented jobs. If the Spanish had known that, I would have been kicked out once and for all!

The *Legion Condor* was, by this time, ready for operations. As an old hand in the Spanish Campaign, I was put into the *1st Staffel* under *Oberleutnant* von Knauer. *Major* Fuchs was the *Kommandeur* of the *Gruppe*, which was named *K 88*.

From Granada and from Melilla in Spanish Morocco we flew night attacks on Cartegena, where the Soviets were landing mainly war equipment. Our warships, under the command of *Admiral* von Fischl and stationed there to supervise non-intervention, were kind enough to point the way to our target with their searchlights. Friend Storp also managed to get himself involved in these raids, to gain experience of bombing by night. He said to me later that the many bright flashes quite unnecessarily made the whole affair seem more dangerous than daylight operations.

When we were moved north later, I had to say goodbye to Storp, who still had to keep an eye on the Straits and the open sea with his 'flying clog'. We set up shop close to Salamanca on the nearby airfields of San Fernando and Encinas, from where we flew day and night operations against Madrid and airfields and railway junctions in the rear. As an observer I was allocated *Leutnant* (later *Teniente*) Roebling, newly arrived from Berlin. Now I had a full crew and was an established bomber pilot. My jobs as inspector of anti-aircraft artillery and transporter of troops ceased.

Our daylight attacks in close formation, escorted by German He 51s and Italian Fiat Cr 42s, were tough going. The Reds, many of them Soviets, would hold back until the last moment as we approached slowly in our Ju 52s, then they would shoot up from below in their bright green Ratas (Polikarpov I-16). They had the most up-to-date ammunition — phosphorous, incendiary and tracer bullets. Against this we had the thin, unarmoured, aluminium walls of our fuel tanks only, and I have seen many of my comrades dive to the ground as if in a glowing ball.

It was then decided that we should operate from airfields further north in order to attack important targets in Bilbao and the oil storage plants at Santander. I was sent ahead to recce the aerodromes at Leon and Burgos and to prepare them for night operations. Having discovered that there only were a few very low-powered lights available at Burgos, I asked the mayor if I could have some street lamp bulbs together with fittings and a sufficient amount of cable. When he answered, '*Mañana*', from deep down in his chest, I decided to look elsewhere for sources of light. I had noticed already that the cathedral in Burgos was surrounded at a number of points with big lamps designed to floodlight the building. These, it seemed to me, were surplus to requirements and that is what I told the high ecclesiastical dignitary, stressing repeatedly that we of Burgos must embark upon the struggle against the atheistic Soviets and the equally atheistic Communists. A number of these splendid searchlights were presented to me, and I was able to pronounce the airfield clear for night flying.

In the course of a daytime raid on Bilbao the crew of *Leutnant* Herrmann (the same name as myself) was shot down and taken prisoner. The Red Spaniards broadcast the news, the French repeated it in German from Strassburg, and my poor parents, who used to listen to the wireless eagerly for the latest news from Spain, suffered an awful shock. For a long time they had suspected that my disappearance was connected with Spain. I was told about this by *General* Wilberg who visited Spain from his Special Staff 'W' in Berlin. My father had asked for an immediate meeting with him. He had been unable to give my father definite news. The General ordered me to sit down at a desk and write a letter immediately with the date and time on it and assure my parents that I was in the best of health and at liberty. *General* Wilberg put this letter in an envelope and took it back with him by air, via Rome, to Berlin the same day.

Winter came to high Castille. On the airfield at San Fernando our Ju 52s sank into the soft ground. We were condemned to military inactivity, but a situation such as that cannot deter a German officer or unit commander from looking for work to do. It fell to me to study Spanish history at the University of Salamanca and to give a talk — as brilliant a one as possible — to the *Staffel*.

The six weeks that *Major* Maass had told me my trip to Spain would last were long over. If I had expected to stay longer I would have listened more attentively to the Spanish from the very beginning and not taken refuge in French. However as time passed the language, which had at first seemed to me like prolonged machine-gun fire, no longer got on my nerves but filtered into the language centre of my brain, schooled as it was in Latin. I began to study a newspaper occasionally, to listen to the news on the radio and try to decipher the various hymns that the military bands in the more important villages and towns used to play at the end of the communal walk-about, the *Correo* — three or four Spanish ones, then German and Italian ones, all listened to standing up. They seemed to me to be beautiful and rich in imagery.

In addition to listening, I had long been able to express myself, in the kitchen of our hacienda in San Fernando, on the subject of hard-boiled or soft-boiled eggs, olives in oil and other such delicacies. I had done reasonably well on guns and flying; my *Co-Capitano* had imparted quite a lot of useful knowledge to me when we had been speaking French. On other topics, I was condemned to silence.

At the University I came into contact with a young scholar who spoke very clearly, not to say very slowly. His sentences, I realised, were sentences just like any others. A panorama of rich pictures passed before my eyes. What he was saying to me was suddenly as clear as if Julius Caesar himself were reading out to me the beginning of his *De Bello Gallico*, studied years ago and never forgotten. I found the young man's language (Castillian) splendid, classical and full of character. There's more to these people, I thought, than meets the eye. Now I experienced great joy in the study of their history, the scholar helping me each day.

We were living a modest existence in San Fernando, thirty kilometres west of Salamanca; an existence that could scarcely be described as that of country gentlemen, but now I no longer felt envious of the fact that the members of our 3rd *Staffel*, commanded by the swashbuckling *Hauptmann* Eberhard Krafft von Dellmensingen, occupied a floor of a luxury hotel in the town and were able to take a walk each day along the classic facades of the Plaza Mayor and admire the spectacular mounting of the Moroccan Caudillo bodyguard. I had reacted perversely and had been unwilling when my *Kapitaen* had suggested that I should do some research work, but my experience was enriching. There must have been still something of the child about me, seeing only the labour and not the reward. I soon came to realise the truth. Even the worst of bullshit that is heaped on you in the armed forces will help something useful to grow.

Christmas 1936 in a foreign country. Christmas at war . . .

We had to have a Christmas tree — a *Tannenbaum* — but the silent, snow-covered winter woods of Germany were lacking. Behind the lust for adventure and masculine combat there grew a tender shoot that strove towards the light and recognition. Homesickness and a yearning for peace emerged, and memories of childhood days. A German Christmas is not complete without a *Tannenbaum*. Someone recalled seeing, in the centre of a small mountain town, a meagre park in which there was a stunted growth not unlike our fir tree. Suddenly, everybody remembered seeing it. One couldn't have wished for greater enthusiasm for any official duty than that which we devoted to that secret, nocturnal excavation. So we dug up our Christmas tree (it would be replanted later equally clandestinely) under the hidden gaze of a sinister member of the *Guardia* Civil who appeared suddenly from concealment. Seldom can a policeman have looked out on the world with such stupidity, such lack of comprehension, as that one did when we explained to him that we had hired the tree!

On the afternoon of Christmas Eve we drove to Salamanca to see a German film. Its title was *Leise flehen meine Lieder* ('Softly Plead My Songs'), in Spanish *Vuelan mis canciones*, and it starred Martha Eggert. It was evocative of house and home, country and loved ones, so much so that, when it was over and we were on the way back, most of us sat in the bus subdued and silent. The lights of our *Tannenbaum* gleamed out to welcome us. Later we sang *Stille Nacht* (Silent Night).

From the mud of San Fernando we transferred with the last few litres of fuel to Encinas, and subsequently we flew operation after operation. We flew in tight formation against airfields and defended positions in Madrid. Each Ju 52 was fitted with extra machine-guns, pointing ahead and to the sides, against airfields and defended positions in Madrid. Our principal fear was the Ratas, the poison-green, low-winged, big-engined monoplanes that took off at the last possible moment and zoomed up from below. Even though our own fighters used to dive down, with great valour, onto them, still one or another of the Soviet-piloted Ratas would get through to us. In technical terms the enemy were superior, and neither the German nor the Italian biplanes were a match for them. One of the venomous machines once went into a climb before my eyes and swept towards our formation upside down, unmistakably aiming for me. Then came a rattling all around me like that of empty milk cans. Ouch — my hand's been hit! When the first shock was over, I saw that the centre throttle had rammed into my hand with considerable force and was now back in its neutral position. It was clear that the Rata had severed the linkage and had holed the fuselage in many places. Nobody was injured. The cloud of sulphur or phosphorous disappeared and we made a smooth landing, thus confirming what Roebling had already checked visually from the under-turret — that our tyres were undamaged.

In April *Staffelkapitaen von* Knauer said it was time that I, as a veteran of the Legion, went on leave. Being a *Leutnant* my leave was calculated in days, with Saturdays counting as duty days. I packed up my personal belongings, handed them in to the Sergeant Major and, somehow or other, found my way to Seville, the starting point and finishing point of the Berlin-Rome-Seville return route. The route was being flown by my former blind-flying instructor from the *Reichsbahn Strecke* at Tempelhof, *Oberleutnant* Giseke, who allowed me to pay him back with Spanish delicacies for the visits to the Savarin (he intoned the word with a nasal accent). I 'earned' so much more than he did, he pointed out.

We took off at dawn and flew, at a safe distance, over the mountains past Malaga, then down low towards the Mediterranean after altering course eastwards. Through the rear windows I looked back at the rough, jagged mountain peaks above the coastline. How devoid of life it all looked. But what life there was down there! What passion, joy, hate, great courage and vast indifference! Behind those steep mountains lay a world rich in experience. If there was such a thing as universal human love, then the Spanish had made me conscious of it to some small degree.

Lower and lower sank the mountain-ridge on the horizon. Fainter and softer it gleamed through the haze, until at last it merged with it and was lost.

Chapter Three
Back Home to the
Goldene Aue, 1937–1939

Following the plebiscite in the Saar the people's right of self-determination is realised for a second time in Austria. The Greater German Reich is created, and the Sudetenland becomes part of it. In England, the Parliamentary Opposition stirs up feeling against Germany. Czechoslovakia, which the victorious powers had created as a new state in 1918/19 from peoples of the Austro-Hungarian Empire, is divided into the Czechs and the Slovaks. The Czechs attach themselves to the German Reich in the form of a Protectorate. Britain guarantees Poland's existence against an attack by Germany. The Germans propose that there should be a free vote to solve the problem of the Danzig Corridor. But negotiations do not take place.

My homeland felt strange to me as I scrambled out of the Ju 52 at Tempelhof. When I thought back to the ragged suits that the Spaniards wore, and particularly to their wretched footwear, the people in the U-Bahn looked as if they were in their Sunday best. And how very differently one's own folk behave and speak. To learn about yourself you must not only have been in a foreign land, but you must also have worked with the people there. It is only when you have fought at their side, or even against them, that the picture is complete. Historians imagine that they know better from books.

At the *Reichsluftfahrtministerium*,[1] *General* Wilberg gave me my instructions: I had to report punctually to him for my flight back. Furthermore, I was to 'maintain radio silence' about what had happened in Spain. Nevertheless, my colleagues at Nordhausen knew better. The emergence of the *Legion Condor* in the footsteps of the Union Tour Group could not be disguised as a holiday trip. They wanted to know whether I had just come back from a skiing holiday, and whether the people in Switzerland said '*Caramba*' and '*Si Si*'. It was a pantomime. My delicatessen shopkeeper, Herr Binder, used to give me the latest news about developments on the Spanish Front — delivered to him at home, courtesy of the Strassburg Radio Station.

After my parents had been reassured by seeing me in the flesh, I reported back to *General* Wilberg. I was very punctual because I was afraid that if I were not they might start looking for someone else to go instead of me. All my friends were waiting eagerly to be called upon.

At *Sonderstab 'W'* (Special Staff W) they pressed into my hand a flight ticket for the route Travemuende-Lisbon. I would travel as a passenger on board a flying boat. Not bad! From Lisbon I would make my way across the Portuguese-Spanish border by rail, via Ciudad Rodrigo, to Salamanca. Take-off was to be the following day. First, I was to report to *General* Kesselring, then Chief of the General Staff, and give him a brief account of my experiences in Spain.

I had been speaking for ten minutes when an officer came in whom I knew only too well from the Air Display at Bamberg and from very many photographs in newspapers and magazines — Udet. Then the questioning began in earnest. It must have lasted an hour. Kesselring asked whether I wanted to go back. I confirmed, enthusiastically, that I did. When he asked me why, I replied that out there I would be able to gain further flying and tactical experience. I had long been unable to get it at Nordhausen, I said, and I wouldn't be able to get it there in the future.

Then, the cross-questioning. I vented my dissatisfaction with the abstinence from flying that had been imposed upon me at Nordhausen by stating that in the entire time from March to July 1936, not counting the three months on the *Reichsbahn Strecke*, I had flown a grand total of four hours and twelve minutes. In such circumstances I would rather be in Spain, I said. Then I repeated it precisely — four hours and twelve minutes. My flying times were entered perfectly correctly in my flying log book, and I had added them up accurately, which went without saying for a pilot mad about flying and existing on basic rations.

At that moment, I didn't have the slightest suspicion that my meagre flying times would arouse fearful wrath in the breast of the Chief of the General Staff, which he would bring to the ears of other people in tones of thunder, and that those people would in turn visit me with squalls of hail. In any case, why should it worry me what was going to be done or not done here? I was flying back to the sunny South.

Kesselring had made one or two notes. I couldn't make out the murmurs that he exchanged with Udet. Then the Chief of the General Staff announced that I was to put my experience to use at Nordhausen. It was quite clear, he said, that I was of the same opinion as he himself was: that something had to be done there. It was the time for others to go to Spain to learn. I gave my air ticket back to *General* Wilberg. Gone was the dream of a passenger trip to Lisbon, and I was on my way back to my unit and the company of friends proven in danger.

I was permitted to put my operational and flying experience to use at Nordhausen as a *Kettenhund* (wing man) to a young lieutenant who had had no war experience but who, as Head of Training and Technical Officer,[2] was my superior. Unfortunately, I hadn't been returned to my old *Staffel*. My new *Staffelkapitaen*, *Major* Maier, reprimanded me if I didn't hold the door to the *Staffel* offices open for him when he was following fifty paces behind me. After a reasonable time I asked if I might be allowed to lead a *Kette* occasionally. A *Kette*, literally a chain, was a formation of three aircraft, and a *Kettenhund* translates into English as a dog on a chain. Maier told me that I must remain as a *Kettenhund* because I was someone who had to be kept on the leash.

Again I had to use my experience in Spain, this time in the *Staffel* clothing store counting socks and underpants, and I found myself detailed suspiciously often as Station Duty Officer or for courier trips to Gotha, where I had to travel on the stopping train in order to hand a locked metal box containing secret material to the *Geschwader* adjutant. It seemed that something was brewing, and no doubt the recommendation contained in my assessment when I became an officer — 'must be watched and kept on a tight rein' — had something to do with it. I felt unutterably miserable, having all this bullshit heaped on me, but I consoled myself with the thought that perhaps one day I'd be a *Staffelkapitaen* myself, and then there would probably be no harm in knowing something about admin.

When the OC Flying had checked my flying time from the previous year in the central records and compared it with the entries in my log book — and found that the two agreed completely — I realised which way the wind was blowing. The OC Flying couldn't avoid dropping hints about my breach of flying discipline at Wenigenlupnitz. I was labelled as someone with a disciplinary record: at the same time I was perceived as someone who enjoyed privileges he didn't deserve. I drove around the aerodrome in a splendid, light green BMW, built in Eisenach, and on Sundays I would sometimes overhaul my *Staffelkapitaen* or the OC Flying in their two-stroke DKW or Adler-Triumph and leave them behind on the slope from Netzkater to Braunlage-Harz. My beautiful motor car, a thorn in the flesh of my *Kapitaen*, was my pride and joy. I had bought it from the car dealer Gebhard in Nordhausen for 4950 *Reichsmark* of Spanish provenance. Gebhard had got me my driving licence after about two hours practice, but he had taken into account the unofficial driving I had done in Spain.

Another ray of light was the new bomber aircraft, the Ju 86, which was better armed and faster than the Ju 52, fitted with bullet-proof fuel tanks and Jumo 205 Diesel engines that gave it a greater range. In the course of my very first hours' flying it there was an awful vibration in one of the motors, during blind flying of all things. Vital parts had fractured. I got down in one piece at Cottbus, but only with some difficulty.

The next engine failure could have cost me my neck. I was taking off from the airfield at Westerland on the island of Sylt for firing practice when my port engine packed in at an altitude of about 100 metres. I had already begun a left-hand turn, and I had no option but to tighten it up, which was contrary to the rules of flying. I turned down-wind, then on to the approach after flying a base-leg at 30 metres, crossed the boundary fence at a height of 5 metres at the most, and made a skid mark of about 150 metres. There was some slight damage to the radiators. When they and the airscrews had been changed, the aircraft was airworthy again. If anyone doubted that my landing was as smooth as butter, it wasn't my wireless operator. When he had stood up to begin firing he had unstrapped himself, and he didn't even fall over. Shortly afterwards the Ju 86 was destined to cause me even greater misfortune.

There arrived at Nordhausen on an official inspection the Senior Air Commander from Dresden, *General* Wimmer, who was accompanied by the *Kommodore* of our *Geschwader* from Gotha, *Oberst* Foerster. The inspection was conducted by *Staffel*, and went into considerable detail. As it was nearing its end Roth, the Adjutant, came up to me and, pointing the way, said 'To the *Kommandeur*!' The *Kommandeur* was standing with the two senior officers near to a Ju 86, out of earshot of the others. It was clear that they were talking about Spain. I welcomed the opportunity to be able to shine. I was asked to compare the Ju 52 with the Ju 86 on the basis of my war experience. I praised the Ju 86 on many counts, but felt that I had to mention my double misfortune with the engines: I said I had flown far more than a thousand hours on the Ju 52 in Spain, and nothing like that had happened, no engine failure, even though on one occasion we had had to fill up with rotten, evil smelling petrol that had come from

Tangiers. Here, at home, I had almost broken my neck twice within the space of thirty hours' flying. The engine was no good: it wasn't up to operational standards.

What I didn't know while I was getting so worked up was that the Senior Air Commander had, when formerly Head of the Technical Service, very strongly promoted the development and construction of this 'crude-oil burner'. In a very friendly fashion I was asked to continue. I found no great difficulty in embellishing the accidents I had had. All three listened attentively. Finally *Oberst* Foerster brought up the matter of my conversation with the Chief of the General Staff of the *Luftwaffe*, mentioning particularly my four hours and twelve minutes' flying time. I was severely reprimanded by him and the Senior Air Commander. I had no overall view; my assessment was immature.

After this knock-out blow I was numb to the further slings and arrows. I felt that I hadn't been left the lickings of a dog. There was no other way to describe my condition. Then I heard *Oberst* Foerster, his voice raised so that I can still hear it to this day, 'You have done your *Geschwader* a great disservice.' With that I was dismissed to yet further menial duties. I was shattered. Did the gentlemen feel that they had been unjustly criticised by the Chief of the General Staff? Had they attempted to justify themselves to him? If my critical words in Berlin had been unwarranted, I would have liked to know. Still I had not been given any explanation for the lack of flying in Spring 1936.

My misery changed to courage out of sheer defiance. At midday, by now changed into civilian clothes, I drove up in my BMW in front of the *Staffel* Office in order to collect my mail and to tell the Duty Officer that, in addition to the service caps I had been told to count, I had also counted the boots and had found the inventory correct. I should be obliged if he would so report to the *Staffelkapitaen*.

After a short time had passed the *Staffelkapitaen* ordered me to put my number one uniform on: I had to report to the *Kommandeur* in fifteen minutes. All the omens were against me. How was one supposed to live like this? After all, I was only human. As usual, the *Kommandeur* was smoking a cigar. I begged to report to him as ordered.

Major Maass was bending over the text of a telegram, and from it he read out, or possibly summarised: with further reference to the discussion he had had with the Chief of the General Staff in Berlin, *Leutnant* Herrmann was to be requested to submit a handwritten report on his experience of Exercise Ruegen. The report was to be treated as a headquarters document. It was to be sent under sealed cover to the Chief of the General Staff. For the purposes of carrying out this work, *Leutnant* Herrmann was to be relieved from all other duties for a period of three weeks. The *Kommandeur* dismissed me with instructions to begin at once.

I could not imagine that the Chief of the General Staff, once having had an oral presentation, simply wanted to enjoy irrelevancies by reading them for a second time, so I concluded that he wanted to put my report to good use. It seemed that the notes he had made at the time had not been detailed enough.

So, to work, wee military writer. To work in the Merry Month of May, with your comrades outside the Scharnhorst accommodation block shouting out, of an evening, 'Come on down — we need your car!' There was no chance of that. For me, life had begun in earnest. I wrote and I wrote, about air transport, about flak inspection, about bomber operations, about fighter escorts, about the Spanish and about the Italians.

A few days before my time ran out an order arrived from Berlin to the effect that I was to produce a second copy of my report. Even without that, the sweat was running from my forehead and my fingers so that my pen kept slipping from my hand. I asked the *Kommandeur* to give me someone to help me with the writing by copying it out page by page in my quarters. After authority from higher up had been obtained, *Oberleutnant* Martin Kaestner, a man noted for his excellent handwriting, was attached to me, and at last I had someone I could talk to about the matter. He was pledged to secrecy, just as I was. Finally, Kaestner and I handed over the work, with me certifying that I had burnt both draft and notes.

My *Staffelkapitaen* seemingly didn't know the reason for my unprecedented release from duties. Nevertheless, I began to sense a certain slight change. In navigation instruction I no longer had to sit at a school bench with the other crews when the instructing officer was addressing us from the desk. I was even allowed, occasionally, to do a bit of stand-in teaching myself, but my tedious supplementary duties didn't stop altogether.

By and large, one might well have described my overall position, as far as the Service went, as drifting in water with my nostrils barely above the surface. One day a tool box fell through, or out of, the hatch in the floor of a Ju 86. The worst thing about it was that a tool box shouldn't have been taken on board at all. What had that to do with me? I was an unoffending pedestrian on the hard standing in front of our hangar when the hellish noise sounded from above. But I was wrong: the trail — how could it have been otherwise? — led to me because, shortly before, I had flown the aircraft from Sangerhausen to Artern to calibrate the airspeed indicator. Could *Leutnant* Herrmann be the one who had so grossly neglected his responsibilities as an officer to the detriment of the State by the destruction of property and the hazarding of human life? It turned out, however, that the real delinquent made a clean breast of it. Nevertheless, a few days later the order came again — best uniform, report to the *Kommandeur*. This was getting monotonous!

Again *Major* Maass was smoking a cigar, and again he had a telegram in front of him. This one, it was quite clear, he was reading out word for word. From: Chief of the General Staff, Berlin. The *Kommandeur* of the *Gruppe* was requested to inform *Leutnant* Herrmann of the following in suitable form. I was wearing the high boots that went with my best uniform, but I stood there with cold feet. They still had something against me. Never in my *Luftwaffe* career had I ever been summoned to hear praise or promotion. Now, however, my chill melted as if under the influence of a good, stiff grog. It warmed me from the inside and inspired my spirit to yet finer deeds when I heard that the Chief of the General Staff had found special pleasure in reading my report, and that he had said that my judgement was sound. And so it went on; a whole page . . .

I was dismissed without discussion, without any word of personal congratulation. I could not help wondering how my *Kommandeur* found it, being obliged to read this telegram out to me after his superior officers had gone on to me about my immaturity. At the time, he himself had not said anything, even though it was on him that my lack of flying hours must have had the most impact.

After some weeks I received a letter bearing the stamp '*Kommandeur*'. I was invited to go for an evening drink with him and his wife. Nobody else was invited.

We didn't talk about what had happened; that was, in any event, made impossible by the presence of the lady of the house, an ethnic German from Transylvania who had the knack of conducting a stimulating, friendly and amusing conversation. The invitation seemed to indicate that the *Kommandeur* bore me no ill will, that he wished to make me acceptable at court and that he apparently wanted to put my over-strict *Staffelkapitaen* in his place.

Shortly afterwards *Major* Maass was replaced as *Kommandeur*. At his farewell party his favourite tune, The Knights' March of the Great Kurfuerst, rang out from the gallery in the Officers' Mess. As it sounded, I cast my mind back and I tried to understand my commanding officer. I realised, quite suddenly, that I had let him down in Berlin. My overwhelming desire had been to get back to Spain, but it had been entirely selfish. If I had wanted to get more flying practice so that I could make progress, why on earth hadn't I spoken up about it at the time — out loud, instead of grumbling? And when I thought about it more closely, with the kettle-drums rattling from above, it was he whom I had to thank for getting me to Spain in the first place. I had imagined that that had been a sideways move for me — with an extra thousand *Reichsmark* in my pocket!

To be a superior officer must be difficult sometimes, and disappointing, but to be a subordinate and to identify with the emotional problems of your superiors is also a cross to bear. However, life must go on, and duty, in particular, must go on. I carried my head a little higher, but I thought more carefully.

At last, under my new *Kapitaen*, Martin Schumann, who had come to us from the *Reichsbahn Strecke* at Tempelhof, we started flying in earnest. I became Technical Officer and responsible for continuation flying training, with my friend Hanke supporting me energetically. Another friend, Schroeder, occupied the chair of Operations Officer directly below the *Kapitaen*: he was fully entitled to that by reason of having had his commission as an officer a few months longer. Seniority was universally recognised, even in the smallest degree, as legally binding. The *Kommandeur*, poised above the *Kapitaene*, now was *Major* Wilhelm Evers, for whom, in the course of my training flights hither and thither, I had to go looking for Camel cigarettes, of doubtful quality and a waste of money, as our propaganda had it, a fact behind which the man with the hole in his shoe had to hide, shamefacedly.[3]

Since Spain, in particular since my adventures with the wild man Storp, and as a result of many discussions between observers and pilots after operational trips, I had always wanted to find out for myself just how to score hits with bombs. I didn't much relish the idea of being an airborne taxi driver and flying into danger, if my observer was only going to land his stick of bombs off target.

So I embarked upon the task of becoming a bomber observer, a job that pilots in general denigrated, as I myself had often done from the very beginning. Transmitting and sending Morse at sixty a minute I mastered after two failed attempts. Photography from the rear gun position — a windy, open-air location that was alien to a pilot — produced quite tolerable photos of the railway marshalling yards at Sangerhausen, some oblique, some vertical. Firing at a towed drogue was great fun; but bomb-dropping just didn't work out properly. The aiming cross, made up of two wires on the bomb sight, wobbled indescribably over the ground. It must have looked like that when I was at the controls myself. The lesson I learned was that the pilot plays a fifty percent part in the success or failure of a bombing mission.

I passed the examinations in the various aircrew specialisations and was now an all-round operational flier. Those men who, more by their ability to creep than to fly, had got their pilot's ticket from having been observers, were known as 'Weder-Noch' ('Neither-Nor') a name given maliciously to them by the Pilots' Union. The brevet that went with it, also called the 'Weder-Noch', now decorated my battledress tunic, at the level of my bottom rib, but I christened it, 'Sowohl-als-auch' ('As well as also').

I didn't lose sight of the necessity to improve myself as a pilot, and I turned up at the desperately boring, but much sought-after, place Wesendorf on the Lueneburger Heide, the famous blind-flying school for would-be instructors. My own instructor, Oberleutnant Fischer who had, by then, developed his own very splendid landing technique, worked me very hard. For my passing-out flight, I took off in visibility of barely 100 metres. A car led us out to the take-off position.

A lot more work was waiting for me back at Nordhausen. New pilots, over and above the establishment strength of the Staffel, had been posted in and had to be kept busy. First of all there had to be a cell division: a new Gruppe was to be formed at Liegnitz.

In addition, my interest in the French had not diminished. I was aiming to become an interpreter in that language because I would be able to put my nine years of French study at school to professional use. In no way did I let anyone know that I had hopes of being able to crawl my way to a post as Air Attaché in Paris. But first of all I crawled my way through long lines of French printer's ink studying Le Matin, which I got by postal subscription in place of the Nordhaeuser Generalanzeiger. A secondary-school teacher, who used to prepare short-service soldiers about to leave the army for a professional life outside, regularly gave me oral and written instruction during the midday break whenever I could get away. We used a small hut that was not unlike an incubator, except that in winter we got frozen feet.

Monsieur Dubois who, together with German officers, gave me my oral examination at the Reichsluftfahrtministerium in Berlin — I had already taken the written examinations at Nordhausen — asked me to translate an article from a French military magazine. It was about the dense French balloon barrage between the Swiss border and the English Channel. Its main theme was that an attacker from the East would not be able to climb above the barrage. In the ensuing discussion I said that it followed, therefore, that the French wouldn't be able to penetrate into Germany either. He came right back at me with a question: was I not aware that French aircraft had a far greater operational ceiling?

I went back, successful, to Nordhausen, and there, for the first time, I received due congratulations. That encouraged me to look for something fresh to do in my spare time. By a stroke of good fortune, a competition landed in the office from Berlin. Our Operations Officer, Schroeder, immediately held it under my nose: 'From what I know of you, you're a compulsive scribbler.' Hanke was of the same opinion. The subject was tempting:

> How does the author assess the prospects against an enemy air force in war?
>
> What is the most effective way of fighting a war?
>
> What are the organizational, technical and tactical prerequisites for the achievement of rapid results?

That, I thought, is excellent. I could contribute as a member of a bomber crew — both pilot and observer — as a flak gunner, and even from personal experience with our own and enemy fighters. I could put in something about transport and how to improve organization on the ground, above all airfield lighting. At that time it was a working assumption, as was apparent from our exercises, that our bombers would be used for the task of combatting an enemy air force: that is, for air defence. I produced about 150 pages. Whenever I saw a clerk sitting around doing nothing I grabbed him by the scruff of the neck. I employed more subtle methods also, including the offer to come along with me on a weekend training flight, which I could arrange quite easily to pass over the house of the clerk's grandma or sweetheart; or, perhaps, a bottle of *Nordhaeuser Korn*, the local Schnapps; or last, but least expensive, extreme politeness.

When the opus was finished, all that was left to do was to affix my self-chosen pseudonym. The judges were to make their first assessment without knowing the name, rank or position in the Service of the competitor. Finally, however, each of these factors would be revealed, in succession, and only then would the final decision be made. (I was told this by my later *Kommandeur*, *Major* Neudoerffer, who was a member of the commission.) I chose the pseudonym 'Varius', the name of the largely unsuccessful Roman general. I had rejected (for reasons of prudence) Arminius, who was a victorious general but whose name related to my own, Herrmann. 'You mustn't show off to the gentlemen,' I told myself.

The gentlemen took a very long time considering the matter. One day, the *Kommandeur* summoned me and told me that I had won the third prize. 'A bit thin,' he said. I thought so too, above all because I believed that, parcelled up in my 150 pages, I had given the judges a very special tit-bit, an epoch-making invention: how to hit a target obscured by cloud. When I had been dropping cement bombs on the *Fahner Hoehe* (Fahner Heights) it had always irritated me enormously when the aiming cross, at first visible, became obscured by drifting clouds or haze, compelling me to stooge around for one fifteen-minute period after another until the target was clear again and I could drop the next bomb. Whether I was flying as a pilot or as an observer it was just as frustrating for me, my crew and the following aircraft, which couldn't start until I had announced '*Ende*' on the R/T.

Rage over the time lost can have just as creative an effect as 'Rage over a ha'penny lost' (Beethoven). Suddenly, my earlier mortar exercises at Potsdam brought me inspiration. Didn't we use to shoot at some target or other without being able to see it, from a hollow in the ground, with a hill crest obscuring the view? With a few reference points behind the mortar and a map you could hit your target. Therefore, if I could see Gotha, or Weimar, or whatever else there was to see down below, I should be able to hit the *Fahner Hoehe*. The range safety officer said he thought it was mad, but he came to a favourable decision, then disappeared into his concrete 'pointed hat' instead of standing nearby and watching the approaching aircraft through his binoculars. In the event, he couldn't see anything, he could only hear the '*Zebos*' (the cement bombs) as they came screaming down.

Consequently, bombs were sprayed about all around the cross; on the bombing proficiency table that hung in the *Staffel* offices I had moved not the slightest bit nearer to the head of the marksmanship table; but I told myself that it wasn't every target that was only 100 metres in diameter. I overcame what was unsatisfactory and imprecise in the whole business by dint of a revolutionary realisation, a by-product of my idea and, at the same time, novel. We would fly in formation above the clouds towards our target; we would take our back-bearings at leisure, and the flak couldn't see or hit us. Cover thine Heaven with clouds, O Zeus, I gloated. I had been very excited when I had thought the whole thing through to its conclusion and had written it down in the competition that had been set by the Commander-in-Chief; because it seemed to me, the idea could be decisive in a war, if it should ever come to that.

A short time later a clever Frenchman robbed me of my inventor's pride, and Germany of a military secret. Camille Rougeron described, in a thick tome which I had bought immediately, a practice attack carried out by French aircraft on cloud-covered targets in Upper Italy, using Montblanc, the Matterhorn and other giants as sighting points: not with the aid of an unstable compass and two points, as in my procedure, but without a compass and using the intersection of bearings from three fixed points, which was much more accurate over long visual distances. The book *L'Aviation de Bombardement* was older than my thesis! So much for my inventor's dream! I comforted myself that Monsieur Rougeron, being a Naval Chief Engineer, was professionally bound to be more accurate than a very ordinary Air Force *Leutnant*. *Morbleu!* I had almost overlooked the fact that a seaman had stuck his nose into airmen's business. I found that exemplary.

But my inventor's dream was not completely lost. In conditions of cloud cover, when there were no landmarks visible, I had put the bomber force flying above the cloud, under the orders of an artillery observer flying at low-level at the same time and reporting to the aircraft flying above the impact position of coloured test bombs. The bombers would be able to follow the correct course into their target, with the aid of this 'downward-looking periscope'. I thought that this system — which, thank God, I didn't find proposed in M. Rougeron's work — was very significant. The flak would be rendered largely ineffective and the enemy fighters would have difficulty getting up through the clag.

Well, I thought, the prize is admittedly rather thin compared to the quality of my invention, but perhaps they don't want to draw attention to it by giving me a higher prize. Perhaps our senior officers are, even now, hatching out even better plans than those of Monsieur le Frenchman and the good *Herr Leutnant*.

In any case, this small success gained for me a prize of 150 *Reichsmark*, which Major Evers supplemented with a further 150 from some element or other of his budget — to be used in the interests of the Service, he added. I interpreted such interests in the form of a trip to Paris at the end of 1938. What was more, the Military Attaché there, *General* von Kuehlenthal, had invited me, when I had made the acquaintance of his family in Davos the previous winter, to visit him. We met on New Year's Eve, in fact, in the Hotel Belvedere into which I walked wearing a dinner jacket, 'Deutscher Wald' brand.[4] I was a non-smoker but with a lighted cigarette specifically carried for the purpose I burst the plump, coloured balloons that were floating above their table, to the alarm of the lady and her daughters. Quite unconcerned, I asked if I might join them at the table — a waiter in tails was already holding a chair for me — and received their permission, which was given in French. I saw this as a lucky break because it gave me an opportunity for linguistic practice. I said that it was *merveilleux* here, and more in similar vein, upon which the gentleman, who had a very cultivated appearance, observed, in exquisite German, that I needed a little more practice! It was still before midnight and I expressed my pleasure at the elderly gentleman's geniality somewhat boisterously. The next day I rode up in the ski-lift to Strela with his two daughters, both of whom were fully qualified French interpreters. My descent was not quite as elegant as theirs was.

To have a point of contact in a foreign country is at least fifty percent of one's security. In addition to the Attaché, I had another. Herr Stoehr from Leipzig, a prominent man in the wool-weaving business, was a reserve officer in the Nordhaus *Gruppe*. He gave me the name of a French business friend in Paris who supplied him with sheep's wool from Algeria and said I should pass his regards on to him. This address was the other half of my security. Nothing could go wrong.

Both the General, who hadn't revealed his true identity to me at Davos until several days had passed, and the wool dealer wrote back to me to say that I would be very welcome. So I set off, not having heard of the assassination of the German Counsellor at the Embassy in Paris. I had only had hearsay reports that many window panes had been broken in Nordhausen on the day I left. I had assumed that this vandalism had been an unfortunate local aberration.

Soon after we had passed through Forbach in the French train, wooden-seat class, I found myself in the company of a number of soldiers travelling on leave. They were very friendly to me, offering me some of their bread, cheese and wine. I looked at their young faces to see if I could discern any hostility in what were our bitter enemies of the First World War. There was none to be seen.

In Paris, my first action was to report to the French Town Commandant, who let me speak French to him but answered me in perfect German. In the streets the strong reaction to the assassination had generated considerable excitement. I was confused by the hectic voices of the French that spoke of German threats against them. Projectors cast the map of Europe on to the walls of houses. One after another displayed those countries which we would have conquered, it was said, by 1942. I took it for pure propaganda. We had our Greater Germany now that we were united with Austria and the Sudeten Germans. I stood in the excited crowd and tried to make out what the arguments were.

I went to a cinema and saw the film *Are We Defended?* It gave the French a reassuring insight into the secret defensive power of the Maginot Line. I read a lot of newspapers and I attended lectures, one by the well-known politician Herriot, who was speaking on the subject 'Napoleon in Egypt', as if there was nothing more interesting at that time. I also went to a talk given by a Jesuit priest on the subject 'Hitler, the German Mohammed'. I asked myself what the French wanted. Nobody in Germany was thinking of attacking them!

The Attaché said I would not have to go back home; nothing was going to happen. He ought to know, I thought. My French hosts reassured me, too. They invited me home to lunch and to the finest restaurants in the Faubourg St Honoré where I was surprised to note that the husband addressed his wife with the formal *Vous*. A striking French girl, a teacher, who tried to teach me the 'Lambeth Walk', which was just coming into fashion, in the Café Bagdad, was very much in favour of Franco-German understanding, but in so doing emerged as a fiery imperialist. No war in Europe, she said, but we should attack China where we could both play our part. *'Voilà un bon morçeau.'* That was her watchword.

The subject of *Kristallnacht* (Crystal Night, November 1938) had receded slowly. The Military Attaché gave a reception at which the senior military dignitaries of Europe, softly clicking heels and bowing politely, greeted each other and circulated in a leisurely fashion, sipping at their glasses. They all looked pretty much alike: men with distinctive features as though they were all from the same family; similar in their bearing, their haircuts and their way of speaking. Each wore his uniform with the same pride, as if they were all from one great nation, their uniforms differing less from each other than did those of the Uhlans, the Cuirassiers, or German Naval Officers of the Kaiser's time. Each of them wore his medals with the same composure — medals from the last war: scarcely to be believed! Neither was it to be believed that those same officers would go to war against each other again, whether ordered or volunteering to do so. The beautiful ladies completed the harmony with the *staccato* of their laughter or the *glissando* of their conversation. I was very happy to be there, and I envisaged a bright future for myself in a sphere such as that which I saw before me.

After I had walked round the International Air Show with close interest, had climbed the Eiffel Tower — what the birds see can be of use to an airman — after I had visited Napoleon's grave and done everything else that the average European was wont to do, I took my leave from my Frenchman, whom I had grown very fond of, and from the Attaché, who was hoping soon to be back home and in command of an Army Group.

The railway journey was long and entertaining. After my first week, when the torrent of French had taken my breath away, I could now hold my own in conversation, to a certain extent at least. Nevertheless it was a relief to hear German voices again at the border. My arrival was timely, too, because my last franc, for which one could drink so much more coffee or wine in France than in Germany, had been spent and a few German *Groschen* formed my emergency fund. I had to walk from the railway station at Nordhausen to the airfield on foot, carrying my suitcase.

Airborne again over a Germany that had expanded in size. The Heinkel 111E was the bird that carried me across the Baltic to Koenigsberg, round Heligoland and Borkum to the *Grossglockner* and the *Venediger*, through dawns and sunsets, moonlit nights and starlit skies, side by side with my aircrew students, the keen ones and the quick ones, the clumsy ones and the bad-tempered ones: all fine fellows.

In between all this there were classroom lectures and ground exercises. *General* Kesselring, who had in the meanwhile become *Chef der Luftflotte*, participated in one of these together with senior — and very senior — Army officers. The theoretical and practical theme was 'Winning air superiority by destroying the enemy air force's bombers and fighters on their airfields, so that our own forces fighting on the ground are not impeded'. There was not a letter, not a word, no official instruction, that mentioned residential areas or civilian populations. Men, women and children as targets for our bombers — such a thing was unthinkable.

In the course of this important exercise, *Major* Evers introduced me as a star turn. From the music gallery I was permitted to unroll a visual aid, about two metres wide and five metres long, strengthened at each end with wooden laths, which enabled me to present, to an admiring and interested audience, in impressive detail my idea of formation flying in conditions of cloud. The fact that in so doing I deviated considerably from what was laid down in the 'Instructions for the Command of Bomber Formations' would have caused *Oberst* Foerster considerable annoyance again, because it was he who had ordered the printed instructions to be produced at the Training *Geschwader* at Greifswald. Now, however, *Oberst* Doerstling was sitting in his place, and he listened with enjoyment as I chopped about with his predecessor's work. 'Quite remarkable,' he ejaculated, more than once. Coming from someone who had just been posted from the General Staff to a Front-line command, this was praise indeed; but I valued more the critical questions that *General* Kesselring put, which I had to answer and discuss.

It became apparent to me, two weeks later, that the General's interest had been more than just friendliness, because I was ordered to go to Berlin and repeat my presentation. On landing at Staaken I got into the waiting Mercedes from the *Luftfahrtministerium* and sat down next to *Hauptmann* Trautvetter, who had come from Greifswald to participate in the same discussions. I discovered later that he had played a major part, under *Oberst* Foerster, in working out the guidelines. As we were driving round the Victory Column[5] in the open car, he asked me what the long roll that I had between my legs was, erect and proud, stretching into the air with the windstream whistling through it like a flute. New guidelines? 'Get those out of your head, my dear fellow!' He patted me, quite incongruously, on my thigh, kindly but insistently. To avoid any complications I took a seat some distance away from the *Hauptmann* in the big conference room until I was asked to explain my modifications to the circle of gentlemen with red trousers.

I spoke a few sentences and then went to unroll my diagram but the senior officers stopped me (*General* Kesselring was not present). The ceiling was too low, they said. The table was too small. I was to leave the thing there, label it, then I could disappear. When I had written 'Herrmann, *Oberleutnant*' modestly on the roll, *Major* Neudoerffer (later to be my wartime *Kommandeur* for a short time and who had been decorated with the Golden Spanish Cross with Diamonds) hissed, 'Nonsense! Not your name — your *Geschwader!*' What, I wondered, had become of strategists' copyright!

Back to Nordhausen at high speed with a seething radiator and a seething mind. Only a year later I would learn that those amendments that I had proposed were already in need of improvement.

A few days after German troops had marched into Prague I began to ponder over the expression 'Greater Germany'. The union of the Sudeten Lands had fired us with enthusiasm. On our low-level parade flights over Eger, Marienbad, Karlsbad and other towns we had seen masses of waving people and a sea of waving flags in the streets and the squares, but after Prague there was no such similar atmosphere. Everything happened so quickly, came about so unexpectedly. I do not remember going onto standby at Nordhausen in March 1939. All we knew was that a Czech, Dr. Hacha, had signed an agreement in the same circumstances as Graf Brockdorff-Rantzau had signed one in Versailles in 1919. Weakness was punished, strength was rewarded — hard facts such as these, not high principles, seemed to me to be what counted in the life of nations. Was there, in truth, only the choice between the anvil and the hammer, as Goethe had written?

Our demand for a solution to the question of Danzig and the Polish Corridor seemed, to me, to be based on pure principles. The fate of the population there had been decided on the basis that the victors were all-powerful. Fresh elections were the very least that should be agreed upon. Anyone opposing them was guilty of betraying the people's right to self-determination, as at Versailles.

Encouraged and incited from outside, the Poles rejected the peaceful solution. The anger that I felt inside at their unreasonableness matched my sacred conviction: that of the German rightness. A people who were not incensed by the unreasonable demands of Versailles did not, in my opinion, deserve to be called a people and have its own sovereign state. Any other nation would have been incensed. Did we Germans want to be nothing more than a collection of individuals? Was I in my battledress, without the right to vote, a political soldier? What else? He who is put before a nation as a guard, to protect its life, its freedom and its property, to win back what has been stolen from it, whose heart beats for it — in war and in peace he is implementing the foreign policy of his country.

There was much activity in the last days of August. Mussolini intervened, and there was hope that the great political powers would be able to negotiate the German demands. We were to learn that they did not wish to do so. That was the perpetuation of brute force under the cloak of the law that had been established at Versailles. Consequently we rose up against brute force. On the 1st of September 1939, therefore, I flew in my He 111 at the head of a *Staffel* under the command of my *Staffelkapitaen*, Martin Schumann, in the company of like-minded comrades, across the German-Polish border.

The war had begun. It was a war in which we fired the first shot and dropped the first bomb, in order to overcome brute force.

Notes

1 *Reichsluftfahrtministerium*: the German Ministry of Aviation which was responsible for all aspects of flying, both military and civil.
2 Technical Officer. The jobs of both a Technical Officer (*Technischer Offizier*) and a Signals Officer (*Nachrichtenoffizier*) of a *Staffel* were secondary duties performed by appointed aircrew, usually a pilot and an observer respectively.
3 'The man with a hole in his shoe' refers to a well-known advertisement for Camel cigarettes in the 1930s. It showed a man lying back and enjoying a smoke and displaying a hole in the sole of his shoe. The caption read, 'I walked miles for a Camel'.
4 'Deutscher Wald' brand. Literally, 'German Forest'. In the pre-War era in Germany synthetic fibres were used widely, manufactured from wood. Clothes made from such fibres were of poor quality, obviously.
5 Victory Column: the Siegessäule commemorating the German victory over the French in 1870.

Chapter Four
Germany at War,
September 1939 — February 1941

*The first stage of the war between Germany and Poland lasts from 0435 hrs on 1
September 1939 until 1100 hrs on 3 September 1939. At that point in time England
declares herself to be in a state of war with Germany. The French follow suit. On
17 September 1939 the Soviets march into Poland from the east. November/
December 1939, the Soviets attack Finland. The Western Powers plan to cut off
Germany's imports of ore from Northern Sweden via Narvik. Germany, Britain
and France fight in Norway. Germany gains the ascendency. Holland and Belgium
are occupied and France is forced to capitulate. The British escape via Dunkirk.*

In the last weeks of August 1939 we lay with our Bomber *Gruppe III./KG 4
'General Wever'* on a forward airfield at Langenau near Breslau, ready to take off
at an hour's notice. One start was cancelled. I don't know whether it had been
meant seriously. In the next few days, after Mussolini had intervened in
international negotiations, it appeared that the danger of war might be averted.
Even when we were awoken on 1 September, about two hours after midnight,
nobody knew that the die had been cast.

Take-off was set for dawn but had to be put back because of ground mist.
There was still a ground haze at around midday when approximately thirty He
111s took off from the airfield, formed up by *Staffel* above the haze in a brilliant
blue sky, and made a wide curve on to an easterly heading, climbing slowly.

From the air you can normally make out everything on the ground: fields,
woods, meadows, villages, rivers, roads; but not, in general, the lines about which
men quarrel so passionately — political boundaries. We could see the German/
Polish border, its course clearly recognisable from the air almost exactly to the
metre. The road, tarred or paved, suddenly took on a different, lighter, colour
like that of sand and gravel. Similarly, the small river, which had been
straightened out on our side, reverted to its original condition on the eastern side
in a series of bends. The meadows, too, drained by narrow ditches and fenced off
on the German side, looked far bigger on the other side, and they had bushes
growing on them.

We were over Poland. I was deeply aware of the historical nature of the hour.
This time it wasn't Spain that was at stake. It was ourselves. It was we who were
challenging the future. It was we who were not prepared to submit. From now on
it was to Fate, and to her alone, that I would yield.

We unloaded our cargo of bombs on a railway line to the north of Biala, in the
region of Krakau. The High Tatras, rising in majestic solemnity above the haze,
were a silent witness to men's thunderous, raging conflict.

Approximately noon the next day saw us carrying out a high-level attack by *Staffel* in line astern on the airfield at Deblin on the River Weichsel. We were expecting to see a river like the Oder or the Elbe flowing on a reinforced bed strengthened with groynes, but its width surprised us, spreading as it did into a number of arms, with islands of sand and boulders shining brightly in the sun.

Late in the afternoon of the same day we attacked the airfield at Deblin again, where there was an officers' school. The flak was quite accurate up to our flying height of 5500 metres, but still the fighter pilots in their PZLs came at us even more aggressively and courageously. One brave airman attacked me head-on and shot out my port motor, so that I had to crawl homeward on one engine. The other members of my *Kette* slowed down too and gave me cover until we landed, somewhat late.

I flew eighteen operations in Poland, all against purely military targets — marshalling yards, railway lines, marching troops, airfields, enemy positions and, once, against the defenders of Warsaw, who were refusing to surrender. The vast battle picture impressed itself deep in my memory — the flashes and the flames of the guns, the burning villages, the steamroller of destruction moving forward, day by day, from the north, the south, the east and the west towards the centre of Poland. Never before had any general enjoyed an overall view such as we had from a height of thousands of metres over the battlefield of Poland.

During the attack on the Kutno pocket we lost a crew, that of *Oberfeldwebel* Deckert. A direct hit tore him, his crew and his aircraft apart twenty metres away from me. My friend Hanke collected a direct hit at the Lysa Gora that put his elevators out of action. He put his aeroplane down with a mighty bang on the Langenau airfield, but he and his crew crawled out of the wreckage with no bones broken.

After our last attack we drove to Breslau. The market place in front of the Rathaus was thronged with excited people, confident or jubilant. Hanke and I both had the Iron Cross Second Class dangling on its ribbon from our buttonholes. We were in a cheerful mood, as might have been those people on this very spot in 1813 when the King of Prussia made his call to the people. We were moved deeply when an old mother hurried up to us with two small bunches of flowers and cried in a piping voice, '*Heil*, you heroes!' There were tears in her eyes as she looked up to us. She had lost her husband in the First World War. There we stood, two heroes very much by chance, each with a bunch of flowers in his hand. I looked again at the medal that was inaugurated on this spot and had since been worn by hundreds of thousands of front-line soldiers of many generations, and now I thought about what it meant. To this day, it remains my best, most memorable decoration.

It was still September when we moved back to Nordhausen, then to Bracht near Marburg an der Lahn, ready to fight off the English and French, who had declared war on us on 3 September. Everything remained calm, and we were moved to Vechta/Oldenburg, then to Barth on the Baltic coast to convert from the He 111 and re-equip with the Ju 88. We continued this process at Luneburg. The Ju 88 was a beautiful bird, but it was said to be dangerous, and we had to test it by flying it at night, first of all on circuits and bumps. I suggested that we might start straight away on long, cross-country flights, up to five or six hours' duration, so that we could get accustomed to the monster in the air. Landing would be less dangerous then, and if we did crash we would at least have gained some experience. That is what happened. I set out for Pillau in East Prussia, from there over the Baltic and round Bornholm back to Lueneburg, where I made a three-bounce landing, but without any damage. I taxied off the runway and climbed out, moderately pleased with myself.

On 8 April 1939 we moved to Westerland on the island of Sylt (still operationally equipped with the He 111), in the assumption that we were going to attack Scapa Flow. I was more than a little surprised when, at two o'clock in the morning, our *Staffelkapitaen* — by this time *Hauptmann* Erich Bloedorn — announced that our target was to be Norway.

We started in the black of night with a covering of stratus, headed northwest towards the North Sea, and then north, parallel to the Danish coast, steering for Kristiansand in South Norway. The other aircraft, which were following at close intervals, were to join up into *Staffel* formation on course for the target when it became light. We were to carry out a carpet-bombing attack on the island fortress that lay in front of the town. A number of aircraft succeeded in joining up. Below us, shining blue, lay the Skagerrak, behind it were the snow-clad mountains; a world of Gods against the red sky of morning. Down below, there was raging a war of men. Our speedboats were zig-zagging fast into the fjord, spreading swathes of artificial smoke to shield one of our troop transports that was listing heavily to one side.

The first bursts of flak appeared in front of our windscreens. My observer, *Oberfeldwebel* Laska, set the bomb release mechanism to its minimum interval, as instructed, and as the others had also been ordered to do. And so we went in to the attack!

The wide-vision cockpit of the He 111 gave an excellent view forward and obliquely downwards. I saw the guns firing from the fortress up towards us and towards the speedboats, weaving their foaming way deeper into the fjord. Our leaders had expected a different reception: on board we had containers which, when dropped over the target, would burst open at a set height and release a confetti-like rain of pamphlets calling for surrender. There was no question of that now.

We thundered ahead on our approach. With one observer's and one pilot's eye I held the machine steady. Laska's voice came through calmly. I corrected my heading. Then the bombs were falling. They were all clear of the aircraft in a matter of seconds. Laska kept his eyes on the bombs as they fell downwards in a long Jacob's ladder. He kept them within view until they vanished as tiny dots. The uncertain time it would take until he would see them again as explosions, success or failures, tore at the nerves.

'Right in the middle! The other sticks as well!' Laska shouted. Both *Kapitaen* Bloedorn, sitting next to me, and I were delighted. I couldn't see what was going on down there, as it was directly below me. 'What a balls up!' shouted Laska. 'There's somebody else bombing!' Some dozy bastard hadn't set ten metres: he'd set a hundred metres. Consequently his bombs spilled right across the fortress and the water, two of them slamming into the town, despite strict orders that dwelling houses were not, in any circumstances, to be damaged. Bloedorn was in despair. 'Out with the pamphlets!' he yelled. What good that would have done when the bombs had landed already, I couldn't imagine. With houses burning down there they would surely think that a call for peaceful surrender was a bit cynical. Dropping the leaflets was a reflex action, but both the wireless operator and the engineer were pleased to be rid of the heavy ballast. However, it served to be an example of the ironies of war that the 'dozy bastard' forced the fortress to surrender when it had, in fact, withstood our attack. Fearing further bombs on the town, the Mayor ordered the fortress commander to cease resistance.

I felt partly responsible for the error. The observer was new to the *Staffel* and I had confined myself to giving the order 'ten metres interval' without testing to see whether the newcomer could set the shortest and longest intervals with his eyes closed (in his sleep, as one might say). I was consoled by telling myself that it was the young officer's excitement that had been the deciding factor. The facts of the case were soon recognised, even by the man who had committed the successful miscalculation, but when he came up with the statement that it had been a decisive success and he should, therefore, get the Iron Cross, at least, my *Staffelkapitaen* went purple in the face and exploded, uttering blasphemies that I can no longer recall with any precision.

That afternoon we flew our second mission against barracks on the outskirts of Oslo. It went according to plan. We flew back low over Oslo Fjord. As we pulled up over a wooded islet, there was a banging noise. The gunners on our cruiser *Bluecher* must have been absolutely on the ball. Too late did we recognise our own warship and they their own aircraft. When we were coming in to land at Lueneburg in the gathering dusk we discovered that the flak had damaged our undercarriage. It wouldn't come down. The *Kapitaen*, the observer and the engineer heaved and strained a good half-hour until finally the manual handle engaged and the three of them either fell over or banged their heads. The undercarriage was down, and we landed smoothly.

The following day our task was to harass the English, who had landed at a number of points in Central Norway and were pushing forward. In order to do so, we had to move to the airfield at Oslo-Fornebu with a full load of bombs, there being none stored there. We were not told the dimensions of the airfield and so it was quite reasonable for me, piloting the *Kapitaen's* aircraft, to expect that the runway would be long enough — but it wasn't!

As I overflew the airfield for the first time I could see that the longer runway had been shortened at each end by a number of aircraft that had collided with each other. I orbited, had a close look, and decided to use the shorter runway, which was free from obstacles. Throttling back to an almost criminal degree I came in over the fjord and, to my great satisfaction, touched down just over the airfield boundary. I rolled, and rolled, and rolled. The brakes seemed to have little effect. I could already see the edge of the field along which there ran a narrow defile. A terrible feeling of helplessness overcame me, and I could see that I didn't have a chance — I could have wept! My beautiful He 111 collapsed with a cracking noise. I was paralyzed. As if from a distance, I became aware of my crew on the outside of the cockpit, waving and shouting, 'Get out! The crate'll explode!'

I couldn't have cared less (a captain must feel like that when he decides to go down with his ship). It isn't a sense of duty, or of shame, or of honour: it's nothing more than the natural, dulled consciousness of one of life's losers, accepting release in the form of the *coup de grâce* by Almighty Fate. Slowly, I switched off the ignition, unstrapped myself and crawled through the fuselage, past the bombs, and out of the tail section, which was reaching up towards the sky. That black day continued its course with one tragic event occurring after another.

Without interruption the Ju 52 transports swept in to land and broke into pieces, soldiers leaping out in utter confusion. One Ju 52 dived from a low altitude into the forest, came to rest on its nose and burst into flames. With firing still going on around us we tried to save the soldiers. Then mortar shells began to explode inside the fuselage. One detonation followed the other. A blonde Norwegian girl in ski trousers who had come to help burst into tears. The pine trees all around were on fire. The heat scorched through one's uniform to the skin. We drew back. When one is powerless the strength that desperation gives evaporates.

Then the G 38, the giant Lufthansa airliner, landed: bringing not bitterly needed reinforcements but the band of the Staaken Airfield Headquarters Unit. Drums, winds, Drum Major. They formed up in front of the airport buildings and started to play military marches while, to the accompaniment of banging drums, aircraft costing hundreds of thousands of Marks were reduced to scrap. Some hours later a patrol set out from the airfield and, some distance behind it, a column of men followed by the band playing 'Preussens Gloria'. We brought up the rear with machine-guns we had unscrewed from the aircraft and pistols with their safety catches off. From the hills we could hear the sound of firing. Oslo fell the same day.

The planning had not been General Staff work. Details of international airports were published, giving all their dimensions. Why didn't I get a map? I knew how long my aircraft's landing run was; so the General Staff must have known too. If the General Staff knew how big the field was — and it is fair to assume that they did — they had committed an unforgiveable error. My aircraft, which took thousands of man-hours to make, was gone. Further aircraft had been destroyed, men cast into the jaws of Death. It was, of course, intended to be a strategic surprise and so had to be kept secret: but from the enemy, not from us.

The previous day the *Bluecher* had also fallen victim to inadequate reconnaissance, shortly after she had fired on us. At slow speed ahead she had presented herself broadside-on to a torpedo position dug into the banks of a fjord at a point where, every year, hundreds of cargo ships passed, many of them German.

The remainder of our operations as far up as Stavanger, Bergen and Andales were not flown from Fornebu but from Aalborg in Denmark. The British were driven out. Norway was occupied. We took off at dawn on 10 May 1940 from Delmenhorst, flew low out over the North Sea across the Ostfriesian Islands, turned towards the west and later, altering course southwest, flew parallel with the Dutch coast. Climbing sharply up to 3000 metres we turned through a right-angle in the direction of the coast, to the airfield at Bergen an Zee that lay just behind the sand dunes. Our *Staffel* was now equipped fully with Ju 88s. We made a diving attack from 3000 metres. We had achieved surprise. The Dutch fighters were unable to intercept us, and we left the dust behind without any damage to ourselves. One aircraft from the *Staffel* with four crew had crashed on take-off; all of them were killed. It was a very dark night and the take-off aids were very poor, certainly not adequate for a more temperamental type of aircraft. The development of ground aids lagged well behind that of aircraft.

So began the campaign in the West. In rapid sequence, we directed our attacks on transport ships off Ostend, Dunkirk and Calais, with a short peak of activity off Dunkirk, which the British were evacuating, on 10 May 1940. At about 2300 hrs on that date I saw, in the light of the full moon, a large freighter leaving the harbour of Dunkirk and setting course north. I hesitated about committing myself to a diving attack, because I could see that when I broke off it would take me over the English pocket with its searchlight and anti-aircraft defences. After I had waited about half an hour and formed a picture of other shipping movements, the transport had left habour and turned on to an easterly heading parallel with the coast, no doubt intending to keep to a channel that had been swept of mines before later turning north for Dover.

Then I committed an error that Storp had indoctrinated me into in Spain: I set out to hit one ship with each of my 250-kg bombs. There were more ships lying at the quayside. One was just casting off. I went into attack at right-angles to the longitudinal axis of the vessel, into the moon. I set the fuse, dived, pressed the release button, and pulled out. My rear gunner reported that I was ten metres short.

I climbed again, then dived; twenty metres out. My observer, a new man flying with me to gain experience, a *Feldwebel* with a good head on his shoulders but something of a pessimist, said that he could have told me so and suggested that I should drop the two remaining bombs at once, so that we could go home with a 'kill'. As I was pulling up again, I had just about decided to do as he said when my *Feldwebel* started needling me again, so that I became angry and said, 'Negative. I'm dropping them one at a time!' There was an element of a gamble in it; but there was a bit of rationality in it, too. First, I had gathered more experience since Spain than Storp and I had had at that time; second, I had come close to my targets with my two bombs and could reckon with a hit the third time.

I dived, and the bomb hit. I saw it. There was a flash from below. As I pulled up again I saw a small fire on the deck, and that made me toy with the idea of putting my last bomb in with it. After ten minutes the fire had spread over the whole length and breadth of the ship. The vessel was a write-off. We looked down on the corvettes and launches coming to its help and assumed that the soldiers were jumping overboard *en masse*. I reported the tonnage of the ship as 8000. Others assessed her as 10,000 tons. Diving even lower I put my fourth bomb on a second, smaller freighter I had already had my eye on. The vessel didn't catch fire: she sank.

Subsequently the passenger docks at Le Havre, Cherbourg and Brest were targets for us, but the critical point remained Dunkirk. Fate and I came close together there during the afternoon of 31 May 1940. We had taken off in a large battle formation from Schiphol, near Amsterdam, in order to attack the Dunkirk pocket from the land side, from the direction of Belgium, in particular the troops and the ships and boats clustered at the quay and the makeshift piers. As my own aircraft had proved to be unserviceable before take-off I had taken a spare aircraft, and hadn't had time to test it. Dunkirk could be seen from a long distance off, marked by a giant cloud of smoke that was rising from the burning oil tanks in the port and combining with a narrow band of cloud. This unusual picture was to become significant to me.

Our fighter and destroyer escort kept the enemy fighters away from us, so I quite happily held my position with the *Staffel* in the middle of the formation. We approached the diving line. Flak. The leading aircraft started to dive. I pulled on the air-brake lever, but the brake didn't come out. I rushed downwards, at headlong speed, past the lead men. The slipstream whistled, high-pitched, past the cockpit. The aeroplane vibrated. I tugged at the brake, but nothing happened. Can't go on like this, I thought. I pulled out in a long curve so that the aircraft wouldn't break up. Below me, the others were falling like stones into the depths, their bombs raining down; but my crew and I were all alone in the firmament.

Get after them, try again! The nearest ships were situated close to the bank. Suddenly the silhouette of a Hurricane swept past; then another. Up into the safety of the smoke and cloud formation! I'd made it! It stank. Whoops — I'd come out on top! Back in again and out at the bottom. The banner of smoke was very thin. A burst of fire lashed through the fuselage. Wires sprang out towards me from the instrument panel. Jettison bombs? No: both motors were still running. Back into the haze. Keep a lookout above, don't climb too steeply through it. If you do, they'll get you. There's another strange bird on the scene. A French Dewoitine? Saw something like that in Spain. It's a nippy beast. But so am I! Let down, but not too steep.

There was more banging. Christ, an engine's gone! The wireless operator cried out; the under-gunner groaned. I had a dark-brown trail of smoke coming from astern. I dived downwards steeply, but the fighters hung back. Either they were saving ammunition or being chivalrous. I couldn't make up my mind what to do. Land on the beach where the Tommys are? Negative! Suddenly, I thought, '*Alles schietegal!*' ('What fucking difference does it make!') and dived down even more steeply. My port engine was idling because I couldn't help it; my starboard engine from choice. I aimed at a medium-sized transport, anchored close in to the coast, and released my bombs, but they were ten metres off target.

I put my wreck of an aeroplane under power on one side: I wanted to get out of this! But the Hurricanes were there. The pilots knew that they had been fooled, and they were mad about it. There was another bang, but that one hadn't made it; he was too fast, and he zipped past overhead. Every second was vital. I flew further east, away from the pocket where bursts of machine-gun fire were splashing into the water. None of us were firing any more. Those at the back had taken cover. I cringed down behind my armour plate. The *coup de grâce* must come now. There was a sound of cracking, but I didn't know where it was coming from. Water burst in through the brittle cockpit, causing my breath to stick in my throat. My *Feldwebel*, the nit-picker, jettisoned the roof in the nick of time.

I thought, 'I'm under water! What am I doing here? Get out!' I tore everything off: life-jacket, overalls . . . I was out, believe it or not, and standing, head above the water, on the aircraft's fuselage. A further three heads appeared above the surface of the water, near to me. Artillery thundered from the shore. The two of us in the front were unhurt, but both of the men from the rear of the aircraft had got metal and glass splinters in their faces and hands. We set about getting to the shore. We let ourselves down from the aeroplane and floated, dog-paddled into the shallows, crawled into the gentle breakers and looked around us. A German steel helmet emerged from the grass. Mate — I could hug you! I'd made it. That was my 40th operation in this war, not counting the half-century in Spain.

By 17 June operations against targets on the European mainland were finished. In the meanwhile, I had been made *Kapitaen* of the *Staffel* and *Major* Bloedorn had become *Gruppenkommandeur*. We were allocated important strategic and military targets off the east coast of England, the oil refineries at Thames Haven and the nitrogen works at Billingham. We dive-bombed them under a full moon, with strict instructions either to bring our bombs home or look for shipping targets if we were unable to identify our main target quite clearly. I always flew on ahead and gave the others clearance to attack only after I had recognised the target positively and had put down one or two benzol bombs.

Particularly difficult was an attack on the Vickers-Armstrong Works in Newcastle-on-Tyne, which was of great importance to the British war effort. By that time the moon had waned to half and the east coast was covered by several layers of cloud, so I decided that I could carry out the strike by day with the help of cloud cover. For the operation we moved to Bad Zwischenahn in Oldenburg from where, after a thorough discussion, we flew northwest in loose formation, in beautiful sunshine and above a deep-blue sea. By the time we arrived over the middle of the North Sea, flying in conditions of radio silence, we had reached our maximum ceiling and were in the light shade of high cirrus clouds. We were approaching the critical zone in which the Hurricanes and Spitfires could intercept us. To our good fortune I made out, in the distance, the first banks of cloud at medium altitude; at first thin but then swelling to 100-300 metres thick, but only half covering the sky.

Soon we had a sufficient body of cloud beneath us. If those black, swiftly moving and ever-growing dots should appear suddenly above the grey below or beneath the cirrus above, which was already darkening the sun, we would dive into the clouds, each man taking his own cloud and orbiting in it, bobbing up and then down out of it to see whether the sky was clear yet. After my experience with the lack of cover off Dunkirk I would feel confident that I myself, my crew and my *Staffel* would be quite well hidden there.

The Met man had been correct. The layer of cloud below us, which was developing into a level floor, and the smooth ceiling at twice the height of a church tower above us, conjured up the feeling of a vast hall — a Valhalla, I thought. That was what I had always imagined when I was a boy, when my father, his eyes directed upwards towards the sky, spoke of someone who had been called up to join the Mighty Host: a hall with many, many beds. In German, hall is *Halle*, pronounced *Halla*, and in the Valhalla of my imagination the heroes slept while Wotan kept watch with his one eye and his spear. Today, that vast hall that was the sky is empty of pictures, and empty of men, too. Thanks be to God!

It is a great comfort to the heart of a bomber pilot not to be the target of a tyrannical fighter pilot armed with fat cannons; he can cold-bloodedly exploit his skill at blind flying to triumph over heavy-calibre superiority.

Suddenly, there they were. Two of them; all-weather fighters. I hadn't expected to meet them there in the top storey. My chums, far astern to left and right of me, dived away. I waited a little while longer. They couldn't fire yet — they had to get into position first. Break! They were showing their teeth. I dropped down into the clouds at high speed. 2300 metres — 2000 — then I was out and the cloud ceiling seemed to be sweeping upwards away from me. Ahead of me was the coast, a fine land, blue-green in the near-evening of five o'clock. There, in the distance, was Newcastle. That was enough to orientate myself, so I ascended into the cloud again.

At 2500 metres in the intermediate layer of cloud I snatched a breather and paused for thought. Up there was my opponent. He saw me and curved in at full power, a black banner flying from his exhaust. I assumed that he was in a hurry. *Nein, nein, Junge!* Not so fast, today of all days! The radio operator kept up a running commentary, but I kept turning my head from side to side as well. I wanted to see him with my own eyes, to wait right up to the last second. I had to get to the target. In a second or so he would be on my tail and gunning for me. The wireless operator shouted; 'He's coming!' I could see him. Down again to the ground floor!

Then things started to get uncomfortable. I came out through the cloud ceiling at 1800 metres. Fat, horrible, monstrous balloons swept past below me. Too bad, if there were some of these jellyfish swimming about in the clouds! All at once a cable saws through your wing without you knowing what's happened. But the stiff wind was laying them flat like a stream does to water weeds. Where there were fighters flying, the upper sky must be clear.

I flew up the Tyne, past the target area. Despite the balloons, the rapid-firing flak got me in its sights. They'll shoot them down as well, if needs be, I thought. I flew switchback, along the lower surface of the cloud — in and out. From below, the gunners could see me only fleetingly. I pressed my R/T transmit button, 'An alle. Herumgurken ausserhalb! That means 'To all. Orbit outside', but it was slang. The English translator monitoring our broadcasts would scratch his head!

While the other crews were orbiting over open countryside and awaiting further orders, I looked west of the town to decide the correct course of action. A diving attack or an attack in a steep glide would be madness. When we were climbing back from down near the ground they would make mincemeat of us. Had the cloud base been at four to five hundred metres we could probably have made it. The attack would have to be made flying straight and level in clear skies and along the cloud base. That would be rough also.

First, the wind had to be checked. The plumes of smoke from the chimneys indicated the ground wind, which was a start; but we needed the wind at altitude. Calculating that was not a comfortable business. I had to break cover so that the observer could take the necessary measurements. Later, we would have to emerge from the cloud exactly to the minute and second, spend a few moments making corrections, aim, bomb, then disappear up into cloud again. To calculate the wind we had to spend whole minutes below cloud. It was all up to us, and disaster was waiting. It's hard to make out fighters against a many-coloured and many-shaped countryside. So, Himmelhunde (dogs of heaven), comrades, keep your eyes open! That is exactly what I did also, while the observer was measuring. My glance alternated between my instruments and the countryside. I was sweating. What did Hadrian's Wall down there mean to me? A tourist attraction. I had no time for the landscape. Surely the observer would be finished soon!

At last he had finished, and miraculously we hadn't seen a single fighter. Was it possible that our orbiting over open country had confused the defences? I wondered what they thought was going on when a Ju 88 peeped out of the upstairs window here and there and bobbed back in again. The British fighters had certainly also done their bit towards confusing the situation in the air.

I broadcast the bomb settings to the other crews, which had been calculated on an east-west attack, heading along the River Tyne, on the banks of which the factory could be seen like a very narrow pocket-handkerchief. We passed the starting point on an easterly heading. I pressed the stop-watch and rose up into the cloud ceiling, keeping rigidly to my course. Down below they were listening and lying in wait at their guns, chewing gum while they tracked us, and somewhere, above or below us, the fighters were hovering. The English can't have a clear idea of what we are planning, I thought. Our wild roundelay must seem very strange to them. Now the roar of our engines was reaching their ears from an easterly direction.

The final seconds ticked by. Then — down! The last scraps of cloud flitted past me. There was the Tyne, and there was the target, just as it had appeared in the aerial photograph. The same plump, odious monsters again — the balloons. Then the flak tracers whizzed past us and disappeared into the clouds — '*Buegeleisen*', we call them (flat irons). We were under our soldier's oath: no more equivocation and hesitation. Results were more important than self-preservation. I took hold of my crate. Come on, observer! Finger out! Drop the bloody things! Now, now — it doesn't matter a shit whether you hit the near end or the far end! He had a long fuse and stayed calm. His eye was glued to the eyepiece. He didn't have the slightest idea what was going on to the left, to the right, and all around the area. In his little field of vision the world was relatively well ordered.

At last the bombs were dropped. I hauled the aircraft mercilessly into a climbing turn which made my lower jaw feel like lead. Thank God for the clouds! I was enveloped in them. I drew a deep breath and headed south to take another look. I worried how the others had done. I'd drummed it into them: never stick flat to the cloud base, because there they'll see you before you can see them. You can break cover with a bang and a cheer when the time's up, just short of the target.

Being lighter now I approached the field of battle from the south to take a look and to cause a bit of confusion. I peeped out quickly. There was something going on ahead. Smoke was rising from the ground in a number of places, and it was not from chimneys. Suddenly there was more banging. I sought cover quickly, climbing up steeply to the intermediate cloud layer. I roared over the port at full revs, opening and closing the throttle and I called my crews, 'Stay upstairs. Good luck!' *Leutnant* Weinrich joined in. He had a talent for annoying you very subtly, and he announced in broad East Prussian that he was going to Edinburgh.

The heavy anti-aircraft fired a few rounds of deterrent flak. As if from nowhere, black wads of cotton wool appeared suddenly, indicating that I was in the right spot. For a few minutes more I roared round the area, revved my engine, made it scream and made the exhaust sound like a death rattle. Then, full throttle, I pulled away, homeward bound. As forecast, the clouds had spread further out to sea. I stayed within their cover until the English coast lay far behind me.

We all got back safely from Newcastle. Hard to believe. The British air defence had acquitted themselves well in their first action. They earned our respect. We had been lucky. Or had we? As we were writing our combat reports, almost light-heartedly, a man appeared. He was wearing a uniform that neither I nor any of my comrades had seen before. A provost-marshal. What did he want? He announced that, according to information from the Führer's Headquarters, German aircraft had carried out a terror raid on the civilian population of Newcastle at about 1700 hrs that day. He said that he had been instructed by the General in command of *IX. Fliegerkorps* to find out who was responsible. He was to question the captain of each aircraft and ask him what he had hit.

Suppressing my anger only with difficulty, I told him that he could start by questioning me. I would confess straight away that I didn't know what I had hit. None of my crews knew what they had hit. I had expressedly forbidden them to hang around after they had dropped their bombs to see where they exploded. I asked him whether or not he knew how long the things took to reach the ground from a height of 2000 metres. He said he did not know. I told him that they took 20.7 seconds. With the aid of the second hand on my watch I demonstrated to him how long 20.7 seconds was, and I imitated the noise of a machine-gun softly with my tongue as I did so. I told him that just as he would take cover after the first second, so had we. We had gone into the clouds.

The provost-marshal was at a loss. The Commanding Officer had to report the hits to *Fuehrerhauptquartier*, he said. I advised him to report that when they released their bombs all the crews did so accurately, with their target in their sights. The long-range reconnaissance crews would have to do the rest. If it was necessary to find out where the bombs that had missed the target had landed, one might as well fight the war in the classroom in future.

I was reprimanded by the *Fliegerkorps* for having prevented my crews from being questioned, for my disrespectful attitude and, quite absurdly, because neither I, nor any of my crews, knew what we had hit. The *Kommandeur, Major* Bloedorn, ordered me to write a detailed report. A piece of paper such as that, to which an unpleasant taste of politics attaches itself, suddenly grows legs and rapidly ascends the ladder of officialdom. The long-range reconnaissance boys flew over there the following day, and the story became clear. One stick of four bombs had made two craters just outside the grounds of the factory, and damage had been caused to one or two private houses. Nobody ever discovered who had dropped them. In fact, the pilot responsible owned up to me at once, together with his observer. They said that they had emerged from the clouds to one side of their track and had dropped their bombs, almost diagonally, on the factory area, and that it was then that it must have happened. It wasn't a very good advertisement for me. Before the war, I had trained the pilot in blind flying and the observer in bomb aiming.

Another piece of paper arrived later, having found its way, considerably more slowly, down the ladder of officialdom, and landed on my desk finally. It informed us that we had done very well. Specifically, I was to visit a number of units in Holland and Belgium and teach them how an attack by day using cloud cover should be carried out. The paper was signed by *Generalfeldmarschall* Kesselring.

A series of mining operations against ports and shipping channels followed, which I interrupted on one occasion to attack a convoy near Flamborough Head on the east coast. I made a dashing low-level attack, almost hitting the mast of a steamer, but all my four bombs were near misses. I was so overcome with remorse that that same afternoon — it was my birthday — I did without coffee and cakes in order to attack the same convoy further south, then near Great Yarmouth, whistling out from the low cloud base, bombing and climbing back into the cloud without seeing the effect. From a suitable distance, we took a look from the side to see if one of the convoy was missing — we had counted them earlier — or if, at least, there was one lagging behind or showing a list. Nothing of the kind. From one of the steamers dark smoke was starting to appear; but, quite often, the British would set fire to combustible material in huge frying pans or cooking pots after an attack in order to mislead us.

My crew couldn't even bring themselves to open fire at the single fighter flying around above the clouds, even though he was in an ideal position for us to attack him. It had been a bad day; a really bad day.

The crew of *Oberleutnant* Geisler, a member of our neighbouring *Staffel*, from Riesa, did not return from that operation. Other crews had seen the British putting up barrage balloons from some of the ships. I was only mildly shocked. The results were shattering when compared with the amount of effort we had put in. We were not equipped with a bomb-sight suitable for attacks from a shallow angle of approach. A few weeks previously, at Schiphol, together with a number of gentlemen from the firm of Zeiss-Jena, I had experimented with the prototype of a bomb-sight intended to be used in conjunction with input data, instead of visual judgement. But the bomb deviated from its forecast path only too easily. Practice flights with cement bombs had so far failed to produce satisfactory results, so I wrote an operational report and sent it upwards through official channels.

The entire month of August was characterised by attacks on important military targets, ships, vital war installations on the coast, ports such as Plymouth, the mining of which was a very difficult navigational exercise and very dangerous, because we had to drop the mines from a very low altitude and at a very low speed; in doing so, I came into very close contact with a barrage balloon.[1] Our strict instructions not to attack residential property in the target area continued in force, orders that increasingly aroused frustration on the part of the crews. Every night we saw aeroplanes penetrating into Germany in the direction of the Ruhr, and we heard from relatives and friends that the enemy was not imposing any noticeable restrictions to ensure accurate bombing. Dwelling houses were being destroyed in many places, and there were dead and wounded.

At the beginning of September 1940, we began to attack London. My first raid, my 69th of the war, was on the night of 7/8 September and was against the India Docks, the great loop in the Thames in the East End of London. I was convinced that we had done everything possible to conduct the war as a struggle between combatants and not as the indiscriminate slaughter of women and children. As time went by our anger at the British war of terror — which was how we saw it — overcame our reservations towards repaying like with like in the hope of compelling a return to warfare according to the rules. That was what was preached by our leaders at every level, and I, from bitter personal experience, never had any reason to doubt it.

By 18 October 1940 I had already logged 21 'revenge attacks' on London alone. That same day, while attempting a dusk take-off with two 1000-kg bombs on board, I suffered a major accident. My left tyre was slit by bomb splinters that had not been cleared from the runway after an earlier attack by an English intruder. The heap of wreckage that had been my aircraft lay off the airfield, its engines scattered here and there. Not far away lay the two huge bombs, which the observer had jettisoned at the last moment. One crew member had been hurled from the metal fuselage in the death-dive and the others were trapped inside it. I was dragged from the wreckage and, I am told, babbled, '*Weiterstarten!*' ('Take off again!').

I first regained consciousness in a cool operating theatre in the Wilhelmina-Gasthüis in Amsterdam, and as I did so I heard someone asking if I could feel anything and saw somebody dressed in white who was pinching my big toe. It was a great shock. Was I paralysed? The doctor continued to talk and to pinch. 'Ow!' I said, which he acknowledged with '*Sehr gut!*' Next to me, two of my crew lay on stretchers, while the fourth member was standing at the top of my bed with a bandaged head. They had all been following my return to the land of the living somewhat tensely.

I lay there with one broken lumbar vertebra and one strained one, with concussion and my left hand slightly cut by metal, in a single room in the hospital. The next day I awoke from a deep sleep to recognise our medical officer, Dr. Coburg, near me more from the sound of his voice than by sight. At first I wept dreadfully, with an abundance of tears. Why, I don't know. After a short time I brought my surroundings more into focus and saw something very strange on the bedside lamp. Dr Coburg told me that it was the Knight's Cross and that I had received it three days before my crash from the *Reichsmarschall* in person. I had forgotten the occasion completely.

After I had spent three weeks being forced to lie absolutely rigid I was visited by *Hauptmann* Gaggy Metzenhin, *Kapitaen* of our neighbouring *Staffel*. He had just finished bringing me up to date on the latest military operations when the sirens sounded. Metzenhin switched off the lights in the room and raised the blackout blinds. The roofs of Amsterdam were shining in the light of flares that an English aircraft had dropped. The town looked as if it was covered with snow. A few seconds later there was an ear-splitting crash and the walls literally shook. Our hospital, which was clearly marked with a red cross, had received a direct hit. There was shouting, the sound of feet running in the corridors and of doors slamming. Metzenhin shouted, 'I'll save you,' using the familiar form of address — '*Ich rette dich*' — which was most unusual because we were not on first-name terms. He rushed out and came back with a wheeled stretcher, put it alongside my bed and rolled me carefully on to it and then ran with me through the corridors. All the lifts were occupied. Through the blown-out windows shouts and the sound of whimpering rose from outside up to our level. There were many dead and wounded. Metzenhin carted me aimlessly around until he saw that it was pointless. By that time the flares had been extinguished.

The indignation of the patients and the Dutch nursing staff was understandable, but unjustified. I could honestly deny any intent on the part of the British. A bomber pilot flying at night at a height of 5000 metres, even with flares, could never recognise a red cross on a roof, and he would never deliberately aim at such a cross either in occupied territory or in the Reich. In the several square kilometres illuminated by the flares he would be able to distinguish clearly defined areas and lines only. There was plenty of important targets all around — factories, canals, locks. How could a single bomber pilot — for that was what he was — feel other than as an insignificant being, dazzled by the searchlights, hammered by the flak, threatened by night fighters, looking for a target allocated to him by his leaders, not finding it or mistaking something else for it? The fault lay with military or political leaders.

I spent a further three weeks in the *Luftwaffe* hospital at the Olympic Stadium in Berlin, where I had the opportunity, sneaking from the cellar in which I had been compulsorily accommodated, to experience a genuine terror raid on Berlin. Bombs were scattered over the entire city. Next day my friends told me all about it.

By the end of November 1940 my recovery, which had involved all sorts of treatment and swimming training, was all but complete. I thought I could manage without the ten days still scheduled, and I telephoned and asked to be collected. I diverted from a walk through the corridors and the Adjutant of our *Gruppe*, *Oberleutnant* Sommer, who had come in a Ju 52, gave me comradely assistance. At Staaken I took the controls and bore in mind the doctor's warning that in future I had to avoid heavy G-forces in tight turns.

When I landed at Schiphol my *Staffel* had just completed pre-flight preparations for a further attack on London and were due to taxi out for take-off in an hour. At that moment, I found it very hard to suppress the memory of my last unhappy experience and to imagine myself at the controls, heading out in the same direction as the others. If I didn't take off today, it would be even harder to do so on a later occasion. So let's do it now! Press on regardless! I dismissed a pilot, took over his crew, climbed into the aircraft with them, manipulated the levers and knobs, and was off. If there was ever a time when I had difficulty in overcoming my weaker self, it was then. After the operation the tension was gone. Calm and composed, tired but contented, I reported to the *Kommandeur*, via London, that I was cured.

In the last weeks of Autumn 1940 my old unit, *III./KG 4 'General Wever'*, was taken out of KG 4 and transferred to KG 30, the *Adlergeschwader*, as the 3rd Group, which had been equipped with the Ju 88 even before we had. My *Kommandeur*, *Major* Bloedorn, became *Kommodore* of KG 30 and was replaced by *Major* Arved Crueger, an excellent pilot, a considerate leader and, above all, a kind man, of whom I was very fond. His leadership was relaxed and informal but because of the example he set, it was positive and conducive of loyalty also.

I was destined shortly to deviate from this example. Don't ask why. I would have carried out my orders very nicely and correctly if my gunner, *Unteroffizier* Stiefelhagen from Engelskirchen near Cologne, hadn't given me such a severe dig in the ribs that the aircraft at once took over and flew her own course.

The meteorological situation was bad all over when I had taken off, briefed to take a look at the east coast of England and the shipping channels off it; to discover and report suitable cloud bases, visibility distances and targets, so that the *Gruppe*, vengeful and standing by at readiness with bombs on board, could strike. Weighted down by this highly responsible task and ten 50-kg bombs that I had taken with me just in case, I scoured the coast, the entrances to ports, buoys and mud flats, crept lower and lower beneath rain-wet clouds down to the grey sea, strained my eyes peering through the mist, ready at any instant to make a rapid dart out to sea should sparks begin to fly towards us from some mole or other. To do a recce like that was a difficult and dangerous business, and the weather didn't help. From the Thames to Newcastle there was nothing but the grey monotony of sea and cloud merging into each other. Here and there, a fishing vessel or a patrol boat could be seen, reporting our course, no doubt. Was that the insidious chatter of a machine-gun behind us, perhaps without tracer? No way of knowing. We thought not. We were destined to be very surprised later, back home, when we saw the holes.

Sometimes our boats play-acted down there in the gloom. This time not a single one was reported to have put out to sea, disguised with fishing nets in order to transport a German agent across. What a job: having to trudge through the mud-flats to the land, at night, wearing rubber boots, and, in case of an emergency, having to carry some fish to show and suitable documents to pretend to be a Dutchman or a Dane. We had to be alert to anything under sail or Diesel-powered, pitching on the waves; alert, too, to the wretched minesweeper in the narrow channel cleared for convoys. He was an impudent dog that not only barked but also bit. He knew that I couldn't hit him with my bomb, even if I managed to find him again after I'd turned in to attack. He'd be far more likely to surprise me with a salvo from one side. No. We were better off where we were: we wouldn't bother with small fry. Back home, they were expecting a juicy report from us.

We took a quick peep inland, so that we could observe the little harbours from the rear. Flying was easier there. We could make things out — roads, half-timbered houses, cows with their hindquarters to the wind, a local train, a cyclist who waved at us, perhaps thinking we were a Blenheim: it's a bit degrading, not to be recognised for what you really are. We're not one of yours, chum. We're one of theirs! Where's your command of the air?

We flew out to sea again, to the bigger ports, the river mouths that swallowed the cargoes from Canada and Australia and pumped them to the vast stomachs of London, Birmingham, Leeds. Nothing there. Nothing — that's something worth knowing. It would be awful to lure the *Gruppe* into this morass. We did an about-turn: but did not fly straight back home, along the shipping channel, the path kept clear night and day by the sweepers. Perhaps the visibility had improved further south. Perhaps we'd find something or other, a wee convoy, maybe.

Nothing appeared from the mist. There was nothing worthwhile to be seen. As hope decreased with the increasing geographical latitude, the anger grew inside us: this England, an appendage to Europe, is not only floating in a grey soup but also darkening in mist beneath a layer of dripping cotton wool. I'd had enough and, in the vicinity of Ipswich, I said, 'Let's go home,' 'home' being Amsterdam-Schiphol. To set the seal on my decision I reached for the chocolate in my knee pocket.

I withdrew my hand. What did my man from Engelskirchen just say? He was muttering, 'Those lovely bombs! All this time flying, and now we're just going home!' The man had been lying on his belly in the under-turret the whole time, and he still hadn't had enough. He'd picked out and identified every sea-mark, the lighthouses, the washing on the line, the cyclist, the flak on the quayside, and all the time he'd been waiting to find a resting place for our ten 'little' bombs. Oh, ignominy and shame! My gunner had given me a blow below the belt. Me: his commanding officer and *Staffelkapitaen*!

I was seething with rage: I'll show you something! I was on a westerly heading already, climbing, under full power, into the clag, into the gap between cloud layers, getting my bearings through holes in the clouds. Thames Haven showed up. It was very familiar. I flew further west. Minutes later, I saw a stretch of the Thames. To London, perhaps? Where else? It's big enough. We'll hit that, for certain.

Sometimes we could see the ground below; sometimes we couldn't. Large fragments of cloud were ranging low over the countryside, over chimneys, fields and woods. We knew what it was like to be grounded in weather like this. Enjoy yourselves, you fighter pilots down there! Come on up, if you want: and parachute down! The flak batteries? They'll do their best to make an impression, just as they did at night. They may impress the folk on the ground, but not us up here.

The rain was bucketing down, and we were bumping about. Through the rain, the sleepy grey of a built-up area gazed up. London. That's right: I'm going to bomb London. Nothing more, nothing less. Alone, off my own bat, because my gunner thought I was chicken. I'm going to lay it on really thick for him. The man must be made to realise just what he has started. It'll be good for me, too. I have to wipe out the disgrace. We saw the smoke of anti-aircraft bursts here and there, most of them mingling with the mist and the wet.

I wove my way further onward. I thought we must be over the City by now. Schmetz dropped the first bomb. We took our time before we dropped the second. If the English could appear over Berlin by night, why couldn't we appear by day over London? Cause a bit of disruption. We dropped the third bomb. We were still OK. There were lots of right-angles in the sea of houses. The fourth bomb went. I said to Stiefelhagen, 'If you find it too boring, try to shoot a balloon down'. He let off a few short bursts astern, but without any great enthusiasm. The balloons were 1000 metres lower, at least. The fifth bomb tumbled away. Still no fighters. How could that be? I must keep an eye on the fuel, I thought. I was feeling so good that I broke off a piece of the chocolate in my knee pocket and chewed it. Seventh bomb. I asked Stiefelhagen if he was hungry. No, he'd rather keep a lookout — perhaps a fighter would turn up, after all. Ah, I thought, he's not feeling too good. Eighth bomb. I asked Schmetz what weather we could expect that night. If it stayed as it was we could go to the pictures, perhaps. Ninth bomb . . . tenth bomb.

The Londoners had been in the shelters and the tube stations for an hour and a half. The German radio monitors were puzzled: they had assumed that the British were firing on one of their own aircraft. No German command post knew anything about an attack on London. *Major* Crueger had said that he knew nothing either. Only when he put the receiver down did it dawn on him. Was it possible that his men . . .?

When we had landed I said to Stiefelhagen, 'Don't stir up the shit like that again!' That evening we went to the cinema together. (I think it was Cora Terry). How Stiefelhagen got the Iron Cross First Class the next day, even he didn't know. Too modest!

When, at approximately 0400 hr on 16 February 1941, I dropped two big mines in the entrance to the port of Sunderland on the East Coast, and the flak opened up angrily behind me, I didn't know that I was taking my leave from England for a long time. It was an England whose geography had become as familiar to me as that of my homeland. I had grown familiar with the enemy also. His hardness and his bravery; his tricks and his traps; but his occasional weaknesses and lack of alertness also, which were something to do with tea breaks, possibly! I hadn't noticed that we differed markedly from one another in any particular way. For myself, I had never felt inferior to the proud sons of Albion. At best, I had been able, I thought, to cut off for myself a small slice of their wealth of invention.

At approximately noon the following day all the *Staffelkapitaene* were ordered to report to the *Kommandeur*. When we left the meeting, a new page in the book of the war's destiny had been turned.

Notes

1 On 22 July 1940 Herrmann's Ju 88 collided with a barrage balloon during a mine-laying sortie off Plymouth. Herrmann lost control of the aircraft but managed to regain it and brought the aircraft back safely to base at Zwischenahn.

Chapter Five
War in the Mediterranean,
February-March 1941

Italy, who had declared war on England and France in June 1940 and has joined in the attacks on Greece and Egypt, is experiencing difficulties. The British have landed on Crete and are preparing to invade the Greek mainland. The German armed forces must help.

Ahead of us, glittering in the midday winter sun, rose the snow-covered Alps. Behind us lay the grey days and nights of seemingly everlasting monotony in the air war against England: mines in the Thames, Humber and Mersey; bombs on industrial and harbour installations; nightly encounters with heavy British bombers over the North Sea, their loads even more dangerous than our own. Behind us lay Holland's flat fields, greenhouses, canals, streets covered in snow-slush.

On this particular February day in 1941 our *Staffel* of Ju 88s was climbing laboriously to height. We were not carrying heavy, streamlined bombs under our wings, but big, angular containers in which was stowed the equipment necessary for operations in the South. In addition, we had a fifth man on board, our ground mechanic, and there was a lot of gear squashed into the cockpit. There was scarcely enough room to breathe.

The container-bombs were holding us back as we staggered towards the Central Alps, round the few white cumulus clouds. We glanced left, then right, where our aircraft, flying in the kind of loose formation we vulgarly called a 'Sauhaufen' (I imagine the nearest English equivalent would be a 'bloody shower'), are rising and sinking with the currents. We kept a weather eye on the sharp mountain ridge ahead of us. We'd have to be careful when we tried to clear it. Anybody who had difficulty in getting over it was under orders to turn back to gain height.

We passed the Brenner. Soon, the last mountains were astern of us. I took off my antiglare spectacles and looked at the Po Plain, spreading out far below with not a trace of snow. Italy, land of our dreams. We had made an intermediate landing at Lechfeld, where there was deep snow. Now, there was sun and pure, eternal green. How the kings and their men, the pilgrims in the Middle Ages, must have hastened to shake the snow from their clothes, how happily their steeds must have whinnied at the scent of the fresh grass.

We passed over Ravenna, flying along the east coast. Clouds were massing on the west coast. We descended to 1000 metres. It was getting warmer: we switched off the heating. It was snug inside the cockpit. We were heading for Sicily. On instructions from above, we were being thrown in there to hold the British Fleet in check, in an attempt to give the Italian Fleet operational freedom and to secure the supply lines for our *Afrika Korps* by blocking the convoys that were sailing from Gibraltar and Alexandria to supply Malta. We had been looking forward to the change and the sunshine; to changing the black night-camouflage paint under our wings for light blue; to flying in a light-blue sky.

We were heading steadily down the seam of the Italian boot, all kinds of colourful pictures in the mind's eye. To some small extent we were already prepared for the ships. One of our observers was *Oberleutnant zur See* Friedrich, who was flying 300 metres astern of me to the starboard quarter as *Kommandant* in 4D + ER. He could distinguish between British and Italian warships in his sleep, which is why he had been seconded to us from the Navy. In Amsterdam he got hold of a Baedecker and, in addition, he knew Italy well from educational visits he had made there. Into his lectures on naval warfare and the use of the sextant he inserted the main facts about Sicily. He spoke of the Ancient Greek Syracuse and of Archimedes, who had burnt the Romans' wooden shops with a concave mirror, of the Normans and the *Staufer*[1] and even of Goethe's primordial plant.[2] I wondered if we would ever get time to check some of those facts in the Baedecker.

We had flown well to the south. We had cut off the heel and were tracking along below the sole of the Italian boot, right up to the toe. Our gaggle of aircraft crossed the Straits of Messina and followed the beautiful coast south. To our starboard Etna, 3000 metres high, was flying her banner peacefully in the wind. We rocked in the powerful, vertical currents. We left Catania to the port and headed inland into the plain south of Etna. There lay the small village of Gerbini, close to which was the airfield that we had been allocated, our destination and our future operational base.

In fact, it was not a proper airfield at all. In front of us lay a grass landing strip of uncertain length, apparently bounded to the south by some sort of flat-lying vegetation. There was not a fence, ditch or footpath to be seen. In the direction of Etna, a sparse row of trees suggested, vaguely, an edge to the field. There were small copses and nearby a thin, irregular double, or triple, row of medium-sized trees among which were a few straw-thatched, whitewashed huts. Just as I was beginning to doubt that this piece of landscape could really be meant to be our airfield, Krahn discovered a few covered and camouflaged Savoia bombers. 'Where?' I asked. Then, 'I've got 'em.'

It would have been a very poor show to have had to go scouring Sicily with the *Staffel* looking for our airfield. Similar things had happened before when we had been transferred from one base to another and when we had been switching between theatres of war. A multicoloured wind sock, swinging slack in the wind, caught my eye. We orbited the area, one aircraft after another, looking for parking spots. The roar of our engines filled the landscape, rolled across villages, fields and slopes, and echoed against Etna. Goodbye, secrecy! What the people there learned, including our *Geschwader* identification mark, 4D, painted large on the aircraft, would find its way to Malta. In England they would be pleased to learn that they would be able to sleep more peacefully at nights. At the time, the *7th Staffel* only had arrived, which could be determined from the final letter, R, on our aircraft. The letter immediately in front of the R was that for each individual aircraft. Thus my marking in full was 4D + AR.

One after another we landed. I was the last of the five crews to climb out of the Junkers, and I felt a mild wind blowing on my face and my neck. The air smelled of farmyards, mixed with the scent of a spice I didn't recognise. All the aircraft from my *Staffel* had landed, together with the two Ju 52 transports that had taken off some time ahead of us. They carried our 'black men': the mechanics and other technicians who would help us into the air, there in the sunny south. They filled their lungs with deep draughts of air and looked up at Etna in amazement. 'Boy, oh boy! What a change from flat old Holland!'

A motley collection of men on donkeys, attracted by the noise of our engines, had wound its way towards us from the olive and almond groves and through the cactus hedges. They brought every sort of edible and vitamin-rich commodity, which they exchanged, amid a welter of words, for anything that we could spare. A donkey, for example, changed owners for a pair of high-fashion, laced boots from the *Kurfuerstendamm*. *Oberleutnant* Hans Hanke, from Arnsberg in the Sauerland, the 1a of the *Gruppe* sent ahead with us, had perceived at once that, until our station administration company and our vehicles arrived, quadrupeds would be our only means of transport, not to mention the best camouflaged. He entered into negotiations. The question was: buy or hire? We didn't have any *lire* because our admin. people were not due to arrive for several days.

From where I was standing one of the huts, about two kilometres away, looked different from the others. It was small and had an upper storey with a window in it. The wind sock was located not far from it, so I decided that the building must be some sort of military headquarters. There was no sign of movement, so I decided to investigate. How about a donkey? I scrutinised one of the grey beasts and my action was taken immediately as a sign of intent to purchase. At first I was shocked by the long number of lire the dealer wrote down; but he was a typical salesman and suggested a thousand ways of solving the money problem. One thing that interested him was my astronomical wrist-watch which was probably worth more than three donkeys.

I was not entirely convinced by the herd of donkeys. One of them attracted my cautious interest, but his legs seemed to be a bit shaky, a point which I expressed, very politely, in my best fifth-form Latin; *'Asinus tuus labilis est'*. Upon hearing that, the man with the jet-black hair and dark eyes let fly with a torrent of words, causing me to flinch back. Nevertheless I realised, with a certain pleasure, that communication was possible by means of that 'dead' language, the usefulness of which had so often and so convincingly been extolled by teachers, but had never been proven until then. In desperation the man spread his arms out wide, flung them in the air and, suddenly, with one bound, leaped on to the donkey in such a way that I imagined it would give way at the knees. Nothing of the sort transpired. The donkey went round and round me in wild, galloping leaps, its rider laughing at me, singing and shouting.

I thought, it's a different world here. Something will have to be done for the donkey. I said that I was prepared to take him on trial, which seemed to restore the honour of its owner. In any event, I was completely credit-worthy, as far as he was concerned: I didn't have to put anything down as a deposit. So I was able to ride over to the stone house.

The grass was somewhat damp from the rain. Now and again my donkey paused. His ears scarcely emerged above the tall grass. He had a name already, given to him by our men during the circus routine. The frequent cries of *'tutti'* had suggested 'Toto', a name that I whispered into his ear during my ride, but without any noticeable effect. He stopped and I had to get off and push. Behind me there was much merriment. I took my animal by the halter and dragged him through the prairie. I doubted that it would have been a suitable subject for a war reporter to write on in the *Berliner Illustrierte*.

To my pleasure, the stone house proved to be the Italian Airfield Control Tower. It was occupied by a soldier of indeterminate rank. My stammerings in a mixture of Latin and French immediately caused him to wind the handle of his telephone fiercely and to ejaculate countless times, '*Pronto!*' The soldier gestured like a Field Marshal, and I felt rather gauche and lonely. He passed the receiver to me with an enviably patronising gesture, and I heard a German voice at the other end. With an uneasy stomach I formally reported our successful landing, and I was immediately given an order — I hardly expected anything else. I was to take delivery of bombs and fuel which would be brought to me very shortly, and was to stand by for an operation the following day together with *Lehrgeschwader 1*,[3] the *Greifswalder*, which was already there. My questions as to the distance, the type of bombs and the type of target involved, remained unanswered. The enemy is listening in, I was told. There was a great variety of targets in the Mediterranean, from aircraft carriers to camel caravans.

Having taken the precaution of leaving my donkey in the entrance hall, I led him carefully through the door into the open air. I wondered where they and their great operational plans would have been if I had been stuck at Lechfeld because of the weather and the deep snow on the ground. I could have been sitting in the *Goldener Loewe* with a large beer.

We had been allocated to *Oberst* Knust, *Kommodore* of the *Greifswalder Lehrgeschwader*, as reinforcements. He ruled the roost in Catania. The *8th* and *9th Staffeln* and the *Stabsschwarm* (Staff Flight) from our *Gruppe* were to join us in a few days. I told the *Staffel* what little I knew, sufficient to set into motion a hustle and bustle of organisation and improvization. Hanke would have to worry about the reception of the whole *Gruppe*. For the time being we all had to make the best of what we had.

While I was waiting for an Italian taxi driver who had, we were told, been conscripted, I had a snack from my flying rations; nuts and raisins, Dextroenergen tablets and chocolate. The latter was too bitter for my donkey apparently: he didn't like it! I wondered how Toto would get on with my Bert-Ingo, a full-grown Alsatian, who was going to come with the airfield administration company via the Brenner. Hanke's donkey and mine presented a different problem: they were deeply and passionately in love. We had to tether each of them to a separate almond tree, on lines just long enough for them to rub noses with their necks outstretched. It would not have done for the ropes to have been any longer!

Giacomo, the taxi driver, compensated for his late arrival by hurtling up the final hundred metres of the rough track at full throttle, his countrymen leaping aside with curses while he, deeply conscious of the strategic importance of his mission, trumpeted back on his horn twice as loudly. At that time and in that region, pedestrians, donkeys and oxen all considered themselves to be priority road-users.

I boarded the taxi with some trepidation. We were soon on a very good asphalt road, an incentive to the Sicilian to put his foot hard down on the accelerator of his Fiat Topolino, a small, four-wheeled vehicle, as broad as it was long, and to cut the corners without any inhibition. Sssst! An unsuspecting road-user rushed past us, going in the other direction, only centimetres away. It was no better for

Giacomo than it was for me. Even though he clung tight to the side of the road when taking a right-handed curve, we were beset by like-minded tearaways. I longed to be in my aeroplane. What was concentrated flak in comparison with the torments of the soul that I suffered in that tin box! Every time there was a 'Sssst!' Giacomo beamed at me, his head turned right round. I wanted to scream out loud. Only my good breeding prevented me. With an air of pride and self-confidence (and, quite clearly, expecting high praise), Giacomo came to a halt in front of the operations room. Weak at the knees, I nodded politely and said, 'Fantastico!'

The operations room had been set up in a smart villa on a low hill on the outskirts of the town, not far from the airfield at Catania. To the south one could see as far as the wartime harbour of Augusta; to the north, as far as Acireale, on the coast before which was the great rock that the blind giant, Cyclops, had hurled after the blasphemer Odysseus. Even in those days they exaggerated the dangers they encountered and the deeds they performed.

Oberst Knust, *Kommodore* of the *Geschwader*, received me on the terrace. 'Glad you're here,' he said. He asked me a number of questions, politely but somewhat warily. I looked at him and I could imagine him thinking, 'What's this that they've sent me?' *Hauptmann* Joachim Helbig, the man whose glorious deeds had been carried as far as Holland on the radio waves, joined us and he made it even more plain: I felt sure he was thinking, 'He's from the second team, that's for certain. The *Geschwader* always keep the best people for themselves.'

I knew that a short time previously the *Greifswalder* had bombed the British aircraft carrier *Illustrious* to almost a wreck, so that she had had to crawl from the Mediterranean into the Red Sea, partly under her own steam and partly with outside help, and I had to bow to that fact. Feeling like a slave sold by his master, I was at pains not to try to present myself in a favourable light. I confined myself to standing properly to attention and I made up my mind that I would listen carefully to the questions they put to me and see if I could form a more accurate impression.

The *Kommodore* came to the point, 'At midday tomorrow, the *Geschwader* will attack Malta. Luqa airfield. Dive-bombing attack. I'd like you and your *Staffel* to take part.' Then, after a pause, 'If you can make it. If you and your men can be rested and prepared. There's plenty of time to get fuel and ammunition on board.' I thought, 'Aha! Now they're testing whether I'm keen to do operations or not.'

'We'll put you in the middle of the formation,' the *Oberst* said. 'Immediately behind the *Kommodore* and me,' Helbig added. So, that's it! They're afraid you'll piss off when things get hot! That's how it was when Hannibal was around: the auxiliaries were put in the middle of the regular troops so that they had to fight, for better or for worse. Helbig added, 'The whole thing'll only take about two hours, including forming up — a nice little exercise to introduce you to the Mediterranean!'

The *Kommodore* must have noticed my sour expression. He continued, 'Mark you, we won't let you fly outside the formation or behind us. The Spitfires and Hurricanes nibble round at the edges. I hope we'll get some fighter escort.' It passed through my mind that maybe there wouldn't be an escort; that we could be in for a rough time. The *Oberst* shook my hand, 'I've seen to it that everything you need will be sent over, including food. See you tomorrow, then, 1315 hours, 5000 metres over Cape Passero, on course for the western point of Gozo.'

They invited me to have a farewell sherry, but I showed them that I was determined to take the operation seriously by declining it emphatically. I likewise rejected the abundant fruit that was offered. As firmly as I could manage I marched down the steps to look for Giacomo. I found his Topolino parked in front of one of the basement windows of the villa, from which appetising smells were emerging. He was in the kitchen in courtly conversation with a fellow countrywoman. I went in and smartly shoved a king-sized orange into my trouser pocket, then urged him to get a move on to the car. I had no great hopes that my *'Caro mio, molto lente, lentissime'* would persuade him to drive less nerve-wrackingly. My sole aim was to survive until the following day so that I would be able to acquit myself with honour. I'd show them! They were only human, after all. It'd be child's play to hit the airfield. A bit harder to hit an aeroplane in a splinter shelter. But the runway, which was the *Staffel's* target — laughable! Over a thousand metres long and fifty wide.

Giacomo accelerated away, and I forced myself to concentrate on my orange and to peel it properly so that I wouldn't think about life's hazards. Now and again I heard 'Sssst!' but I managed to keep myself under control and didn't look up. The result was that my chauffeur's desire to show off his skills evaporated. Despite its lack of substance my forced indifference had taken the wind out of his sails.

Meanwhile, there had been much activity on the airfield at Gerbini. I found the aircraft well dispersed and their black night-flying camouflage paint washed off. A start had been made on splinter trenches and pickets. The remainder of the *Staffel* had settled into a well-concealed barrack hut some distance away, from which homely sounds were emanating into the evening landscape. My God — food! The *1st Gruppe* of the *Lehrgeschwader* had sent a field kitchen over. Thanks a lot, *Kommodore*! Unusual that — he'd acted before he'd made a promise. 'Operational subordination' as it was blandly called in the language of the operational command, usually meant a secondary relationship, a sort of marriage of convenience between those who command and those who had to obey. However, it was through the stomachs, even of the lower orders, that the way to the heart lay.

In my absence the senior officer of the *Staffel*, *Oberleutnant zur See* Friedrich, had been in command. Whenever he went off the base he used to change out of his flying clothes and into his naval uniform, true to the traditions of Imperial Germany. He was a fund of anecdotes from Tirpitz to Raeder. Airmen think they are soldiers? The only true soldier is the seaman. Long before the Prussians had discovered militarism, the men in the sailing ships personified soldierly spirit, comradeship and discipline, in peace and in war. He called us underdeveloped soldiers. Words like 'left' and 'right' irritated him enormously. If he saw something from an aeroplane, if he was driving along Dutch roads, if he was seated at table, it was always 'port' and 'starboard'. He tried in vain to convince us that it was impossible to navigate over the sea using kilometres. 'As far as I'm concerned, you can keep your kilometres, your kilometre-stones, your railways, your railway stations with their names on them and other such curiosities on land: but at sea, if you don't mind, it's nautical miles. They are an organic and intrinsic component of the terrestrial globe. Gentlemen, have you ever heard of Thalassian thinking? The sea is the bosom of the earth. That's where everything began — war, trade, piracy: three-in-one, inseparable. Strangely enough, it was the land-lubber Goethe who said that.'

Friedrich had been seconded to us because he knew how the shipping lanes, into which we had to drop our mines, were marked out, and because he was familiar with other nautical signs, with tides, astronomical navigation and types of ship, and because, down here, he would be able to differentiate for us between British and Italian warships in the naval battles we could expect. This highly educated naval officer, who always carried a glass with him — he scorned the expression field glasses — would sometimes play the accordion, and now and then he would suck on a Rittmeester cigar: all of which we found very odd, but very endearing.

The accordion had been supplied from the *Staffel* Welfare Fund, and with it he conjured up the wide ocean, with a touch of grief for comrades lost overboard and a trace of homesickness. 'Yes,' he would say, 'our seamen's songs are the soldiers' songs of the *Marine*. Where are your airmen's songs?' The *Luftwaffe* airmen's songs were composed by professional musicians at the behest of the State. We still preferred to sing the old field-grey songs such as, '*Lippe-Detmold, eine wunderschoene Stadt*' and '*Argonnerwald um Mitternacht*'.

To Friedrich's triumph, we had to confess that we had even borrowed from the *Marine*, because we sang '*Wir fliegen gegen Engelland*', having substituted '*fliegen*' for '*fahren*'. Moreover, he told us, the likes of us hadn't even been on earth when proud frigates under full sail had gone privateering and firing broadsides. There was no denying it: when the foot soldiers went into battle with pipes and drums and with banners flying, and when the bivouac fires flared after the great cutting and thrusting, and when the melody sounded to a background of slashed buffalo-leather jerkins and a small cross over a deep, dark, grave — then it was that a tailor from Ulm, with his winged suit,[4] first attempted a circus trick that failed and sank into the Danube, unhonoured and unsung.

He finished his sermon: we airmen were modern, technical exponents of soldiery, brave enough, admittedly, but we lacked the maturity that would come with age only, and that was all there was to it. Such an objurgation on the part of someone who didn't even belong to our unit caused wild cries of protest: 'Out with him! Kick him out! He's not fit to captain a rowing boat! He can't even swim!' but even they didn't shake our seafarer.

All this amused me. I was born the son of a sailor in Kiel in the time of the Kaiser and baptised, as they say, with *Jade* water, and I still felt a certain regret that the *Marine* hadn't taken me as a cadet before 1933, although I was naturally thankful that I hadn't had to sail on the ill-fated *Niobe* in 1932. Friedrich's Thalassian knowledge served to enrich the narrow experience I had gathered when sailing, canoeing and rowing in Kiel Bay and on the naval course in 1939. Sometimes he spun seamen's yarns. The following tale he told could have been one of them, but I couldn't be certain.

The Fleet visited Singapore and they entertained Englishmen from the *Rodney* in the wardroom, and a lot of 'Bamboos' and whiskies were consumed. In the course of all this, the young Royal Navy lieutenants declared, 'Fellows, one of these days you're going to get a real arse-full. This world isn't big enough for both of us!' Friedrich told us that we shouldn't kid ourselves — Aircraft Carrier Malta couldn't be sunk: it would have to be boarded.

Friedrich had divided the barrack floor into squares and allocated one to a crew. There wasn't a lot of room, and nobody was allowed to drift outside his own parallel and meridian. The atmosphere in the billet after we had eaten was so good that there was no thought of sleep. I was given a bench up against a wall to sleep on; four unshaven pilots' faces looked up at me from below. Long before midnight, heavy lorries and specialist vehicles rumbled up with bombs and petrol. The gunners went out to help the mechanics to get the kites operational by two o'clock in the morning at the latest.

Everyone worked like mad. One only needed to see and hear *Oberfeldwebel* Lorenz, the broad-shouldered, blue-eyed, blond Chief Mechanic, behaving like a slave-driver who, himself a slave, is trying to earn his freedom, and letting fly with oaths and strong language that would have shocked even the least sensitive. Every word, every oath hit exactly that spot of human dignity at which it was aimed, but this wild man loved his men. How can I say that? When his mechanics had accomplished the impossible in the shortest possible time; when they dragged away the chocks and the overladen machines taxied out, swaying heavily, to take off, took up their positions and roared off, every one of them, without leaving a single lame duck behind, then his eyes would light up. 'See them flying. You've done that. You're the best!' When some lily-livered bastard, some useless example of a malingerer, couldn't roll a 250-kg bomb from where it was lying, then 'Horse' Lorenz, as they used to call him at Nordhausen am Harz, would do the job himself, still swearing and with swelling arteries. When he'd done the job, he'd comment, 'When I was your age, I used to carry those things on my watch chain!'

Lorenz did far more than just carry out orders. He always did twice as much. When his men were falling over from tiredness, he let them sleep and did what was necessary single-handed. When he went to work, he looked like a wrestler on the mat who, bending slightly forward with arms apart, touches his opponent on the body and, in doing so, whispers, 'I'll show you, you bastard!' A party wasn't a party if Lorenz wasn't there. If ever there was anyone who could take a joke, it was Lorenz. If someone imitated his Thuringian accent and dialect, an uncontrollable gale of laughter would emerge from deep within his massive chest, and any old, enlisted man could smack him hard on the back without risk.

There was not the slightest modesty about Lorenz when it came to the strength of his physique, the power of his voice or the reach of his arms. He was a taker, but in the best possible sense of the word. He had gradually buttered up his co-equals, the *Oberfeldwebel* in charge of weapons and bombs, and the Radio *Oberfeldwebel*. When I was Technical Officer of the *Staffel* his first act had been to offer himself to me as intermediary to pass on my orders. That suited me well because I didn't want to have to run after all and sundry and in that way I could concentrate on getting ready for operational flying. You can imagine what that led to. He handled his technical warrant-officers no less strictly than he did his mechanics. After I had heard about it, I asked Lorenz in private whether or not he was technically qualified to do so. He said that 'his' people had the technical expertise. All he knew was how long it took to change a radio set and hoist up a 1000-kg bomb. I didn't consider re-introducing the hierarchical system. And that was how we did things in Sicily.

I could hear what was going on outside in the countryside; heard the voices of the maintenance personnel in the distance, and was content. I weaved my way to my bench, wrapped my gas-mask container in my uniform coat, pushed the bundle under my neck, and covered myself with my flying overalls. That was sufficient unto the day. Whether it was the sun heating up the box-like barrack that woke me from sleep, or the cacophony of voices from outside, I didn't know. There wasn't time to think about it. You're in Sicily, I thought. Today's the day it's all going to happen. The door was closed, and a beam of sunlight was falling on the back of my head through one of the windows. I sat up. There were approximately a dozen men asleep and snoring on the floor. The atmosphere was thick — my sole thought was to get outside into the fresh air.

Outside a war for survival was raging. A number of bootblacks were jabbering and jostling each other, barging one another like footballers for the privilege of serving our pilots, to whose boots there still adhered the soil of Holland. The vehemence of the competition was alien to me, verging on violence, it seemed. I strode among them, but at once they began to fight over me, because the surface area of my high boots promised a profitable piece of business. I feared — but my fears were unjustified — that the machine-gun fire of words and the waving of hands would develop into physical violence. Then, unexpectedly, all of a sudden, a smile flashed across a face. I realised yet again that it was a different world down there.

Intent upon doing their job, they didn't let my cry of '*Nulla lire*' discourage them. They wanted work, they needed work, and they generously granted me a '*Domani pagare*', no doubt seeing me as a likely, long-term customer. Would they ever get their money? I found it a warming thought that these people had not the slightest doubt that I would survive. When you are about to go into action, looks of gloom and sympathy feel like the last rites. I placated two competitors as Solomon might have done: each got a half, one leg each, while I sat on a packing-case and waited for the job to be done. The two knelt in front of me and jabbered away in Sicilian, each casting an occasional sideways glance at the brilliance of his rival's work and then applying himself even more energetically to the business in hand.

Why is it, I asked myself, that in Germany you can cross the road wearing dirty shoes without anyone saying anything about it — over the Jungfernstieg, the Kudamm, the Königsallee,[5] and take a seat in a café with a completely clear conscience? Why is it that here the first thing they notice is your footwear? Why don't barbers accost you? It must have been because their culture began with footwear. Most probably because shoes were essential for getting about, for gathering food and for hunting. Only afterwards did the decorative fig leaf come along, then garments, then crowns and authority. As I looked down when the work was completed my theory became certainty. Polished footwear is more than half of the overall impression they call Culture. Shining boots invite you to smarten up the rest. I made up my mind to press my jacket and, once I got a bed, to put my trousers, packed away in my luggage, under my mattress with a damp sheet and sleep on them to remove the creases. Finally I swore to myself that in future I would pay more attention to seeing that my boots shone.

The authority I mentioned was not long in putting in an appearance. Fully aware that he shared the dignity of the King of Italy and the Emperor of Ethiopia, there approached the Mayor of the township of Paterno, situated on the southern slope of Etna, where we could see it about 200 metres above the level of the airfield. The *Geschwader* had negotiated the site for us. First the Mayor banished the mob of traders, shoe cleaners and lookers-on. A Roman prefect, handling the newly conquered Sicilians after the Punic Wars, could not have done it with more conviction. We were impressed. Nevertheless this was the twentieth century, and the black-haired ones withdrew a few paces only, to take up new positions of readiness.

The Mayor came up to us and in a trice Italian dignity was transformed into smiling Italian politeness. Weinreich and Friedrich made a graceful withdrawal, pointing at me, '*Capitano*'. In the flood of words that I couldn't understand I felt completely out of my depth. In stormy breakers you fight for air, but can't find it; there I was struggling for words but couldn't find them. I was floundering between a fatuous grin, in reply to what I assumed was a witty remark, and deadly seriousness, reverence in the face of regal gestures. Our guest, self-confident but naive, assumed that we could understand him. My God, why didn't it occur to him to speak slowly, in simple words and sentences? As if Rome were the centre of the Earth! Rome, my dear fellow, is only one end of the Axis, and the lower one at that!

Friedrich and Weinreich, having had sufficient enjoyment from my predicament, came to my aid. It is surprising how words occur to you when you're not being addressed directly, while the one who is being spoken to is either struck dumb or stutters in search of them. We three had sweated for about ten years over vocabularies and texts in English, French and Latin, and now here we were, overjoyed and surprised because the conference was beginning to make progress. With an outstretched hand the Mayor pointed proudly to the light spot on the weathered, green-flecked lava; that was his town, he said. To call it a town seemed to us to be a bit of an exaggeration, and we cast furtive glances at each other. We were surprised when the Mayor stated that his town had 40,000 inhabitants. *Oberleutnant* Friedrich, through his glass, took a look and said nothing. His face remained expressionless. What we didn't know then was that in that nest of 40,000 souls each room was occupied by four to six people. There were many such surprises in store for us.

Cautiously, we broached the tricky question of where we might live — in private quarters, perhaps. Oh no — you'll be in the monastery! Good Lord, that's all we needed! Nothing like that had ever happened to us before. Sleeping in cells with barred windows? Morning service at six o'clock? No. It's a nuns' monastery — a nunnery. The nuns will cook for you and do your washing. *Donnerwetter!* That sounded more like it! If only blasted Malta was a thing of the past.

Weinreich showed the Mayor to one of our laden aeroplanes, while Hanke showed me the latest photographs of Malta/Luqa which had just come from the *Geschwader* by despatch rider. With them was a sealed envelope, marked 'Secret/ Operational'. We inspected the photos closely with a magnifying glass. Aeroplanes could be seen again in the splinter shelters, those that had been there previously having mostly been destroyed by the *Geschwader* in a series of heavy attacks. The British used to bring up replacement aircraft half way to Malta in the carrier *Ark Royal*, which was stationed at Gibraltar, then they would fly the remainder of the way. That must have been done overnight and in the early morning. It was possible that other aircraft had reached Malta during the night, flying in over France. Our new aiming points were the shelters, the hangars and the headquarters' buildings.

It was 1000 hrs. If we were to be over Cape Passero at 1315 hrs we would have to start at 1245 hrs at the latest. I ordered take-off for 1230 hrs. We hadn't taken on our maximum fuel load, but I wanted some slight time in hand so that we wouldn't miss the join-up. It would be useful also to have a look round the area. Perhaps we would be able to see Malta from the southern extremity of Sicily.

I can't remember what we did about food that morning, but there was something sweet for the donkeys. During the night they had wound their ropes around the tree stupidly and were standing opposite each other on a short lead. Toto pricked up his ears and looked at me expectantly. What impenetrable eyes you have, you dim creature, you soulful thing. I must get to know you. You're sold, my friend! Hanke decided that his lady donkey should follow the example set by my donkey: hire became purchase. A rosy future was ensured for them. They were given a lovely, many-coloured Sicilian donkey cart adorned with allegorical pictures, and they enjoyed being harnessed to it and carrying foodstuffs, laundry or light pieces of equipment. Later, in France, they were to discover Paradise on Earth in the lovely grounds of a château.

Between briefing and take-off we had to clear up the matter of our accommodation in Paterno. Our *Staffeln* could arrive from Holland any day. I asked Hanke to find out how things stood while we were away. Before I took over the *Staffel* and gave up the job of Technical Officer I had worked with Lorenz at Nordhausen am Harz in a way that had proved to be satisfactory. When I was promoted to *Staffelkapitaen*. I asked him whom he would like to see as Technical Officer. He replied that it had to be Weinreich: he was so calm and relaxed when he was speaking, interfered less than anyone else, and could recite such splendid Ringelnatz[6] poems — he could even sing them to the accordion. Yes. Weinreich could do that, and he liked doing it, in defiance of his father, who was head teacher at a Gymnasium.[7] So, Weinreich became Technical Officer. The previous evening, with the most melancholy look possible, he had recited:

> 'And on the peak of Sicily,
> Pondered Kuttel Daddeldu,
> All about the sad, sad story
> Of his many families.

After the briefing we relaxed a while outside, sitting or lying on the grass. Friedrich called it '*Gammeln*' (loafing about). There they were, all those brave campaigners who had flown operations over Poland, Norway, Holland, Belgium, France and England. We had lost many comrades along the way. *Leutnant* Kuehnle had come to the *Staffel* from the personnel reserve, a broad-shouldered man of medium height and with a pink face, who accepted the most dangerous of missions with a beaming countenance. He personified what was laid down in that object of fun, Service Regulation No. 1: 'The soldier always faces a new day with a cheerful face.' There, was *Leutnant* Saure, an observer from Bremen, taciturn and ever-obedient, whose facial expression never changed whatever came along — suicide mission or special leave. Never a cheerful beam, never a sullen look, the only thing that counted was a job well done, no matter what that job was.

Feldwebel Mosbach was a big, sturdy man, rather thick set, an experienced pilot plagued by a series of young observers over the *Fahner Hoehe* near Gotha where we used to practise bombing with our cement bombs. He was never down in the dumps. However, he came to me one day — Friday the 13th, I think. He said he couldn't fly that day. I laughed in his face, 'Mosbach, do you want me to take your aunt instead of you?' Mosbach stood there in front of me, strictly to attention, not saying a word. Only then did I look him keenly in the eyes. 'What's wrong with you? Are you sick?'

'No. I'm not sick, but I know I won't come back from this operation.'

'I guess you've done too much flying. You should go into a Reserve *Gruppe* to recover.' He didn't want to do that. He wanted to stay with the mob. But that day he just couldn't fly so he stayed behind. Nobody made fun of him for it, and nobody else took advantage by trying to emulate him. I don't know just how I came to that decision now, if indeed it was one. It was quite unlike me. It's possible that Hanke intervened, as he did many times, with an appropriate comment — 'Don't make a bloody fool of yourself!'

We were waiting for the latest wind report. The banner of smoke from Etna showed us the wind direction, more or less exactly, at our intended diving height of 3000 metres, and no great alteration was to be expected on the short run to Malta. We urgently needed the wind speed and direction at 1000 metres above sea level because that was the height at which the bomb would get the decisive shove from the aircraft. In the case of a wind from astern, a light breeze was all we could cope with. If there was a strong wind from the rear, it would force us out of a 50° to 60° dive into the vertical, or even beyond it. If we let the bombs go then, they would hit the propellers.

The weather report arrived. It said that there was a light, prevailing, stern wind from the northwest, and no change could be expected before 1400 hrs. Nevertheless, success depended on my aircraft going into its dive correctly, and on the accuracy of Helbig's eyes, so that we could dive down on the target in battle order and storm through, still in tight formation. If we scattered we would waste bombs and be like a herd of sheep, easy prey for the fighters lying in wait for us below, camouflaged and scarcely visible against the ground. Down there, they didn't have to get mixed up too early with our fighter escort. They wanted to shoot us, the bombers, down and then disappear. We had experienced and mastered tactics and difficulties such as that on other Fronts, so there wasn't a lot to discuss. We didn't set a delay on the bomb fuses because we didn't want to crater the airfield and the runways. The setting was 'Impact' because we wanted to cause splinters for maximum effect against the aircraft in the shelters and hangars.

We were gratified to learn that we were to be escorted by the German fighter *Staffel* led by *Oberleutnant* Muencheberg, who had already earned the respect of the Hurricane pilots in the sky above Malta. In addition, there was an Italian fighter unit. That gave a feeling of confidence among the crews, and there was a relaxed atmosphere to the hands of *Skat* that were being played. *Unteroffizier* Knobling, a pilot in *Oberleutnant zur See* Friedrich's crew, asked 'What do we do, if one of the aeroplanes down there starts taxying or takes off? Should we dive down on him and drop our bombs?' It was not a dumb question. Our attack had been planned against stationary aircraft. Nobody had given any thought to moving ones there to fight us, those poisonous hornets the Spitfires and the Hurricanes.

The man who had asked the question was a native of Vienna; a man who foresaw and forecast the many vicissitudes of war with much pessimism, if not intelligence, and who was always happy when he could discomfort his officers. I had been a target of his since I had detailed him to go on an operation with a slight head wound. In a thick Viennese accent he had expostulated, 'My God! What's this then? Why don't you try it yourself, putting an R/T helmet on with a bandage like this round your head!' Everybody had to wear one when flying operationally, so as to be able to communicate within the aircraft and to other aircraft. 'My dear Knobling', I replied, putting on a Viennese accent, while the others looked on with some amusement, 'think it out for yourself. What would happen to you if a Spitfire took off down below and you went after it while we carried on diving on the laid-down heading? You'd be hopelessly out of formation, a lamb for the slaughter, and they'd have you!' He replied in broader than ever Viennese, 'Sure, I didn't want to do it, but I just wanted to make sure you wouldn't have done it either!'

Our small band of fighters had command of the air over Malta because the English fighters preferred to remain on the ground, unless the *Greifswalder* came with their bombs. So small formations of bombers were sent as bait occasionally. If the Spitfires took the bait, then the German fighters would dive down from height, out of the sun, aiming for the RAF roundels. That was the Battle of Malta described to us by the old hands. In a couple of hours we would experience the reality.

The reality was coming closer. The motors were running noisily, warming up. Full and melodious, the sound waves surged towards us over the tall grass which was waving in the light wind. Now and then they reached a full-throttle crescendo. The first crews had set out already for the aircraft, which were parked some distance away. All the crews had to be at their positions and ready to taxi ten minutes before take-off. Schmetz, my observer in 4D + AR, his navigator's satchel slung from his shoulder, went on ahead with Wireless Operator Krahn and Rear Gunner Alles. So far, everything was going very smoothly, according to plan. A good operational pilot even calculated the speed for the walk out to the aircraft so he knew how long it would take to cover the distance — as much as 2.5 km, in our case. That was how long the airfield was, and our aircraft were dispersed along its entire length. In that way we were reasonably well protected against destructive bombing attacks.

I waved goodbye to *Oberleutnant* Hanke. We had been good friends since we had been at Nordhausen am Harz together in the same *Staffel* of *4th Geschwader 'General Wever'*, where we had enjoyed the happy days of our flying youth going together on Sundays on the Harz Railway up to Braunlage, or later, in my six-cylinder car, into the Thuringia Forest to Bad Friedrichroda or Weimar, and all the other wonderful places, the names of which I forget. Together we had encountered a great deal of bad weather, not to mention technical problems, flying blind, wing-to-wing, through cloud, lightning and hailstorms. We had no secrets from each other. We discussed the military situation, as far as we were aware of it, without inhibition. If we got orders from above that were hard for us to understand, we found ourselves in a corner when we couldn't answer the question we asked ourselves — how else could things have been done? We usually had to give in at that point. Then there was no other guideline but the simple motto: orders are orders.

I remember Hanke giving me a terrible fright in September 1939 when he thumped an He 111 down from 10 metres to land. He had recently been withdrawn from operational flying and made 'chairborne' as 1a of the *Gruppe* Staff. 'Armchairborne', as the joker, Weinreich put it. He used to say, 'Hanke, please see to it that the orders that come to us from on high, through official channels, are nicely written out.'

I set out towards my aircraft, AR, along the freshly trampled path. She was standing about 200 metres away. Both her engines had been run up and switched off. Silence reigned far and wide except for the chattering of birds, and the scent of almond blossom filled the air. The donkeys were grazing peacefully. In our overalls, we took up our positions, life jackets and parachutes strapped on. Our oxygen masks hung ready. Schmetz had fastened his pencil, protractor, circular slide rule and navigation satchel in position. Left and right, the sliding windows were still open for take-off, so that we didn't roast. The entry hatch was closed with a dull thump. We checked the intercom briefly, then switched it off.

The Number One Mechanic, *Feldwebel* Hans Buhmann from Woerrstadt in Rheinhessen, was standing approximately ten metres in front of the cockpit. A little further away I caught sight of *Oberfeldwebel* Lorenz, who was positioned so as to be in visual contact with all his mechanics. Everywhere there was silence: even the four of us were silent. We checked the time. No point wondering what would happen in the next hour, or even before that. We had a job to do. It would begin when the hands of the clock pointed out 1224 hours.

1224 hrs: I called from the window, 'All clear ahead!'

'Clear ahead!' Buhmann confirmed.

I switched on my engines, and Lorenz waved his arms to all sides. Everybody started up. Both my engines were running. *Unteroffizier* Alles looked out and checked that everything was OK. I gave the hand signal for 'Chocks away!', throttled back to tick-over, and trod lightly on the brake pedal so that the chocks weren't under pressure. Buhmann reported, 'Chocks away!' and moved to one side.

From then on everything went swiftly. It was 1225 hrs. I opened the throttles and taxied to the head of the other aircraft. One after the other they moved into place behind me: there were nine of us altogether. I taxied to the east of the field, roughly where the boundary should have been, turned towards the west and came to a halt. My left and right wing-men formed up with me. The second group of three positioned themselves behind us and to the right, and further behind and to the right the third group of three formed up. The wind was blowing from the starboard quarter, which made it possible for us to take off in groups of three, at minimum intervals. The slipstream from the aircraft's propellers was blown to the left, and those taking off behind were not affected by the turbulence.

To the right of me were Friedrich and Knoebling; to the left, *Leutnant* Dr. Kratz, who had just joined us from the Test Centre at Rechlin. His job was to test the new bomb sight, the BZA, in operational conditions, the bomb sight which had a self-adjusting aiming marker. He was very keen to test his development. The rest of us were equipped with the fixed reflex sight. To use the fixed sight you needed to bring more intelligence to bear — too much intelligence, in Kratz's opinion.

I looked back and to the right. They were all there, in proud battle-order. Weinreich was leading the second three; Piëch, the third. Behind them the high grass was flattened to the ground by the wind from the propellers, which gleamed in the sunlight. I gave hand signals to my three, half-opened the throttles and began to roll. My example was taken to be an order: full throttle after a few seconds. The drill had begun: they all followed. I put the control column forward and aimed for the distant mountain peak. I'd covered about 800 metres. I pulled back slightly and felt the weight come off the wheels. The airscrews hauled their burden forward — 180, 190, 200 kph. That was enough for lift-off. At that speed we could get the two 500-kg mines and the two 250-kg bombs into the air. The almond trees and the olive trees were coming nearer every second. I hauled back on the stick. The aircraft was in the air, sloppily but safely. Undercarriage up. *Unteroffizier* Alles looked at the indicators on the wings and reported, 'Undercarriage retracted!' In the cockpit, the two lamps shone red.

The crowns of the trees below us rushed past astern. We flew straight ahead. I throttled back slightly. To the right and left my wing-men were closing in a little above me. Krahn reported, 'Second three airborne . . . third three airborne.' I held my course and throttled back to cruising speed so that the others could catch up with me. There was a gap of 500 to 700 metres between each group of three. After flying two or three kilometres I made a flat turn to port to avoid the mountains ahead and to let the aircraft behind cut the corner and close up on me.

We were flying on a reciprocal heading, east, stepped up in threes line astern at 1200 metres, below the peak of Mount Etna. The *Geschwader* Staff at Catania must have seen us. We made a port turn onto a westerly heading, and Etna was then to our starboard. We climbed to 2000 metres. We turned south above our own airfield, conscious that our men would be watching us. We could see the southern tip of Sicily, Cape Passero, where we were to form up and from which we would set course. We didn't want to arrive there before the *Geschwader* and our fighter escort. The British fighters had made surprise attacks before on weak bomber formations and single aircraft flying along the southern coast of Sicily. Schmetz took a bearing on a datum point on the ground that we had to overfly if we were to be over the Cape on ETA. The 'Greifswalders' would be coming on a direct heading from Catania, and we would have to filter in on to their course.

We had reached the designated altitude. It would not be easy to pick out the armada coming from the north in good time. They would be climbing up to our height and it would be difficult to make them out against the rugged countryside with its countless small fields with buildings on them or surrounded by stone walls. We had to keep a good look-out. We could only spare a quick glance across Etna which we had by then overflown, to the Straits of Messina and back to Calabria. We could not let ourselves be carried away by distance and the splendour of heaven and earth. We had to use our eyes to their maximum effect, to scan the fields and brown mountainsides, to watch for our comrades' approach.

'There's something there! Ten o'clock!' Schmetz pointed with his protractor to port and slightly ahead. I strained my eyes and after a while I saw them: dark, elongated shapes, little more than pencil-strokes, moving like a dotted line over the ground. 'Keep your eyes on them!' Rear-Gunner Alles climbed down into the belly turret. We flew on a collision course, but way above them. The pencil-strokes grew thicker. Our groups of three were neatly in line astern — an expression we'd agreed to use to placate our sailor. We would normally call it '*Staffelkolonne*' (column of flights). We had strictly rejected such expressions as 'abeam' when talking of broader formations, such as echelons. Thus far, we had stuck to expressions such as 'right' and 'left' — right echelon, for example.

The leading aircraft of the *Geschwader* crossed us on a southerly heading about three kilometres ahead. The formation was suspended, clearly recognisable, and climbing with noses still well up. I turned carefully to the right and was soon positioned some distance directly behind the *Geschwader* Staff Flight, and higher. To the right and left of us were other *Staffeln* of the *Greifswalder*, flying in loose formation but beginning to gain height on us.

1310 hrs: Cape Passero was below us and slightly ahead. The Staff Flight had reached altitude and was beginning to increase its speed. I put my nose down a shade and followed, keeping my throttle settings constant. We joined up and crossed over Cape Passero. I couldn't see what was immediately below me. I was no longer watching anything except the *Geschwader*'s lead aircraft. It seemed that Helbig was maintaining his speed stubbornly. The pilot in front had to be the best formation flier, always alert; holding his speed, height and course spot on. If he didn't, all sorts of confusion was likely to develop behind him — juggling with throttles, swearing, a general breakdown of confidence. We called it the 'concertina effect'.

Cape Passero lay five minutes behind us and we were on course for the western tip of Gozo. All around there were aeroplanes, cruisers of the air, as if on parade. Only a gentle rise and fall was perceptible. Where were the fighters? Nobody had seen them. It was the old story: the bomber wanted to have his escort as near as possible alongside — on both sides, if it could be so arranged. That calmed the nerves. But the fighter pilots, with their advantage of speed, had a different viewpoint. They liked to hang high in the sky, seeming to appear as mere dots, preferably in the sun so that they disappeared completely. The main thing, they said, was that we see you. The enemy would also come out of the sun and then we would get him! All right then: nothing's possible without faith. We'd try hard to have faith.

Schmetz had taken a back-bearing on Cape Passero and was calculating the drift. By the time we got to Gozo he would have calculated the wind at height. We couldn't let the attack throw us into confusion. We stayed on our southwest course for Gozo. To the left and ahead, about 10 o'clock, I could see Malta quite clearly, the jagged coastline and the notched inlets to Valetta harbour. Far below us, the sea was calm. Only Schmetz could make out the odd white horse through his bomb sight. Not a ship could be seen, far and wide. Both my engines were running smoothly. I looked left and right and over my shoulder. I saw our men sitting there, wearing flying helmets and oxygen masks, transformed into monsters, but monsters with hearts full of a sense of duty and comradeship, a little afraid of the unknown. I had to smile a little when I saw Knobling: his sinister garb was quite out of keeping with his Viennese charm and blarney. I thought 'You don't fool me!'

Schmetz, still flat on his stomach, turned on his side and looked up at me in such a way that his oxygen mask stretched the skin on his face. I couldn't bear to think how slant-eyed I must have looked to him. He checked the wind: from the northwest and moderate. The lead aircraft was turning slowly to the left from its southwest heading and preparing to attack. Malta lay immediately behind Gozo. In the middle we could see the airfield at Luqa. We could also see the second airfield, Halfa, past Luqa and to the right.

Schmetz got up from his prone position. There was nothing more for him to do at the horizontal bomb sight. When we made a diving attack he sat beside me and read off the diving angle from the quadrant on the side of the windscreen. 'Can't see anything taking off, yet!' he announced. We had been briefed that any aircraft taking off from the airfield would create clouds of dust that would be visible from a long distance. We wondered where the British fighters were. They couldn't know whether we were going to dive-bomb, or to attack from altitude. In the latter event they would have to dive down out of the sun: otherwise, if they had started to take off, then they would never catch us. Malta would have been a long way behind us. If they knew that we were going to dive, they'd wait down below, patrolling. For the time being: eyes aloft! All of the radio operators had put on their sun glasses and were staring into the bright light, their twin machine-guns pointing upward, their safety catches off.

We pressed on towards the target, changing from line astern to vic formation. We formed a vic within the *Geschwader* vic. To the British that could have indicated either a diving attack or a horizontal one. The breadth of the formation matched that of the target on the ground, of which we had each been allocated a particular sector. There were still no fighters to be seen, either ours or theirs. Was it to be the calm before the storm? Their fighters were all staying on the ground, perhaps creeping into their splinter shelters, which were supposed to be constructed very solidly. Were the fighters giving this time a miss, hoping for a better chance later?

Then the British heavy flak was thundering up at us full belt. The *Kommodore* was surrounded by bursts. If he blew up, that was the end of our planned synchronised attack. In that event, we would have to dive-bomb individually. I followed him through the smoke, about 100-150 metres behind. There was no more shrapnel there. The smoke would show the Spitfires where their targets were. They should be coming in now, if they're up above us, I thought, and I shivered. I watched the aircraft in front of me, nervously. Will Helbig stay on course, dead ahead? Now we'll see what he's made of. I followed him. The film was running. Still there was no sign of him beginning his dive. It looked as if it was going to be bloody steep. Come on, mate! Dive, and let's get out of the heavy flak! It can't follow us if we dive.

There were hundreds of guns firing at us, as if they'd been brought there from the entire Empire to guard the artery of world power. Flashes appeared from all over the island. It was a veritable wasps' nest. Through the glass of the cockpit I could see the airfield at Luqa steep below me. We were not going to make it! Then Helbig's aircraft tilted down, and the entire Staff Flight went with him. The light-blue underbellies of all the aircraft showed simultaneously. No waverers! A second later I lowered my dive brakes, put the nose down and throttled right back. Out of the corner of my eye I watched my wing men. I look ahead. I was right behind Helbig in the vic of the Staff Flight. The Staff Flight aircraft were racing down ahead of me but seemed to be poised, motionless, over the target area, their wings like narrow lines, as if on an aerial photograph. Press on! Don't look at the two threes to left and right. It's up to them to keep in position. They'll do so, just as if it were an exercise.

Schmetz reported an angle of dive of 60°. God — no steeper, please! The lead aircraft adjusted slightly to the side and seemed to move over on the picture. I followed it. We were both on the same target. The red tracers of 4-cm flak were whizzing through the formation. I swallowed quickly. Closing my left eye, I looked through the bomb sight with my right. The shelters were dead-ahead; right on the cross.

We had not descended to 1200 metres yet, and the klaxon still hadn't sounded. I hoped that because there were so many of us the flak would be scattered. The leaders were still poised steady in front of us, drifting slowly across the target area. Drop your bombs! Pull out!

At last! Ahead and below me there was movement in the formation. Almost as if they were rocket-propelled the staff aircraft, pulling out of their dive, swept out from the target, so that in a flash I could see the imperial crosses on the upper surfaces of their wings. Our turn now! I held my aim down to the smallest ring of light in my sight. The alarm klaxon blared out: that meant that I was 800 metres above the ground. I could see my target clearly. The bombs dropped by the Staff Flight hadn't detonated yet. I pressed the bomb-release.

Pull out hard, automatically, dive-brakes in, and let's get out of this witches' cauldron on the heels of the Staff Flight. Schmetz was at the machine-guns, ready to hammer the troublesome light flak. *Unteroffizier* Alles shouted 'Jesus! Look at the explosions down there! There's more. More!' I said, 'Shut up! Look out for flak and fighters. There's certain to be some round here.'

The Staff Flight was making a flat turn from its southerly heading towards the sea, so that we could cut the corner and join up with them. We pulled our oxygen masks down onto our chins. A couple of stragglers joined the formation and the *Staffel* formed up into a column again. Ahead of us, very high, an aircraft was dropping like a stone from the sky, another behind it. What is it — whose is it? Suddenly white smoke appeared from the first one, turning quickly to black. Bits flew off the aircraft. The second aircraft broke out of its steep dive, pulled up and disappeared aloft. There was a parachute. We didn't know if it was a friend or a foe.

Still accelerating, we flew out over the coast and its many flak guns. All of the machine-guns were manned. We descended, down to sea level, down to one or two metres, so that the Spitfires couldn't attack us from below, and the rear gunner could help to change the ammunition drums. We still didn't dare to think that it was all over. So far, it had all gone too smoothly. Our fighters knew our route and there was nothing else for them to do up at altitude. They were only too ready to go looking for the opposition. They said that if they could shoot some down, then there would be fewer of them for us to worry about next time. We were nearing Cape Passero where Italian fighters were supposed to patrol. The British were quite capable of sweeping up unexpectedly from a mountain valley and clobbering us on our own doorstep.

We could hardly believe it. Breaking off from the *Geschwader* we roared in over our airfield unmolested and landed at 1503 hrs. The historian recorded that eight Wellington bombers were destroyed and a further seven badly damaged. The airfield was out of action for forty-eight hours, at a time when German and Italian reinforcements were being moved up from Palermo to Tripoli.

We had made it! That made the feeling of being alive even better and made us feel friendly towards everybody. I was very pleased with my aircrews. They were not as bad as I sometimes thought they were when the spectre of an operation loomed ahead of us. Then, I was always afraid one or other of them was going to make a balls-up, and that always got me worked up or made me severe. However, I didn't wish to appear to be too exuberantly happy: I wanted to seem relaxed. Who knows what tomorrow will bring? I suppressed my true feelings.

Hanke came back from Catania, via Paterno, but hadn't brought any new orders with him. Our *Kommandeur*, Arved Crueger, and the remainder of the *Gruppe* were due to arrive in three or four days. We were looking forward to seeing our comrades; also to the arrival of the administration people, to getting some money and to being looked after. The warrant officer had got some food for us: a dozen oranges per man and some dry, white bread. He'd also organised some agricultural equipment. We needed protection against splinters, so we had to dig. The aircrew had to do their bit. We wouldn't be able to go to Paterno until later that afternoon.

I walked with Hanke from aeroplane to aeroplane and he collected their combat reports. When the smoke and dust had cleared from Luqa, the *10th Fliegerkorps*, to which the *Geschwader* belonged, would send a reconnaissance aircraft to overfly it and take photographs from the glacial heights. Then the photos would be compared with the reports.

Behind a cactus hedge on our field I discovered a flat, whitewashed cottage, more a bungalow than a farmhouse. A slim woman, clad in black and wearing a Calabrian slouch hat, was busying herself at a small tree. I greeted her in a mixture of French and Italian, but she bade me welcome in choice Austro-Hungarian. Soon, I knew her whole life-story — daughter of an Austrian civil servant, married to an Italian who was killed fighting for Italy in the tenth to thirteenth Battles of Isonzo, her brother killed fighting on the Austro-Hungarian side in the same series of battles: 'And now you're playing kids' games again, great big men that you are!'

She must have been a countess, at least, if not a duchess. She spoke French and Italian, was educated and well-read. She invited me in. From the garden we went directly through open French doors into an airy room that had a tiled floor and was adorned with plants and paintings. She walked ahead of me. I saw the hem of her long black dress trail over the dust of the garden and then over the tiles, and it seemed to me somewhat slovenly — but I couldn't see her as being a slut. Her movements and her speech were too precise, too imperious, and she acted towards me like a royal princess.

'There! Look at these', — the heads of her Italian and German relatives painted in oils. 'Tell me how life has been treating you, you young blood. Come and see me whenever you want. I make the tea myself — a bit weak nowadays. And I've got a cow for fresh milk.' She looked at me quizzically. 'A big hero, are you? And you're going to win the war? You'll never do it!' That was my cue: 'We're going to win, that's for sure. It's completely different from 1914/18 this time. We're here in Sicily, and I've just come back from Malta.'

'Yes,' she said, mockingly. 'I know. I've just heard about it on the BBC. I heard the noise you made when you were coming back.' She took hold of my arm. 'My dear boy. My husband and my brother. Take a good look at them. They were young then, just like you are today. In their prime, and they killed each other.' She looked at me and seemed to be from another world. Was she like a Cassandra, trying to frighten me? I thought, I've had enough for today. I'd rather be alone and ponder the riddle we call the future in my own way. But perhaps that would be pointless. Perhaps it would be better if someone gave me a hefty shove in the direction of some trouble spot or other, some cock-up that would provoke me into furious action. That eradicates all the deep-rooted problems that one doesn't have solutions for.

'Two aircraft unserviceable,' reported Lorenz.

'Why aren't they serviceable?' I asked angrily.

In a silky, matter-of-fact voice, Lorenz told me that it was because of flak damage, and that there was no way of telling what structural parts could be affected. I began to get angry. I wanted all my aeroplanes serviceable by the following morning. In a flat voice Weinreich answered, *'Jawohl'*.

The good *Leutnant* Weinreich had an expert, cunning way of showing it when he considered my ideas to be nonsense, and he did so with a self-deprecating and forbearing manner. Young lout! It was not easy to get the better of him. He sailed pretty close to the wind. Damn and blast it! If I announced what I thought was a good idea, he cut me down to size by singing his *'Jaaaa-wohl'* on a descending note, long drawn-out. I swallowed this insubordination and thought: just you wait, my friend!

I said that I wanted the aircraft to be worked on through the night. 'What? It's not full moon? Then get the standby batteries. Tap the mains power somewhere or other. Organise some cable. Where's Lorenz?' Bad news didn't get me down; it had the opposite effect — it made me angry. There would be time to relax later. After I got everything off my chest, I put my arm round Toto's neck. I was at peace with the world again.

By evening, I had completed the operational report. When I came to the aircraft availability report I wrote — and I made sure that Weinreich heard it — 'All aircraft serviceable', but I whispered to Hanke, 'Minus two, perhaps.' It was his job to explain it to the *Kommodore*.

My Giacomo was waiting, together with a few similar vehicles of cheap design and a ramshackle bus with a motor that sounded as if it was on its last legs. Springs protruded through its upholstery and some of its windows were broken or missing completely. Nevertheless, the aircrews' joy was boundless. The driver jumped out with enthusiastic shouts, as if he were meeting old friends again after a long time, his pride not in the slightest diminished by the sad condition of his vehicle.

Four of us travelled with Giacomo — *Unteroffizier* Alles stayed behind on the airfield to do some technical work — along roads that didn't deserve to be called such. We were squashed and shaken up until we felt a more-or-less solid road beneath us on the outskirts of Paterno. Ahead of us, in the Market Square, was a throng of people. The square, the road and the pavements were flooded with a sea of men clothed in black. They were standing in groups, discussing, with considerable excitement, what surely must have been something very important because, when Giacomo sounded his horn in a peremptory manner, they showed neither the slightest agitation nor sign of movement. The horn blared out a long blast. Giacomo stuck his head out, shouted and swore. Nothing moved. Then something happened that we didn't expect. Giacomo drove up to the nearest man at a walking pace and gave him a shove in the back of the knees with the car's bumper, shouting even more loudly while he did so. Lo! There was movement in the crowd. It opened up, then closed up behind us, the people swearing. We forced our way onward. I thought, God! What a carry on! They'll tear us into pieces! Nevertheless, we were through. There was more breathing space on the road between the market place and the convent. I wondered how the bus would get on in the crowd, always supposing it hadn't broken down somewhere out in the countryside.

The warrant officer met us. He had been waiting for us for several hours.

'Where are the nuns?'

He pulled a long face. 'Invisible!' he announced with a worried look. 'They do everything through a serving hatch!' He said that only one had been seen, and she had crossed herself.

Two-tier bunks had been erected in a spacious, cool room, probably the refectory. They were made of wooden frames and had tightly stretched, coarse, linen cloth to lie on. We asked ourselves whether or not the nuns slept like that all their lives. Our aircrew arrived and their pleasure at being there was short-lived; their faces darkened. They were even less happy when an almost invisible hand passed out macaroni in a metal bowl. Surely, today of all days, they deserved something better? We went out for a stroll. Lights out was at 2200 hrs. We could never tell when a higher authority might wake us from our bunks. I fell asleep wondering what the important business was that the black-garbed men had been discussing on the piazza. I awoke with the same question in my mind. Giacomo had tried to explain, but I'd hardly understood a word.

I didn't give a thought to breakfast, even though there might have been manna or some other such delicacy. I was eager to be out of the sacred precincts and with my aircraft. I told the warrant officer to follow on with the crews. It was perhaps 0900 or 0930 hrs when Giacomo drove me into the Market Place. Good Lord! The black men are there again, standing around. I spoke somewhat snappily to my permanently good-tempered driver. 'Is it like this every day? Just to gossip? Why aren't they in Africa — Benghazi or Tobruk?' Giacomo explained that there weren't sufficient boots for their soldiers.

I was shocked. They'd joined in a war without being able to kit their soldiers out with boots? What else haven't they got? Poor Germany, I think. Giacomo was playing battering-ram with the crowd again. The men had put up umbrellas to shield themselves from the sun. My sense of order and diligence cried out against their inactivity. I became angry and tetchy. I swore. I just couldn't understand idleness. What I was not used to, couldn't imagine, didn't expect — in short, anything foreign to me — threw me completely. I just couldn't think, by any stretch of the imagination, that it could be like this all of the time. It was beyond my understanding that this non-productive, gossiping mass should go on streaming into the square each morning and stay there until they dissipated in the late evening, only to congregate again the next day. It was unimaginable that on beautiful Spring days such as that, our drivers had to force their way, time and again, through the inertia, that solid mass of layabouts, so that we could embark upon hazardous raids against British naval units or against Malta and then come back from our operations, having lost some of our best comrades, only to see in front of us that idleness and sleepy indifference. They could at least have been working in shoe factories!

I consoled myself with thoughts of my boys in the *Staffel*. In the light of what I had just witnessed they seemed to me to be as busy as ants. How did one set targets when a job had to be done: at what seemed possible, or higher? Who had the right to set standards? Who had the right to acknowledge what had been achieved, be it with criticism or with medals? It dawned upon me that the standards were usually set for the many by a few, who were mostly invisible, high-up individuals. Therefore I could not avoid accepting the fact that, within my own small area of responsibility, I was a man who set rather demanding standards.

All was quiet on the airfield. Here and there a farmer could be seen with an ox or a donkey, moving leisurely through the cacti and the trees. Weinreich was still in the hut, asleep. Lorenz was sitting by an aeroplane, his back against an ammunition box, and he was peeling an orange with oily hands. I suppressed an oath, not wishing to seem unjust. I said, simply, '*Guten Morgen*', and lay down in the grass about ten metres away. The sun warmed me agreeably. Gradually I submitted to the feeling that time and patience would do what had to be done.

After a short while Lorenz said, 'Today seems to be one of the *Herr Hauptmann's* sociable days'. He had picked up that form of words from Weinreich, who was in the habit of using them when I had nothing to complain about. It was an act of impertinence on the part of Lorenz of course. I sensed that Lorenz knew that he was in a one-up position. He continued: 'Both aircraft will be operational in an hour'; I was right! He added that during the night he had been to Catania to get a spare part. That gave me a pleasant feeling; but I was never one to give lavish praise. I didn't like speeches of gratitude myself: ninety-percent of them consist of lies and ulterior motives. My *Kommodore, Major* Bloedorn, once said to me, after he had praised me in his own way, 'There's no need to look at me as if you wanted to call me a cheating bastard!' Lorenz and I knew each other. I squinted up at the sky, and after a moment I said, 'I guess you're a bit tired now, aren't you?' Receiving no reply, I lifted myself up a little on my elbows and looked across at him. He had fallen asleep, still propped up against the munition box.

The knocking noises outside and inside the aeroplane, the warmth and the way things had turned out well made me nod off. When I looked at my watch, a full hour had passed. Hanke was plodding towards me through the grass. 'Medium-sized British naval formation from Alexandria heading west in the direction of Benghazi. Finger out! Get cracking!' Our *Staffel* had to carry out the attack alone. We were to wait until the ships came within our range, probably in the Tobruk area. It was thought that they would make harbour there about evening and spend the night under the protection of the coastal flak before pressing on further west to tempt the Italian fleet out. 'You've got to be over Tobruk at dawn. Dive-bomb with armour-piercing bombs. Great, isn't it?'

A fine way for the *Fliegerkorps* and *Geschwader* to treat us. They could have left us in peace for a couple of days. We hadn't even arrived properly yet. We were still living out of our suitcases, so to speak. Time after time during the war I'd thought, 'That's that. Now I've time for a breather,' only to be clobbered with more orders. By now I was used to it. I'd made myself get used to it by asking myself what action I would take to get at the enemy, or by anticipating unpalatable orders.

A dawn attack meant a night take-off. I was on the ball. 'No paraffin lamps? Then make fires out of potato leaves, or maize leaves, or tobacco leaves, or cactus. We'll take off to the left or the right of them. Scrounge the stuff. Paraffin lamps would be no good anyway. They'd be swamped by the grass.' Hanke said I was round the bend. We were still waiting for the PC 1400 armour-piercing bombs. The lifting vehicles hadn't crossed the Brenner yet, so the bombs would have to be hoisted up under the wings with a block and tackle. Everyone had to lend a hand, including the aircrew. Then we topped up with fuel. There wasn't a lot left after the flights over the Alps to Malta. Briefing was set for 1900 hrs. I ordered 30 minutes readiness from 0100 hr.

I set about organising lights to help us on take-off, which would be towards the west. A few cars were to shine their headlamps on the olive trees in the direction of take-off, and others were to illuminate the ground with their beams further west, outside the airfield, That would make it easier for us to see three-dimensionally when we got airborne. Above all, I needed a vertical searchlight to act as a beacon for us to aim at and as a marker at which to turn. It would also show us where the rising ground started. The course to Tobruk was south-east.

It grew warmer. I ate one orange after the other. The aircrew, rested, arrived from Paterno. I called *Oberleutnant zur See* Friedrich over to me. '*Achtung!*' He always reported like that, in accordance with naval custom, whenever I sent for him. I put him in the picture and he busied himself. The transition from astronomical twilight to first dawn, the short, decisive period between it being still too dark and too light, so that we can avoid being seen, had to be calculated with a high degree of accuracy. We could not arrive too early in darkness because we would have to search for our target in the dark, nor must we arrive too late, in daylight. The fighters would make short work of us. At our latitude the transition phases were short.

It would have been very risky to rely on the forecast wind alone for our long flight. The wind could have slowed us down or speeded us up. We would try to get bearings from the radio station at Athens, and possibly from one in Turkey. But night and twilight often played havoc with the invisible radio waves. Astro-navigation was also out of the question. Encouraged by Friedrich, it was true, we had messed about with our sextants during our flights to England, and we had shot many a pair of stars at night-time outside our barracks. But it was like black magic to us, and frequently our measurements had shown us to be in Greenland rather than in Holland. But we had gradually cut the error down to a few miles.

The skies could have helped us — if its servants the astronomers had produced tables for this part of the world and sent them to us. All that we could rely on was our eyes and our sixth sense. Friedrich focused on this *ultima ratio*, albeit with a certain amount of jocularity. He concentrated particularly on the observers, the bomb aimers and the men who would man the under-turrets, because they were the ones who would be looking outwards and downwards.

While all this was happening I had made a quick trip to Catania. I tried to explain to the Italian flak commander that I needed one strong searchlight, at least, to aid take-off. The highly decorated officer pointed in the direction of Malta and gave me a tragic look. He was afraid, he said, that the Wellington bombers would come. I told him calmly that they wouldn't be coming that night: we had put them all out of action the previous day. At last I made some progress, but I had to give my word of honour that I would send the searchlight back the next day with its cable length unaltered. The smallest searchlight possible was wheeled up on a most unusual undercarriage. Giacomo attached the trailer to his car and I took my leave with a '*Millie grazia*', telling my driver to take the greatest care as I did so.

I was very proud of my victory, and was looking forward to showing my comrades just what could be done when one really tried. 'What's that thing that looks like a cross between a field kitchen and a saucepan?' asked Weinreich. 'Ah! It must be the night-light we've heard so much about.' When you were among aircrew, you had to exercise a measure of self-control!

The crews did not go to Paterno that evening. I was not prepared to risk dangerous night-driving over unmade, bumpy roads in clapped-out vehicles. We had to sleep as we had the first night: like sardines in a tin. Some of the aircrew made themselves comfortable in the bus that was to take us to our aircraft that night. The atmosphere in the barrack, after sunset, was so terrific that nobody thought of sleep. In the distance I could hear bursts of laughter as I went out to the dispersals with Weinreich and Lorenz. The final armour-piercing bombs were being hoisted up, the bowsers were rattling from one aircraft to the next.

At about midnight Hanke brought the latest reports on the enemy and the weather from the *Geschwader*. There was no fresh news about the enemy, which wasn't surprising because the nights were dark. The expected wind at an altitude of 3000-5000 metres was from the north-west, moderate at 15-20 kmph. It became quieter in the barrack block. The three of us sat down on packing cases and ate oranges, the staple diet thereabouts. I felt a bit tired, but not sleepy. The main thing was to get off the ground and into the air. Then everything would go according to plan. The warrant officer was responsible for what happened until then. It was his job to wake the crews up. They had to be up and out of their 'sardine tins' by 0115 hrs.

'Wakey, wakey!' I looked into the barrack, in the middle of which two lanterns were burning. I saw small eyes and pinched, unenthusiastic faces, and I heard curses. 'Mind where you're treading, clot!' 'Shut your face!'

The bus rattled and then pulled away. I walked out to my aircraft together with my crew. The air was invigorating. All the crews were in their aircraft by 0130 hrs. By 0145 hrs we were in our seats, ready to taxi out for take-off with the aid of the headlights and the position lamps. The Italian air traffic control officer was to fire a red flare if an attack came from Malta. We had to wait for a green flare before we could move off. It was Hanke's job to see that everything was coordinated.

Our runway lights, the paraffin lamps, formed a nice, tidy line. Weinreich had even had a path cut in the grass. It was not wide enough for the aeroplanes, but at least we could see the lamps and keep straight. I taxied out past the line of heavily laden aircraft. One by one, they lurched out and filtered in behind me. A thin pencil of light from the searchlight shone vertically into the sky, and I thought that it was better than nothing. The headlamps were more useful. They lit up the landscape, enabling us to judge distances.

Take-off was still set for 0200 hrs. I was ready to get airborne, had all the internal lights turned up bright and made a signal with my right hand. Krahn repeated the signal for those behind. Lights out. The luminous marks on the instruments shone softly but clearly back at me. Brakes on — half throttle — three-quarters throttle — brakes off! Full throttle and off we went. After rounding the feeble searchlight, I looked back towards the airfield where I could see one red port navigation light after another moving across the ground. Krahn counted them. They were all airborne. After three or four minutes they switched off their navigation lights. The game was on. We climbed steeply to 3000 metres.

We remained at that altitude so that we could fly without using the uncomfortable oxygen masks and not freeze unnecessarily, maintaining staggered heights of plus or minus 300 metres. After half an hour I was dog-tired. I had been on my feet, tramping all over the airfield, the whole day. I hadn't eaten anything solid. I checked the course and our heading with Schmetz and, with parachute and Mae West on, made sure I was strapped in tightly. Held in place by that corset, I handed over the controls and responsibility to Schmetz. I told him to wake me thirty minutes before the ETA over the target. I fell into a deep sleep. Neither the noise of the engine nor that of the crew as they went about their business disturbed me. I knew I was secure and in good hands.

We had to fly 1150 kilometres to our target, Tobruk, which we calculated would take three and a quarter hours. When I was awakened I squinted at the instruments and at the stars. My hands and feet had gone to sleep. I did a few small gymnastic exercises within the embrace of my seat belts, then I opened the throttles to gain height, and I put on my oxygen mask. Schmetz had been navigating. Radio beacons and broadcasting stations were either not available or too weak, or else night effect was making it difficult to get bearings. Consequently, navigation consisted of nothing more than setting our course according to the estimated wind we had got from the Met. office in Sicily and letting the automatic pilot look after steering it. All we had to do then was to keep an eye on the clock.

Ten minutes to go. We peered downwards. The African coast should have been somewhere directly below us. There was nothing to be seen. An indefinable background of black and grey yawned up at us. One indefinable feature changed into another. Why should we imagine that our nocturnal earth should not be visible or that it should look the same everywhere? The half-darkness over mud-flats is different from that over the North Sea or over England. When the faint light of the stars falls on what is below, on water, meadows, woods, steppes, clouds or mists, it is either swallowed up or reflected back upwards. Millions of stars with occasional bright planets endow our earth's night-coverlet with an infinite variety of patterns and shapes, sometimes black, sometimes grey, threatening or comforting, lasting or ephemeral. And from them a human being can only get impressions, and his sixth sense has to set them against its five rational sisters. It was a new experience for us to be flying from the darkness of a southern night into the dawning day.

Time was up. Schmetz thought he saw something below like a line, a shape; but it was nothing. More shapes. Clouds, or banks of fog below us? I began to get angry. The weather man had forecast clear skies in the target area. How were we to pick out warships from altitude in weather such as this, then dive-bomb and hit them with armour-piercing bombs? We were a few minutes past our ETA already. I hadn't decided what to do. I thought of the others following on behind. They were close behind and were hoping to be guided by the defensive fire from the warships and the coastal flak and, if possible, by the light from bombs detonating on their targets. In the east the dawn was painting the horizon red. I became uneasy and shouted, 'Keep your eyes open! Can anyone see the coast?'

The thought that the attack could fail and that we could fall prey to fighters made me hot under the collar. I had to be able to see something. I strained my eyes, peering into the darkness. I saw nothing at first, then vague outlines. I closed my eyes and opened them slowly in an attempt to conjure up images from the depths, as one does when sitting in front of a dark stage waiting for a great spectacle to begin. Nothing! There was no coast to be seen. Then I saw something. A scarcely perceptible undulation. The mist below us was turning gradually brown, then brownish-red. And then we all saw it at once — desert. Nothing but desert. No coastline, no sea, no fog, no clouds. I had a radio message sent at once: 'To all aircraft. Reciprocal heading immediately. Low level.'

A wind, stronger than forecast, had taken us past the target, deep inland to the south. To have stayed on the old course a minute longer could have made our return impossible; neither could we have searched for the target. We were flying individually, and the defences would have cut us to pieces. We must have been on the British radar screens for a long time, and the Spitfires would be vectored on us when the sun was up. We would have to fly nearer to the ground and take advantage of the slower winds there. We flew on a north-westerly heading, right down over the sand dunes and undulating ground, the sun bathing the endless wastes red. I was bringing up the rear. I hoped against hope that the *Staffel's* aircraft, lightly scattered as they were, would manage to cross British-occupied territory and find their way out to sea.

In the meanwhile, we thought of how we could get rid of our heavy bombs profitably and in such a way as to cause damage to the enemy. It was pointless to think of following the coast and looking into every bay, even the harbour at Benghazi, in the hope of finding a supply ship or a naval vessel. A plan that involved climbing up out of the radar shadow near the ground and then clambering up to height for a diving attack would have been assessed as unsatisfactory at the Military Academy. Calculated risk was the watchword: save the aircraft and the crew for future operations with more hope of success. So we put off the decision, but not without the uncomfortable feeling that we might have to cross the coast, thick as it was with flak and fighters, with an unused cargo, risking our necks while running the gauntlet. It was, in any case, far from clear whether or not we and our sophisticated machines would ever see the Sicilian beaches again, let alone reach them. Should we drill a hole in the desert sands with our bomb? Should we let it splash into the sea?

The decision was struck from our minds like a spark from a stone even as we were toying with it. 'Fighters!' screamed Krahn, the radio operator.

OK, I thought, here goes. Self-taught to stay calm, I asked, 'How far? How high? Direction?' But Krahn was already reporting, 'Four or five o'clock, two thousand metres above.' They were astern and to our right.

Krahn continued, 'Closing. Range, two kilometres.' I twisted my head round to look until it hurt. Then I saw the section of fighters. They were flying towards us, but not diving down at us yet. They were almost in the sun. Aha! I thought. It's going to be a surprise attack. I looked ahead at the sand dunes I was racing low over, and then back at the Hurricanes.

Now was the moment they should be committing themselves to the attack. The closer they came, the quieter we spoke. 'God in Heaven,' I whispered. 'Make them sleep, or make us invisible!' We hadn't even painted a desert camouflage on our aircraft before we took off. And there was also a bird of doom in the form of black shadows cast by our aircraft on the sand ahead. I crouched down in my seat. The infantry soldier could crawl into a hole in the ground, throw himself down in a furrow, cower behind a bush. We were travelling through the air in a glass blister. We were sitting ducks; unfortunates. Time crawled by. I wished that it was night.

The Hurricanes were exactly above us. Please don't turn! Then they were a short distance ahead and above. They flew off to the left, heading west. They hadn't seen us! We had survived! We didn't dare to ask for how long. Every minute was precious. Slowly the Hurricanes faded into black dots in the distance. We carried on, right down on the deck. What we had experienced was the victim's mute expectation of the executioner's axe. In a renewed state of high tension, we drew nearer to Cyrenaica, its mountains visible in the distance.

The sun was making us very warm, when suddenly red tracer shells came up at us, shells from 4 cm automatic flak. Before I had a chance to make a mistake, the

r the cockade of the Hamburg Police. On manoeuvres in the Sachsenwald.

Summer 1935, after the lifting of the camouflage, as an Infantry Lieutenant.

As a trainee pilot, by now a Lieutenant in the Luftwaffe. Kitzingen/Main August 1935.

Pilots' Course at Kitzingen, in front of a W 34. Under the propeller boss is the Course Leader, Major Weller, a First World War pilot. On the left-hand edge of the photo is Karl Huelshoff, and at the right-hand end of the back row, Rudi Kiel. Two officers later became successful fighter pilots: Willi Gaeth (2nd row, right-hand side) and Rolf Pingel (front row, 4th from the right). The author is in the centre of the rear row.

Major Maass and Major Graf Luckner take the parade on the Nordhausen Corn Market, Spring 1936.

View of the airfield construction site from my lieutenant's accommodation.

One of the 'Pedros' ' He 111s at Burgos.

Two fixed forward-firing machine guns, one on each wing, defence against the increasingly frequent attacks by Soviet 'Ratas'. The idea was that of Hauptmann Krafft von Dellmensingen.

As a Leutnant after my return from Spain, in front of a Ju 86, the new but already ailing bomber. Nordhausen, Summer 1937.

On the Bilboa Front in the North, April 1937. A bombing attack on the almost impregnable enemy positions constructed on the slopes in the background of the picture, which are visible as light lines.

Aircraft and troops parading on the East-West axis of Berlin in honour of Prince Regent Paul of Jugoslavia.

Oberst Fiebig. Kommodore of KG 4, 'General Wever', in conversation with Chief of the Luftflotte, General Felmy (right).

August 1939, in quarters in Schloss Langenau near Breslau. Back row, from the left: Oberleutnant Hans Hanke, Hauptmann Martin Schumann, Oberleutnant Koehne. The author is in the front on the right.

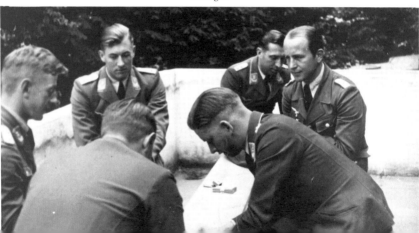

Above and below: The 9th Staffel of KG 4 on operations during the Polish campaign, 1 September 1939.

Above right: Damage on the Polish airfield at Deblin after attacks on 1 September 1939.

Above left: My mechanic Buhmann in front of 'his' He 111. He was a skilled craftsman.

Centre: My He 111.

The He 111 that was the Geschwader Commander's aircraft, 5J + DA, after making a belly-landing on the Amsterdam-Schiphol airfield after a low-level attack. It had been hit 200 times, and the Kommodore, Oberst Fiebig, and his crew spent 5 days in captivity.

Above left: Oslo-Fornebu, 10 April 1940. There was not enough room — quite clearly!

Above right: Leutnant Weinreich attaching the heavy luggage container to his aeroplane.

Left: Officers of the 7th Staffel of KG 30, the 'Adler' Geschwader, on the sea-front at Scheveningen. Left to right: Piëch, Weinreich, Herrmann, Friedrich, Kuehnle, Schmetz.

Below left: With comrades at Gilze-Rijen. Left to right: Roehricht, Richtering, Hanke, Schmidt, Crueger, Holler, the author, Haase, Sommer, Dahlmann.

Below right: Despite appearances, this crash on 19 October 1940 was not too serious.

*My faithful Ju 88, 4D + AR, taking a rest at [the]
foot of Etna. Bullet-wounds have to be healed, a[nd]
the creases on the upper surface of the wings[, a]
legacy of pulling out of diving attacks, have to [be]
smoothed out.*

*With my observer, Schmetz, in the cockpit sett[ing]
off on an operation. This is how our mechar[ic,]
Buhmann, sees us when he gives us the 'all cle[ar']
signal.*

*Over the Mediterranean and heading for Crete[, in]
loose formation in the interest of preserving ner[ves,]
engines and fuel. We will close up before we re[ach]
the target.*

Carola Hoehn, a beautiful film actress, vied for by fighter pilots at Gela, Sicily. Major Muencheberg is the second from the left.

The supply of bombs by the cactus-hedge is not always well camouflaged or part-buried. It costs time and effort to hoist bombs, and there's a very rapid turn-over.

Technicians working in icy cold on the airfield in the Bardufoss basin. The mountains reach up to 1400 metres.

The King of Italy and the Emperior of Ethiopia with 111./KG 30.

The newly engaged couple, Carola Hoehn and Major Crueger on the isle of Capri, April/May 1941.

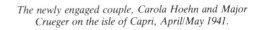

Flying from the basin towards the sea. The beginning of the fjord can be seen in the middle distance. In conditions of low cloud we used to fly out to sea at low level.

The fjord broadens out. Tromso can be seen bottom left. Far to the north the way to the sea is over scattered clouds.

The formation turning on to its approach heading.

On the approach to Bardufoss.

*It is not until some time after the battle the
German U-Boats come back home. This
is parading in front of the Admiral i/c N
Sea. Prisoners — rescued from the sea —
lined up on deck (left).*

Goering talking to victims of the air raids in the Ruhr district, 1944. He could still trust himself among the people.

Above left: Schloss Allner on the Sieg, near Hennef.

Above right: 'Wilde Sau': the Company Sergeant Major in the orderly room.

Left: A 'Wild Boar' in its sty.

Pilots of I./JG 300 in front of the spa-house at Hennef. The Commandeur, Major Stamp, wearing the Knight's Cross, is in the centre.

Above: Friedrich Karl Mueller by a camouflaged aircraft shelter.

Below: Some of 'Wilde Sau's' opponents. Arrowed: G. Taylor, shot down, taken prisoner, then a visitor to some of the old Wild Boars in the seventies.

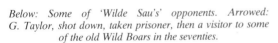

Below: On the left, Hermann Goering, Comm in-Chief of the Luftwaffe and Reichsmarsch conversation with 'Wilde Sau' men.

Planning and production, an eternal and tiresome subject. Talks at the Junkers factory in Dessau. Omitting the factory managers and engineers, from right to left in uniform: Oberst von Below; Staff Oberst von Lossberg; Major Baumbach; General Vorwald, Head of the Technical Office; Aircrew Staff Engineer Professor Steinmann; Generalfeldmarschall Erhard Milch; Herrmann (in high boots and speaking for both bombers and fighters). In civilian clothes: General Director Dr. L. S. Rothe (extreme left) and Director Walter Jander (second from left).

The Control Room of the First Fighter Division in Doeberitz, photographed from the 'stage'. But it is not an audience that is sitting in the rows of seats that slope upwards, but presenters who are equipped with microphones and headsets and are creating a picture of the air battle on the screen. The controllers themselves are sitting in the back row, which is smaller than the others: at the moment there are fewer of them than there sometimes are because only reconnaissance flights have been reported.

Wind von oben wird dir verdrießen
Da Wilde Tau...uns nicht beim Tiefangen

Above: Our twin-engined fighters join in — but they are in competition with us. An interesting item of wartime propaganda — among friends!

Right: Marshal of the Royal Air Force, Sir Arthur Harris.

Below: There were only 21 copies of this envelope, signed on 1 February 1972 by one-time enemies and much sought-after by philatelists.

radio operator and the observer loosed off a few hundred rounds from their twin machine-guns. I saw shots from a vehicle standing alone on a hillock of sand spraying past, while other vehicles made themselves small under a cloud of dust in a depression. I shouted out, 'Bomb ready!' lifted the aircraft slightly and released the bomb. As the bomb raced down to the earth, I saw, through the haze, camels, a caravan headed by a jeep that was firing at us bravely. I turned to port, all guns firing. A column of sand rose up into the sky from the armour-piercing bomb that had been intended for a battleship. Heavily laden camels scattered widely in all directions. Suddenly tracers came at us from three, four directions. There was no doubt that the caravan wouldn't reach its destination that day, and the ammunition it was carrying wouldn't reach the front and be used against Rommel.

We made haste so that we wouldn't fall into the clutches of the Hurricanes. They could be called up by R/T and be on the spot in a matter of minutes. After a short time we made a wide turn south onto a westerly heading in the hope of reaching the nearest airfield on our side of the German/Italian lines, or alternatively of getting to Tripoli. So much had gone wrong, but so far we had been lucky. We didn't want to take a bath in the Med.

Then something very human occurred. Before taking off, hungry for vitamins, we had each eaten ten, fifteen or twenty oranges, partly in the form of juice, and now a certain natural discomfort was making itself felt. Speed was of the essence! After a short R/T conversation we made a slight turn and soon headed for the coast south of Benghazi, crossing it at low level. Above a lightly wrinkled sea we made space for a sharp turn south to approach the airfield at Syrte. The field, which was occupied by Italians, was only a few kilometres behind the Front. It was near to the Via Balbia, and we could only recognise it as an aerodrome by the one or two Italian aircraft parked there. There were a few palm trees. Except for them there was nothing but sand. Even the excellent Via Balbia was covered with sand in many places.

The landing gave me the awful feeling that we were going to tip over. The wheels didn't want to turn: they were held by the sand. Although I held the control column against my stomach with all my strength, the aircraft made a number of hops before it came to a standstill. Our limbs were cramped but our spirits were high as we clambered down the ladder. We stamped in the sand and became aware of an Italian officer seated high on a camel. He dismounted in front of our aircraft and gave a formal military salute. We had always envied the Italian aircrew their beautifully styled caps. They looked sporting, fashionable, yet masculine. Our caps were simply behind the times. While the Italian saluted, we made embarrassed gestures and retired to the shade of the wings, where we relieved ourselves near the undercarriage with sighs of satisfaction. Shortly afterwards we took off from the desert sands, aided by a fresh wind from the sea. We landed in Tripoli to refuel and then made our way back to Sicily.

The feeling that I had of having been a protective shepherd to my flock was, unhappily, misplaced. Dr. Kratz's crew had gone off alone to take a look at the area around Benghazi. Kratz had been anxious to try out the new bomb sight, the ZBA, brainchild of his inventive mind, in operational conditions. He had dived down at high speed on a large ship moored alongside the docks, and the wolves had got him. However, he survived. Sometime later we received news of him from Australia via his parents.

Our *Gruppe* arrived at last, the aircraft swooping down on the field like crows in the evening. Then they were taxying, the 8th and the 9th *Staffel*: there was the *Kommandeur*. Each made for its allocated place. When they got out of their machines, I thought, how they would stretch themselves, how they'd sniff the air; how they'd stamp about, how they'd shout for joy. They would have lots of things to tell us, and we them. Things were going to be a lot better now: there would be proper food, there would be spares, there would be mail.

Where was our mail? We wanted it at once. It still had the old field post number on, Bentheim on the German-Dutch border. Come on, accounts officer, we thought — make with the *Lire*!

Arved Crueger, my *Kommandeur*, was tall and good-looking, which was why he had been chosen as an aide-de-camp to Emmy Goering in Kampen, on the Island of Sylt. We used to joke about him handing her beach robe to her, passing her cooling drinks, until finally, it became too much for him and he went to the front. Apart from the fact that he led us to ice-cold Olympian heights operationally, I had nothing against him.

Hanke received friendly praise for his planning. *Oberleutnant* Holler, the signals officer, had brought with him new and more accurate charts, together with the frequencies of all the possible friendly and enemy transmitters. Packing cases full of paper were off-loaded from the Ju 52, together with teleprinters, typewriters, telephones and radio sets. We toasted our comrades' arrival with orange juice. How they drank! Reverently and happily, we watched them swallow it down. Suddenly, I thought: where is my dog, my Berto-Ingo, my sturdy German Shepherd? Is he following on by rail? I was told that he had been left in the care of naval pilots at Schipol. They hadn't been able to guarantee a place for him on the goods' train. A pity! But the rest of us were united in the nunnery at Paterno, with much joy and jubilation.

Ahead of us lay difficult operations against naval units and convoys, and against Malta. We scoured the stretch of sea south of Crete to the limits of our range. We flew to Derna and Tobruk on the African coast. We came to know the British as seamen of the first order. With their heaviest vessels, the battleships *Barham*, *Warspite*, *Valiant* and *Queen Elizabeth*, they held their courses in formation, cold-bloodedly, until the very moment we came tearing down in our dive. Then they gave hard rudder, visibly heeling over, almost invariably avoiding our slim, armour-piercing bombs as they did so. When, as experience taught us to, we got right down on the surface of the sea after pulling out of our dives to escape the intentions of those fighters that had taken off from the aircraft carrier *Formidable*, we found the heavy or middle naval flak banging away at us, its shells creating a barrier of fountains in front of our noses. Running into one of those pillars of water meant being smashed into pieces and going down to a watery grave.

Fending off the fighters demanded the utmost from our crews. We flew in tight formation over the water, wing-tip to wing-tip, belting off ammunition until the barrels of our guns glowed red. The fighters kept at a respectable range from our guns. With the foaming spray caused by our fire in front of their eyes, the single-engined fighters felt the damp too clearly to risk close combat. They preferred to be higher up, where they could fight more easily and with more dash. Sometimes, in an emergency, the fighters would glide down to their carriers, airscrew stationary, or the pilot would make a quick R/T call so that a swift destroyer could come to his aid and fish him out of the water.

We suffered losses. *Leutnant* Piëch was caught by a fighter as he pulled out from a dive-bombing attack; even though his aircraft was badly damaged he managed to press on for several kilometres on one engine. Two of us kept him company. Then, in front of our eyes, he dived flat into the sea and disappeared in a mass of foam, only to come back to the surface almost immediately. I turned back and flew past at low speed, and was relieved to see that the crew had inflated the dinghy and were clambering aboard. The unfortunate men sat there in the raft, with us up above, powerless to help. They were in an area of the sea that it was almost impossible for our ships to enter. The only way we could help the luckless crew was to pass on their precise position.

I sent my No. 2 off, and I flew south on automatic pilot, timing myself with a stop watch, taking the shortest route to the North African coast. Heinrich Schmetz calculated the drift and groundspeed. We were lucky that we were equipped with the splendid *Lofte* 7D bomb sight, unlike the other crews. Schmetz was able to pinpoint exactly the place on the African coast at which we made landfall. While he was calculating the position of the crash we flew on to Benghazi, landed and passed the coordinates immediately to the *10th Fliegerkorps* in Taormina, Sicily, by radio. The staff there were in direct telephone contact with the air-sea rescue *Staffel* at Syracuse.

We filled up with fuel at Benghazi, and I flew back to the dead-reckoning position, arriving there when the sun was down low on the horizon. No matter how much we strained our eyes we could not see the dinghy. There seemed to me to be no point, therefore, in transmitting from the spot so that the air-sea rescue aircraft could take bearings. I flew round the position time and again but the search was fruitless. In a mood of depression we returned to Sicily. Nor had the air-sea rescue aircraft had any success. But the following day good fortune seemed to favour the pilot. He found the dinghy at the exact spot we had given, curved in to make a landing on the water — and then lost sight of it. The pilot flew round and round, circling the spot, but without success. It was not until the next attempt, in the afternoon of the same day, that the rescue operation was crowned with success.

We collected our shot-down, shipwrecked comrades, some of them wounded, from Syracuse and took them back to base with much rejoicing. It was only then that we learned, incredibly, what had happened. The search aircraft, our own included, had been within one or two kilometres of the dinghy either without seeing it, or had seen it and then lost it from sight. The lives of those in the dinghy had been on a knife-edge because there wasn't a Very pistol on board. They reported an unusual phenomenon. Under the fierce rays of the sun, our comrades had almost lost their reason. At sunset they had thought they could see the African coast, which was almost two hundred kilometres distant.

There was another occasion on which my *Staffel* lost a crew of four. They too took to their dinghy. Our rescue operation was more successful than we had hoped: we picked up five pilots. An English fighter pilot was in the dinghy with them. The bomber and the fighter had shot each other down simultaneously.

Our operations were planned to prevent the British Fleet from crossing the Eastern Mediterranean and giving cover to the troops which were being withdrawn from North Africa and shipped to Crete; to make it difficult for the enemy to bring up supplies; and to give the Italian Fleet room to manoeuvre. After each of our operations the huge, steel-clad, heavily armed, fire-spitting monsters would withdraw to Alexandria, giving us a welcome breathing space in which to overhaul our motors and repair any damage. We ourselves had the opportunity to cast a glance at the fertile landscape and the ancient witnesses to European culture. As I looked at the old, weathered ruins, in an uncertain mood made up of both hope and resignation that operational flying generated in me, they seemed to me to emit life and meaning. I remembered how different I had been, how much more naïve and uninspired, when I had stood in front of works of antiquity in Berlin and Paris and had then taken a quick look at the newspaper and a cup of coffee. There had been no feeling then of floating on the long swell of the centuries.

Under the bright Sicilian sun the joy of being alive could not be suppressed. We had an unexpected visit by a group of German artistes to the theatre in Catania. Two complimentary tickets for the royal box were sent to the *Kommandeur* (no doubt that fact that he had recently been mentioned in a special report on German radio had played its part). He delegated me to go as his representative together with his Adjutant, *Oberleutnant* Sommer. It was a splendid performance, and the high spot was the appearance of the much-loved film star, Carola Höhn, in all her radiant beauty. During the reception that followed I was able to pass on to her the best regards of my *Kommandeur*. I did not neglect to mention that he had been the subject of the latest special broadcast report, and *Oberleutnant* Sommer expanded on the theme by describing the particular attack on the aircraft carrier. Given that northern, feminine beauty under a southern sky, it was little wonder that the hearts of the airmen beat faster. The highly decorated fighter pilot, Muencheberg, a gallant campaigner, vied for the lady's favour; but the bomber pilots triumphed. Carola Höhn said graciously that she would like to meet the brave *Kommandeur* of the successful *Gruppe*. Hiding my own interest in the meeting, I hurried back to the *Kommandeur* to suggest an intimate meal, to be attended by just a few of us. Instead the *Major* despatched me — me, of all people — with a bouquet of red roses and a note expressing his own devotion: I, a *postillon d'amour*, handed it to her with due ceremony and formality.

And so, instead of a meal for a select few, what actually took place was a tête-à-tête supper on a flower-decorated terrace in Taormina, from which the rest of Carola's would-be suitors, including me, were excluded.

Notes

1 *Staufer*: the *Hohenstaufen*, the imperial line that produced such outstanding figures as Friedrich I, Barbarossa, Heinrich IV and Friedrich II.
2 Goethe's primordial plant: *Kennst du das Land wo die Zitronen blueh'n*? Goethe, '*Mignon*' (Know'st thou the land where the lemon trees bloom?).
3 *Lehrgeschwader*: literally, Teaching *Geschwader*, were units formed to try out new aircraft and tactics under operational conditions.
4 'A tailor from Ulm with his winged suit'. Legend has it that a tailor from the German city of Ulm made himself a suit of leather with wings in an attempt to emulate the birds. He fell to his death, so the legend goes.
5 The Jungfernstieg, Koenigsallee, and Kurfuerstendamm were fashionable streets in Hamburg, Düsseldorf and Berlin respectively.
6 Ringelnatz: Joachim Ringelnatz was the pseudonym of Hans Boetticher (1883-1934) the humorous poet. He wrote '*Kuttel Daddeldu*' in 1923.
7 Gymnasium: equivalent to the British Grammar School.

Chapter Six
A Mini-Odyssey,
6/7 April 1941

March 1941, military putsch in Jugoslavia. On 5 April the country renounces its military treaty with Germany and signs a friendship pact with the Soviet Union. On 6 April 1941 the Germans march into Jugoslavia. In the meanwhile the British have landed on the mainland, but by 30 April they are driven out to Crete. Crete is captured, the German Air Force playing a major part.

Wise were the Gods to conceal from men what their fate would be: whether or not the day would bring for them triumph or death. The fear of death and the certainty of success could both paralyse motivation and action. The Delphic Oracle skilfully combined fear and hope in its predictions, so that mortal man, bewitched by both desire and fear, heeded only that which he wanted to hear.

It was the night of 6/7 April 1941. Had I consulted the Oracle that evening before setting off on my flight to the place where, 2500 years before, the sea battle of Salamis had been fought, she would surely have spoken thus: 'Stranger from the North, in this night shallst thou inflict a deep wound upon thine enemy. Fear the wrath of the Gods!' I would have thought, 'My God! Temptation calls, but there's a warning as well, and I mustn't ignore it.' So ran my thoughts as I relaxed, lying in an Italian officer's deck chair in the shade of olive trees at the foot of Etna. Whom does curiosity drive on to the morrow? Surely only a man who has a plan to carry out and a success to win, who is ready for the best, or for the worst. So must it have been always. So he dismisses the evil omens from his mind and stumbles, unsuspecting, towards his fate.

It was the day on which German troops had marched into Northern Greece in support of the Italians, who were attacking from Albania to drive the British out of the country. The Third *Gruppe* of our *Adlergeschwader*, III./KG 30, was still deployed on a grass field near to Gerbini, on the plain stretching south of Etna to the coast of Catania. Our *Gruppe*, equipped with the Ju 88, had been tasked to lay mines in the narrow entrance to the harbour of Piraeus, where the British were landing troops and supplies. It was hoped that the mines would sink ships which would then block both the way in and the way out. Our *Kommandeur*, Arved Crueger, had the aircraft loaded with two mines each. To me, *Kapitaen* of the *Staffel*, this seemed a bit on the modest side. I had flown a series of attacks against Malta and on that short run I had increased my bomb load and decreased the amount of fuel on board, both gradually, so that I had a payload — which is what we called our deadly cargo — of three tonnes. So I asked myself while I was sitting beneath the olive trees in the early evening and listening, through the metre-high cactus to the sound of my aircraft warming up, why should we simply let two mines float down on parachutes and plop into the water, and then rush off back home in the pious hope that at some time, maybe hours or days later, a ship would blow up on one of them? Why should we kid ourselves with such a piece of play-acting? I wound the handle on my field telephone and ordered softly but firmly, 'Put on an extra two 250-kg bombs. Understood?'

'*Jawohl, Herr Hauptmann*,' came the reply.

The *Kommandeur* hadn't ordered it: but he hadn't forbidden it either. As the crow flies the distance from our airfield to Piraeus was approximately 750 km, so we had to carry enough fuel for 1500 km, which was a fair load. If my calculations were correct we could get away with it. I climbed into the Packard I had commandeered in Belgium, drove round the widely dispersed aeroplanes and watched the heavy extra load being put in place. I found the crews in good fettle. The flight plan and the plan of attack, not to mention the mine-laying, were quite familiar to the experienced pilots and crews. They had already carried out dive-bombing attacks by moonlight in a number of theatres of war.

As secondary targets we were given British shipping in Suda Bay on the north coast of Crete, and our emergency diversion airfield was Gaddura on the Dodecanese island of Rhodes, an Italian strongpoint near to the Turkish coast. I was impatient for darkness to fall so that the bombs under the wings wouldn't be noticed. I was afraid that the *Kommandeur* would pay a visit to the *Staffel* to see that all was correct.

That is exactly what happened. He came too early. He saw the bombs under the wings and he said, 'I thought as much. If an idea occurs to me, you can bet that the *Staffelkapitaene* have thought of it, too. I'm telling you — take them off! You know very well what the weather's like: heavy cumulus over Greece up to a great height. We'll have to overfly them, and it can't be done with the extra load.' Shit! I've been caught out again, I thought. They've had their eye on me, just because I've pulled the odd fast one now and again. The *Kommandeur* waited to see what I would do.

I told my Chief Mechanic to unload the bombs. *Oberfeldwebel* Lorenz had been responsible for technical services ever since Nordhausen am Harz, and he had kept his aircraft in immaculate order. He usually reacted to an order with an enthusiastic, '*Jawohl, Herr Hauptmann*,' but this time he only managed to produce a flat grunt from his throat. With equal reluctance his men began to carry out the order. The *Kommandeur* looked at me winningly, laughed and, as he drove away, said, 'And try to look a bit happier next time!' I felt like a little Hercules at the crossroads. How does the story go? The noble lady named Virtue promised him immortality, while the other, the tarted-up woman named Pleasure, fondled his head of curls and eyed him seductively.

I had to make a choice. Standing in front of me was a big, solid man in black, sweat-stained overalls, his hands calloused. I showed no emotion: I did nothing, said nothing. I had my foot on the first rung of the ladder and I didn't say a word. The conflicting impulses within me united into firm resolve. I lifted my other foot slowly onto the next rung. A foot that feels the rung of a ladder has a mind of its own, an irresistible urge to climb upwards, then both feet take over and lift that minor appendage, the brain. So I found myself in my seat without really knowing how I got there. I put my parachute on over my Mae West and strapped myself in, neither looking at Lorenz nor saying a word.

It was Lorenz, born in a little hamlet at the foot of the Kyffhaeusser in

Thuringia, who chose the way I was to go that night. My *Staffel*, the 9th, took off ahead of the 8th. During the day there had been a few spring showers. Now it was a clear evening, fresh and cloudless. We took off at intervals of a minute or a minute-and-a-half from the big airfield, overgrown with high grass into which a few lanes had been mown. It was shortly before sunset. Initially we flew east at low level so that we wouldn't be picked up on the Malta radar and attacked by Beaufighters. Gradually we climbed to our flight-plan height of 800 metres, intending to stay there until we reached the Greek coast.

At this point it is worth explaining the plan of attack. At the flight planning the *Kommandeur* had discussed with his *Staffelkapitaene* whether we should fly through the barrier of clouds over Greece in order to reach Piraeus, whether we should climb over them or go round them via Cape Matapan to the south. I had made another suggestion: couldn't we go beneath the cloud-base, which was forecast at about 800 metres, enter the Gulf of Patras and fly on to Corinth at the same height? There, according to the weather forecast, there should be broken cloud, with clearer skies further east. There was a half moon. The *Kommandeur* had thought that that way was too uncertain because it was difficult to know what the visibility below the clouds would be like. Therefore we were to fly direct to Piraeus, climbing over the higher cumulus clouds, which should not be a problem in the moonlight.

I had to take into account the fact that as a result of my undeclared intentions my aeroplanes would be more heavily laden than those of the other *Staffeln*. In addition, my own view, based on the weather forecast, the most recent reports and my own calculations, was that the upper limit of the clouds over Greece would be so high that we would have difficulty in getting over them. To fly through them would cause heavy icing to the aircraft. The time of year and the synoptic situation meant that the icing level would be at approximately 2000 metres, a level below which it would be foolish to descend because of the majestic mountain peaks north and south of our track. So I had suggested that we disregard safety regulations and fly to the Gulf of Patras between the island of Sakinthos to the right and Ithaka and Kefallinia to the left. The *Kommandeur* had rejected my proposal. Now I thought, 'Just wait and see!'

I always preferred a low approach, whenever that was possible, for a number of reasons. For one thing the oxygen mask on one's face in no way felt like a warm towel applied by a Parisian master barber. Second, it was tedious in those subtropical latitudes to have to force oneself into flying overalls and fur boots only to sweat as soon as you started to taxi — if not as soon as you climbed into the aircraft — before you hauled the 13.75 tonnes of aircraft into the air. By the time you were aloft you were wet through, and then you began to shiver. It was far better to stay close to the bosom of Mother Earth.

The success of my own plan depended on my finding a clearly defined point on the coast that we could aim for and which would serve as a signpost for us. Only with such a pinpoint would we be able to weave our way through to Corinth. The south-east tip of Kefallinia, a small island to the north of the Gulf, would be a good pinpoint that we could all head for and set our onward course from. It would only be dangerous if we didn't stick precisely to the plan.

We had worked everything out in beautiful sunshine, under the olive and almond trees in the monastery garden in the little town of Paterno, which was built on volcanic ash on the slopes of Etna. We had written down the course and times, and, in the evening, after take-off, we checked the wind and did our sums again. While we were flying over the sea and could still see the surface we measured the drift and speed. Consequently we felt confident that we would reach the place we were aiming for.

We did just that. *Leutnant* Schmetz, my observer, eagle-eyed by day and owl-eyed by night, saw it after a quick glance at the map. 'There it is!' I couldn't see much, but from the tone of Schmetz's voice I knew that he had got it right. When we reached the point we fired off a flare as planned, a flare that would burn for approximately ten seconds. That would make orientation easier for the others, who were following at distances of 5 to 7 km. To make doubly sure Schmetz fired off a further flare. I set a course of roughly north-east, heading as planned for Araxos, a sharp promontory on Peloponnisos pointing north-west. Shortly afterwards the radio operator, Krahn, reported that the aircraft immediately behind us had just fired off his signal flare dead astern. That was what had been arranged: each aircraft would send up a flare at the south-eastern tip of Kefallinia, to serve as a beacon for the one behind — a nocturnal torchlight procession that the stout goatherd on the mountainside must surely have watched wide-eyed.

Over the islands the visibility was still good and the clouds were scattered, but as we travelled east they closed up progressively, so that the moonlight scarcely penetrated them. It was then a matter of navigating to the exact minute and second, not giving in to feelings or guesswork, trusting implicitly in the automatic course-steering and the clock. We saw the surf round the Cape of Araxos emerging from the darkness on ETA. This was the second point at which a signal flare was to be fired. Schmetz fired ours, at the same time giving the next heading and starting his stop-watch.

Now was the moment of truth. As the earth rotated, night crept to meet us, and we sped into it. It became dark. There was no glimmer of light from human habitation to help us judge distance and heading. There was no beacon to guide us. Greece was at war, and there was a complete blackout.

The straits became progressively narrower, down to three kilometres, and the second hand on the watch approached the time to turn. Another signal flare, and then, to the accompaniment of a satisfied cry from Krahn, yet another one appeared astern, then the second, then the third. 'I can see everything now,' Krahn said, 'and the water's glittering.' But Schmetz and I were flying into darkness. I didn't dare to look right or left. I was tempted to make a steep turn to starboard in order to fly close parallel to the mountain slope. But out there in the pale moonlight a veil of darkness was rushing by. Alter course. Fire a signal flare. Restart stop-watch. Maintain height. Was I mad? At least I had an advantage over those aircraft that were higher up. I was completely safe from night fighters. Nobody had yet invented a method of operating fighters below Mount Olympus and Taygetos. But my confidence that I had made the correct choice diminished by the second. In keeping to my plan, we were putting ourselves in the hands of Fate. Turning point. Signal flare. Stop-watch.

Suddenly a vivid light illuminated everything around for a split second. Our first instinctive reaction was to think that we had run into a thunderstorm; then we realised with relief that we were over the sea and could see where we were heading. Before our thought-processes were fully under control, however, a shock of wonder, of superstition, caused a shiver to run through us. We were in the world of the Gods and the Titans. Humans, insignificant beings in the cosmos, seized and taken over by superhuman forces. Damn it! I thought. There's no such thing as the supernatural; but it would be easy to think otherwise and give way. I took hold of myself: there was my watch, there was my compass and my airspeed indicator. They were my servants: I had to keep my mind on my job.

It became totally black again. Then the same display again — and a miracle! In the light from heaven we saw, stretching out before us, the water of the Gulf of Korinthos. The unknown was behind us, and with it the fear. A light drizzle misted my windscreen. Schmetz fired some more signal cartridges. The boys behind had to stay right on track. It seemed that we had made it. If the weather got thick again we could overfly the Isthmus using our instruments and we'd have Salamis ahead of us.

Within the cockpit we had all stayed calm. The only sound had been that of numbers being called out and repeated. We could breathe more deeply. We had no way of knowing what the natural phenomenon had been. It wasn't that mighty hurler of thunderbolts, Zeus. It was, in fact, our comrades from the 8th *Staffel* following behind us, higher and faster. They had had St. Elmo's fire on the tips of their airscrews and had begun to ice up in the clouds. The only thing they had been able to do was to jettison first one mine, then another. Somewhere in the mountains they had hurtled down and exploded as programmed. Sea mines dropped on to dry land self-destruct for reasons of secrecy.

We were not far from the Isthmus. One or two lighter patches were appearing on the surface of the sea — moonlight! A few minutes later — we scarcely dared to believe our eyes — the Aegean Sea was gleaming in front of a backdrop of a flat mountain ridge, with only a few thin scraps of cloud floating above it. We had relied on the Met. man, and he had been right. Our morale was high, but there was one adverse factor — our worry for the other eight crews. Had they made it? Had they done their sums properly? Had they fired off their signals at the right place and at the right time? Had they stayed on course?

The visibility being good, I reached Salamis by flying low over the mountain peaks of the narrow land-mass of Korinthos. For the first time in my life I saw those places that we had discussed so often during our schooldays, from class to class, in history, legend and poem. There they all were — the battlefields of Leuktra and Platea. By the pale light of the moon I saw Marathon and Athens. Phidias, Plato and Aristotle all lived and worked there. Wonderful scenes, made living by youthful memories.

I returned to the business in hand: full throttle; start to climb. We overflew southern Salamis at between three and four thousand metres and passed the entrance to Piraeus harbour heading east, parallel with the coast. Searchlights reached out towards us. We curved away to gain more height. An increasing number of searchlights lit up and reached further out towards the west where our other aircraft were following behind us. We became more daring and turned towards the harbour, full throttle, to act as bait for the searchlights and the flak. There was no better navigational aid for the approaching crews than the enemy's display of lights and gunfire. There was something of an art to it: turn left, then right, throttle back, then full throttle all at once. It added spice to the game of hide-and-seek, and was exciting for us.

Given that the entrance to the harbour was very narrow, our mines had to be dropped from low level. If they had been dropped from too great a height, the parachutes could have been driven on by the wind so that the mines would miss the water altogether and detonate on land, which was not what we had planned. For aircraft coming in at low level the harbour entrance and the harbour itself, which spread out into a broad circle, represented a veritable trap. One would have to fly directly into the searchlights and the rapid-firing anti-aircraft guns mounted at the harbour entrance and on the harbour installations, then do a neck-breaking half turn out again. An additional danger was that the mines could only be dropped at reduced speed, approximately 300 kmph, otherwise the parachutes would tear apart and the thin-skinned mines would break up on hitting the water and would therefore be of no use. To any flier speed is half of life, and ours would have to be cut by half.

But there was a better alternative on offer: to approach quietly from the south, fly inland, then make for the harbour entrance in a steep dive on a westerly heading over the harbour flak and the searchlight zone, cross the harbour, drop the mines and leave the mousetrap behind. When the mines had been dropped, our aircraft would be lighter and we would be able to try to avoid the flak and the searchlights by jinking and pumping the throttles. The first aircraft from our *Staffel* would dive into the harbour area and towards the entrance. The others, stacked at various heights, would kick up a hell of a noise around the port and create a diversion by firing off the occasional white flare. The searchlights would be attracted to them instinctively, and it would be several seconds before anybody realised that they had been deceived.

The defences were certainly alert, so I allowed myself to break radio silence. I called up the aircraft behind me and was relieved to get the reply, 'Target in sight.' I throttled back fully and, flying almost at stalling speed, propellers all but standing still, I glided through scattered flak bursts and past a searchlight which was wavering upwards. I turned sharply and straightened out onto the attack heading, west, as if on a special kind of final approach, not to land but to overshoot. What we had to put down were those weighty objects hanging beneath our wings. The 'runway', the narrow stretch of water that was the entrance to the harbour, was easy to make out. The scattered light from the searchlights made the quay installations and the mole stand out better than the reflection of the half moon did.

Schmetz, by this time lying flat on his belly in the bomber aimer's position, reported, 'Mines ready for release.' The radio operator and the rear gunner reported, 'Machine-guns all clear.' Gliding a little further on, the harbour dead ahead of us, we were flying at just three thousand metres when we reached the point at which I would have to begin the steep descent.

Now! Dive-brakes out! But we're not going to nosedive. I went into the most grotesque manoeuvre that a pilot could imagine. I pulled the control column back into my stomach, so that the wild steed that was my aircraft strove to stand on its head and rush towards the earth. But I had it on the rein, its nose pulled back as high as the strength of my arms could hold it. That object — it couldn't be called an aircraft in that condition — that monster, groaning and vibrating, fell downwards.

Stand by! It's nearly time! Still 600 to 800 metres to the target. Brakes in! My aircraft was gliding, happily, flat over the final stretch of the harbour. Had they spotted us? We were down at 300 metres. They must be able to see us with their naked eyes! Cautiously I opened the throttles, and the searchlights reached out towards us just before we reached our aiming point. I gave more throttle. We were bathed in light, dazzling light from ahead, astern and both sides. Schmetz released the mines. The radio operator and the rear gunner let fly at the searchlights with all they'd got. Schmetz joined in, firing into the blinding light ahead of us. Throttles wide open, I danced my way, curving wildly, through the searchlights' beams and the tumult of tracer, and reached the open sea. Suddenly they were shooting at us from the cliffs, from boats below us, from Salamis, from God knows where. They'd still got us in their searchlights. I was weaving for our very lives. Tracer from the rapid-firing flak flashed above the cabin roof, below us, to our left, to our right, glowing chunks of metal. Christ Almighty!

Suddenly we were out of it. Someone said, 'Whose idea was this operation any way?' There was no time to think about that. We went into a full-throttle climb. Flying lighter, we had to give supporting fire to our aircraft above, and create a diversion. Our Number Two just escaped from the jaws of the trap. From higher up the tracer shells looked like thick, glowing wires stretched across the ground. From above, our boys fired into the unfriendly beams.

I throttled back viciously, then opened up again. We created a backdrop of noise. Out over the harbour again. The crew fired all their guns into the sea of searchlights. We climbed, curving. My aircraft felt light, only the 250-kg bombs weighed it down. I made orbit after orbit, sending the sound of my motors down into the cauldron below. A solid burst of tracer from above just missed us: the British night fighters from Tatoi were on the job. Was it only because we were lucky that we had been able to run the gauntlet without being hit?

Our *Staffel* should have finished the job in ten minutes or thereabouts. Then, unladen, the pilots would climb rapidly on a westward heading so as to gain sufficient height in clear air to reach the Ionian Sea, flying above the cumulus clouds over the mainland. Then they would let down and head for Sicily, flying low level over the sea where there was only a light head wind against them. It wasn't necessary, and it certainly wasn't an inviting prospect, to fly a second time through the dark, twisting gorge . . .

In our aircraft, 4D + AR, we were poised in the night sky of Greece with the remainder of our load, over the bay between the island of Salamis and Attika, slowly gaining height and circling. Weren't the mines enough? We felt homesick for our cosy monastery garden in Paterno, the smell of blossom in the evening, the clear notes of the violin and the accordion played by the artistically inclined members of our *Staffel*, conversation in a circle of friends, a glass of wine and the murmur of voices from the unseen nuns who had given up a part of their nunnery to us. Stop it! There's nothing to argue about: the things that the *Oberfeldwebel*, and *Oberwerkmeister* Lorenz had let us have were to be put to proper use. While the *Staffel*'s aircraft coming up behind were presumably in the searchlights and under fire, we had to decide whether or not to attack a ship moored alongside the quay using a diving attack — this time a proper one at high speed — or in horizontal flight. According to the aerial photos that we had seen before we took off, ships were moored along the entire length of the quays, particularly on the west bank of Piraeus. We had been able to confirm that fact while we were making our mining attack.

A diving attack approaching from land would have been less dangerous than the mine-dropping because we would have been able to break out of the flak and searchlight zones at a much higher speed. Nevertheless, we decided to attack in horizontal flight because we considered that it would be more accurate to sneak in and bomb at a speed of no more than 250 kph and from a height of 1000 m. We would be able to calculate the wind at that height quite accurately while flying a short distance away from the harbour, outside the flak and searchlight zones, and then we could set the calculated values on the bomb sight. In addition, the prospect of being able to leave the defended area silently and unobserved after we had bombed, remaining higher and heading out to sea, seemed more attractive to us because if we dive-bombed we would end up only about 200 to 300 metres above the ground.

The decision taken, Heinrich Schmetz had to do his job. He altered the air pressure setting on the altimeter so that the correct height was shown, then he directed me to a dark clump of rock which stood out from the glittering surface of the sea. When he had it in his sight he told me to start circling and he took a note of height, course and stop-watch reading. After we had completed a full circle and were back on our previous course, Schmetz calculated our displacement in two dimensions, then used sines and cosines to calculate the wind velocity. It was an odd figure and would have surprised even the most experienced meteorologist — 237 degrees, 18.7 kph. For safety's sake, and much to my annoyance, Schmetz carried out the manoeuvre again. He was an engineer by trade and wanted to make sure he had it right.

Everything was set. We spiralled up again to three thousand metres over the bay between Salamis and Piraeus, made a similar turn to the one we had made previously and approached the port from the rear — through the tradesmen's entrance, as it were — to finish the job. The firework display put up from below intensified, but it didn't affect us directly. In the meanwhile, we knew that other German aircraft from bases in Bulgaria had arrived on the scene. A magnificent piece of theatre was being played out. The lights and the dome of fire must surely have enticed the Gods hither from high Olympus, away from a life 'eternally clear, crystalline and undisturbed,'[1] and tempted them, in their curiosity and each according to his specialisation, to intervene to show favour here, to trip someone up there. What would they have thought was happening as they appeared on the scene, in silent formation and clad in flowing robes? Troy had been different. Then the Greeks had striven to recapture the beautiful, kidnapped Helen; but what about us that day?

That day, men from the far north were making war. Men who had no business being there and who did not revere the Gods of Olympus. Some time ago, it had reached the ears of Zeus, the Father of the Gods, that a Barbarian by the name of Goethe had slanderously declaimed that there was nothing more wretched beneath the sun than them, the Gods! Without a doubt the watchword of the Gods would have been, for once, unequivocal: Nobody may win. We will punish the one through the other. But *we* did not intend to play a submissive role. *We* would decide what was to happen. We were convinced that Fortune and Right were on our side.

Softly we flew in, turning towards the West, the moon ahead of us, flaps half down. Softly as a night bird, workmanlike as a craftsman. It was the moment to weigh up the prospects. I held my speed exact to the kilometre, letting down flatly, with the heading on the automatic course-setting but making slight readjustments when told to do so by Schmetz. All I could see was my instrument panel. Searchlights played. Below, guns flashed; above, shells exploded dark-red. Our Ju 88 glided smoothly towards our target. The enemy's attention was on other aircraft. We stole onward, in the darkness. We wouldn't take any evasive action. We would stick to our programme and rely on Fate and the instructions given by our computer, which is taking us onwards to success . . .

There was no point in wasting thought. Danger being no longer a factor, there was no point in thinking about it. The final technical adjustments were carried out as if by an external hand. The barrier of lights and anti-aircraft fire ahead was more subdued now. I told myself to remember what I had always impressed on my crews in quiet moments during pre-flight briefings: it's not the red-glowing tracer lines that are the most dangerous, but the afterglow that is left on the retina of the eye. If you tie a piece of rock to a string and whirl it round and round, it appears as a circle, yet it can only be at one place at a time. If you're hit when you're flying through flak, it's nothing more than bad luck. The more you understand that, the less you need to call on courage.

Black cloudlets from heavy flak sailed past us, minutes old and of no danger. Occasionally they were lit by searchlights. We felt the wake of other propellers, but our computer corrected confidently. Nowadays they would be called near misses, but our rule of thumb in dealing with them was that when you felt them, the danger was already past. To quote Descartes a little freely, 'I think, therefore I exist — still.' The more we yearned to get to the target and be rid of the burden, the worry and the uncertainty, the longer our approach seemed to take. The seconds ticked by slowly. We were flying below 1500 metres. I juggled with the flaps in order to be at our bombing height of 1000 metres just when we reached the release point. The speed, height and rate-of-descent indicators, reflecting the ultra-violet light, were my only taskmasters. My hands transferred their instructions automatically to the control column, flaps, propeller pitch and throttle. I held the course steady. Schmetz, lying flat in the bomb aimer's position with his eye to the lens of the optical bombsight, gave his commentary, cool as only a Westphalian can be: 'Ten seconds to go.' I flattened out and opened the throttles a fraction. A last glance at my instruments. If the searchlights picked us up, the flak would pick us off like a sitting duck or a night fighter would get us like a pike swooping on a slow-swimming carp. Far worse than the thought of the lurking enemy was the gnawing feeling of guilt that we could be shot down making an extra run and that I was risking the lives of my comrades. Oh God! If only I hadn't . . . My mouth was dry.

Thank God — at last! The longed-for, relief-bringing upward lurches of the aircraft as the bombs were released one after the other in rapid succession. Confident that both bombs would hit their target, a good-sized freighter, fair and square, we had come in at a slight angle to its longitudinal axis. Schmetz had set a short interval. I switched off the automatic course steering, my feet tensed, ready for action, on the rudder bar. I was ready to execute immediate violent manoeuvres if the angry flak and searchlights should try to search and destroy above the spot where the bombs fell. They hadn't impacted: they were still on their way to earth. It would take fifteen seconds before our fate and that of the people below was decided. If we saw one or two big flashes from down below, we would know that we had hit something. If not, it would mean that the bombs had fallen into the water, with nothing to show but short-lived fountains of foam.

The time was nearly up. Everybody who had dropped cement bombs in hundreds of practice flights had the ensuing tension fixed in his subconscious. I put the Ju 88 into a steep turn to port so that I could look down, along the wing, to see the impact. A pilot always wants to know what success his observer has had.

There was a massive, bright flash. Someone shouted 'hurrah'. Our joy knew no bounds. Then, hard on its heels, there was a clap of thunder, a vast sound, and wild gusts of turbulence from below. We were hurled about violently. Will the aircraft break up? What will be first to go? I dared not to use my controls. As if determined to meet its fate, out of control, the aircraft came out of its turn somehow or other. Still no cracking? Still no breaking? Still no wind rushing through a shattered cockpit? Two, three, four seconds pass. Is is possible? Can a machine of aluminium sheet survive such a pressure wave? Very tentatively, I applied a small amount of rudder; tried to straighten out. To my astonishment and my delight the Junkers responded. Hope returned. I applied opposite rudder; again, the aircraft responded. Very carefully I gave throttle very slowly, and the aircraft followed through. I retracted the flaps, and the aeroplane behaved perfectly. Thank God for German workmanship! Now for the open sea!

Our surprise was even greater when we saw that the searchlights round the port and along the coast were pointing straight up into the sky. Not a single gun fired. From the stricken ship and the cargo discharged onto the quayside further explosions erupted and white glowing masses were hurled aloft. We breathed deeply and watched the spectacle. What had happened? I gave throttle and we climbed higher. The defences seemed to have given up the ghost. We returned to the scene of the crime to observe carefully and without interference. What we saw we later entered in our combat reports:

Two mines laid in the harbour. One munitions ship made to explode with one SC 250 bomb; one ship burnt out; one ship damaged (but not yet confirmed); one SC 250 on quay installations; 2 warehouses burnt out; several warehouses severely damaged; goods trains set on fire.

That entry in the War Diary was based on our own observations and those of crews of other aircraft from the *Gruppe*.

The following is a report written by the English historian Alfred Price after careful investigation and published twenty years after the event. To a very large extent it corresponds with aerial photographs taken a few days after the attack by our reconnaissance aircraft.

The ship Schmetz hit was the 12,000-ton freighter 'Clan Frazer', just arrived with convoy AFN 24 carrying 350 tons of explosives in her hold. 100 tons had been offloaded when work ceased at dusk: it was the remaining 250 tons that had just gone off, with a roar that smashed windows in Athens seven miles away. 'Clan Frazer' herself had disappeared, and ten other ships totalling 41,000 tons were also destroyed in the explosion. This was bad enough, but the ships could all be replaced. What was far more serious was that in this bang of almost nuclear dimension the port of Pireaus was wrecked from end to end. It would take several months' work to make good the damage. The explosion was, in the words of the Mediterranean Fleet Commander, Admiral Cunningham, 'a shattering blow'. In one stroke it had deprived the British of the one reasonably equipped port in Greece through which supplies could be passed to the army there.

The English suspected that we had had information from agents on the type of load that the *Clan Frazer* was carrying, but that was not so. We did not even know her name and tonnage. Schmetz had aimed at her simply because she was the biggest target.

We had lost our sense of danger, and so we overflew the port area several times so that we could observe and report as accurately as possible. The less our enemies reacted, the more secure we felt. We had been lucky: if we hadn't turned the aircraft on to its side so that we could get a better view of our bombs landing, the bombs' shock waves could have struck the Junkers directly on the undersurface of its wings and would probably have shattered them.

As we decided to set course for home, the first British soldier awoke from his inertia, got up from the ground and aimed his 40 cm gun at us. There was a short, hefty thump, and a bang; our feeling of euphoria disappeared. Salamis, on which there were one or two searchlights, lay ahead, and we had to avoid it. The rear gunner, who was also the flight engineer, checked all the control equipment. Everything was in order; neither could we see any sign of damage on the wings. We breathed again. As we climbed onto a westerly heading in the direction of Corinth, Fate showed her hand. The coolant temperature of the port engine began to rise slowly; that of the starboard engine stayed steady. I throttled back on my port engine and we watched intently. The temperature continued to rise, and it rose ever higher until it passed the permitted maximum. We had to stop the engine immediately to avoid a seize-up and a possible fire. Just as hope had returned swiftly and invigoratingly after the thunderbolt, now it dissipated equally rapidly. Gloom took over; but the best way to get rid of it was by activity. So: Throttle back. Ignition off. Propeller feathered, and press on on one engine.

There could be no thought of climbing over the cumuli over Greece or flying through cloud, nor could we imagine flying beneath the clouds through the dangerous narrows in our condition. What caused us the most worry was the thought of the long flight on one engine across the Ionian Sea, a distance of approximately 500 kilometres. Who would fish us out if our starboard engine packed in? Who should ever find us? A far more attractive idea was to cross the Aegean, navigating from island to island, to reach our allocated diversion airfield on Rhodes and seek hospitality and assistance from the Italians. Then, if we had to take to our dinghy, we might be able to reach one of the Cyclades in a matter of hours or days, depending on the wind.

Our minds were made up: destination Rhodes, the airfield of Gaddura on the southeast side of the island. So about turn, course roughly south-east, distance to fly about 450 kilometres. We had climbed to approximately 1000 metres by the time we had switched off the engine and set course for Rhodes. The Ju 88 A-4, a thoroughbred among aircraft, was not easy to fly on one engine. We began the painstaking task of trimming her. At 200 kph she lost height slowly. We switched the instrument lights on to full so that we could check our flight conditions and the performance of the starboard engine. I tried to level out slowly in order to maintain height. The airspeed sank to around 170; between 150 and 160 kph the aircraft would stall and take us down into the sea with her. There was nothing else for it: I had to give in and allow the aeroplane to lose height, in the hope that near the surface of the sea we would find denser air, which would give us more lift. We sank lower and lower. Schmetz worked over his charts with a protractor, compasses and a slide rule, while Krahn tried to establish radio contact with Rhodes. The moon was almost down on the horizon. The wind now seemed to be blowing from between south-west and south. We still hoped that nearer to the sea we would be able to maintain height. The altimeter showed 100 metres.

Suddenly, out of the darkness ahead of us, we saw a wall of rock. A swift manoeuvre was impossible. The silken thread on which we hung was snapped. In the emergency situation I operated the fuel jettison handle. I shouted out, 'How much can I get rid of?' Schmetz yelled back, '500 litres!' As if hypnotised, we watched the pointer moving back. 'Halt! Stop!' yelled Schmetz. I turned the handle to 'Off'. To my horror, the pointer fell still further — 400 litres left, 300, 200! In desperation I pushed the lever backwards and forwards, on and off; but the fluid continued to drain away. Rear gunner Alles reported that there was a trail of petrol behind us. The indicator for the fuselage overload tank, which had held 1200 litres, read nil. We were poised above and near to the surface of the sea. Carefully, as if treading on eggshells, I made a gentle turn towards the south, where we could see the end of the cliff. We passed very close to it. It was a most pleasant surprise when a gentle up-current took us about a hundred metres higher. We breathed out.

I said to Schmetz, 'That was a bloody awful piece of navigation!' He replied, 'You've got to allow for the conditions. I'm using a one in two million chart, and these pesky little islands aren't shown, nor are the heights.'

'Have we still got enough fuel to get to Rhodes?' Schmetz peered at the wing tank fuel gauge, manipulated his circular slide rule for some time, then said drily, 'No.' There was silence in the cockpit. Silently, we asked ourselves where it would all end. Schmetz fumbled with the inflator tube on his Mae West: 'Shall we ditch right now?' The water didn't look very inviting to me, although it seemed to be calm and there were no white horses. To both sides the sea wrinkled in the pale light of the setting moon.

Alles, the flight mechanic/gunner, standing behind us at the wireless operator's side, said, 'I'm for flying on. Who knows what'll happen?' We thought of our good air-sea rescue aircraft that was stationed at the port of Syracuse and which, only a few days previously, had fished out one of our crews, that of *Oberleutnant* Piëch from the Tyrol, south of Crete after they had been paddling about for more than 24 hours in their rubber dinghy. But who would fish us out? Nobody else knew if we were still alive or where to start looking for us. Our miniature war council decided quickly that we should postpone our cold bath. We would give it more careful thought later.

Suddenly we were talking of Turkey, the nearest non-enemy coast, which would be much quicker to get to than Rhodes. That would mean a left turn on to about north-east. Towards Smyrna or Ephesus, I said. 'There's nothing in it,' said Schmetz, after taking a quick look at his chart, 'but the direction is about right.'

Internment! That word meant that the war would be over for us. The loudest protest came from *Unteroffizier* Alles. 'Let's get back to the boys!' Schmetz contributed a thought: he wanted to get his report on our successful attack back to headquarters. The East held no attraction for me, either. We decided to press on towards Sicily via Rhodes. One thing was quite clear: before the moon set we would have to use its glittering reflection in the sea as a 'runway' to land as close as possible to Rhodes. It was an unbelievable relief to have reached this decision. We were no longer vacillating between fear and hope. We knew what we had to do and where we were going. Again we had our own little world of intentions and ideas. That was enough to live on for the moment. That would give us strength to find the ways and means.

We threw empty and full ammunition drums overboard in an attempt to lighten the aircraft. The more fuel we burnt up, the longer the aeroplane would stay on the surface of the sea and the easier it would be for us to climb out and get into our inflatable dinghy: we might even be able to keep our feet dry, but in the worst event we would be able to walk along the wings. We would not have to break into our emergency rations, raisins and chocolate. We would have to save them up against the possibility of days afloat.

Krahn had given up trying to contact Sicily on short wave radio so that they could notify our Italian allies of our situation. He had not had any success. Perhaps the mountains of Greece had impeded our transmissions. But our generator voltage had been reduced. The automatic course-steering that had to even out the thrust from the single engine had consumed too much power. The one generator in the engine that was still running couldn't cope by itself. The batteries had had to provide the necessary extra power, and consequently they were running down. In addition, the instrument lights were growing weaker. So I switched off the automatic steering and thrust the rudder bar far enough forward with my right leg for us to stay more or less on course. We were still too low. Ahead of us lay the island of Naxos, over 1000 metres high, to say nothing of further obstacles of unknown size. With the wisdom of experience I steered to the right, towards the south, as soon as we saw rocks above the surface of the sea, and in so doing took advantage of the welcome up-currents coming from the south. Every time we made that manoeuvre the currents took hold of the aircraft beneath its wings and gave it a friendly lift.

My right leg was getting hot because my left-hand 'horses' were lame while those on the right were pulling with all their might on the harness and I was having to fight against them until I was perspiring freely. I will get cramp soon, I thought, and that will be the end of the whole business. But the Flight Engineer knew what to do. He took off his belt and, squeezing forward, tried to attach it to the left foot-pedal on the rudder bar. 'I can't see anything,' he groaned. '*Herr Hauptmann's* leg is in the way.' Finally, however, the relief of my right leg was accomplished. I could breathe again. I wiped the sweat from both my forehead and neck. We had things under control.

The atmosphere on board was calm. Nobody gave any sign that he might be drifting on the sea like Odysseus, keeping a lookout for the nearest desert island, on which he might hunger and thirst, with no Nausicaa to look after and shelter him. That facile, home-spun precept, 'Wait and see,' was the uncertain tight-rope under our feet. Only by looking straight ahead could we find strength and confidence. There was no time for doubt.

In the meanwhile we had clambered up laboriously, a little at a time, to perhaps 600 or 700 metres. It was getting darker and darker, and our eyes were fixed on the cockpit windows so that we could see any obstacles. Striving to see didn't help: one had to switch over to the detachment channel, otherwise no pictures could be received. But we couldn't rely on sight alone. Schmetz got out his sextant, and he sighted on anything and everything — Betelgeuse, Castor and Pollux — then passed the instrument back to Krahn so that he could shoot another star, if possible at a ninety-degree angle to the first one. The cockpit of the Ju 88 was fitted here and there with special parallel-ground panes of glass, both ahead and astern, so that the altitudes measured with the sextant would be accurate. While the star-shooting was in progress, I had to fly steady and without accelerating, a difficult job when the aeroplane had to be balanced on a single engine. As usual, Schmetz's fixes were within three or four minutes of arc, or five to seven kilometres. Newly indoctrinated into the 'black art', we had practised a great deal at the foot of Etna, sitting in unsteady chairs and trying to wind the sun, the moon and five of the stars available at any one time down into the middle of the bubble, while a friendly instructor shook the back of each chair to simulate turbulence. And so we navigated our way through the islands, keeping as straight a course as was possible to avoid lengthening our flight unduly. In an emergency we would be able to reach one of the other Italian islands in the Dodecanese and ditch there.

Suddenly, what looked like lightning appeared in the sky ahead of us. What could it be? Hardly a storm, because none had been forecast for that area; in any case, the sky was clear to the horizon. After a short time we concluded that it must be bombs detonating, or possibly gunfire. Yet we couldn't make out positively flashes or muzzle-fire. It was interesting, but could hardly affect us, we thought. After some time, when we had clawed our way up to between 800 and 900 metres, we began to make out the crest of a row of hills against the lightning. Schmetz said that on the basis of our flying time it must be Rhodes. For the hundredth time we swore at Krahn and encouraged him to call up the airfield at Rhodes/Gaddura. I also told him to transmit 'Pan, Pan, Pan,' — 'We are in distress.'

No result. I swore. I suspected that Krahn was not operating his equipment properly or that he was on the wrong frequency. We drew nearer, and against the lightning from the far side of the mountains we saw that they formed a high, jagged range. 'Rhodes', reported Schmetz, laconically. God in Heaven! The British are bombing the airfield, the place where we want to make an emergency landing. What have we done to deserve that? Do we have the choice between fire and water only, Scylla and Charybdis? Things are not being made easy for us. The engine continued to turn. Our pulses continued to beat. We continued to fly onward, our hopes subdued. The minutes slid past.

Gradually the sheet-lightning behind the mountain curtain died away. Our fuel gauge showed almost zero. There was no point in aiming for an airfield we couldn't reach; but what was the point of heading for an airfield that would swallow us up like a pit? To hell with an airfield that could be covered in craters! We would head out to sea.

Soon we could make out the southern tip of Rhodes from our starboard bow. There, a dark, massive mountain range stretched to its left, straight ahead of us. The landmass seemed to be close enough to reach out to and touch. To our right, the cool water shimmered in the moonlight. What about our brave plan now, our thoughts of gliding down at 180 kph on to the surface of the sea off Rhodes? Did we still want to, or didn't we? Or did we lack the courage to perform that trick? *Hic Rhodos, hic salta*? Our resolve evaporated, and we hesitated. Each of us thought alike: defer the inevitable, wait and see what happens. Against all reason, we rejected a calculated risk in favour of blind irrationality. We began to think crazy thoughts. Perhaps our fuel would last long enough for us to reach the airfield. Perhaps the field wasn't too badly damaged by bombs. Perhaps we would be able to sleep in proper beds. Drifting about in a dinghy came a poor second —

and who could say that Tommy hadn't damaged our rubber boat? It was a compulsion, but at the same time a relief. We would head for Gaddura! No sooner said than done. We couldn't fly right round the southern tip of the island in order to get to the airfield, which lay further to the north. That could be a fateful diversion. Our fuel gauge showed empty. The west coast of Rhodes was below us. We flew into the interior of the island, intending to cross it at the point where it was approximately 20 km wide, and reach the far coast south of Gaddura. We did not look at the yawning precipices below. Ahead of us, the mountain ridge was black against the horizon. What would happen if our airscrew stopped now? We would have to turn out towards the sea and ditch. We could still make it. If we maintained our easterly heading for a further two or three minutes, until we were just this side of the ridge, we would no longer be able to reach the sea in a glide should the fuel run out. Nevertheless we flew onward, maintaining a stoical calm and equanimity in a difficult situation, as the Latin verse has it. We didn't put it quite like that. We thought, 'Let's see what happens,' not knowing whether, burnt to a cinder in a deserted ravine, we would be able to see at all.

The mountainside grew closer. How does a flier act when he's short of height, short of clearance? He stands up in his seat, as far as his straps permit. It is the deceptive feeling that you can make the aircraft lighter and help it over the hurdle. It was only a matter of seconds. The uncertainty was hideous. There was nothing more to see of the starlit sky. Was I high enough? The seaman asks how much water he has beneath his keel: the pilot, how much air he has under his wings. I didn't fully trust my altimeter, and I didn't know where I was trying to fly across the long mountain crest. There were no heights marked on the map. The highest spot on the island, north of the airfield, measured 1200 metres.

I glanced quickly below. There was no depth. Dark surfaces and shadows swept past close beneath us. My breath came in short gasps. Schmetz avoided my eyes. I hated those worried, uncertain looks that compelled me to act the part of an ice-cold, inflexible person. Schmetz, well trained and the epitome of a good soldier, kept his agony to himself.

We had made it! The crest slid away below and astern of us. Ahead, the land fell away to the east: we sensed it. Suddenly we were flying high in the air. We could talk again, now we experienced relief. If the engine were to fail now, fair enough! We would glide down to the sea to the east. The fuel gauge still showed empty, but the motor was still turning. Schmetz, a trained engineer, guessed that an intelligent designer had built a small safety margin in the indicator. That was probably the answer. Until then we had never had to try it out.

We were approaching the coast, and we thought that we could make out the sea. In the distance we could see a Turkish lighthouse flashing. We looked down. What we had thought was the sea was a sea — of clouds! A layer of stratus stretched along the east coast of the island, several kilometres wide. It covered the coastline. We could see the mountain peaks protruding above the cloud. A moment ago we had been in high spirits: we had crossed the mountains, reached the sea, and had the prospect of reaching Gaddura. Grey hopelessness struck us dumb. There were no cries of frustration, no curses. Again we were living from second to second, just when we had thought that we had put that experience behind us. The idea of having to glide down without power through the layer of fog and come down in complete darkness somewhere in the water robbed us of the power of thought. We were incapable of reacting to the situation.

Krahn was sending out SOS calls. This is the end, I thought. Who would feed my donkey, my little grey Sicilian rascal? He had always come running for sugar at tea-time on hearing the rattle of the cups. I could have wept. Live dangerously: what a stupid way to advise anyone to taste ecstasy! Not to have ditched when we had had the chance, close to the western coast of the island shimmering in the light of the pale moon, had been pure stupidity. By now we could have had dry land beneath our feet. We only had ourselves to blame. How thick was the clag? Was it sea-fog? What difference would it make whether we crashed in darkness or in fog, or in a ghastly mixture of the two? Our anger at our own lunacy overcame our dread of the inevitable. We were left with the bitter acceptance of a fate we deserved, a touch of determination to die like men. There were four of us, a long way from home: four German soldiers, dying like men and silent.

As we flew onward in silence, still breathing, I saw fleeting images. Where do ideas come from; ideas which if they succeed are lauded as bravery, but if they fail are denounced or cursed as stupidity? From somewhere in space? I did not agree with the ancients who believed that they were controlled by the influence of the Gods. If you have a tendency towards, a hankering after, stupidity, is that the fault of nature? No! The fault is your own, you crazy man! My brow was sweating.

With the help of the flight engineer my right foot held the aeroplane on its course. The uncertain, dark greyness of the fog continued to cause us agonies. That is what death must be like, and eternity. I was 27 years old. *Dulce et decorum est* . . . The Roman who wrote that didn't know what he was talking about. Bitterness, regret, sickness — swallow them, if you are still able. This is the end: the walk out in front of the firing squad. My heart was beating like a drum. The fuel gauge had been on zero for 10 to 15 minutes. We were flying towards the north-east, towards that moment in time when the engine would stop.

Suddenly, Krahn shouted, 'I've got a bearing! I think I've got a QDM!'

I came round, we all came round. We began to think again. There were still men who could save us. There were still men in the darkness, on the edge of Europe, who would stretch out their hands to us! Everything was fine. Bearings were received: numbers, information. We were in our element. A miracle had taken us into its arms. Bearing followed bearing, until we had the airfield directly on our beam. I pressed the stop-watch. The last fuel tank was still showing nil, but still we flew on.

The stratus extended along the entire length of the east coast, as far as we could see from the cliffs that rose up through it. Below the cloud was the airfield, constructed on a small, level area at the foot of the mountain slope. You could only land there coming in from the sea and take off with the hills behind you, heading out to sea. That was how that one-off diversion airfield was described to us. Our bearings indicated that the field was behind us and to the left. It was time to make a turn to port on to a reciprocal heading, parallel with the coast again, so that we could make our approach. We proposed to take the risk of starting our port engine shortly before touch-down. That was the outline of our plan.

I had barely begun my turn to the left when the starboard engine cut out. Fuel starvation. Empty! My heart missed a beat. I hissed at the engineer, who was conscientiously holding the pedals under pressure; 'Let go!' The stoppage came too suddenly. He understood. Looking ahead through the windscreen, the aircraft gliding down, I sensed the pressure equalising. We were in cloud. Because the nose of the aircraft was pointing down, the few remaining litres of petrol shot from the tanks into the injection pumps and brought the airscrew to full revs. The aircraft threatened to swing away off line. The turn-and-bank indicator was right over against the stop. I trod hard on the rudder bar and straightened out to some degree. Suddenly the engine stopped again. I turned further on to a heading parallel with the coast. The engine howled again for a few seconds. I applied full opposite rudder. All the time we were getting bearings. QDM 270 degrees. The airfield was west of us, ahead and to the right. The dark grey we were in turned into deep black. That was the ground — the underworld. We were still flying at an altitude of 200-250 metres, but below cloud. The starboard motor burst into life once more.

What was that? Ahead of us and hard to the right, lights appeared. Four, five, six yellow lights. We were very close to them. Without thinking, I turned towards them. Whether they were approach lights, boundary lights, runway lights, I didn't know. Nobody knew. We stared fixedly, expectantly, at them. Nobody was helping me to land. Nobody read out the airspeed — until I swore at them. Then, the last desperate effort, the ultimate act of bravado. I began to believe that a miracle had occurred. Suddenly I had a feeling of great peace. It was as if there was nothing wrong at all. I decided against making a belly landing, the procedure laid down for making a night landing on one engine. Nobody had yet got round to laying down the procedure for a landing *without* engines.

So much had gone wrong and then gone right that night. I ordered, 'Hand-pump clear. Wheels down!' *Unteroffizier* Alles pumped for dear life, like a madman. I didn't know whether or not we would make it. I thought we would! Alles jostled the wireless operator, whose hand was on the Morse key. Curses flew backwards and forwards in the cockpit, usually so quiet. 'What's the point of transmitting now? You should have started earlier!' He was correct. What was the point of thinking about barometric pressure at that stage? Before Schmetz had set the reading my wing-tip could have been digging into the ground.

We were low — that was a fact; but too high to make a decent landing. We were too close to the lights. There was an offshore wind blowing, a tail wind, as we could see from the way the fog was piled up. I side-slipped down towards the ground, all caution discarded. If we went too far we would smash against the wall of rock on the edge of the airfield. Flaps down! The green light flickered, then settled down; a bit dull, but it was steady. We'd made it. The undercarriage was down and locked. Look ahead! I side-slipped hard to starboard. Nose up! I saw the yellow lights describing a gentle curve. I held the aircraft close to them, thinking that we would be safe from bomb craters there. We passed the first light. Our landing lamp was no good: it was too weak. The second light zipped past. Then the third. We were still flying too fast. Ahead, beyond the next light, darkness yawned. Better to put down here and risk writing off the undercarriage than smash ourselves against that wall of rock.

I shoved the Ju down on her wheels, so hard that we felt our backbones compress. The instrument panel vibrated and rattled. Something was banging about in the cockpit. I applied the brakes immediately; the Ju tipped forward. Brakes off, quickly, control column back into my stomach. Brake again, another pitch, then apply left and right brakes alternately. The Junkers swung back and forth. So let the tyres burst! We passed the final light. Ahead of us, everything was pitch black. We couldn't calculate how fast we were travelling. The brakes squealed. The aircraft settled down gently and came to a standstill, rocking briefly back and forth.

We didn't say a word. We just sat there. In the last, dim-yellow light of our landing lamp we saw in front of us, a few metres away, an Italian Savoia bomber, on its nose and gently smoking. I switched off the ignition for the starboard engine, then the internal power. The high-pitched whine of the gyroscope descended to a lower pitch, then cut out. The second hand on the stop-watch was still moving. I pressed the button, and it returned to zero — back to its rest position. The silence was complete.

It was 2 o'clock in the morning. Nobody slapped me on the shoulder saying 'Good show!' or, 'That was some landing!' That was what usually happened with my crew. When that happened, every pilot got a good feeling from knowing that he had brought his crew safely home. Our landing on Rhodes had been far from smooth. It had been a very poor performance indeed. But for us it was the happiest, the most emotional return to Mother Earth that we had experienced during the one to two hundred occasions we had flown together in the war. Who should congratulate whom? Fate had played a game of dice with us. We had all, stubbornly and coarsely, tried to load the dice our own way — *Oberfeldwebel* Lorenz, we four in the cockpit, the Tommies at their guns, the man in the radio station; but it wasn't we who had thrown the dice.

'Out you get, men,' I said, taking off my microphone and my helmet. I realised that I was hoarse. The other three got out, opened a bottle of *aqua minerale* and drank it; it was indispensable, indeed compulsory, in those southern latitudes. I was the last to leave the aircraft. I climbed down slowly and took a deep breath. The ground sloped down gently to the right. I could see shapeless trees. Like a dark stage-curtain the steep mountainside spread behind the Italian aircraft. There had been very little room to spare. I looked up towards the point where the mountain was lost in grey fog. Outlines and forms swam and blurred like those we had left behind us — Sicily, Piraeus, the explosion, Naxos. I got a bottle, lay flat on my back on the stubbly grass, closed my eyes and drank until the water ran down my chin onto my neck.

I sat up and propped myself on my hands. Between the trees I saw a figure moving here and there, watching our aircraft. The figure didn't come any closer. After a while, I called out, 'Come here, you bastard! Help us!' The figure hesitated a moment, came towards us and addressed us in broken German: 'I not bastard. I *professore* and have studied in Germany.' The cautious man, whose peaked cap and epaulettes shimmered with their mass of gold, had thought that we were British pilots making either a forced or normal landing after the bombing attack. He told us about the attack, but nothing about the splendid landing lights. It was left to a German *Feldwebel* of the Air Communications Branch who put us in the picture.

He drove up in a VW, guided by the *professore* flashing a torch. That splendid German had been reading our signals in his radio station on the mountain slope for a long time, but there had been no power for his transmitter, even when the attack was over. To make the blackout one hundred percent, the Italians had switched off the entire power supply to the airfield, and it hadn't been switched back on. He had received our SOS and, after the bombing was over, had had his petrol generator started up. It was he who, in defiance of the Italians' blackout, had collected together the lamps and hurriedly set them out. 'Yes,' he said

'Working together with our Allies is a bit difficult at times.' He introduced himself as Head of the Radio Monitoring Service for the Middle East. He spoke the local language and was a professor. He was our saviour, pilot and bringer of light.

A small gathering of academics this night and on this island. 'Welcome to Rhodes,' the two of them say. There is only one possible answer, '*Vivat academia! Vivant professores!*' The professor murmured, 'I'd better collect the lamps. Otherwise someone will pinch them.' We climbed into the car beside him and it lurched across-country, then along a winding path. We stopped outside the Italian Officers' Mess. The professor lit our way in with one of his lamps. We drank the rest of the bottle. Nobody wanted to eat. We wanted to sleep.

In a room lined with tiles, with a bed in the middle, I let all my clothes fall to the ground. An Italian batman helped me. I lay down, pulled the light blanket over me, and closed my eyes. I saw islands, lights, *Oberfeldwebel* Lorenz's big hands resting on the bombs. Then nothing more.

Never had I known a more wonderful awakening. The sun was shining into the room through a snow-white mosquito net, which I noticed for the first time. Outside the wind rustled through sparse bushes, behind which the sun was mirrored in the sea. The scent of Spring filled the room.

'It's past ten o'clock,' said an Italian soldier who was opening the window. The black, curly head gave me a friendly nod. His movements were unhurried. Man and Nature were at peace with one another. Barefoot and clad in a shirt and underpants, I walked across to the open window. I had the urge to be an heroic Italian tenor and give vent to my boundless joy of life and the world with a high C. I wanted to be able to do what I had sometimes dreamed of doing: soar into the air with outstretched arms, swoop over the hills, circle and glide forever.

I said to the Italian, 'Look! Isn't it beautiful out there?' He peered out, as if looking for something. He looked at my bare feet and my underpants and chuckled: '*Si, Signore Capitano!*' Then he picked up the various items of my uniform.

I stayed a while at the window. The sky was a deep blue. The sun shone strongly. 'Homer's sun shines on us, too,' wrote Schiller. It was true. It was shining down from the very place where, thousands of years ago, the blind poet sang of men's wars, their sufferings and their victories. It all came back to me, and with it a gleam of the beauty, cause and cost of faded turmoil. Very faintly I heard, from far away, the voice of my teacher enthusiastically scanning verse: Dum-di-di, dum-di-di, dum-di-di. Suddenly, it occurred to me that the ancient dactyl had taken on a new life in our airmen's language, as 'Dora', or 'Delta': —·· —·· —·· (Da-dit-dit, da-dit-dit, da-dit-dit).

A pair of heels clicked together behind me. Flight Engineer Alles reported, 'Radiator mended. Aircraft serviceable. Bombed up as well.' Nobody wanted to think about our diversion airfield in Suda Bay on Crete at that moment. I pulled on my trousers. 'Let's think about it after breakfast.'

And that's what we did. We let our eyes wander far and wide over the green, flower-covered countryside around us. I lay back, my face towards the sun, in an Italian officer's deck-chair covered with a traditional pattern, in a row with Schmetz, Krahn and Alles. The warmth on our khaki shirts felt good, spread slowly through us and gave us new strength. We drank *cappuchino* and ate pieces of chocolate from our flying rations. As we did so, we looked up at the mountain slope. It looked much more forbidding than we had imagined it to have been during the night. That had been just as well: less for us to worry about. Ahead of us, south of the field, there was a promontory of rock, majestic but very dangerous, on which stood a temple to some Greek God or other. When we had turned in on our approach we must have scraped very close past it. We marvel, we are happy and grateful, we feel light as air.

Over the terraces, swallows soared and glided, and brightly coloured birds flitted from bush to bush. Half-a-dozen kittens played around our feet. One began to stalk, its covetous eyes fixed on the tiny birds. It leapt three feet into the air. Like lightning a small paw flew through the air, but missed.

Bad luck! Good luck!

Notes

1 '*Ewig klar und spiegelrein und eben.*' Friedrich von Schiller.

Chapter Seven
Aircraft Carrier Malta,
April-May 1941

The Axis Powers blunder in not taking Malta. The British use fast naval units and aircraft to disrupt the German and Italian supply lines to North Africa.

We had a short break and then we set about the steady job of blocking the British flow of supplies to North Africa from Egypt and Crete. We operated by the full moon and in the cloudless skies over Greece. Large ships could no longer be unloaded in Piraeus, so they anchored or cruised between the mainland and Salamis. We made a night trip over the bay and found that a large freighter, obviously damaged, had been beached on Salamis, and that there were several smaller vessels sailing in the bay in various directions. I decided to attack a ship that was sailing in the moonlight, approaching it, throttled back, along its longitudinal axis. I set a delay of five to seven seconds on the bombs so that we would not be caught in the explosion. I was so low when I dropped the bombs that I heard the crack as they struck the ship's superstructure. There was a sound like wood splintering, something seldom experienced when attacking from the air. The explosion followed after a few seconds, tearing the ship apart.

Two days later, on 13 April 1941, we had a similar success in a low-level attack: that time the captain succeeded in beaching his vessel. The defences had grown stronger. Flak spat up at us from the ships and from the guns on shore, while night fighters took off from Tatoi to try to stop us doing our job. *Leutnant* Saure, a splendid man from Bremen, and his crew were lost during one of those attacks, as was a crew from the 8th *Staffel*, that of Oberleutnant Wimmer, the son of my former OC Flying from Dresden. They were laid to rest in the cemetery on Salamis, by the side of fallen enemies and the brave warriors who, in the first decades of the previous century, had come from several European countries to help the Greeks in their war of liberation against the Turks.

Once more Malta became our prime target. The island had to be kept under constant pressure so that German and Italian reinforcements and supplies of war materials from Palermo could safely cross the Straits of Sicily and reach Tripoli along the coast of Tunisia. One day, when I checked in at the Operations Room, the Adjutant, *Oberleutnant* Sommer, informed me, beaming with pleasure, that our *Kommandeur* had been kidnapped and taken to the Blue Grotto on Capri, where he was to enter the state of holy matrimony. It was Sommer's duty to tell me, he said, that I was to take over as Deputy *Kommandeur* of the *Gruppe*. The appointment came as a complete surprise.

My first task was to appear over Malta and drop bombs in order to draw out enemy fighters. Our fighters would then engage them in aerial combat and shoot down as many as possible. I arranged it with our fighters that we would approach from the north-west at altitudes of between 5000 and 6000 metres, as we had done on 28 February, but we would not dive. We would bomb from the horizontal. Our target was a particular area of the quayside where an enemy cruiser and other ships were moored.

When the flak opened up, we were flying with a fair degree of separation from each other, and I had switched on the automatic course-steering equipment. It was my intention that after dropping our bombs we would turn north and close up into tight formation so that we could use our combined fire power to provide mutual protection against enemy fighters. I had laid that down emphatically at the pre-flight briefing.

All went well until shortly before we arrived at the target. My wingman to my left, *Oberfeldwebel* Lorra, was hit by flak and his windscreen was blown in, so that he had no protection against the slipstream. Nevertheless, he managed to stay with us until he had bombed, but then he lost his self-control and pulled to the side, out of the formation. What happened then, as I learned subsequently, caused great amusement, not only to our crews but also to the British, who were monitoring our radio transmissions continuously. I shouted to *Oberfeldwebel* Lorra, on the R/T, something along the lines of, 'Come here you bastard, you stupid clot! If you're not back here at once, I'll give you ten days in the glasshouse!' The good Lorra, who had been disorientated completely by the flak attack and who had broken formation involuntarily, got such a shock that he was more afraid of being locked up than of the English fighters. All around us, there was a wild circus of Spitfires and Me 109s. Our fighters couldn't cover everything. They had to adjust their tactics according to how well we kept formation. We joined up and flew home in good order, without too much trouble from the fighters. As Lorra had obeyed my order promptly he did not fall a victim to the Spitfires — or his Acting *Kommandeur*.

Nevertheless, I wasn't particularly keen to use my *Gruppe* to play decoy again. Admittedly, our bombing had been accurate — the cruiser was one of the ships that had received a direct hit — but it was clear that our leaders' principal aim was to destroy the enemy fighters. I said that we could do that equally well by night.

One of the about twelve attacks we made is worth describing.

'Night-time's not only for sleeping,' sang Friedrich and Weinreich to the accompaniment of the accordion, imitating Gustaf Gruendgens.[1] Gradually, a small breed of young officers had evolved. It would not be unfair to describe them as civilians in uniform: they were completely lacking in traditional military attitudes, and it was only on ceremonial occasions that they stood to attention with their heels together. They all had the habit of expressing themselves somewhat uninhibitedly, whereas I, for example, was always at pains to address my superiors in properly phrased, formal language.

One evening Paul Hecking, who came from the Lower Rhine, hobbled into the room that we called the Officers' Mess, impersonating Josef Goebbels. He sat down on a chair, giving a slovenly Nazi salute, and proceeded to deliver a propaganda speech in a Rhineland dialect that made us split our sides with laughter. Similarly, an Austrian officer marched in to the accompaniment of the accordion playing the Badenweiler March. His hair had been combed down so that one eye was covered. It would have been an injustice to put us in prison. We were not rebelling against the State. We stood apart from the politicians, and even from our own opinions. For us one thing came before all criticism, all joking, all personalities: to win the war, or at least not to lose it.

For that particular raid on Malta, the night offered us cover from troublesome anti-aircraft fire. But the deciding factor had to be whether or not it would allow us to bomb effectively. Staff *Oberst* Harlinghausen, Chief of Staff of the 10th *Fliegerkorps*, a man who did not spare himself — he had flown on operations against convoys and the Suez Canal — would tear off us a hell of a strip if his reconnaissance aircraft went out the following day and found only holes in the sand. His fundamental principle applied not only to the infantry but to pilots also: it's results that count, not self-preservation. But to achieve results, we had to be able to see what we were doing. We needed target illuminators.

I telephoned *III./KG 4 'General Wever'* in Comiso, which had been reformed in Autumn 1940 from the remainder of the *Geschwader* with the addition of a number of new recruits. The *Gruppe*, in common with the whole *Geschwader*, was equipped with He 111s, which could each carry thirty-two parachute flares that burnt for a length of five to seven minutes each. I was told that flares were in stock. The *Kommandeur* of the *Gruppe* was *Hauptmann* Kuehl, who had been at the Military Academy with me and together with whom I had done my flying training at Kitzingen. He said that he was prepared, in principle, to send me one of his best pilots on the afternoon before the attack so that I could brief him, but first I had to promise to hand over to him, at the next opportunity, our standard. This had been presented to *III./KG 4*, he said, and not to *III./KG 30*, the *Adlergeschwader*. I stated the contrary: the standard had been carried ahead of the Nordhausen aircrew in 1936 when they had marched into the town, not in front of a name. I was the standard-bearer and its custodian. It was in its place among former Nordhausen men, and there it should stay. The silken white banner with a yellow stripe and the Iron Cross in the middle had long been a bone of contention, which had not been resolved. It would be some time before one *Kommandeur* or another would yield. I finished by saying, 'First of all, let me see what sort of a show your apology for a target-illuminator puts on. Then we'll continue the discussion.'

The illuminator aircraft landed in the late afternoon and a young *Leutnant* reported to me, standing stiffly to attention. He would have been a perfect example of a supervising officer at a military academy, which caused me and my staff to suspect that his formally correct bearing might be his only military virtue. While briefing the *Staffel* captains I made it clear to him that we would be attacking the airfield at Luqa in three waves, and that he would have to make three runs, dropping ten flares each time. He would have to weave his way through the searchlights, and the success of the entire attack depended on him. As I spoke, the *Leutnant* interjected '*Jawohl*' a dozen times at least, his face beaming with joy. It became apparent that in front of me I had an innocent, dashing theoretician. Summing up, he repeated, 'First stick of flares at 2330 hrs; second, at 2336 hrs; last one at 2342 hrs. *Jawohl*! Sticks to drift gently over the target area. Bombing wind to be passed by R/T. *Jawohl*!' The *Leutnant* departed and Hanke gave me a quizzical look. We had our hireling, but he appeared to represent a poor bargain.

The illuminating aircraft took off, and I followed fifteen minutes after, at 2255 hrs, the first aircraft of our *Gruppe* to do so. It was 29 April 1941. Again, the target was Malta. Over the beacon at Cape Passero, Schmetz calculated the wind at our mean altitude, and we transmitted it to all our aircraft. There was nothing to be secretive about. In Malta they would already know that we were on our way. All we had to keep secret from them was how we were going to carry out the attack.

This was our plan: our aircraft would attack simultaneously, approaching the airfield at Luqa concentrically from preselected sectors of the coast. We would time the approach to arrive two minutes after the flares had been dropped. Those two minutes would allow us to make certain that we had identified the correct target. We would attack in a gentle glide and at speed, our airscrews turning slowly and almost fully feathered. Our bombing height would be between 800 and 1000 metres. We would attack the hangars with shrapnel bombs, and the aircraft shelters with 500 and 1000-kg high-explosive bombs, because we would expect results from the blast and flying debris even if we were unable to achieve direct hits on the shelters. We didn't need much fuel for the operation, which would take barely two hours to complete, so we loaded each aircraft with a total of 2000 kg of bombs. I experimented for the first time with a bomb-load of 2500 kg.

I flew round the island in a southerly direction and circled at a height of approximately 4000 metres in my sector, waiting for the performance to start. Here and there a searchlight reached out towards the sea, trying to catch whoever was disturbing the night, but I was relieved to see that it had no success. Our pilots had been told to keep their distance, as far as was commensurate with their being at their precise bombing position on time. Time passed. I looked at my watch. If our hireling was going to light his ten-armed candelabrum over the centre of the island at 2330 hrs, he would be on his way at any moment: the searchlights should show signs of his activity.

The performance began. The beams from a dozen searchlights shot into the sky to the east, from where our man was due to come. A further dozen augmented the brilliant display, and we saw a tiny, bright point, at first lit up and then lost. Then it was captured mercilessly by sharp pencils of light from every direction. The whole island was projecting light at the invaders.

The Heinkel was flying at an altitude of at least 6000 metres, and was moving very slowly. I suspected that it was to be the turn of the night fighters that night, because the flak was momentarily silent. Then the thunderstorm erupted. The sea flashed the reflections of the galaxy of light, and I saw the jagged line of the coast, appearing as if on a map. I saw the pinpoint from which I was to begin my bombing run, and approached it in a gradual curve, throttling back gently and carefully, watching the clock, holding back . . .

The time came for me to start my run-in, and for the *Leutnant* to drop his flares. I looked up and saw him, bathed in vivid light, flying in a cloud of flak bursts. Stick on that heading, I said to myself, and I slid in over the coast without anyone paying any attention to me. The flares appeared: 1 . . . 2 . . . 3 . . . they hung, swinging gently, right ahead of me in a perfect line above the airfield. I saw it as if I was seeing it in bright sunlight. Now, into the attack; hope I'm not picked up by the searchlights and dazzled. Fortunately they were fully occupied with the big aircraft above, which was curving to the south, towards me but far above, in order to begin its second run.

Schmetz had everything under control and the aerial photograph clear in his mind. The precision of his instructions helped me to relax. One, two, three lurches: our bombs had gone and we were flying lighter. Unhindered and undetected, we had flown almost right through the canopy of light. Below us, there was an inferno, testimony to our work. The flak gunners seemed to wake up, angry and wild. They swept the sky with their searchlights, here and there, high and low, separately and in cones. The flak gunners fired wildly towards the flares and sent up a barrage over the airfield while I approached the finishing line of my obstacle race on the coast. I knew that the 8th *Staffel* were already moving on to the stage that I was leaving. Once over the sea I opened up and climbed to height. There was still work to be done.

I had scarcely climbed to between four and five thousand metres north-east of the island when the searchlights reached out again to the east, trembling, searching, sweeping. Then they settled down. I looked at my watch: the second run-in was beginning.

The searchlights picked up the *Leutnant's* aircraft precisely over the coast. The storm broke. I flew towards him, approaching the target below him and to one side, and opened up my engine to full revs. A number of searchlights swung round towards me, searching but, the aircraft seeming as light as a feather, I changed direction rapidly. The searchlights held the Heinkel in their beams, and concentrated flak rose towards it. I saw the He 111 large and clear; its cockpit sparkled like a diamond.

Christ! They've hit him! A long trail of fuel streamed away from one wing. Now that the searchlights had enabled blood to be drawn, they wouldn't let him go. The Heinkel, losing height, descended towards me. Don't turn away, man! At least, drop the second stick! He did so, and they lit up the sky. Well done! Well done! The He 111 turned away. Off you go! Back home. Away from the island. Course for home is north! What is the fellow doing? He turned towards the south. The searchlights were on his tail, but the flak couldn't follow the turn he made, thank God! Gradually, they lost him. He was in the dark.

There had been another storm of bombs below. Here and there, a dark column of smoke billowed from the bright background. Once more our boys had flown through the fire without harm, with only the odd gun following them out to sea with its fire. When the last flares had burnt themselves out I thought, uneasily, about the third wave. The searchlights sprang up again towards the sky, pointing east. Could he be — is he — going to make his third run? I couldn't believe it: he was approaching at an altitude of 2500-3000 metres. I moved into position alongside him. I went crazy — he was flying on one engine.

Help him, Heaven! I called Weinreich and told him to start jamming at full power. I feared for the lives of the men in the He 111. Using all the tricks I knew, I curved in close, dived, desynchronised my motors, applied full throttle and switched on my navigation lights for an instant. The searchlights picked me out. So what? They won't hit me! I am doing my damnedest, and so is Weinreich. He had seen everything and said 'My God! Just look at that!' Flak was bursting very close to the Heinkel. The *Leutnant* was like Winkelried,[2] letting his own breast be a target for the enemy spears. They would surely get him. But he turned away north-east and flew out to sea.

Has he dropped his flares, or hasn't he? Terrific! I saw them, a wonderful majestic row. The heavy cargoes of the 9th *Staffel's* aircraft crashed down. Weinreich and I followed the Heinkel north-east. The searchlights from La Valetta latched on to me. The flak couldn't follow the steep turns I made, flying on instruments, and the searchlights couldn't harm me. It is as bright as day inside the cockpit. It's an easy number here compared to the cross the illuminator has to bear. From 2000 metres firing at searchlights is no problem.

The illuminating aircraft was flying over the sea. Still in the searchlights and scarcely 1000 metres high, the aircraft turned, seemingly tired. Then I couldn't see it any more, nobody could see it. I called up base in plain language. In plain language, Krahn radioed, 'Emergency at sea,' and gave the time and the Heinkel's course. We landed safely at Gerbini, but the illuminator had not returned. He was to have returned to Comiso, the airfield from which he had taken off.

Depressed, I picked up the telephone to call *Hauptmann* Kuehl at Comiso. It was about one o'clock in the morning. I asked tentatively whether the aircraft had returned or if the crew had been in radio contact with him. Neither! I described what had happened. The aircraft must have been riddled with holes. *Hauptmann* Kuehl was on the point of hanging up, but I asked him not to: I wanted to wait.

Then Kuehl yelled out, 'There's been an explosion here!' All I could hear over the phone was loud voices. A quarter of an hour later, Kuehl rang. The damaged aircraft had crashed on the edge of the airfield. Everything was u/s: the radio, undercarriage, lights and the remaining engine. The *Leutnant* was in a critical condition. I have since forgotten his name. He was my Unknown Warrior of the Second World War. It is very difficult to judge a man. Some men act big: some men are big.

Malta, island fortress and naval base, had to be defeated. My orders were to continue with our attacks. By 16 May 1941 we had carried out ten, with the *Gruppe* starting twice in a night on three occasions: the first before midnight, the second after. The stubborn defences made different attacking techniques necessary: high-level; gliding; diving in waves, or in one concentrated blow; or a mixture of methods, all using frequent changes of spoof and jamming techniques. Aerial photographs showed subsequently the *Gruppe* had caused not insignificant damage. We lost one of our crews.

In the middle of May our *Kommodore*, *Major* Bloedorn, arrived at Gerbini from Evreux in France. At the same time *Major* Crueger returned from his honeymoon. I was told that I had been wanted by Department 1 of the General Staff, but *IX. Fliegerkorps*, to which our *Geschwader* was subordinate, had been uncooperative. I was to be posted there as 1a Op in the Operational Planning Department. With a wink, *Major* Bloedorn whispered to me that the posting was in my best interests, because I would certainly be noticed in the *Fliegerkorps* and be put on the *Kommandeur* Reserve, ready to fill a post immediately when one became vacant.

The prospect of being *Kommandeur* pleased me, but why should I go the long way round via the Staff of *IX. Fliegerkorps*? I would sooner stay with my *Staffel* and move directly from there to an appointment as *Kommandeur*. Bloedorn took the opposite point of view and said that that was not on. The alternative was that I would be taken from my *Staffel* and never heard of again, a victim of high-level bureaucracy. I didn't want that to happen so I withdrew my objections. I was very pleased when the *Kommodore* told me that in any case the *Gruppe* was shortly going to be moved to France, into the area of responsibility of the *IX. Fliegerkorps*, to be reallocated to the *Geschwader*. At the *Korps*, therefore, I would be able to do much for the *Geschwader*.

It was pure horse-trading at high level, and I was the horse! I would rather have stayed where I was. Admittedly, the war had become something of a strain for me. Our most recent operations, flown over the sea, had clocked up almost 150 hours on the engines, whereas the permitted limit was 100 hours. Each time a motor faltered we thought instinctively that our time was up. In dicey crates such as those I had lifted as much as three tons of bombs, two weighing 1000 kg each, and two weighing 500 kg each, off the deck. Now they wanted me on the Staff. That was no place for me in a war. Of course, I had written many papers, reported various experiences, and had sent this proposal and that suggestion up through official channels. But I wanted to be in the front line, a fighting man: for it was, in my opinion, mainly the fighting men on whom victory or defeat depended. On the Staff during a war? No! All I wanted to do was to stimulate the people there. I imagined that the officers there would read my reports carefully and act on them efficiently: there were plenty of people in the Directorates, the Departments and the Sections, who could surely take the ideas of an experienced front-line officer, work on them in detail and put them into effect: and so one day my aircraft would carry the sort of equipment I had always dreamed of, and our leaders would be so wise as a result of my advice that everything would go like clockwork. But I had neglected to take into account the boss, Chief of Staff of *IX. Fliegerkorps*, Staff *Oberst* Czech, known as the Red Commissar, whose job it would be to indoctrinate me into the intricacies of staff work.

Most distressing, however, was the separation from my *Staffel*. What bound me to these officers and airmen was not the years we had been together. It was the totality of our shared experience, the successes and the dangers, now part of history, which had left their mark on our individual characters, superior officers and subordinates alike. Seeing the heads of my crews in their cockpits; flying with them, wing-tip to wing-tip; giving them orders; making reports, listening to their questions — and their curses; cheering them up when they were low; preaching caution or subterfuge when one of them was too rigid, too unimaginative or simply too much of a daredevil — all that had been my life, my reality. The thought of having to follow events from behind a desk or having to read about them afterwards caused me much soul-searching.

Our operations had only been accomplished with hard discipline. There had been differences of opinion, of course. When arguments had arisen, I had joined in the debate. The plans put into operation when at last we opened the throttles were in no way wholly my own. Many of my ideas were discarded; what emerged finally was a combined effort, as far as that was possible within the framework of orders from higher up. Our experiences in action had consisted of a pulling together, not a dragging along. This was to be the one exception. Only the profit and loss account — which Clausewitz had said was to be found at the bottom of the final page in the great ledger of War — could convince either me, or, I believed, the most stupid of men. That had been the guideline which I had followed over the months, and it was, in my view, the best way to prepare and look after ourselves, the *Staffel*, our totality.

Above all else was our shared memory of fallen comrades. The proximity of Death united the living and the fallen with bonds which, painful though they might be, inspired us to determination and bravery, bonds that we hoped we would retain when our days came to an end. Old Duphorn was gone, an observer in the First World War and a volunteer in this. He had been the *Buergermeister* of

Poessneck in Thuringia, stolid and indefatigable. During exercises at Nordhausen, he used to type his official letters in a room with the window open, while I, one storey higher, was working on my report. The irrepressible *Hauptmann* Neumann, *Kapitaen* of the 8th *Staffel*, had been hit by flak and his aircraft had plunged from 5000 metres into the harbour waters of Tobruk, impacting close to the side of an enemy ship. Our dead comrades lived on among us, and we were all members of a happy and contented circle.

Finally, after the *Kommodore* promised to transport my donkey and its mate over the Alps in a Ju 52, I agreed. As I climbed into my Ju 88 I was helped on by the hope that I would soon be back. The following was how others saw me: it was what my *Kommandeur* wrote about my Mediterranean operations after I had left; to it he had attached photographs of Piraeus:

> *In action Hauptmann Herrmann does not spare himself, nor does he set any store by personal popularity. He acts uncompromisingly according to hard, soldierly tenets and intelligent tactical principles.*

Major Crueger's hope had been that this assessment would result in my receiving the traditional silver-framed photograph of *Reichsmarschall* Goering. But it didn't. It was aerial victories that impressed that *Pour le Mérite* fighter pilot of the First World War.

Notes

1 Gustaf Gruendgens, born 1899, was a well-known actor and producer in pre-War Berlin.
2 Winkelried: the Swiss folk hero Arnold Winkelried is said to have ensured victory in the Battle of Sempach in 1386 by sacrificing himself to the spears of the attacking Hapsburg knights.

Chapter Eight
On the Staff of the
General Officer Commanding,
May-June 1941

Sowing mines in British supply lanes. Disruption bombing raids. War on the Soviet Union. Air Force units are transferred from the West to the Eastern Front. Heavy battles of encirclement.

I landed somewhere in Holland, and my aeroplane was taken for a major overhaul while my crew went off on leave. At about the same time the *Korps* moved to Brussels, to the Hotel de l'Europe, if my memory serves me well. There I began my new job as a minor cog in the wheels of bureaucracy and a sharpener of pencils. I seem to remember that it was in the dining-room that the operational maps were spread out or displayed on the walls. I played no part in operational orders, which were looked after by the 1a or his assistant, 1a Op, *Hauptmann* Lauer. At nights, when the bomber force was airborne, I had to be in the Operations Room (the *Gefechtsstand*) and keep an eye on the weather. I had nothing else to do until the bomber crews' operational reports came in.

During the daytime, I had to work on various problems set for me by the Chief of Staff, and I usually had to present my solutions in writing. On one occasion, I had drafted a paper of this sort with meticulous care, underlining what seemed to me to be the salient points in coloured pencil. I had no sooner placed my paper on his desk when the Chief of Staff began to bawl me out. He asked me if I was mad. I learned that green pencils were reserved for the General Officer Commanding alone, and red pencils for his Chief of Staff. To my question as to whether an exception might perhaps be made on this occasion I was told that there could be absolutely no exceptions to the rule. And so I began to work out for myself a new range of priorities — pencil-related. Outside, the priority was to stay alive if at all possible.

I was on duty during the night of 21/22 June 1941. The duty signals operator passed me a teleprinter message. It read, 'War with Russia with effect from 0300 hrs.' That, I thought, was all we needed. I cranked the handle on the telephone and woke the Chief of Staff. He gave me the honour of informing the GOC. The senior officers did not seem to be at all surprised. The General and his Chief of Staff had both served with the Navy, and in *IX. Fliegerkorps* they had occupied themselves almost exclusively with the war at sea against England and, in particular, with the invasion plan 'Seelöwe'[1] in Autumn 1940, which they spoke of occasionally as being historically parallel with Napoleon's plans to invade that country. After the die was cast, they expressed themselves more unequivocally. They understood the British, they said.

I heard no criticism of Operation Barbarossa: on the contrary, the general hope was that it would be successful. I shared those hopes without being able to form my own independent assessment. Napoleon had marched on Moscow in 1812 after his defeat at the Battle of Trafalgar, in order to avoid a stab in the back. Our Russian Campaign seemed to me to be a daring enterprise, but fully justified. I was not at all ideologically biased. I did not see Russia as the world enemy, nor did I believe that the Russians were an inferior race. My view of history was founded on the Holy Alliance in the struggle against Napoleon and later against the revolutionary movements, on a Russia drawn into Europe and still not rejected after the October Revolution. Even our teachers did not know what had been happening in Russia in the past twenty years.

About the beginning of July 1941 the Staff was transferred to France, in the centre of the few units remaining in the West. We occupied the Château le Francfort near Compiègne on the River Oise. I rapidly forgot my small hotel room in Brussels. I could now rest on a wide four-poster bed with a canopy, like Louis XIV, looking out over a magnificent park. My old *Gruppe* was located not far from there, at Melun south of Paris, and I was able to renew my acquaintance with the good Toto, who quickly became a favourite among the members of the Staff. Now and then the slit-eared beast would peer in through the great windows, which reached almost down to the ground. Should a door be left open he would walk in and cross the red carpet in a stately manner.

Sometimes, on Sundays, I would go out at the crack of dawn to the Oise to watch the patient anglers lined up at regular intervals along the banks. There was a Frenchman who, if he didn't get a bite within five minutes, would launch into voluble explanations: I should have come an hour later; or I ought to have been there yesterday; or if only he were a bit further upstream, where the others were, I would see what he was capable of. Almost without exception the fishermen talked a great deal and, like fishermen the world over, they had a fund of excuses. I would hand cigarettes round: it was a lonely spot by the riverside and I was not armed.

On a number of occasions I had to make a duty visit to the *Luftflotte* in the Palais Luxembourg in Paris, and my route took me past the homes of my peacetime acquaintances. Nothing seemed to have changed there. But I didn't call on them. It could only have been embarrassing for them to have to greet a member of the occupying forces.

Gradually I came to understand a little more about the work of the Staff. Staff *Oberst* Czech proved to be a very strict teacher, but comradely. Sometimes he would invite me to join him in the evening, when he would sit on the chair in which, legend had it, Matthias Erzberger had sat during the Armistice negotiations in 1918. In the course of talking with him I learned a great deal about organization, communications, supplies and strategic leadership — things a front-line officer doesn't normally concern himself with. The leitmotif of these conversations was always ships, ships, ships. They had to be sunk: anything else bombed in England simply didn't count.

Once I had to accompany the GOC to the airfield at Buc, where certain recent innovations were to be demonstrated to *Reichsmarschall* Goering. I had with me a briefcase stuffed with secret documents of all kinds, which I was to pass to the

General when the Commander-in-Chief started asking questions. Unobtrusively, a member of the retinue of senior officers — another *General* — came up to me and asked in a friendly way if I was Hajo Herrmann. He had, he said, asked for me to be posted to the First Department, and now he had seen me here. *Kommodore* Bloedorn came bustling up and embarked upon a torrent of words, which only came to an end when the aircraft carrying out the demonstration created a very welcome diversion. I was told that the *General* was the Head of the Office of Personnel, *General* Kastner.

One warm, sunny afternoon in August I was taking my coffee in the shadow of a mighty tree in front of the château and reading a racy, trashy nineteenth-century French novel, thus combining the labour of translation with stimulating relaxation. Toto was grazing nearby. The *Major* from Reserve X who worked in Department II — Personnel — came up to me, walking unusually rapidly. In his hand he had a piece of paper which he waved in my direction and told me to take a look at. Good Lord! I had been appointed *Kommandeur* of my old Nordhausen *Gruppe*! *Major* Crueger was to take over a light bomber *Geschwader* on the Eastern Front. I jumped to my feet, causing the cups to rattle, with the immediate and positive realization that there was nothing more for me to learn on the Staff.

Notes
1 *Seelöwe*: Operation Sealion — the planned invasion of Britain by Germany.

Chapter Nine
Kommandeur,
July 1941-July 1942

German troops are deep inside Russia. Japan cannot be persuaded to enter the war against the Soviet Union. The USA supply war material to the Soviet Union via Iceland-Murmansk and Persia. In September 1941 Roosevelt orders his fleet to fire on German ships, even though the USA is not at war with Germany. Germany declares war on the United States following the Japanese attack on Pearl Harbor on 7 December 1941.

The airfield lay close to Melun, a place which I knew in my first year at secondary school from the verse:

> *À Paris, à Paris*
> *Sur mon petit cheval gris.*
> *À Melun, à Melun*
> *Sur mon petit cheval brun.*

I would arrive at Melun, not on a little horse as in the verse, but with a grey donkey instead. There would be a wonderful reunion with my comrades. Seldom had I packed my bags as rapidly as I did then. I couldn't wait to be off and away. *Major* Crueger was as pleased with my appointment as I was with his, which he richly deserved. We exchanged our best wishes.

Feldmarschall Sperrle ceremonially handed my command over to me on 2 September, Sedan Day, in the presence of the *Kommodore*. After that, I came up against the realities of life, initially in the persons of my *Staffelkapitaene*, Paepke, Metzenthin and Schlockermann, all three senior to me in both age and service. Each of them could have reasonably expected to take over the *Gruppe*. How was one expected to overcome a situation so fraught with potential disaster?

Military discipline, enforced by means of punishment but sweetened with the help of honours and awards, is the most primitive substitute for leadership. The same applies to training. Leadership means taxing oneself to the limit in order to achieve effect and set examples, without a sideways glance for others. Fundamentally, leadership is a silent, ascetic and honourable posture owed by a man to himself: leadership is joy in the overcoming of both internal and external resistance, joy in achievement — not only in military success, which is so frequently a matter for sadness. This is the kind of leadership that brings out the best in others, without compulsion or reward.

My uncomplicated existence as a front-line officer came to an end when I left to the discretion of my *Staffelkapitaene* the question of whether or not they should fly on any particular operation. I never experienced a single instance of misuse of that discretion. I made it the responsibility of each *Staffelkapitaen* in turn to alternate with me when planning operations and giving briefings, and when they did so I attended solely in my capacity as leader of the *Stabsschwarm* (Headquarters Flight) and obeyed their orders. This arrangement satisfied everyone, and, at the same time, ensured that any one of them could take over, if the need should arise.

We carried out mine-laying operations in the dismal, narrow harbour-waters of the Tyne and the Humber, in the Thames, at Bristol, Cardiff, and in the Mersey between Liverpool and Birkenhead. We also bombed the harbour installations, which was less difficult.

We didn't forget how to laugh. One warm, sunny day at the end of September or the beginning of October, the GOC was scheduled to give a talk to all front-line commanders in the Château le Francport, and I turned up late. I knew my way around the château and decided to slip in unobtrusively through one of the big French windows and take a seat. I had just reached the heavy curtain when I heard the Chief of Staff — at that time Staff *Oberst* Herhudt von Rohden — mention my name in the course of his address. The *Oberst* was a very strict and much-feared senior officer, who had been my *Kommodore* in the *Kampfgeschwader General Wever* the previous year. He could issue reprimands, sharply and concisely, without raising his voice. When in his presence I had always experienced an uneasy feeling in my stomach, and I had finally made a determined effort to overcome it by contradicting him on a point of tactics. I based my contradiction, I told him, on something I had read. Yes? Where? In black and white, I said, in the red-bound brochure *Military Science Review*; and above the article had been printed 'Herhudt von Rohden', although no rank had been given. Marvellous! His pride in his authorship triumphed over his dignity as a senior officer. Since that incident, it appeared, the *Oberst* had looked upon me as an adult.

From my position of concealment, I pricked up my ears, fully expecting a reprimand *in absentia*. Instead I heard blatant flattery. I was praised to the skies for the most unexpected reasons, so that I felt just as Mark Twain's rascals, Tom Sawyer and Huckleberry Finn, must have felt when, after going missing, they returned unexpectedly to find the Pastor extolling their virtues in glowing terms at their own memorial service. However, I was shrewd enough to realise that what the *Oberst* was doing was attempting to stimulate his audience, not eulogising me. I withdrew and entered the château formally through the main door, accompanied by one of the guards, and I was admitted to the hall. I was immediately on the receiving end of a blast: unpunctuality, the first step on the downward path, disregard of basic principles. I tried to remain serious, but my new fellow-commanders burst out laughing, as did the GOC and the Chief of Staff.

Even though when I was a *Staffelkapitaen* I had contrived mostly, or at least adequately, to take cover from the barrage of paper that poured down from above, as a *Kommandeur* I was forced to recognise that I was in the front line of the lightweight war of bureaucracy. I was somewhat daunted by the knowledge that my first *Kommandeur*, poor *Major* Maass, had, when building up the *Gruppe* in peacetime, been so overloaded with keeping the paperwork under control that he had hardly had any time at all to instil a love of flying in his young officers. Confronted with the abundance of papers that Adjutant Sommer and the

1a, Hanke, piled on my desk, I began to suspect that the red-green nonsense on the desks at High Command was not perhaps such a nonsense after all. And so I began to rationalise the business side of things with the laudable aim of speeding it up. If I told Hanke to do something this way or that way he would answer, with mock formality, *'Jawohl, Herr Hauptmann!* Has the *Herr Hauptmann* any further orders?' 'Yes. Do this, do that.' *'Jawohl, Herr Hauptmann!* Has the *Herr Hauptmann* any further orders? Jesus — that lot up there's made a proper ink-pisser out of you!'

Equally, our irregular style of night-life caused problems: how could one possibly set a time for lights out and then enforce it? One result of this difficulty was that the clandestine paths to the beauties of the nearby village were worn smooth, and they were out of the view of the guards. Now and again passion claimed its sacrifice when certain precautions were not observed, resulting in the necessity for action of two kinds: one disciplinary, the other performed by our Dr. Coburg. Those who were doubly afflicted were not excused from operational flying. Indeed, they didn't want to be, because that would only bring them boredom and loneliness; and it would mean that they couldn't share the flying meals which, at that time, were supplemented with tasty partridge or pheasant.

One of my aircrew showed more initiative than common sense when, emboldened by tenderness, he followed his girl, despite her protests, into her parental home. Slightly tipsy, he took his place in the family circle under the lamp in the kitchen. Most unfairly, her father was convinced by his daughter's protestations of innocence in the matter, and he summoned the German *Feldgendarmerie*, who carted the delinquent off and brought him to me. A court martial resulted in a mild sentence for the pilot, which re-established the honour of the girl and her family and compensated adequately for the invasion of the family's privacy.

The British night-fighter defences had become much stronger. The fighters were controlled from the ground and vectored on to our aircraft with considerable accuracy. The number of aerial combats escalated. I recalled an evaluation memorandum that I had read in General Headquarters. In it, all of the British ground-to-air R/T traffic for a period of several months was tabulated. The traffic information had been collected by the monitoring station *Meldekopf Birk* near Cherbourg on the Channel coast. I instructed our signals officer, *Oberleutnant* Holler, to visit the station and see whether there was any possible short cut by means of which we could evaluate the data being received immediately and pass warnings to our aircraft. Holler remained there a few days, then returned with a plan he had devised with *Hauptmann* Birk, the CO of that unit. The idea seemed a bit fiddly, but I was very enthusiastic. First, however, we would have to try it out.

We did so in the course of one of our next operations. A number of our aircraft flew over the British coast at different points. Swiftly, the night fighters were vectored into position and given the heights and courses of our aircraft; then, they moved in to attack. At that point their ground station ordered 'Flash your weapons!' Safety catches to fire! Not until they heard that instruction did our ground station, which had been listening in carefully and taking bearings, transmit, 'JJ — 48 — M.' The bomber flying at 4800 metres and located in grid square M would make a tight turn and shake off the fighter. The capital letters were printed on our charts, and it was only a moment's work for the ground station to convert feet into metres. We enjoyed the resulting security even more a few days afterwards when we read a record of the curses that had been heard over the English fighter controllers' R/T.

While Holler was occupied with clarifying the procedure and training the sceptical radio operators and aircrew, a telex arrived ordering us to attack the docks at Liverpool. There was a full moon and almost clear skies. The orders from the *Luftflotte* were quite specific: we were to fly around Cape Lizard and the Scilly Isles and fly low over the Irish Sea before climbing to height to make our attack. I told the *Kommodore* immediately that I would not fly that route because it would take us over the bright surface of the sea with the moon behind us. All the British would have to do was to patrol over the sea and pick out the approaching bombers, which would stand out dark against the background. I preferred to fly over the land, which would be dark, dodge round the searchlights and rely on our new fighter-warning equipment. The *Kommodore* sent my counter-proposal up to the *Luftflotte*, but it was rejected as out of hand. I was relieved to note that the *Kommodore* had kept quiet about my refusal to fly the route.

We took off, leaving the poorly blacked-out city of Paris below and astern. We gained height rapidly in the direction of the Channel, and crossed the south coast of England on a front of about 100 kilometres. Another *Gruppe*, flying He 111s, took the tedious route around Land's End and over the Irish Sea. We received approximately a dozen warnings and managed to avoid combat with fighters. We kept as silent as mice so that we would hear our 'JJ' (*Jaeger. Jaeger!*) signal giving heights and grid references. Nothing out of the ordinary happened. No ball of fire or aircraft going down behind us was reported by the radio-operator or the rear gunner. But in the latitude of the island of Anglesey, out to sea, a drama was being played out. Fires were seen to erupt at low altitude, then extinguish almost immediately. We saw seven or eight planes go down within a short time.

We decided to return at low level for a change; not over the sea but over Wales, with its countless lakes and streams glittering in the moonlight. Then we would fly below the level of the mountain-peaks, cross the Bristol Channel, and speed off over Cornwall keeping at heights between 100 and 200 metres. Monitoring our altitudes carefully and navigating with precision, we flew too fast for the searchlights to follow us. Over the Channel we listened again for the 'JJ' warnings. We were not flying into the moon but towards the south-east, diagonally to the bright paths it made on the sea. We only had one serious combat encounter. The rear gunner of one of our aircraft was killed by a bullet through the head from a night fighter and the machine seriously damaged. The pilot was able to land on the beach near Caen, however, and the remainder of the crew were unscathed.

Occasionally the *Herr Baron* visited us, in order to check the condition of his stately property and the two manor houses in which some of our men were accommodated. He was very pleased with us, and his only request was that the donkeys shouldn't be allowed to follow us indoors at night and warm themselves at the open fire. We were able to help him, particularly when we became beaters when a hunt was in progress: on one occasion the tally was 238 hares.

As higher authority had by and large given me a free hand when it came to planning operations — day or night, and indeed the precise timing — we were occasionally tempted, if we got back to base early in the evening, to set course along the dead straight road that Napoleon had so thoughtfully built from Fontainebleu to Monmartre — or, to be more precise, to the Chantilly night-spot, where a bevy of delicious young French mademoiselles awaited us. We were never quite sure whether it was us they loved or the bread and hares' legs we brought with us. On one occasion, little Madeleine burst into tears when we couldn't bring ourselves to answer when she asked, '*Où est Erneste?*'

One fine day we drove in relays by lorry to Paris, and there, with my previous knowledge, I was able proudly to act the part of a guide. It was a great pleasure for all of us, not to say an enriching experience.

And so it was with some disappointment that we learned that we were to leave *la belle France* for flat Holland. We shared the airfield at Gilze-Rijen with my old comrade-in-arms, Karl Huelshoff, who was commanding a *Gruppe* of long-range night fighters that was carrying out raids on English bomber airfields, while my *Gruppe* flew equally hazardous bombing and mining operations. We looked back wistfully on our earlier, happy, hell-raising, flying days at Kitzingen am Main. Now it was a matter of clenching our teeth.

When I returned from one particular operation I was met by a delegation from the Junkers firm, who presented me ceremoniously with a sleek, silver model of a Ju 88, complete with an inscription, to mark my 200th operational mission.

One day during the Christmas holiday period we had just returned from a mining operation, in the course of which we had avoided flying over land in deference to the seasonal spirit of both friend and foe, and had sat down to our Christmas dinner, when I was called to the telephone to speak to the Chief of Staff of *IX. Korps*, Staff *Oberst* Herhudt von Rohden. He ordered us to fly immediately across the North Sea to Stavanger in Norway, where we were to take on bombs and intercept a British naval formation that was at that very moment engaging German strongpoints on the coast with heavy gunfire. Our meal, untouched, was left on the table to go cold. I took my leave from my dog and my donkey, and within the hour we were storming out into the night. We all landed safely on the airfield at Stavanger, which had been itself under fire, and began to prepare for the attack on the ships the following morning. In response to our report confirming our safe landing, we received a telex congratulating the *Gruppe* for our rapid action. Such commendations had become cheap, and many of us were beginning to ask themselves how much longer this sort of thing could go on.

We were back in Norway, and up against the British again: us, the landsmen, against them, the seafarers. What is it that brings us together, but always on opposite sides? The fact that four-fifths of the surface of the earth is covered with billowing seas, spreading here, there and everywhere, scarely seems to be an adequate explanation. The answer lies in the fact that Britannia, the ruler of the waves, has become accustomed to overseeing — or has taken it upon herself to oversee — the remaining fifth part, manipulating those who frequent the rest of the world so that she can hold the balance of power. This is a well-practised, ancient tradition, it seems, proclaimed by the proud names of warriors and heroes that are written on the sides of their naval vessels. While other people are at each other's throats, all that John Bull needs to do is the minimum necessary to ensure that the scales are tipped in his favour.

That was the gist of our philosophising on New Year's Eve 1941/42 in Oerlandet, a flat, rocky peninsula off the Trondheim Fjord, where we could have come under gunfire from British warships at any moment, as had our people in

Stavanger at Christmas. We hoped, however, that we would have been able, by means of daylight sweeps, to reconnoitre the sea adequately. Out there it was cold and stormy, but here, inside, the oven-plate was warming me blissfully from below. I was sitting on it alongside my comrades in a huge, tiled farmhouse kitchen, in the middle of which was a long oven with numerous grates.

The original 'a toothbrush is all you'll need' had long been overtaken by events and the passage of time, and also by our new brief: to make our way far north, across the Arctic Circle and only just south of the Polar Cap, to the airfield at Bardufoss, which was used by the British in 1940 against our Narvik Expedition. We had to head for even colder latitudes. Everything seemed to be against us. A storm raged round the farmhouse; the weather continued to be atrocious. East winds brought hard frosts, and west winds pushed mighty storms of big, wet snowflakes against the thousand kilometres of rocky coast. Clouds and waves met; together, they raged and surged against the reefs and the mountains to such an extent that dogs crept, howling, behind stoves. But man, that unpredictable being, allowed himself to be lured out on orders from above: during the ensuing few days we swept low over the sea in threes, heading west to where the clouds, broken up by thermal currents, gave us sight of the sky so that we could climb and head north in better visibility. That was what we did. With the mid-day sun low on the horizon we headed for the North Cape, leaving to our starboard the towering shower-clouds crowding each other and the coast, now shining treacherously bright, concealing disaster. When we took off in the morning it was dusk, and it would be dusk when we come in to land. Already I could see the sun declining on the southern horizon. To the north, polar night held sway, while here, at noon, we were in a timorous half-light.

I held my course to the north-east, climbing over the cumulus clouds. The ground station sent a message: 'Coast mostly closed in, broken cloud over base.' I set my altimeter. Below us lay a stretch of snow-covered, wooded, mountainous landscape. A sharp hill crest loomed here; a steep peak, there. The visibility was improving. From below, green Very lights rose into the air. We landed rapidly, so that the aircraft behind could benefit from the half-light. The runway resembled a narrow mountain pass. Left and right, the snow had been pushed back to a height of three metres. The taxi-tracks had also been cleared for traffic. The airfield commander seemed to have things under control.

Once out of our machines we gazed around us. The mountains, reminiscent of the high Alps but only about 1400 metres high, made a homely picture of the hollow in which the airfield lay and reminded me of Garmisch-Partenkirchen. One after another the aircraft swept in over the dam-lake just above, let down over the hillside and landed in good order. There were aeroplanes everywhere, and the noise of engines filled the air.

The airfield was situated on land which lay at the centre of a semicircle formed of enemy convoys protected by warships, stretching from Iceland via the white volcanic island of Jan Mayen, the southern tip of Spitzbergen and Murmansk, to Archangel, where the convoys would discharge war material with which the Soviets could fight against us. The convoys were due to sail along the edge of the pack-ice, sometimes venturing into it, as far as possible from the coast. It was not hard for them to get as far as the southern tip of Spitzbergen in the month of December, during which time, with the help of the Gulf Stream, still effective even in those latitudes, the boundary of the ice receded further north. But April would bring the enemy seafarers many difficulties because April pushed the blanket of ice victoriously to the south — towards us.

What sort of a world was this for a Central European, when, at midday, he saw the stars gleaming in the twilight of the Polar Sea; where, at night, the Northern Lights shot aloft from the depths of the horizon, or spread their brilliant colours across the arch of heaven? To our primitive forebears in grey prehistory, neither troubled by the paleness of thought nor swayed by knowledge, the world must have seemed to be populated by militant, all-powerful beings. Strangely enough we pilots, familiar with magnetism and electrons as we were, rushed out from our huts and gazed up at the Lights as if they were some sort of miracle.

At first we did not fly long operations. The orders that came to me from the *Fliegerfuehrer 'Lofoten', Oberst* Roth — whom we soon christened '*Lofotenheini*' — were to send aircraft out on reconnaissance, singly and in pairs. Our 7th *Staffel*, which we sent ahead from Oerlandet to Trondheim, was doing the same job further south.

The Chief of *Luftflotte 3*, based in Oslo, was *Generaloberst* Stumpff, one of our neighbouring air commanders was *Oberst* Bruch, and the officer commanding the flak was *General* Feyerabend, so that ready tongues — among which Weinreich's was always to the fore — rapidly coined an appropriate phrase. Conveniently for punsters such as Weinreich, Stumpff sounds like '*stumpf*' which can mean dull or monotonous; '*Bruch*' means a mess; and Feyerabend sounds like '*Feierabend*', which can mean the end of the road. So their phrase comes out something like this, 'Here, everything's a mess (*Bruch*), monotonous (*Stumpf*), the dreaded end (*Feierabend*) — here at the A-d-W.' (A-d-W stands for '*Arschloch der Welt*' — the arsehole of the world!) The solicitous airfield commander encouraged them to stick it out, there at the anus of the globe, with the promise of a certificate of commendation.

Our ground staff followed by rail, making the short journey across the water at Hälsingborg, Sweden being kind enough to allow its neutrality to be breached by letting the train, its trucks sealed and the soldiers unarmed, to cross their territory. And so we were rapidly ready for action. Ingo-Berto soon made friends with the snow, leaping about me when I went on skis from the barrack hut to the operations room. We had handed the donkeys over to Huelshoff's night-fighter boys for safe keeping in Holland.

During the winter months small convoys had passed through almost unmolested under the cover of darkness and of the weather. About the time of the equinox, larger formations had begun to come through. Together with torpedo aircraft and U-boats, we began increasingly to attack them, our capital ships in the northern fjords exercising their threat as a fleet-in-being. But the larger the convoy, the more strongly it was defended by naval vessels, among which were, most dangerously for us, aircraft carriers. The *Victorious* and her retinue usually carried out their sinister business from a position some distance away from the convoy. We had to cater for them too, even though our principal targets were the freighters.

The convoys, in narrow formations of several rows wide and compact in length, with corvettes and fast ships surrounding them and weaving in and out, were iron-spouting and fire-spraying entities. But now and then a single bomber and a single ship would find themselves in dramatic one-to-one combat. A bomber diving and a ship under steam looked to each other like a moving dot in their respective sights. The difference was that on the ship's deck there were numerous heavy-calibre guns pointing at the bomber, while the bomber had only one feeble machine-gun, pointing forward. It seemed to me to be advisable to augment the single machine-gun fitted as standard in the cockpit with two fixed guns that I could fire when I was at the controls of the aircraft. During steep or shallow diving attacks I could fire at a rate of 1800 rounds per minute from each gun, aiming at the upper deck and the flak crews, who were usually unprotected, before releasing the bombs using the same sight. We equipped all our aircraft in this way, and whenever we attacked the convoys in either *Staffel* or *Gruppe* formation each crew was under orders to pick out its allotted steamer and engage it with a brief burst of continuous fire. As long as a ship was busy defending itself, it couldn't provide defensive fire for the others.

But we also had the fighters to contend with. Our rear-firing armament comprised twin MG 17s above and below: because that configuration was insufficient, I proposed that we should fit one of Udet's inventions, the so-called '*Ente*' (duck). This was a rotating, flashing contraption on a long wire that was towed behind the aircraft and was intended either to scare a fighter off or to collide with it. Because this patent device could not be produced quickly enough I fell back on something that was cheaper and readily available in quantity — toilet-rolls. These, allowed to unroll out of the window and then let go, were whisked astern looking for all the world like a wire entanglement, and a pursuing fighter instinctively assumed that they were something sinister and potentially dangerous, because at the speed the fighter would close in they couldn't be recognised as harmless white paper. Anyone who had experienced it didn't find it funny.

We had to use all our ingenuity. The distances we flew over the sea were long, and the water was very cold, approximately zero degrees Centigrade. Anyone who fell into it froze to death, even if he were able to get into his dinghy straight away. Moisture on the body and a stiff breeze of between minus 10 and minus 30 degrees Centigrade killed within twenty minutes, as U-boats that came to the aid of survivors learned. The most important thing was to increase the accuracy of our bombing. Our very considerable operational effort must not be wasted. That entailed increased practice-bombing. I gave the order that, in addition to routine training flights, cement bombs were to be carried on every air test, on all calibration and radio-testing flights, on short trips between airfields, and so on. They were to be dropped and the results recorded on film. Any rock in the sea or any small ice-floe would serve as a target until such time as we had positioned a target float made of empty beer barrels in the fjord. I pretended not to hear the barrage of oaths — 'Always bloody cement bombs!'

Our commanders kept a very careful eye on the convoys as they formed up in the Reykjavik roads, where they were under close observation by long-range reconnaissance aircraft and agents. As they set sail they were allocated PQ numbers. In the Spring we were engaged with PQ 15 to PQ 17, which sailed into the North Sea on their dangerous journeys at intervals of a few weeks. At the beginning of March 1942 we deduced that a convoy had completed its forming-up, because a fast naval formation, an aircraft carrier with an escort of cruisers and destroyers, was sighted heading north by our 7th *Staffel*, which had taken off from Trondheim. We calculated that the British intended to hold our capital ships in check with this flotilla and so provide cover for the convoy.

In his operations room, situated on a hill above the airfield, the *Fliegerführer Lofoten* showed me a large sea chart. The position of the convoy was still unknown. The weather was as usual: snow showers and occasional bright intervals. The enemy warships were following their usual route along the semicircle at the extremity of our range. If they turned away at that time or forced their way through the pack ice we would have no chance, but would have to grind our teeth and turn back. That's no sort of mission for an attack in formation with a large proportion of young crews. But the Admiral Polar Coast and the Commander-in-Chief Surface Forces urgently wanted us to show the enemy our teeth. If we could force the escort to turn back our capital ships could emerge and annihilate the convoy of cargo ships. Most of all the Navy feared the torpedo bombers that would take off from the carrier. They were familiar with the fate of the *Bismarck*.

The *Fliegerfuehrer* showed me the last report he had received from the aeroplane shadowing the naval units; location, course and speed, together with the weather. I thought to myself that if the lone flier was still alive he must long ago have taken cover in the clouds. I suggested that we send out a small form-ation — one aircraft carrying armour-piercing bombs, two carrying medium HE bombs — mainly to assist the reconnaissance.

I took off about noon with a full load of fuel and carrying a 1600-kg armour-piercing bomb. My two crews from the Staff Flight followed close behind me. We gained height above our hollow in the lee of the foothills and flew out to sea above the clouds. My two companions turned off, one to the right, the other to the left, and took up courses parallel with mine, heading west-south-west with a 50-km separation.

Unteroffizier Baumgartner, who for a long time had been trained by Schmetz as his replacement, was flying with me as both navigator and observer. He broke off his education while still at elementary school and volunteered for the armed forces. He knew his job, astro-navigation included, which was most important in those latitudes, where sudden compass variations and radio interference made the life of an aviator difficult.

I was far out over the sea, some 500 kilometres from the coast. The aircraft shadowing the enemy reported that the naval flotilla had turned on to a reciprocal heading, in the direction of their base. Baumgartner plotted, made his calculations and scribbled. He announced that we could make it, if we were prepared to forgo part of our fuel reserve. We had to go below the cloud: we had to be able to see. The foaming sea, of which we had caught only occasional glimpses far below, was covered to a height of 4000 metres with towering cumuli. As we approached the next gap in the clouds, I throttled back and descended: we were down to approximately 600 metres. Here and there black showers reached down to the surface of the sea, but between them the visibility was perfect. We dodged round the perilous masses of water drops and snowflakes that were as big as the palm of a man's hand. We zig-zagged our way ahead. Baumgartner used his compasses, plotted on his chart, measured the drift and calculated.

Alarm! The shadowing pilot hadn't spoken for some minutes. Have they got you, you poor devil? This is a dangerous mission, I thought. I was happy that my adjutant and the third man were keeping their distances. I was worried about fighters, too. What else could have silenced the shadower? He would have kept out of the range of the ships' guns. I rejected instinctively the thought of flying into one of the showers to avoid the fighters. That would be madness. Our de-icing equipment was no match for the Arctic climate. In those polar showers we would have been several hundredweights heavier within three minutes, and the ice would have destroyed our aerodynamic characteristics. And in addition the airscrews would have become so unbalanced that the entire engine-housing would have shook. And the sea was bloody cold! I could imagine how a rubber dinghy with a full crew in it would rotate in all directions in the seething breakers. There, at the end of the world, life was as hard as steel, as cold as ice, and lonely.

Suddenly, through the curtain of showers, I saw the aircraft carrier. She was sailing on the horizon, looking to all the world like a flat chest of drawers. Baumgartner congratulated himself on his accurate navigation. I flew close to a shower. The first, fat snowflakes sped past. Then the sun broke through. I must have been standing out against the lightness of the clouds and the snowfall like an inkblot on a white tablecloth. Look out, men! We might get visitors.

I altered course for where the clouds were casting their shadows. There, too, sheets of snow were driving through the foam. We had to climb to be able to attack. Throttle open, but keep close to the cloud. Perhaps I'll nip in there for a minute if the Hurricanes attack. Have they taken off yet? How many? I glanced to one side, towards a frayed cloud that didn't look as wet, and a little brighter. I would have been very happy to hide in it; but I had to press on. It was becoming brighter, and therefore more dangerous. If there were any fighters airborne they would be up at height, and they'd see me sailing across the white sea of clouds.

We were at about 3000 metres and weren't wearing our oxygen masks. Our necks turned faster than sparrows hopping across a road. What was going to happen? I hadn't a clue how to begin. The warships were hidden again. The British must have seen me by now. They knew what a shadowing aircraft meant. I had been told to show them our teeth. Hadn't I done that already? Hadn't we done enough? The law of inertia carried me forward. In two or three minutes the paths of the ships and aircraft would cross. Abruptly, the mountainous landscape of clouds I was skimming across fell away. I looked down onto a cold, magic sea, bounded to the left by steep, blue-black banks of cloud; to the right, by brilliant white ones that looked as if they were covered in snow.

Suddenly, to our right, out of the kingdom of snow, one steel colossus after the other loomed into the sun-bathed stretch of water, almost as if to plan. The gigantic aircraft carrier followed and the muzzles of her guns had already begun to spit fire in my direction. If only that were all we had to fear! I shouted, 'Look out for fighters!' I looked alternately into the sun and at the warships. I weaved, then flew in a tight curve along the southerly bank of the clouds. To attack then would have been madness. The armada would have blown me out of the air before I had started my dive.

The scene below was a proud one. The aircraft carrier and its close escort of cruisers and destroyers were steaming ahead at full speed, butting into the waves, foam cascading over their bows. The carrier too thrust its bows deep into the sea, so that they were covered in spray. Where are the fighters? Are they waiting down below? Are they worried about the weather and whether or not they can get back again? If so, a *Rotte*[1] of our aces would soon sort them out. The flotilla approached the opposite edge of the break in the clouds. If they reached it they would disappear into hiding. I flew ahead of them and reconnoitred the cloudscape. After a few minutes the cloud became more broken, and here and there I caught a glimpse of the sea below, between the cumuli. I would wait there for the ships. I circled at an economic cruising speed, close to the slopes and peaks of the clouds.

I had been hanging about there for roughly twenty minutes. I told Krahn to broadcast the position of the warships, their courses, speeds, total strength, and the time, all in plain language. He could keep a lookout while he was doing that, and could scan into the sun because he wouldn't need to look at his tables to work out the coding. Every second could have meant the difference between life and death. I sent an R/T message to my other two crews, telling them to go home: I didn't think that they were up to the job. I continued circling, lying in wait. They must emerge from that cloud, just about now. Have they altered course so that they can stay in the protection of the heavy clouds?

There they are! Through a grey veil of cloud, I recognised the slim form of the cruisers looming out of the fog: and then came my most majestic quarry — the mother bird of a flock of hungry predators. The ships didn't see me straight away, but I had them in sight. For a while the advantage was mine. I knew my strengths and could assess my chances. I looked quickly to the left, to the right, astern, ahead, planning where I would race to for cover after my dive if the fighters appeared on the scene. I set the wind velocity and the target's speed and heading in a split second. I was committed — dive brakes out. I was forced up from my seat as the Ju 88 stood on her nose and rushed down on half throttle. I saw the long monster through the veil of cloud that came to meet me. I kept my target in the circle of light. The excitement of anticipation took hold of me as I adjusted my heading slightly to keep the target in my sights and throttled right back. 600 kph! I'm going to go down low. This one is mine.

I raced through the curtain of cloud. Large as life, as if I could almost touch her, the huge vessel stood in front of me. Tracers flashed past the cabin — iron and phosphorus. She was showing her teeth — but I had teeth as well! We were fighting, eyeball to eyeball. I pressed the machine-gun button. The guns rattled, but I couldn't hear a single explosion. All I was aware of was a violent vibration. Then a bang and a clattering noise. My aircraft pulled round to the left. The starboard engine accelerated to full revs: the throttle had no effect. I kicked the rudder bar as far as it would go and applied full aileron with my teeth clenched. I couldn't hold the target any longer. The claxon sounded — 800 metres. Bombs gone! I felt myself being pressed into my seat. We were pulling out. I applied full throttle on both sides and headed for the scraps of cloud. My rear gunner reported that the bombs had missed by ten metres, and he sprayed the ship's decks with his twin machine-guns.

Where were the fighters? Our guns and toilet rolls were at readiness. No fighters? What about my aircraft? It was still flying at full throttle. No change. It'll go *kaputt* if I don't do something! But first, let's get out of here! We'll take a breather behind a mountain of cloud at about 1500 metres. *Unteroffizier* Alles checked the engines. A throttle linkage had been cut. The engine was running automatically at full revs. Solution: climb, then the power will drop back to normal.

We flew our homeward course above the clouds. There would be barely enough fuel, but we'd make it. I couldn't land at full throttle, so I switched the motor off and landed on one engine between the walls of ice. At the end of the runway we stopped and waited to be towed away. I switched off the ignition. Hanke turned on to the runway in a car and stopped near to the Ju 88. Berto jumped out and clambered up the ladder, wild with joy. He knew that it had been a long day for me. He didn't know about the good fortune that we'd been aiming for but had failed to achieve. Luck had been on the enemy's side, but so had nerves and cold blood.

What had become of our 'toothbrush' mission, for which we had interrupted Christmas dinner? Another *Gruppe* from our *Geschwader*, accompanied by the *Kommodore, Major* Bloedorn, had been deployed to a nearby airfield, ready to attack the convoy that was approaching from the mild West, to Banak, a God-forsaken Lapp village in a treeless, tundra-like area at the end of a fjord.

We attacked the next convoy heavily, combining with torpedo bombers and U-boats to do so. Our *Gruppe* won a few 'sinking certificates': the *Kommodore* always took great pleasure in presenting such pieces of paper with due pomp and ceremony.

In April there was a pause in the convoy operations. It happened that at this time *Hauptmann* Dieter Pelz, a former Ju 87 Stuka pilot, was running unit leader's courses in Foggia, Italy, and I hadn't been able to find time to go on one up to that point. With *Kommodore* Bloedorn's agreement I had my Ju 88 fitted with overload tanks for the flight across Europe to the spur on the boot of Italy.

It seemed, to me — and, incidentally, to my fellow aircrew and the *Kommodore* — that it was quite unthinkable not to add a little spice to such a boring flight by coupling it with some sort of supplementary, self-imposed undertaking, and so my first staging point was not Foggia but somewhere even further ahead — Tripoli in North Africa. Why? To prolong the boredom? Of course not. It was to be an experiment. Would the machine fly from the seventieth parallel down to the thirtieth: would it do 4444 kms? Was it just because the distance read as four of a kind, or an even dafter idea? Of course not! If one flew from Norway via Petsamo in Finland on the great circle, over the ice-floes and the loneliness of Northern Siberia down to Manchuria, one would reach our Japanese allies. There was an urgent need for some sort of courier service between us. There had been a number of attempts to find suitable routes by air and sea, but the routes had all been very cumbersome. The *Kommodore* had suggested on one occasion that I might make such a journey as a change from my normal work; but I had dodged the excursions that had been proposed — some of them by U-boat — and had concentrated on finding a more comfortable route. And so the idea of going to North Africa was to discover an easier way to East Asia, which was only a mite further from Tripoli.

So I burdened myself with two overload tanks each carrying 900 litres, so that, with a total of 5400 litres of fuel on board, I could go from the northern end of the world to warmer latitudes, crossing as rapidly as I could over a bad-weather front that stretched from central Norway to the north of Italy. But that was no problem. From Trondheim I flew into cirrus, which let diffused light through, but I could not climb above it. The weather reports that Krahn had received from Oslo, Copenhagen, Berlin and Vienna were wretched, ranging from sleet in the north to continuous rain in the south and a cloud base of 100 metres. I felt sorry for my poor compatriots down below, and was in a most agreeable frame of mind as small crystals of ice ticked against my windscreen — until I noticed that my oxygen was running out. Damn! I'd forgotten that I'd given instructions that half the maximum amount only should be carried when flying operationally, in order to minimise the risk of explosion when under fire. I'd neglected to tell my mechanic that I was doing a special trip. Anything I did, I tended to do there and then, without equivocation. If it had been otherwise I would have issued a printed order with a full distribution list.

I began to gasp very badly. Where were we to go in weather like this, when if we went down we flew into icing? We all sagged tiredly in our seat belts. My head throbbed; inside, it felt like pins and needles; a hangover after a night's boozing felt good in comparison. We had to descend. It was an emergency by any standards.

As I am writing this, something else has emerged from the grey cells of my brain, something long suppressed and shameful that cries out to be aired. I will not keep quiet about it, even though it impinges on my professionalism and the qualities of leadership that have sometimes been attributed to me. Over Norway we had flown the first overload tank dry, and I had switched over to the second one. I gave the order to jettison the empty one into the Kattegat. What happened? The full one dropped! The jettison-circuit had been mistakenly connected arse-about-face. What price my care, my supervision, my leadership now? Two major boobs in one peaceful, smooth job. In fact, it hadn't been necessary to jettison at all; I could have kept the tank on and flown ahead just the same. Because I thought I had dropped the empty one, I tried to fly on the other, which was empty, of course. What rotten workmanship. I had wanted to keep one tank on in any case, so that I could bring fruit back in it from North Africa. It was the end of my African dream, and the end of the East Asia experiment. I barely had enough fuel to reach Foggia — and we all had stinking headaches!

Over the Alps, the high clouds vanished. The tops were at only about 4000 metres, and rather lumpy. We descended below them immediately. We could breathe again. We called Klagenfurt and took bearings on the transmitters at Vienna, Budapest and Milan. We got a good fix. On a westerly heading along the valley with the Karawanken Mountains on our left, I descended through the clouds: ten-tenths with base at 600 metres, as forecast. Horizontal visibility was good.

After we landed, all that we could think about was sleeping — 'perchance to dream'. I knew then how the tormented Hamlet must have felt. All I wanted to do was to shuffle off this mortal coil — my king-sized hangover! I fell asleep in the little officers' barrack block on the airfield and began to dream, but the shrill note of the telephone next to the bed woke me up. 'Guess who's speaking — an old friend!' A bloody old friend, I thought. It was Theo Blaich from the *RB-Strecke* at Berlin-Tempelhof. Together with Giseke, Huelshoff and Rudi Kiel we had sat together over many a glass of beer late into the night at Martius' *Savarin* on Budapesterstrasse. Theo had seen my Ju 88 when it was coming in to land. Any airman who didn't ring up Air Traffic Control to find out what stranger had wandered into that quiet valley in a bomber wasn't fit to fly an aeroplane — only a desk. It was a stroke of luck, he said. It was his wife's birthday and thirty guests from round about were just sitting down to feed their faces. He had just returned from a bombing raid on American bases in Chad. 'What?' I asked. 'From Chad? Are you crazy?'

What price sleep now? That fascinating Black Africa shock cured me within a second. I climbed into my trousers, put on my tie together with its regalia, and heard the car draw up. I managed to stay awake through the celebratory meal, then fell asleep. I came round when it was one in the morning. I lifted my head from my plate to find myself alone at the table in the row of carved, high-backed chairs. From a neighbouring room came a pleasant hum of conversation and soft laughter.

It was true. Theo Blaich had taken off from Tripoli in an He 111 with bombs on board, escorted by several Ju 52s, and had flown deep into the Sahara and landed there with his convoy in order to refuel. A former farmer in Africa, he was fully conversant with conditions there. All along the road that the Americans had built, from Cameroon to Kenya, he had visited, in broad daylight, fuel depots and other installations, and had set them on fire with his bombs. Soon afterwards his very interesting photographs appeared in the German illustrated magazines.

In addition to celebrating Theo's wife's birthday the fact was celebrated that two fellow airmen had chanced to come together over a distance of 80 degrees of latitude or almost 9000 km — Spitzbergen to Cameroon. But that in no way spoilt the evening. On the contrary: it was as if a night of happiness in the midst of the turmoil of the times had been granted to us by a benevolent Heaven. The following morning I reconciled myself to the fact that I had been fated to fail, but I was determined to carry out the experiment on the return run. So down to Foggia and serious duty, the splendid banquet in a pretty room nothing more than a memory. On to the metal bowls filled with spaghetti and Parmesan cheese, the spartan basis of our aircrew fitness training.

Dieter Pelz was a year younger than I was and had a record of considerable success as a *Stuka* pilot on Ju 87s, now converted to standard bombing and the Ju 88. He was the first young man in high authority that I had come across — and, sometimes, into argument with. He was very relaxed, in contrast to our senior officers of the old, imperialist school, who found difficulty in coming to terms with the challenges of technology and the younger generation. Pelz's lectures were graphic, humorous, optimistic, and always thorough as far as detail was concerned. It was a pleasure to be with him.

In using the Ju 88 as a dive-bomber I learned important new technical and tactical methods. From the very beginning Pelz had a more flexible attitude of mind than we stolid exponents of horizontal bombing, who used to approach our targets in tight, rigid formations, rather like the pattern of the Germanic wedge on the battlefield. This equated with the style of leadership of the older officers. But there was a grain of wisdom in it too, and I considered it to be not too unseemly to bring up in a course for unit leaders. If it was possible, I said, to hit a target from height no less accurately than in a dive, then choice should depend on circumstances. I would like to demonstrate. Using the same methods as I had used at Piraeus, and with a Zeiss-Jena specialist on board, I calculated the wind, then we dropped our bombs very accurately from a considerable height. At that time the accurate results which were being achieved on the Eastern Front with the new bomb sight Lofte 7 D were beginning to make an impression. I expressed the opinion that ponderous, lengthy convoys of cargo vessels could be attacked from medium altitude just as well as they could be in a dive. I drew attention to one great advantage, even though most of my attacks had been diving ones: the formation leader only needed to aim accurately and carefully, one pilot only needed to be experienced, the leader of the vic or the *Staffel*. The others — the young ones and the green ones — needed to drop their bombs only when ordered to do so.

Pelz and I, far below the dizzy heights of command, engaged in a fruitful exchange of views sitting together at lunch-time over a bowl of spaghetti or a game of chess. Neither of us imagined — Pelz had very rapid promotion — that, before the year was out, he and I would be working very closely together in Berlin, and that he would be my boss.

One day, when the weather was bad and dive-bombing was impossible, I requested permission to go to Sicily to call on the staff of *Feldmarschall* Kesselring in Taormina. I also wanted to get from my former *Kommandeur*, Evers, then an *Oberst*, the necessary *lire* to buy some oranges: I had spoken to him about it on the telephone in advance. I took a 900-litre fuel tank with me. I didn't bother myself with the question of how the clearing system between the *Luftflotten* and the currencies would be handled. As I was taking my leave from *Oberst* Evers after a meal in the Hotel San Domingo, a smell, suspiciously like that of fresh coffee, began to pervade the corridors and drift in through the windows. It prompted me to raise the subject of the meagre supplies of such delicacies to the troops in the field. Leading on from this, I tried to cadge a few kilograms of the brown beans that had been taken from the English after the fall of Tobruk. In reply my dear *Oberst* said that if I asked for anything else he would kick me in the backside.

As evening approached the weather all around, and particularly in Foggia, became worse. Drizzle, bad visibility and a cloud base of 50 to 100 metres did not deter me from taking off with my load of oranges. Because I had to cross the Apennines I had to fly at an altitude above 2000 metres, but the approach lane to Foggia was flat and so I could let down there on instruments. I intended to show my fellow pupils on the course how this should be done: their jokes about my Africa-East Asia excursion had upset me.

Ground control advised me that the cloud-base was at 50 to 100 metres, so I was rather put out when I was still in the clag at 50 metres. Overshoot. Request confirmation of atmospheric pressure. I had the correct data; but the cloud-base measurement was an hour out of date. A second approach: down to 30 metres. Still no sight of the ground, but I had caught a glimpse of shimmering, green Very lights. According to the latest visibility report I should have been able to see the far boundary of the airfield. My third approach, which I carried out using the Fischer system, which had been taught to me by its inventor at Wesendorf, went perfectly. Having got good bearings, I lowered the undercarriage again and descended carefully, one or two metres at a time. From a height of fifteen to twenty metres I saw the near perimeter lights in front of me and those on the far side glimmered just above them. I throttled back and landed — without sliding in on orange juice! I have often told this story to pilots of Jumbo jets who have carted me off to distant diversion airfields in much better flying conditions. Yes, yes, things are different in wartime, they said.

Off Reykjavik, the next convoy was weighing anchor. Time for me to go back across the Arctic Circle to the noodles and gulasch. I spared myself from the big showpiece of a flight from Tripoli by means of a devastatingly simple consideration. I could calculate, from the fuel consumption between Foggia and Bardufoss, what fuel would be used on the longer flight from Bardufoss to Manchuria. So I had to forgo the prospect of supplying Junkers with a report that would be good publicity for them, and perhaps getting from them in return a silver or even a gold-plated model of the Ju 88.

At Bardufoss, our tonnage-score mounted.

At short notice we transferred to Kemi in Finland, at the northern extremity of the Baltic, which I knew better from its western extremity. Our task was to attack railway traffic which was going to Leningrad carrying war material that had escaped our attentions on the sea-crossing and discharged in Murmansk. Many were the locomotives we saw tumble head over heels into our bomb-craters. It was remarkable how quickly the Soviets cleared away the debris and repaired the railway line. The line had been laid during the First World War by prisoners of war, mainly Austrians. It was quite likely that foreign workers or condemned 'enemies of the people' were doing the work this time.

The German Army Corps located at Kemi had requested a special type of operation. The army geologist of the *Korps* had given it as his opinion that with a few small-calibre bombs the stretch of road running above the river bank along the edge of an area of marshland could be so unsettled that a wave-effect would be created in the marsh which, after rebounding off the firm bank on the far side, would return to the embankment carrying the road with such a force that it would push a considerable length of it into the river.

I listened attentively to what he said, but I could not believe that a few 50 kg bombs would be sufficient. I said I would like to load the aircraft with two 1000-kg bombs, and *Generaloberst* Stumpff, who had a battle headquarters detached in Kemi, agreed with me. Our reasoning was that if the ground-wave did not rebound, we would in any case have destroyed the embankment with our first strike. But the good geologist's only thought was to prove his theory. He said that he had been able to prove it to a modest extent, further north, with a howitzer battery of smaller calibre. Sometimes one had the impression that wars existed for the good of scientists: only when they were in a war did they really seem to get into their stride.

To cut a long story short, we carried out the attack at low level with a total of thirty 1000-kg bombs. We had good cover from our fighters, and our bombs struck deep into the embankment, which was about ten metres above the level of the river. After five seconds, by which time we were over the marsh, a wall of mud, together with lumps of earth and wood, rose up behind us. We made a wide turn and flew over the embankment at a different spot. Our aerial photographs showed that the marsh had poured down like a stream of molten lava into the river valley on a broad front. Whether it was our strike or the wave effect that had caused the phenomenon was never explained satisfactorily. The geologist, of course, had his own opinion.

At Bardufoss we had to mount operations against the next convoy. After that I had to send a *Staffel* to Kemi again, and I chose that of *Hauptmann* Stoerchel. He took off in the early morning, and I went back to bed to catch up on my sleep. I had slept for an hour when the telephone rang: it was *Generaloberst* Stumpff. He shouted at me with such vigour that my pyjama trousers fluttered and my dog began to bark. He said that my *Staffel* had calmly flown more than three hundred kilometres across Swedish territory: church-goers had seen the crosses on their aircraft and had read their squadron numbers. He, Chief of the *Luftflotte*, now had the job of reporting the culprits, the thick-heads, to the *Fuehrer's* Headquarters, and explaining what they were supposed to be doing.

Before I can explain what had happened it is necessary for the reader to know that in the area of the Swedish border a large number of rivers run, virtually parallel to each other, in a south-westerly direction towards the Baltic. Stoerchel had pinpointed the wrong one. The correct river was that which ran directly on the border, but he hadn't identified it as such. So, instead of flying to the left of it, he had flown ten kilometres to the right, well into Swedish territory, in blissful ignorance, sailing over the natives of a dozen villages in their Sunday best, as if on a ceremonial fly-past. It was not until he reached the Baltic that he realised his error.

The written report I submitted went something like this:

> The *Staffelkapitaen* whom I detailed is an outstandingly gifted and experienced navigator. For the flight he carried only the officially issued maps. The lines of magnetic variation printed on the maps have proved to be incorrect. In the area of the Swedish border they are up to 30° in error, as a result of iron-ore deposits on the Swedish side. I request urgently that more up-to-date and accurate maps of Sweden be provided in order that unavoidable border infringements such as this, which both I and my crews much regret, shall not be repeated.

Generaloberst Stumpff was most pleased and said that the Foreign Ministry could send the text to the Swedes without comment.

Later I returned to Kemi, this time with two *Staffeln*. We were able to stop a serious Russian penetration of our Allies' lines. The *Generaloberst* passed on to us a case of German champagne that the Finns had donated. The simply but tastefully uniformed Finnish *Lottas* served our aircrew, and a good time was had by all.

It was a difficult mission. We had to drop our bombs 100 to 200 metres in front of the Finnish lines. The Russians had crawled up to the lines in close order, ready to throw themselves forward when ordered to do so in an attempt to break through a narrow sector, the most passable spot in the monotonous area of miserable landscape made up of mud, water-filled craters and ragged trees, in which friend and foe alike wallowed, filth-covered, in the dirt. In this porridge of a landscape, an eagle-eyed photographic interpreter had made out on the aerial photographs, with the aid of the Zeiss magnifying glass, a red line — the front line. But just how were we to find it precisely within the area? A massacre would have ensued if there hadn't been the bank of a lake, eight or ten kilometres on our side of the Front, over which we were able to fly, take a wind measurement, sight on, and use as a datum point from which to make our bombing run. The *esprit* of Monsieur Rougeron, transformed into deeds by Teutons, hit the 'canaille', as Napoleon had arrogantly called them, in the small of the back. The calculation was easy, but it was hard to feel confident of the result. It was the dilemma of the arrow aimed at the apple,[2] and after it came relief.

I was summoned to the telephone: then I went into my room, sent for my crew and had my aircraft made ready to take off. Once landed in Bardufoss, I asked to be shown the area on the map in which the attack had been made. The wind there was weak and the Gulf Stream was running slowly. It was midnight and still light when I arrived, but the wide area of sea in which I searched for my friend Hanke seemed cheerless — Hanke, who had never believed in victory. He had argued strongly against me in December 1939, between training flights from the icy winter camp at Vechta. Verdun, Flanders, the blockade, he said, all had been historical landmarks and evil omens for us. I had angrily thrown his pessimism, which had its origins in Spengler, back into his face.

Finally, I had snuffled in the musty smell of the 'Decadent West'. When I had finished the book — it was towards the end of the Phoney War, shortly before the Norwegian campaign in April 1940 — I shoved it in front of Hanke's nose, indicating the part where it said '*Ducunt fata volentem, nolentem trahunt*'. 'Look there, pacifist! That says, "The Fates lead him who tries: they betray him who doesn't."' In other words, if you do something, you have a chance: if you do nothing, you're buggered. The only questions are what to do, how, where and when.'

In this case, words were inadequate for such an argument.[3] There are thousands of answers to the questions of existence. Should Germany have played Hamlet in 1939 before the victors, enthroned on gold and tributes, lording it over stolen land and subjugated coloured races? Should she have knuckled under to those who had promised equality but never granted it, those who callously let that stab wound known as the Polish Corridor fester? Should she have resorted to sulking, to clever words, to written protests, eventually to have been sucked into the whirlpool? Should she have renounced enterprises that merited the name of action?

Hanke, my dear friend, you who were as troubled as the Prince of Denmark: how much more difficult must it have been for you to do your duty for the Fatherland than for those who thought less deeply about things but went to war with the wrath of the have-nots, the despised and the deceived. I was one of them: a man full of personal rage.

Hour after hour I combed the sea, and again the next day, thinking of our talks while looking for a tiny rubber dinghy, distress flares and waving arms, electrified with hope a dozen times and each time deflated. Recalling the days in Friedrichroda, Schierke, Breslau, and the icy cold of 1939, when we heard the Christmas Oratorio in the Cathedral in Bremen. His Airedale, his spoilt companion, wandered dismally all day around the barrack hut. He had named him Pax — Peace. It was a long time before curly-haired *Oberleutnant* Dahlmann got him to take food again.

Then came PQ 17, a mighty fleet of freighters, about 40 Liberty Ships of about 7000 tons apiece. We attacked them for several days in a row, first to the west, then via the north to the east. On the first day there was a layer of cloud at about 1000 metres above the convoy. We raced down in formation, diving steeply through the cloud layer, emerging like devils, our machine-guns firing wildly. We descended lower and lower, dropped our bombs and pulled up high into the sun, swiftly leaving the smooth white sheet of cloud below us. Suddenly it was pierced by a dark-coloured cumulus which rose high into the sky as if from a fire-spewing volcano. The Swabian, Herbst, had hit an ammunition ship. The towering cloud was our marker and the signal for the next fierce attack by our last *Staffel*. We returned to base. While they were bombing-up again, we dined on fried trout. Our anglers had been successful in the rapids nearby.

We took off again and flew over the ice floes. In the background, a number of enemy capital ships were lying in wait, but were not coming any closer. We flew with the torpedo bombers and aircraft from Banak. Anything we crippled but didn't sink would be torpedoed by the U-boats; or they would be blown up after their crews had been taken on board another ship, or after they had taken to their lifeboats with the bare necessities for survival. Then the convoy would scatter.

We carried out a sweep over the wide sea. Individual steamers battered their way through the drift ice. We found them. As I flew back from the combat area, one of my pilots called me up: the crew of a steamer had taken to their boats before he had carried out his attack. He had dropped his bombs, and the crew were rowing back to the ship to board it again and sail further on. He asked me whether or not he should fire on the men with his machine-guns. I was at a loss. I tried to picture the situation. What would I do? I couldn't make up my mind. I told the pilot to take a note of the steamer's course, fly back to base and calculate the position of the incident by dead-reckoning.

I telephoned *Kommodore* Bloedorn. He spoke to the Chief of the *Luftflotte*, who then spoke to me. I told him that in my opinion this was not a case of an emergency at sea. The crew had made a tactical evasion and should not be treated any differently from the crew of a scout car who have run away and taken cover from an attack from the air. Such soldiers would be looked upon as combatants, not as wounded or ship-wrecked mariners. The *Generaloberst* was inclined to agree, but said that he would leave the decision to the Fuehrer's Headquarters.

I received the decision from Headquarters about two hours later: the men were to be treated as survivors from a shipwreck. If we had missed with our bombs, that was our incompetence. There was no reason why anyone else should suffer because of us. This was yet another situation that had two sides to it, when you came to consider it: the agony of choice. Soldiers of the whole world, which of you could swear that you would have stayed calm as they climbed the rope ladder, one by one, to bring their guns to bear on your countrymen?

A few days later our signals officer, Holler, came with the adjutant, Sommer, and passed me a telex message with the comment that I was in luck. The blessing vouchsafed me was that the Command Staff of the *Luftwaffe* had ordered me not to fly any more operations against the enemy. Sommer asked how they thought they would be able to punish a drowned man. I was to put the affairs of the *Gruppe* in order and hand over command to *Major* Werner Baumbach, who had been a pilot in the *Adlergeschwader* from the beginning and had made a name for himself as an anti-shipping ace. I was unable to get any information about the colour of pencils I would henceforth have to sharpen and lay on which superior officer's desk. I assumed that up there the pencil system would be even more complicated and colourful than it had been with the General Command.

During the handover there were two happy occurrences. About three weeks earlier one of our crews had been shot down by enemy fighters in the course of an attack on the Murman road, and had been missing ever since. Then the pilot turned up suddenly with the Finns in the very front line, fly-bitten and debilitated. We brought him back to base. His radio operator and his rear gunner had been killed by machine-gun bullets, but he and his observer had waded knee-deep through the flooded woods and the frozen lakes. With their naked hands the two had dredged for fish, which they had eaten raw, and they had chewed on the bark of trees. After a week, the observer had shot himself. *Faehnrich* Arndt had stuck it out.[4] The second occurrence was a happy and celebratory meeting with U-boat crews who put in to Narvik Fjord about a week after the battles. They paraded before the *Admiral* in line ahead. The crews were brought to attention in one rank on the deck, and a short distance apart were their prisoners. At about midnight I was invited to go on board a U-boat. The flotilla set course in the alpen glow and sailed into a narrow, silent fjord at the end of which was moored the luxury liner *King Haakon*, then being used for the rest and rehabilitation of crews who had returned from their perilous missions. First however there was a festive meal, with every delicacy that was to be found in the liner's refrigerators brought to table and there given the *coup de grâce*.

There was another amusing incident. After a delay of more than six months IX *Fliegerkorps*, situated in France, discovered that I had allowed rations, issued for the troops, to be sold for up to twice their price. That smelt of moneymaking. I offered the investigating officer a piece of gâteau with fresh cream — in the mess, not during the hearing, of course. '*Donnerwetter!*' he exclaimed. 'Where did you get that from?' 'From the illegally earned income,' I told him. In Norway we could exchange a glass of cognac, which was in very short supply locally, for a bucket of whipped cream. I had had half the sailors and infantry as our guests, or let them have this or that at very favourable prices. All of my airmen were very satisfied with the arrangement.

Still suspicious, however, he wanted to know how I had been able to know that I would be leaving France and coming up north. That, I said, was very simple: in a war nothing is permanent, neither station nor food nor even life. The only certain thing is that things will soon change, and that is as inevitable as Amen in church. He told me that the way I was talking was not exactly religious, but he spoke rather indistinctly because he was still busy with the *Torte*. He then pointed to a verse that was painted on the wall in large letters:

> *The sword-hilt was his holy cross,*
> *His faith the pistol's ball,*
> *And short and sweet his only prayer,*
> *'The Devil take you all!'*

'Did you write that?' he asked. 'No. It's a crib. How about a cognac?'

Less dangerous but more senior visitors, high-level dignitaries whose hair had turned grey in the gunpowder of Cambrai and Arras, Inspectors and Generals, demanded immediate attention. A number of them who had chosen, or been ordered, to see that things were being done according to regulations in the Arctic Circle, we received with respectful forbearance, even though we considered ourselves to be the technically qualified, modern generation, particularly so when we, prepared as we were to die, saw them climb elegantly into their communications aircraft, sometimes with a fighter escort. Later, Goering was to forbid this practice because it was too dangerous. That followed the occasion on which General Grauert, Commander of *I Fliegerkorps*, was shot down over German-occupied France by British fighters. He had been on an armed shopping expedition, disrespectful young officers said, rather unkindly.

Up there, in the Arctic Circle, Europe's back-of-beyond, suspended between life and death, the young officers developed a precocious Ringelnatz-Morgenstern[5] attitude before the thrones of kings,[6] humorous rather than disrespectful, yet not discarding military proprieties. It was more marked in those fighter pilots who flew alongside us. I was much more military in my attitudes. I often sweated blood when inspecting officers ventured into technical matters and got out of their depth. It was a blessing that the gentlemen in question didn't understand the aircrews' barely concealed irreverences — or, at least, that they pretended not to understand. I never found out and never asked (although I was later in a position to do so) whether or not the General from Paris who bent over our map and screwed in his monocle — monocles were not looked upon kindly by us — understood the disrespectful impersonation that took place. Suddenly, *Oberleutnant* Dahlmann, a fair-haired youngster with a fresh complexion, took out from his pocket a monocle he used to wear occasionally among us for a joke. He screwed it adeptly into his eye-socket, moved his finger over the map and began to prattle on in a nasal voice. I was struck dumb, but I had to play along with him. Until then I had always been fortunate to have in my senior front-line superiors, *Generals* Felmy and Kesselring, Coeler, Harlinghausen and *Generaloberst* Stumpff, leaders whom I could trust completely with my pilots. Respect, too, grows with experience. I had come to learn with the passage of time that a very great deal of staff work had to be done before the first aircraft could get airborne.

The time for my departure grew nearer. Our medical officer, Dr Coburg, showed his interminably long, eight-millimetre film yet again, covering all our theatres of war from the very beginning to date. The dead lived again, as if telling us, 'Stay just as you are now, friends. Just as we once were.' If we hadn't had Dr Coburg, so much would have faded away, even as we were fighting. He was a fighter himself. In defiance of orders he would secretly wangle his way on to operations with blatant forms of bribery, and fly as an air gunner. When I caught him at it he replied that he would have to apply for official permission to fly operationally. How else, when there was a maximum effort on, could he refuse to pass a man with a temperature of over 100°F unfit for flying? He had — or pretended to have — angina, and said he wanted to set a good example. He took his duties, both medical and patriotic, very seriously, and he explained his ruling by saying that the warmer you were and the higher your temperature when you fell into ice-cold water, the better it was for you because you had reserves of energy, a statement that had slanderously been attributed to myself.

We flew a number of bitter operations. Neither doubt nor despair helped the time to pass more quickly. What did we feel as we flew our course from take-off to action, a course along which lurked that monster, Danger, reaching out to seize us? None of us rightly knew, certainly not from ourselves, even less from others. Was there an element of acceptance here, of faith there, of great strength in some, or discipline and a sense of duty, or self-control and clenched teeth in those who were afraid? Or a mish-mash of all those feelings as time was running out, ever-changing, as we moved inexorably to an end we dreaded but never believed would happen to us? Was it a dream, was it a child's game, calling ourselves Goodies and Baddies in a fools' world on Earth's roundabout, in the canopy of ice above the Pole? Begone, fantasy! The only good was what helped us to survive. And that, my dear friend on the other side, means that you must draw the short straw.

We were a rough lot, intent on suppressing any manifestation of weakness, determined not to philosophise overmuch but to present to the world a simple, hard-man image. The officers had to be strong in order to return the walking wounded to their feet. On one occasion, when it was said that one of the pilots had jettisoned his bombs outside the flak zone during an operation against England — his own crew were very upset — I instructed the pilot to fire off a Very cartridge over the target in future so that I could satisfy myself as to his position. Not until he had performed this unpleasant task half-a-dozen times did I grant his application to be posted to a training unit.

Even volunteer aircrew sometimes underestimated what they were letting themselves in for. I gave a few days' special leave to one pilot who had shown cowardice of a different sort, and told him that he should go to his home town and play the big hero there to the best of his ability. He didn't go, and I didn't allow him to fly operationally again. Living with danger was a strange thing. One couldn't think straight. Sometimes, gallows humour was a compensation. When our tame impersonator, Paul Hecking from the Lower Rhine, burst into joyful song, *à la mode de* Mozart, when we were in the thick of things — 'Only a cowardly knave despairs' — the world was suddenly sunny again and hearts were light. And thus many struggled with themselves, secretly, inwardly, successfully: while some were obviously unhappy but held the line nevertheless. For us, the high-jump bar was always set very high; but we all reached it. When we had struggled to overcome it, we looked back at our earlier efforts with satisfaction. We achieved much, and in our battles over the northern seas our losses were comparatively light.

I never invoked courts martial or other disciplinary penalties to encourage operational readiness. With the exception of our over-willing cavaliers in France, I never punished anyone formally. It was my view that aircrew, who had all volunteered for military service, could be led only by means of setting them a moral example day in, day out: and that a catalogue of privileges and disprivileges should be enough to weld individuals into a fighting community. I believed that worthwhile praise only came in the form of medals and small concessions that made life just that bit easier. I found particular pleasure in granting unexpected special leave to a man or to a crew. The *Kapitaene* did the same, as I myself had done when a *Kapitaen* and as leader of my Headquarters' *Schwarm*.

I had also occasionally had to act in the disciplinary role of guide in affairs of the heart, when the cool self-possession of the young Norwegian maidens had begun to melt before the warm advances of our fliers, like the snow in the inhabited valleys and when the merry month of May wafted marriage applications through my window and deposited them on my desk. What was one to do when there was a *Fuehrer's* Order that insisted — Nordic races or no Nordic races — that German women should not be left on the shelf? And so I tried a policy of deterrence: warning each individual that the marriage would soon founder, mentioning postings and their resulting separation, grieving widows, the patriotic duty to put all one's effort into winning victory — setting myself up as a shining example. If all of that had no effect, I ran marriage down, making it — I freely admit — sound vulgar. Any street-sweeper, I said, could marry and beget children: we airmen were the *élite*. It would have met with disapproval in the highest of quarters that I was thereby throwing the German child out with the bath-water, so to speak. Thank God there was no Romeo among our aircrew, no Juliet among the Norwegian maidens, ready to drink, one after the other, from the poisoned chalice. Faced with a crisis of that nature I would have granted special permission very rapidly.

Day by day, my magnificent, shattering experiences in that splendid Nordic world drew closer to their end. Then they were all there, my men, on parade. I took my leave from each of them with a handshake. We broke up into a crowd almost as wide as it was long and marched down the runway, through the barracks area, through the domestic site, the Norwegians and the Russian prisoners working on the roads looking on in bewilderment and asking themselves what sort of a strange procession was passing. At the airfield my Ju 88 was standing, ready for take-off. Together with my crew I climbed in to head for Berlin-Staaken. Then the whining Berto was let loose and he clambered swiftly up the ladder. Usually when I was taking off on an operation he had to watch sadly. Now he was going on a comfortable pleasure-trip, and he could stand in the front of the cockpit and watch everything passing by below. He had never been able to understand why things down there went past so swiftly. He would frequently turn to me, looking as if he was asking me to explain.

We were all on board and the propellers could start to turn. The flag that we used to place at the start of the runway up here in the North when we were taking off on operations was fluttering proudly in the wind. Like me, it was taking its leave from the *Gruppe*. At long last I had promised it to my former War Academy comrade, *Hauptmann* Kuehl, *Kommandeur* of *III./KG 4 'General Wever'*. Everybody on the ground waved. I waved back.

A Special Order, issued by the *Kommodore* on 19 July 1942, contained the following paragraph:

> *In losing its Kommandeur III Gruppe is, at the same time, losing its oldest comrade, who has belonged to the Gruppe for about six years as a young pilot, as Technical Officer, as Staffelkapitaen and, finally, as Kommandeur. His path through these long and portentous six years had taken him through battle and victory, with the death of some of his best and oldest comrades at the side of that path. Just as this period will remain indelibly in his heart, so he will remain in our memories. He is now going to a position in which his wide experience will be used to the greatest effect.*

Notes

1 Rotte: a tactical pair of aircraft.
2 'The arrow aimed at the apple': in German 'Apfelschuss', a reference to William Tell.
3 Goethe, Faust Act 1, Part 1: 'Mit Worten laesst sich trefflich streiten, Mit Worten ein System Bereiten'.
4 Faehnrich: Officer Cadet.
5 Ringelnatz: see Chapter Five, note 6.
6 Morgenstern: Christian Morgenstern (1871-1914) was also a humorous poet, and was known for his so-called Galgenlieder (gallows songs).
7 'Before thrones of kings': a reference to 'Maennerstolz vor Koenigsthronen' ('The pride of men before thrones of kings') — Schiller.

Chapter Ten
At the Top,
July 1942-July 1943

The Crimea is taken. We advance towards Stalingrad and the Caucasus. German and Italian submarine successes in the North and South Atlantic. The Battle of El Alamein. British and American forces land in Algeria and Morocco. The encirclement of the German troops at Stalingrad. The Western Allies demand unconditional surrender.

I arrived at *Gruppe T* of the *Luftwaffe* Headquarters Staff as one of six comparatively junior officers, four aircrew, one from the Flak and one signals officer, all with Front-line experience, all very obviously a different breed from the red-trousered, grey-haired gentlemen of the Quartermaster General's Department and *Abteilung 1c*, the task of which was to assess the enemy's potential. Within *Gruppe T* I had to take over the 'Bombers' desk from Staff *Major* von Ditfurth, who was transferring to the Quartermaster General's Department.

The functional responsibility of the *Gruppe* was designated as technical/tactical requirements, which meant that, on the basis of our particular experiences and insights, we were to conceive innovations and improvements which were then to be passed to the *Generalluftzeugmeister* (Director General of Air Force Equipment), to be developed and put into production if possible. We were to work in conjunction with the individual inspectorates of the *Luftwaffe* — Fighter, Bomber, Transport, Marine, Flak, Signals, etc.

My first action was to scour my safe for old plans and ideas that had been formulated under Department 1 of the General Staff. It was only later that the Technical/Tactical Section had been made independent as *Gruppe T* under Staff *Oberst* Storp who like his brother, my bombing strategist in Spain, had come from the Navy and taken part in many convoy battles. In my search I came across the draft of the paper that I had been detailed to write by the General Staff in 1941. A wondrous encounter! I began to work on the subject of bomber equipment.

In Wildpark-Werder on the Havel, in the old Imperial hunting estate, surrounded by beautiful countryside and in the height of summer, we set about germinating our ideas, our windows permanently open to help things along. Once a week Storp drove with me to Berlin to the marathon meetings chaired by *Feldmarschall* Milch, Director General of Equipment. Many clever people, aircraft constructors, engineers, professors, civil servants and officers, brought their wares to market, at which there was only one customer — the German Reich, represented by the Field Marshal. He enjoyed his role: 'You, *Herr*

Professor Messerschmitt, want to sell me this Me 209, but it will only do 650 kph. I think I'd rather have the one *Professor* Heinkel's made — it can fly two hours longer at the same speed. But what am I saying? Here's *Professor* Dornier's Do 335, which can fly 100 kph faster!' So it went on: weapons, bombs, radio sets, anti-aircraft guns, rockets; every sort of equipment was evaluated. I used to return to Wildpark at night with other people's brilliant ideas in my head, and going to sleep, which had been no trouble at all in the front line, became harder and harder for me.

Staff *Oberst* Storp fell victim to differences of opinion between the Director General of Equipment and the Chief of the General Staff, Jeschonnek, and more often than not thereafter I sat in the exalted circle as the sole representative of *Gruppe T*. I soon noticed that the Field Marshal treated me very civilly, probably because I usually used to give him my strong support, or at least didn't contradict him; or perhaps because he wanted to prove to me that he had no in-built objection to a representative of the Headquarters Staff.

Later individual members of *Gruppe T* were sent to each appropriate Inspectorate — I went to the *General der Kampfflieger*, the Bomber General. At first this was *General* Fink, then Staff *Oberst* Peltz, then *Oberst* Helbig, and finally *Oberstleutnant* Baumbach. My function, technical/tactical requirements, remained unchanged, as did my participating in the Director General of Equipment's conferences.

It did not take me long to form my own opinion on a number of important questions. However, given the incident of *Oberst* Storp, it did not seem advisable to express myself too loudly until I had gained the confidence of senior officers. Soon the Field Marshal would often ask me for my opinion on certain questions. So I, a mere *Hauptmann* in the *Luftwaffe*, got to know senior officers — the Chief of Staff of the *Generalluftzeugmeister*, *General* Vorwald; *General* Galland; *General* von Axthelm from the Flak; our famous aircraft constructors; and the Minister, Albert Speer. There were occasional discussions in very small circles, even *à deux*.

As I crept deeper into exalted circles, my Front-line officer's nose, not yet dulled by the dust of files, sensed that there was something going on that was not quite right. Was it me being a know-all again? I couldn't help my nose. Events to which I did not, or could not, contribute, would show whether what I set out to do was for the better. I must place on record that my proposals, which I considered to be of burning importance, were put into effect to a very small degree only, because I had been too weak, too restrained by reason of my military upbringing, too polite and too easily swayed to put them across strongly. Sometimes I let off steam in the wrong place or at the wrong time and offended others, with the result that I was shown the door. In particular, I am speaking of the priority between bomber and fighter production.

In the Summer and Autumn of 1942 there was a general call for more fighters. I had taken over the Bomber Programme from Storp and Ditfurth, and that too had envisaged an increased demand. But we all knew that resources were not infinite. Every branch of the *Wehrmacht* was fighting for priority in the allocation of men and materials. Within the *Luftwaffe*, indeed within all the armed forces, there was a pecking-order among the various branches. For me, having been a bomber pilot, the basic question was whether anything could be diverted from other sources in order to make good the shortages that I had become aware of when at the Front through both my personal experiences and those of my comrades.

To that end I considered it necessary to make sense of the flood of figures in our production planning, figures which to me, as a simple front-line commander, had seemed so impressive when I had commenced to work on the Staff. The first questions were: What was the enemy doing? What was he planning? What was he achieving in the same period of time?

I enquired at Department 1c, just a few steps away from our hut, what information they had concerning British production of bombers and fighters. What I learned from *Oberstleutnant* Dewitz worried me a great deal. He said that in a year the Western Allies were producing a maximum of 29,200 twin-engined or four-engined aircraft, against which our own fighter production figures of 10,000 a year appeared rather pathetic: even if planned increases were achieved it would still lag behind. Therefore it could well be that our industry, and in particular the aircraft industry, would be smashed, or at least damaged, before the increased production both of fighters and of bombers that we were planning had even begun.

In any event there were good grounds for fearing that our increased fighter production would be overwhelmed by the enemy's increased number of bombers: in other words, that we would lose the race, and that the 10,000 fighters we hoped to produce would never go into action against the enemy's total of 29,000 bombers. The figures applicable to both sides would have to be translated into front-line strengths, but in the process the ratio would remain the same. As I saw it at the time, this danger could only be neutralised by changing the priorities in production. In the section I was the officer responsible for bombers, and so I suggested that the bomber fleet should be cut by two thirds and that the production capacity thus released should be used to build fighters. Only the remaining one third of the bombers should be further developed and improved.

The 29,000 Allied bombers were roughly divided between the USA and Great Britain, and each period of 24 hours was divided similarly into day and night. But it could not be ruled out that one fine day the entire Western bomber fleet might attack in concert. In addition the attackers would be able to call on cover from their forecast fighter production of 19,000 per year, giving a total capacity of 49,200 aircraft from which to build their assault force; against which, believe it or not, our side would be able to deploy a front-line strength of 10,000 fighters. It did, in fact, come to this tragic position eventually: a ratio of five to one, and even worse.

In 1942 I discovered that this worst-case situation had not been considered in the planning of aircraft production. The war in the air was looked at from the point of view of a strict division between day and night. Not only was equal priority overall given to the production of bombers and fighters, but fighter production itself was divided into day and night. The day fighters and the night fighters looked upon themselves as having equal rights, while remaining independent. If I considered the air war by night alone, the British had an annual production potential totalling 15,500 twin- and four-engined bombers, while our night-fighter capacity totalled only 1700 per year. This comparison was disturbing. It was clear that the Inspector, *General* Kammhuber, recognised and was demanding that an increase in production was essential, as was the introduction of new systems of fighter control.

An even worse situation would come about if the USA and the British combined for night operations. Then the total Western production of 29,200 bombers would be faced by only 1700 night fighters. In my view, this adverse balance represented a real danger. We had already become aware of the argument between the British and Americans as to whether precision targets should be attacked by day or by area bombing carried out at night. Today we know that US General Fred Anderson flew on two RAF night raids, against Hamburg and Essen, to evaluate the feasibility of Flying Fortresses participating in night attacks. Anderson was apparently a level-headed man who reckoned with the possibility that reverses in the course of daylight attacks could compel the bombers to be used for night attacks, as had happened to us after the high losses we had suffered in the Battle of Britain in 1940.

One expects to hear from one's leaders what they would propose to do when faced by a serious threat. If they skirt around a threat blindly and without planning, and afterwards look back and curse their bad luck, that is a matter for shame.

It was a matter for great concern that if my conclusions were correct not only was our night-fighting capacity against the British hopelessly inadequate, but also, at the same time, that our day-fighter force could be condemned to inactivity. Our day-fighter crews were not trained for night flying and did not have any ideas of how they might operate in the dark. On the other side of the coin: if the British decided to swing their mighty hammer by day alone, how would, or could, our twin-engined night fighters counter them?

And so the following conclusion was forced upon me: the three elements of the *Luftwaffe* that put the greatest demands on the production of aircraft — bombers, day fighters and night fighters — were each demanding a higher proportion than could be granted to them within the foreseeable future. Because the Chief of the General Staff had neglected to set priorities or demand sacrifices, the onus was put on the Director General of Air Supplies to consider their demands. I tried to form a clear picture for myself, and I put down my thoughts on paper. Not only should the escalation of bomber production be stopped, but the existing bomber capacity should also be ruthlessly cut, and from the capacity so released fighter production should be greatly increased. My proposal envisaged that seventy fighter *Gruppen* could be formed from thirty-five bomber *Gruppen*, and a further nine fighter groups could be formed from nine *Stuka* groups.

That was not a betrayal of the bomber arm. It was not my job to put the special interests of any one element above the general interest as I perceived it. Further I was convinced that my former bomber crews would fly a single-engined fighter or a fighter-bomber with the same enthusiasm. I even believed that with such aircraft bombs could be dropped onto targets more accurately, and that the pilots would have a better chance of getting back home. Admittedly, to drop the same weight of bombs they would have to make two trips. My solution was, therefore, a multi-purpose aeroplane, a single-seater that could fight or bomb by both day and night.

When I spoke officially to high-ranking members of the Night-Fighter Staff in Autumn 1942, in the course of a discussion of a provisional paper on armaments, I was told, in connection with my single-seater proposal, that I, the cobbler — i.e. the bomber man — should stick to my last. Further discussion went by default because the Section Chief, Staff *Major* von Ditfurth, gave me a sharp kick on the foot under the table. Even in the Day-Fighter Section my fine *exposé* was dismissed as a naïve fallacy. In connection with my proposal, I had already been able to persuade the optics firm Steinheil in Munich to fit a bomb sight in an Me 109 to help to overcome the restricted view, a sort of periscope, and I tried it out one Sunday when I dropped cement bombs on the airfield at Oberweisenfeld.

It was in fact not a very propitious time to get anything far-reaching accepted, because our victories were generating general optimism. The British had been thrown out of Dieppe, our troops were deep inside Russia and elsewhere within Africa and Europe. Sometimes I asked myself whether or not all our problems could be solved by means of a decisive victory, because then politics would have the main say.

But my doubts persisted. I could not bring myself to be reassured by the words, 'The *Fuehrer* will know what to do!' Would any harm be done if we did pursue the multi-purpose idea — of both machine and man — and then either politics or a miracle weapon proved decisive? No harm would be done. It is always right to take precautions. I tried to make my plan attractive to the bomber men as well as to the Quartermaster General, *General* Kleinrath, and his colleague, Staff *Oberst* Eschenauer, by pointing out that our latest fighters would not be wasted if they were equipped to carry bombs, because they could be put to better use than our clapped-out medium bombers in support of the Army in the East: for attacks on Malta, for blockading the Straits of Sicily and for defending an invasion. If range should be necessary, I said, the remaining third of the bombers, drastically improved, could be used.

I did not hear any objections proving my proposal to be fallacious. What was against it was an unwillingness to present our competition with the enemy in the form of a graph, time against production, and to see the danger depicted therein. Because I considered my proposal highly important in the light of my specialist knowledge, and when I saw that it was having no effect, I had an extra copy made of the Top Secret paper and I have kept it to this day. I will quote from it:

> *Headquarters, 22 11 1942*
> *The General der Kampfflieger considers the reduction in the potential that has hitherto been made available to the Bomber Force to be very alarming and disadvantageous, and that for various reasons a wide-ranging reorganisation of the equipment programme is necessary as a matter of urgency . . .*
> *It is already clear that by the year 1945 the medium bomber, in utilising its range of penetration, will suffer losses that cannot be made good from industrial production . . .*
> *On the other hand it is possible, by introducing a basic type of aircraft for both the bomber and the fighter arm, to deploy force in the greatest strength, and so to be equal to the operational situation then pertaining . . .*

After this had been duly acknowledged by Headquarters Staff 1c at the beginning of 1943, I produced figures in order to underpin my concept, briefly in graphic and printed form:

> *Secret: 25 03 1943*
> *Making war by despatching bomb-carrying aircraft against the enemy has in the long term one prerequisite, that production sources remain intact and capable of sustaining this form of military activity . . .*

Defence against air attack through 1943 and into 1944 is not secured . . .
The comparison (in the diagram) is however only theoretical, in that its
validity is confined to a situation in which Germany on the one hand and
Great Britain together with the USA on the other hand are the sole
combatants. Both sides, however, are fighting against third parties, Russia
and Japan. If it is assumed that in 1943 the greater part of the enemy's
action will be directed against Germany, while half our forces are tied up in
Russia, there emerges a comparison of forces even less favourable to us
than the one shown above . . .
Not 10,000 against 29,000, but about 5000 against 20,000 . . .
The huge shortfall in night fighters into 1944 can be remedied by operating
day fighters at night, backed up with all possible technical, organisational
and training support.

It was clear that my oral and written submissions to the higher spheres of
responsibility were nothing but sound waves and waste-paper basket fodder
respectively, because nothing of importance could be changed within the Fighter
and Bomber sections, and so I tried to destabilise the pyramid from below. I
asked Staff *Oberst* Eschenauer of the 6th Department in the Kurfuerst Park if I
could have a fighter aircraft, and he commendably made one available to me
at Berlin-Staaken. *Generaloberst* Jeschonnek, with whom he regularly had
discussions, had turned him down flat when he had brought up the idea of cutting
the bomber force by two thirds: how, he had asked, would one be able to
penetrate as far as Alexandria or the Russian hinterland? But Eschenauer had
read my paper and agreed with it, so he let me have the aeroplane and kept his
fingers crossed for me.

And so in the evenings I used to tear along the Avus[1] in my staff car as far as
Staaken, where I used to get airborne. The Flak cooperated by letting the searchlights join in the game to pick out an He 111 which was acting as target so that I
could latch on behind it and carry out flying and target practice. This would not
have been possible if the Commander of the 1st Flak Division, *General* Schaller,
had not given his agreement to this unorthodox undertaking. His 1a, Staff
Oberstleutnant Herzberg, a clear-thinking and very conscientious man who used
to study the Japanese language during his free time on watch, gave us his strong
support.

It did not discourage me that at the beginning the searchlights picked me up as
frequently as they did our friendly bomber. I looked forward to an improvement.
After a few practice flights I said that I would like to take part in a live defensive
action. I suggested that the flak should be restricted to a height of 6000 metres, so
that there would be a clear space above it for me, but the *General* refused. In
heated discussion in the *Division* offices on Fasanenstrasse he said that the
Befehlshaber Mitte (Commander Central Area), *Generaloberst* Weise, had
ordered unrestricted fire — that was a *Führerbefehl* (*Fuehrer's* Order). If I wanted
to continue despite that, then that was my choice.

I wanted to continue. I thought that if I were prepared to dart in and out among
a large number of bombers, then the flak should also be prepared to be less
concentrated. but things turned out differently. A lone stranger was coming our
way, a probing Mosquito, and a hundred guns would open up on it, and on me at
the same time. I rang up, and what I got in the way of an answer was not

comforting. 'You fly if you like: we're not going to stop shooting for anyone.' I heard what they were saying. That was in April 1943, when single Mosquito nuisance-bombers replaced the heavy, slower machines during the brighter, shorter nights, with the aim of preventing the Berliners from sleeping.

Time was getting on. I tore out to Staaken in my car just as a Mosquito was reported to be over the Dutch coast, climbed into an Me 109, or FW 190, and taxied out, the Berlin Flak warned off by telephone, as the fast bomber had reached the Weser. I took up my waiting position between Nauen and Potsdam at about 11,000 metres, on the edge of the searchlight zone that covered Berlin and its environs to a diameter of approximately 60-70 kilometres. Everything depended on the large, two-metre searchlights on the edge of the zone picking up the high-flying, wooden bomber in good time. Then I would be able to clobber him. Suddenly a large searchlight slanted high up towards the west. I made for it right away. Swiftly it went to the vertical, a second one joined it, and then a third.

There's my bright fellow! I turned in. Too late! Stupid fool! I'd miscalculated: I was 800 metres behind him. I opened the throttle wide, pushed the stick forward and descended to his height of 9000 metres. I was hardly gaining on him. Below, an ever-increasing, fire-belching hurricane erupted. The flak, which had been waiting for the right moment, was firing in regiment strength. I thought, 'When that lot gets up here, it's goodnight bomber!' But he knew the game. He turned into a curve before the first welcoming salvo bursts could reach him, but I was able to cut off the curve smartly. I was surprised how big his aircraft seemed, how bright. All the searchlights in the vicinity were drawn to the twin-engined crate as if by magnetism. It appeared that my smaller mass didn't cause any reaction on the ground. I crept behind him in the dark, swerving, hopping over cotton-wool balls — there could still be splinters in them — swiftly coming up on him, getting nearer and nearer. That'll do! I aimed, determined to turn him into a heap of plywood. I pressed the button. Flashes appeared before my eyes: my tracer was blinding me. The belts should have been loaded with night tracer. Bad planning! Stupidity! Inexperience!

My eyes adjusted themselves rapidly: I could see again. He was still in the cone, but they'd got me also; I was coned by our searchlights. The searchlight crews couldn't see that I was following him. Once they picked something up, they stuck with it. Through the milky air my eyes remained fixed on the Mosquito. He was twisting and turning more wildly than he had been. I made a tight turn and was free, in the dark. By then the British pilot knew that something he hadn't reckoned with was happening. Flak — OK, it was a nuisance, but flak and a fighter at the same time — that was not so good. The salvos concentrated close to the nocturnal intruder. The splinters weren't getting any less. I kept on after him. Suddenly the flak stopped its predicted fire and began a barrage, blocking his way and enabling me to get in closer. That's what I call cooperation!

Again I turned inside him, got closer, and closer still, until I was looking down on him. I saw him weaving, and again I opened fire. Another miss — no flames; no splinters. I hadn't given enough deflection. I closed in. Flak bursts sailed past me. Then the Mosquito was in darkness, leaving Berlin behind. The searchlights were behind him, and behind me. Cobbler, why didn't you stick to your last?

I asked myself the same question when I climbed out of my machine and the ground mechanic found a big splinter-hole in the side of the aircraft about a metre behind my seat. I was very quiet. Is it sensible to get into this business, to take other men in with me, to fly in masses into the storm? It will have to be better organised, I think to myself.

Often, waiting to take off on a practice flight or an operation, I had shared a meal with the mechanic and with my driver. They were both from Berlin and had lived through the air raids on the blocks of flats. Both had asked why the fighters didn't go up while the bombers were twisting and turning, for endless minutes, in the searchlight beams, dropping their bombs indiscriminately. I had watched it happening many times. The frightful spectacle of those terror attacks hurled one question into the faces of the sorely afflicted below — why isn't there someone up there? The three of us said nothing about the shrapnel damage. 'Keep your mouths shut, understand?' '*Jawohl, Herr Major.*'

Next morning the marathon session with the Director General of Air Supplies began at 1000 hrs as usual. I had already told the General's Staff Officer, *Oberst* von Lossberg, of the course of events. The *Feldmarschall* was also informed, and at last, after I had been pestering him for months, he faced up to the problem. He said that I couldn't tell him that I had caught up with a Mosquito, let alone fired on it. That wasn't even possible by day, because the wooden bombers couldn't be seen on the radar tubes and the fighters couldn't be directed on to them. He said that if what I had said was true, he wouldn't have to produce the He 219 that *General* Kammhuber had been demanding. What had occurred didn't result in any further help for me on his part. It was hard for him to dismiss the assessment that had been put to him by the Inspector of Night Fighters, which was that collaboration between fighters and searchlights could not prove successful.

But behind the failure *General* Galland perceived success, and he took a gamble by ensuring that a few more fighters were diverted for me so that I could begin to recruit pilots who were both suitable for and willing to do the job. I got the first recruits from the Pilots' School at Brandenburg-Briest, where *Major* Fruhner, my Chief Instructor at Ludwigslust, ruled the roost. During the daylight hours my recruits carried out their duty schedules as flying instructors, but towards evening they could be found at Staaken, practice-flying or sitting in their cockpits ready to scramble. All of this was completely unofficial and based on a personal, non-binding discussion. Two or three young officers from Staff jobs had also joined. Among them was one who told me that he had the permission of his superior officer to do so. I learned the truth of the matter only after he had shot his first bomber down: he didn't want to keep quiet after that!

We were all filled with optimism and enthusiasm. Ten to twelve volunteers, all qualified military pilots. We practised throughout May and June, but no-one came along against whom we could test ourselves.

In the meanwhile the Inspector of Night Fighters had been demanding not only more, but better, aeroplanes, including the He 219, a twin-engined, two-seater which had a nose wheel, an excellent field of view from the cockpit, and was very fast. It was intended mainly to take on the Mosquito. *General* Peltz had the job of deciding whether the aircraft was to be built or not. He was instructed to test the aircraft and produce a report on it. Peltz referred the matter to me: I had in any case begun to think about it. He told me that I was not to show my report to anyone, but that he was to be the first to read it and show it to Goering. I was, and was expected to be, independent and unbiased. I rang up the Inspector in Holland and told him that I had been instructed to go to the Heinkel Works in Rostock to test-fly the aircraft. He reminded me very emphatically that he needed the aeroplane, and that I had a great responsibility to the German people. That should have been the end of the conversation, but I left it to his discretion whether he might send a trusted and experienced night-fighter pilot who could give his opinion independently of me.

At approximately midday one Sunday I landed in Rostock-Marienehe, where I was greeted by one of our most brilliant night-fighter pilots, *Major* Streib. We were both received most warmly by *Professor* Heinkel and his construction team and invited to a lunch of roast goose — obtained strictly legally, the *Professor* assured me in reply to my delighted question. After the meal I thanked him and told him that I hoped his aeroplane would fly as well as his goose had tasted.

The two types of aircraft that had been most used until then for night fighting, the Ju 88 and the Do 217, had been developed from basic bombers of the same designation. They were equipped with items that would have been seen as unnecessary or a nuisance in a fighter. The Me 110, which was basically a *Zerstoerer* — a heavy day fighter — was no longer suitable for various reasons. The He 219 was light on the controls, had a lot of power and excellent visibility, which was very important for night flying. After I had tried all the appropriate aerobatic manoeuvres I handed over the controls to *Major* Streib so that, together with the *Professor* and the other gentlemen, I could watch the aircraft from the ground. At the end of the demonstration I declined to give an opinion, although I was asked very politely for one.

The *Professor* mentioned casually that there was an He 177 ready for take-off, and asked me whether I would like to fly it. He knew me from our meetings with the *Feldmarschall*, and knew that I was a bomber pilot. Of course I wanted to have a go. I went on board with a flight mechanic (in those days there was no great fuss made about converting on to a different type), and took off in the giant, four-engined machine, the all-up weight of which was approximately thirty tonnes. I was not barred from speaking of the aircraft, and I gave my view with conviction and enthusiasm. In my report on the He 219 I included a comment to the effect that Mosquitos could also be combatted by single-seat aircraft, a bold assertion at the time, but one which was to prove to have been well-founded. For *Feldmarschall* Milch that was grist to his mill; but for the Inspector of Night Fighters it was a bitter pill to swallow. One can't please every individual, only a cross-section, and the way to do that is only through the truth.

Back to Berlin. After I had done some more practice with my little band I suggested to the Flak Division that we should move west, because the Ruhr area would be the target of the bombers during the short nights. The move caused my pilots some difficulties because of their routine duties. In addition I had to obtain the agreement of the Flak Commanders in the West; and so I had to go through cursed official channels. At the end of these channels sat *Generaloberst* Weise, Commander Central Region, to whom all the Air Districts, together with the ground defences, were subordinate. *Oberstleutnant* Joachim Helbig, my former comrade-in-arms in the Mediterranean area, put the views I had expressed into a written submission and was ready to go along with them.

In Berlin-Dahlem irreconcilable opinions were put forward one after another. Nevertheless it was a discussion, an exchange of views, and until then there had been no urgent call for such a meeting between the Flak and Night-Fighter Staff, simply because the latter operated in advanced areas and left the job of defending the homeland to the former, a division of responsibilities that militated against fruitful discussion. Helbig gave the introductory address, referring particularly to the need to protect Berlin because the Senior Staff were located there — which was very clever of him — as well as the foreign embassies, the concentrated industry and the population.

Restricted flak fire? No! thundered the *Generaloberst*: he had 700 heavy guns under his control and he wouldn't think of silencing even a few of them for the sake of a handful of single-seat fighters. Flak restriction above 6000 metres? The mass of four-engined bombers flew higher than that, so he might as well send his flak crews home: that was what it came down to. I could see my hopes slipping away. I suggested that we should give the Flak complete freedom to shoot up to 7000 metres, then our pilots would have a small space in which they could breathe freely. Now and then, they could swoop down and pick off a bomber. The *Generaloberst* was no longer growling quite so threateningly; but said he didn't know what my men could achieve. If they had first shown what they could do, then he would have been prepared to discuss the possibilities, even above 6000 metres. For the time being he would have to refuse any flak restrictions, so the planned exercise was pointless.

Without thinking, I blurted out that I was prepared to do it without any fire restrictions. The *Generaloberst* looked at me for a short while, then at Helbig, then at me again. 'Do you know how much metal there could be flying about up there? Tons: thousands of tons. That means millions of splinters. That's not a procedure — that's a . . . that's a . . .'

'It's a *Wilde Sau*[2] procedure,' added Boehm-Tettelbach (1a Ops, Aircrew) and Ruhset (1s Ops, Flak). The *Generaloberst* continued, 'You got away with having a go at a Mosquito. Don't ask me how.' I forced myself not to think of the splinter hole next to the Imperial Cross on my aircraft.

Until then I hadn't given any thought to the quantity of flak, but experience that had been planted in my subconscious told me that the tons of iron spread themselves quite nicely over three dimensions. Not wishing to concede defeat, I mentioned some data gleaned from my acquaintance with enemy anti-aircraft fire, together with the magic words 'La Valetta', looking to Helbig for support as I did so. But he knew what was coming, and kept quiet. Then the blast came: 'That's the bloody limit! You dare to compare *my* flak with the enemy's?' If it hadn't been for the presence of Boehm-Tettelbach, who had studied and practised diplomacy in his dealings with ministers and the highest military leaders, shame and disgrace would have characterised the end of my way through service channels that I had followed according to the regulations. I had learned my lesson: in future I would be more careful when following official paths.

The outcome was that the *Generaloberst* told us that we might try to intercept bombers over the west of the Reich, but without any flak restriction. He told us to try to find a Flak Commander who would cooperate with us.

Strings began to be pulled. Staff *Oberleutnant* Herzberg of the *I. Flakdivision* introduced me to *Luftgau* Commander Schmidt in Münster. He told him that the operational plan had been discussed with the Commander of the Central Area, who had approved it. I confirmed this, in somewhat imprecise terms, in a personal preliminary discussion with the *General* in Münster. He gave his blessing to the project and told me to discuss details with the General Commander *II. Flakkorps*, responsible for the Ruhr Area. I visited this gentleman at Ratingen, near Duesseldorf, and talked over the entire operational plan with him and his 1a,

Major Vogel, a man of approximately the same age as myself and a native of Kiel, as I was. I went away with the promise in my pocket that anti-aircraft fire would be restricted to 5500 metres.

Before I describe how my gratification was in fact premature, I should put on record that I still had my Bomber Section to run. I went on a duty visit to Garz, near Swinemuende, where a handful of devoted men, led by my former flying instructor Ernst Hetzel, were carrying out operational trials of a truly revolutionary weapon, a winged bomb impelled by rockets that could be steered to its target by means of radio impulses.

I was invited to go up in an He 111, and I sat in the cockpit alongside the pilot and observer as we took off over the sea. We approached the target, a beached German freighter that had been damaged by a British mine. Our heading took us past the ship at a distance of 6-8 kilometres, the target moving gradually from our starboard bow to our starboard beam. The observer asked me whether or not I would like him to place the bomb on the bridge or on one of the cargo hatches. I laughed, commenting that I'd be happy if he hit the ship at all. He said he would aim at the second cargo hatch from the bows — it looked no more than a pinpoint. He released his bomb. At first I couldn't see the bomb, which had been mounted under the fuselage, but then it suddenly sped on its way ahead of our aircraft, propelled by its rockets, for approximately seven seconds. At that moment the ship was ahead and to the right of us.

What happened then was both exciting and fantastic. The bomb, with its small wings, went into a curve and headed for the steamer. The observer explained aloud how he was steering it — a little higher, down a bit, a fraction to the right. The bomb, by then flying without propulsion, left behind it a trail of smoke so that it could be seen and steered. Then it struck. Just above the water line, in line with the No. 2 cargo hatch.

What I had been privy to while I was on the Staff, both on paper and in discussions, I then experienced personally: I could say that I had seen it with my own eyes. We bomber crews had to attack the target in an antiquated way. We had to fly into a canopy of fire, only to notch up a few miserable tons of shipping sunk, and in doing so we had to suffer grievous losses: but the carrier of this new weapon could fly past the convoy, outside the flak zone, and was virtually certain of success — one bomb, one direct hit. The four-engined He 177, which had been in service for some time, was the ideal weapon carrier for convoy battles. In my opinion the He 177 would not be affected by my proposed two-thirds cut. If we could inhibit supplies to England, particularly of oil, that would be a good contribution towards the air defence of the Reich.

But back to the West again. *General* Hintz, a Flak Commander who had proved himself with distinction in the Western Campaign, also had reservations about combining his efforts with the fighters in such a restricting way. But he and Vogel had come to one conclusion as a result of their experiences of defensive battles over the Ruhr that could only count to their credit: they cast their pride in their service aside and admitted that they could not defeat the British bombers alone. They questioned seriously whether a correct balance of responsibility existed between the fighters and flak arms. They said that a comparison of effort and results between the two arms showed that the needs of the hour dictated that the fighter force should be strengthened at the expense of the Flak. I was very surprised: if a Flak commander had said it, it must be so.

They said they were prepared to clear a small space for us, then it would be up to us to show what we could do. I sat down with Vogel in the Headmaster's office of a school in Ratingen, and together we began to develop and refine the concept of cooperation between the Flak and Fighter arms in a major raid. One particular decision was that the Flak arm should also hold its fire against individual bombers at lower levels as soon as an attacking fighter fired a light-signal. Other bombers flying in the lower region should be subjected to sustained and heavy fire.

Everybody became enthused of the idea. The *Flakkorps* in the Ruhr promised to make the concept the subject of detailed instructions. I promised to do the same with my pilots in and around Berlin when I got back from the Ruhr.

At approximately sunset on 3 July 1943 we received a warning, 'Enemy aircraft approaching'. From Berlin I telephoned *Major* Fruhner and asked for overnight leave for my men. He gave the OK. The three Staff officers, who were always on the phone to me after nightfall, were also put in the picture. In his enthusiasm, one of them left the Café Kranzler so swiftly that for 24 hours he suffered the odium of having skipped without paying his bill — for *Volk* and *Vaterland*, he said. All of my nine men landed in Moenchengladbach, as planned. When I arrived, the tenth to do so, about an hour later, having flown from Staaken, the last of them was getting airborne to go into action. I refuelled and took off in their wake.

Unmolested by Hintz's flak, we circled at an altitude of between 6000 and 7000 metres over Essen and Duisburg. It was working. We were reassured. The area covered by *II. Flakkorps* stretched from Duisburg, over Bochum and further east. Duesseldorf, in the south, was included in that area, while Cologne was protected by the 7th *Flakdivision*, under *General* Burkhardt, who was not subordinate to *General* Hintz.

In the distance I could see the first bombers going down: our night fighters were at the throats of the attackers. That encouraged us, and the balls of fire showed us the enemy's positions as they went down. The further the stream of bombers penetrated into the defended area, the nearer the frightful messengers of fire came to greet them. That was where the leading bombers must be. They were not approaching the Ruhr from the north, but heading towards the west, past Krefeld, turning suddenly on to an easterly heading. We held our positions. Was Duisburg or Duesseldorf to be their target?

Flames were rising some distance away. The tip of the bomber stream, now outside the defensive belt, was in darkness. Keyed up, I asked myself what was happening. Suddenly a vast sea of searchlights sprang up ahead of me, and while the flak loosed off its barrage, coloured marker flares, dropped by the British Pathfinders, fell to earth. The first heavy bombs began to explode obliquely below me.

We were not flying above *General* Hintz's flak but over Cologne-Mulheim, in the area of the 7th *Flakdivision*, which was illuminating bombers and fighters indiscriminately. They fired on us without paying any heed to our flashing belly lights and navigation lights. Searchlight beams were concentrated around us, and ahead of us we heard the thunder of our artillery. In the intoxication of that summer night's battle we forgot the countless flak splinters and other dangers that faced us, and we tore into the witch's cauldron, hot with anger and spurred with enthusiasm. This was *Wilde Sau*, pure and simple.

By the time the affray was over, twelve four-engined bombers had been downed, and the *Flakdivision*, who until then had managed to shoot down one or two aircraft only, were congratulating themselves on the result — until I claimed the twelve as having been destroyed by my pilots. The horse-trading began. I modified my claim to ten, giving the remaining two to the Flak. The trading ended with each of us being credited with six, an unpalatable result for us but a titbit for the Flak, who then asked us formally if they could be included in our plans. The word got around. The combined battle by fighters and flak generated interest in every *Luftgau*. Soon I became a welcome visiting lecturer everywhere.

First, *Generaloberst* Weise expressed his pleasure at this 'brilliant success' in a teleprinter message to Moenchengladbach:

> . . . *particularly in view of the fact that you carried out the operation over the area most heavily attacked last night on your own initiative and decision without any pre-planning with the Cologne Flakdivision.*

That was rather less than half of the truth. The pack had gone into action before I had been able to give the order to begin. I was the last to take off, and the first to cry 'Horrido!' — the Luftwaffe equivalent to the RAF's cry of 'Murder!' — was Friedrich Karl Mueller, he of the long nose, before I could give the order to attack. If the good *Generaloberst* was of the opinion that we had flown calculatingly into the darting, unbridled fire of his flak, I could only reply that it had been an oversight on our part. Who knows just where he is, when he has been circling and flying here and there in a single-seat aircraft? Only when the battle had been joined did we begin to realise that something had gone wrong, and to wonder what that something was — but even then we had only a vague idea. We simply didn't know where we were. We knew where we weren't — we weren't with Hintz!

Only after it was all finished did we begin to see things for what they were. Wasn't that a pundit flashing down there? What letters is it flashing? Hold it a bit to the left-hand side. Land. Taxi. Where are we? A man with a torch tells us: Bonn-Hangelar.

At seven o'clock in the morning someone shook me out of my sleep. 'The *Reichsmarschall* is on the line.' After Goering had spoken to me when I was a machine-gunner in Doeberitz we had exchanged a few friendly words in Holland in October 1940. This was now the third time we had spoken to each other. He told me to report to *General* Jeschonnek, Chief of the *Luftwaffe* General Staff, and then to him.

Early the next morning I returned my part-time workers back to Berlin so that they could go about their well-regulated daily work. I flew to the *Fuehrer's* Staff Headquarters 'Robinson' which were in the Hotel Geiger in Berchtesgaden, if I remember correctly. For the first time I was able to explain personally my thoughts concerning equipment to the Chief of the General Staff. He suggested that I form a Fighter *Geschwader* of one-engined aircraft. I replied that it would not be popular with the Inspector of Fighters if by doing so we were to weaken his day-fighter force, and I went straight to my idea of reducing the bomber force by two-thirds. Having had experience at the front, I was well qualified to criticise the medium bombers adversely. I added that at that very time *Kampfgeschwader* 2, which was operating against Britain, was suffering such heavy losses that the crews did not survive on average more than twelve operations. By changing from medium bombers to single-seaters one would be killing two birds with one stone.

The Chief of the General Staff listened thoughtfully to everything I had to say, seeming almost to agree, so that I formed the impression that he had already been considering the problem. He closed the meeting by saying that in any event I should form a *Geschwader* of single-engined aircraft and become its *Kommodore*. I replied that it had not been my intention to become involved directly in Air Defence: I had only wanted to stimulate ideas. My own preference would be to operate He 177s equipped with remote-controlled bombs in the Atlantic Theatre. Jeschonnek said, literally, 'You do this first of all. Who else is to lead the Wild Boars?' Of course I was very pleased to be made a *Kommodore* on the spot and not to have to wait until He 177s were available in sufficient numbers.

I took my leave and went to work. *General* Galland, in default of any assistance from the night fighters, helped me generously, even though it meant that he had often to act against his own immediate interests. In addition to a *Gruppe* with a full complement of aircraft, which was based at Bonn-Hangelar, I was given permission to use aircraft from two day-fighter *Gruppen*, based at Rheine and Oldenburg respectively, and I sent the necessary number of pilots there. In this way were born the so-called 'Piggy-back' *Gruppen*, a temporary expedient that made it possible to use aircraft that would otherwise be standing idle for night operations.

I went to Galland's staff for instruction. Edu Neumann, 1a on the Staff, an expert fighter leader in the Africa Campaign, taught me the theory of air-to-air gunnery, at first with the aid of camera-gun films. I could not but be amazed at where one had to aim in order to hit an aircraft in a turn — quite a long way off, in fact. I was annoyed with myself because at Nordhausen I had always skived out of clay-pigeon shooting. Neither had I been very interested in hunting. I had never aimed at or shot a duck, so I had never developed the correct instincts. Nimrod Galland had a better grounding for his air battles.

Goering, Commander-in-Chief of the *Luftwaffe*, was naturally interested in — and had a right to know — what I was getting up to in the night skies in his area of responsibility, and where I was getting my aircraft and my pilots from. 'Do you know anything about it, Bruno?' he asked his friend from the First World War, Loerzer, then a *Generaloberst* and Head of Personnel. He didn't. Neither did he know how it had all happened. The whole thing was *Wilde Sau*, irregular, unpredictable, in organization as well as in the matter of supplies. They looked at each other, then at me, laughed and declared that the whole thing was a gross impertinence, but their handshakes showed me that I was forgiven. Goering told me that he had issued an order authorising the formation of the *Geschwader*, that I had complete authority to choose its pilots, and that I was to visit him at any time.

Fired with enthusiasm, I raced ahead. I had only to drop a hint at schools and operational units and I had more than enough volunteers. I made no secret of the many flak splinters they would have to face, but that didn't put anyone off. Among the people I visited was *General* Coeler, my former OC at *IX. Fliegerkorps*, then commanding the *XIV. Transport Corps* in Tutow. He asked me please not to take too many of his best men away from him. The pilots who applied to join us, even to the extent of begging to be allowed to do so, didn't come spouting 1914 maxims such as 'With God, for Kaiser and Reich', or 'For the

Fatherland' — but simply 'Even if others are worried about their skins, we're not!'

It was the beginning of July 1943. I had asked to be left in peace until the end of September. The pilots had to be able to work together with the searchlights within the flak zone and learn the proper way to approach the bombers that were flying as our targets; not least, they had to learn air firing. Even Wild Boars had to learn to overcome their inborn fears; the Flak Commanders had to get used to the system; and I had to take into account the needs and the capabilities of the Flak arm.

The biggest problem, however, was the situation that we were in: that of mobile warfare by night. The shortage of night fighters, and in particular of single-engined fighters, meant that it was necessary to operate very swiftly, and that we could not afford to stand guard on individual target towns. In that phase of mobile warfare, there could be no question of carrying out tactical experiments. Disporting ourselves in the flak fire over Berlin was a crazy enough idea, but scarcely anyone seriously considered switching about at night, from airfield to airfield, between Hamburg and Berlin. The Air Districts, who were responsible for the Flak arm and the Air Reporting Regiments, had a hard enough job plotting enemy formations. To form an overall view of the air situation had become very difficult. For a long time even twin-engined night fighters were not brought into the battle from long distances away, and by day the areas patrolled by fighters were confined to those near the coast. Anything flying around deep in the Reich could only be hostile.

To be effective against an enemy who was numerically much stronger, you had to concentrate your forces and not bring them to bear until you had done so. To be able to do this we used a simple technical expedient, well known but, at that time, not used often. Under the fuselage of our single-seaters we mounted overload tanks that increased flight times to between two and three hours, so enabling us to cover long distances.

This method of conducting the battle was in clear contrast to the system of radar stations erected in the coastal areas with one fighter, or at the most two, tied to each station and precisely, and usually successfully, controlled on to individual bombers. However, when all was said and done, this system had not been very successful against the narrow bomber streams that the British were using to penetrate our territory in great strength. Even where a second or third defensive line had been built, only three to six night fighters could be employed against the overwhelming numerical superiority of the enemy. The remainder of the night-fighter force stood idle, thereby making the unfavourable balance mentioned earlier even less favourable. I was not prepared to accept that the existing radar system, which drastically reduced the operational potential of the night fighter force, was the last word in defence. My view, which I had put repeatedly to Goering, was that technology should not dictate tactics, but just the opposite: tactics should govern technology. By approaching the problem in this way one would discover techniques and procedures, aids, tricks and dodges, all firmly based on military experience.

The principle of mobility that characterised *Wilde Sau* operations required the setting-up of a wide-ranging navigational system, at first visual only, extending across the entire Reich, and even beyond. Only with such a system could entire formations be brought into action, directed to the target and finally returned to their airfields.

Chance came to my aid when I was setting up the system. During a conference held by *Feldmarschall* Milch, *Generaladmiral* Witzel, who had been invited specially, gave a talk on the experiences of the naval anti-aircraft artillery — the *Marineflak*. He said that when there was a thin layer of high cloud they used to fire flares through it so that any aircraft flying below would be shown up as if against a ground-glass screen. The *Generaladmiral*, an outgoing man and most interested in hearing about the *Wilde Sau* system, was very pleased to let me have several hundred of these flares immediately. I distributed them to a number of widely separated locations, instructing the flak batteries that whenever there was a night raid they were to fire the flares at regular intervals in groups of two or three and set them to explode at altitudes of 7000 to 8000 metres. From Bonn, one could see the flares as far away as Kassel or Münster, from there over Leipzig and Magdeburg, and so on. The man I made responsible for this method of navigation was my former Signals Officer, *Oberleutnant* Holler, who had already given me first-class assistance in bombing operations between North Africa and the Arctic.

And so three fighter *Gruppen* at Bonn-Hangelar, Rheine and Oldenburg came into being under *Major* Stamp, *Major* Kettner and *Major* von Buchwald respectively, equipped with nothing extra save for their overload tanks. *Professor* Tank was the first to hear that his aeroplanes were being operated at night, something for which he, the designer, had not tested them. After some time *Professor* Messerschmitt asked whether he could help me, and whether any alterations or modifications to his aircraft were necessary. The designers were used to being overwhelmed with special requests. In this case both gentlemen were most surprised, but at the same time very pleased, that their day-birds had proved that they could be night-birds as well.

When I thought of the way in which during recent night raids the heavy bombers had been held in the searchlights for endless minutes, and shot at by the Flak Arm without apparent effect, I was firmly convinced that we would be able to inflict considerable losses on the British. Up to that date the radar-controlled night-fighter system had accounted for approximately five percent of the bombers per raid, and I thought that, by making the remainder of the night fighters mobile and introducing single-seaters, we would be able to shoot down at least a further five percent. Following our Moenchengladbach success some of the night fighters had gone quietly over to a form of freelance operating, but they hadn't made a big thing of their successes, reporting their kills in the form laid down in regulations as '*Himmelbett*' successes, to use the official code-word.[3]

At first I continued to work at least half-time in my Bomber Section. Following up my idea of operating over the Atlantic in the new four-engined bomber, I went to see the Inspector of the *Luftwaffe (Marine)*, *General* Moll to consult him about his plans. From him I learned the salient details of the six-engined flying boat, the BV 222, and of the bigger aircraft, the BV 238, which was still in the development stage. Blöhm and Voss had an experimental version of an asymmetric dive-bomber ready to take to the air, so I took the opportunity to fly to Finkenwerder and speak to the Chief Designer, Vogt.

The BV 222 seemed to me to be eminently suited to the task of carrying out successful long-range operations, supported by U-boat tankers and surface supply bases, along the 20,000-kilometre coast of the Western Hemisphere, in which nearly all of the countries were at war with Germany. Admittedly an operational force of half-a-dozen BV 222s would be only able to inflict pinpricks, but they would be no less irritating than the enemy's Mosquito attacks. The aircraft would be able to land in quiet spots to take on fuel and bombs, stay away from their bases for many weeks, and carry out surprise attacks both on enemy coastal targets and merchant shipping.

To a suggestion I made to this effect, *Feldmarschall* Milch replied that one BV 238 would cost him fifty fighters. I begged to differ: it would cost him twenty-five useless medium bombers. If we couldn't change them for fighters, at least let us swap them for heavy aircraft that could tie up a large number of enemy fighters, thus making them unavailable for use elsewhere in Europe. That was air defence. As an example I drew the Field Marshal's attention to our long coastline from the Arctic to Biarritz, along which could be found much unused flak, radar and fighter capacity. Imagine, I said, how the South Americans would scream out for help if just one bomb fell on their country every week. Imagine the outcry in the USA if important targets there were left undefended!

Such was modern-day sea warfare as seen by the strategists of the *IX. Fliegerkorps*, and *Oberleutnant zur See* Friedrich, who had described to us so vividly the effects on conditions in the South Atlantic, from the Argentine to South Africa, of *Graf Spee*'s East Asia Squadron. South Africa, newly freed from British domination, had been on the verge of collapse until Spee's fleet was defeated off the Falklands.

I could find nothing wrong with this concept. I asked the designer, Vogt, to show me the BV 238 in its hangar at Finkenwerder. He asked me if I would like to fly the BV 222. I was taken out in a motor-boat with a flight mechanic, and we got into the flying boat: then we were ready to go. He took the combined throttle in his hand and shoved all its six levers forward and upward. We skimmed over the sea until I heard, 'Right. Now we'll climb, nice and slow.' From then on it was a pleasure trip: across to the Alster, then a nice, gentle curve that a sports plane couldn't have performed more elegantly, then back to the Elbe, where we touched down. I was captivated, and I would willingly have gone to sea as a pirate there and then to conduct a new kind of trade war.

For me, having made a technical/tactical suggestion was not sufficient. I could not overlook the difficulties that would occur in the process of putting it into effect. The more I thought about implementing my plan, and the more ideas that came into my head — and I didn't think they were all that profound — the more I would become excited or start to worry. It was important at the beginning not to start thinking half-resignedly how long it would take to set up a system. The first step was to consider what the aircraft had to offer in terms of success or of freeing other resources. If you could reach a positive conclusion a way, and a rapid one at that, would soon suggest itself.

Another of my ideas caused some amusement. In one of my papers I had written that, after the various successes and failures of the First World War, it would be unwise to play the old U-boat gramophone a second time as a long-term strategy. I had seen it in the Arctic: if we hadn't bombed ships out of the convoys the U-boats would hardly ever have been able to bring their torpedoes to bear, or else they would have been destroyed by the strong escort cover. I calculated that in three weeks an He 177 carrying four remote-controlled bombs could make ten attacks on the enemy, whereas a U-boat could carry out only one torpedo attack in the same space of time, always assuming that it had first been able to locate the enemy. The field of vision from a U-boat was very limited compared to that of a *Staffel* flying a search in line-abreast. Each separate aircraft can see much more than one U-boat could see. This suggested the possibility of transferring production capacity from the *Marine* to the *Luftwaffe*, if not for air defence then to strengthen the offensive bomber force that would be retained — the one-third of which I have spoken before.

Werner Baumbach, a first-class attacker of ships in both dive-bombers and torpedo-bombers who had taken over my dear old *Gruppe III* of *KG 30*, the *Adlergeschwader*, from me in 1942 was now Acting Inspector. He read my paper, jumped to his feet and said, 'You're quite right. We'll get into the car and go round and see *Admiral* Doenitz.' We drove up unannounced to the Hotel am Steinplatz on Hardenbergerstrasse in Berlin and gave our names. At that very moment the *Admiral* came out of his office wearing his greatcoat with blue piping, his cap on his head, on his way to lunch. He asked us what we wanted. In his cheerful, smiling way Baumbach, pointing at me, said that I had been working on some very important ideas and that the *Admiral* should be aware of them. In an anteroom the Admiral sat down in an armchair, took off his hat and said, 'I'm listening.'

I started by mentioning the gramophone record that wouldn't be as good the second time as it was the first, and then I went on to mention my calculations and the better visibility from bombers. I gave a short assessment of the quantity of high explosives in a torpedo compared with that in the bombs, and then, feeling confident of success, I proceeded to demonstrate that the balance of advantage in favour of the *Luftwaffe* over a period of three weeks, the average length of a marine operation, was perhaps ten to one.

The *Admiral* asked me if our aircraft could hit targets any better than his U-boats could with their torpedoes. I was happily able to draw on my own experience with the cargo hatch, and I made a number of other important points relating to the subject. The *Admiral* looked at me very closely. Then he thought a while and asked Baumbach whether or not he shared my views. 'Of course,' said Baumbach. 'Otherwise I wouldn't have come.'

The *Admiral* thought a bit more. By now fifteen minutes had passed. Then out of the blue he said, 'And I'm to be your corporal, am I?' He laughed and stood up. He thanked us for our visit and promised to give the matter his consideration. The gramophone record continued to turn. In the meanwhile, the enemy was working on a lethal countermeasure.

From my base in Berlin I had done the necessary organization for my night fighters. The time was drawing near for me to get more closely acquainted with my *Geschwader*, to go to Bonn and to take part in their exercises. There was still time, however, to take a look at the Me 262, the new *'Wundervogel'* — the 'miracle bird' that was opening up a new technological era and which, given a few hundred of them in the front line, could overcome the enemy's superiority in the air. I expressed my opinion that this aeroplane should, like conventional fighters, be used in a number of roles, carrying bombs if necessary or operating as an interceptor both by day and night. Attempts on my part to be allowed to fly it met with all sorts of obstacles, and I tried to overcome them forcibly. But a letter dated 28 May 1943, from the *Chef de Cabinet* to the Controller of Air Supplies, Vorwald, addressed to Staff *Oberst* Peltz, made my blood boil:

I request you to draw the attention of Major Herrmann to the unmilitary nature of his behaviour apparent in his use of certain idiomatic expressions when speaking to subordinates, as set out in the attached report.

The report that accompanied the letter is no longer in my possession.

Ends can sometimes justify irregular means, but they do not justify even valid anger. So I clenched my teeth, put a brave face on it, asked nicely, and one brilliant, hot July day with no wind and clear air, I found myself at Lechfeld at the controls of an Me 262. Taxying was awkward and the speed half-way along the runway was only moderate, only just high enough to get airborne when I reached the end. Then the aeroplane leaped forward, 550 kph and climbing at nearly thirty metres a second. Ahead of me was the jagged backdrop of the Alps, while below me the mountains were rapidly becoming a bizarre, speckled mixture of brown and white. The ASI showed speeds undreamed of — 800, 900 and, believe it or not, 1000. Lord God of Hosts, give us 600 of these and we'll sweep the sky over Germany clear, we'll decimate the harbingers of terror on their own airfields with bullets and with bombs, and the invasion fleets as well, should they come our way.

The voice of the controller on the ground awoke me from my dream: I was to show myself over the airfield. I heard him say that with the Me 262 you could fly perfect rolls. He told me to try it at low level. It was an experience that my five senses were incapable of taking in all at the same time. It was a unique experience, and I had had it. I was able to say to myself, 'You've been there!'

Among the roles that I had envisaged for the aircraft was quite certainly that of a night fighter. Then I began to have reservations: would it be wise to fly an aircraft that left a trail of fire behind it at night that could be seen miles away? Could one operate an aircraft as fast as that in darkness? It would close with a bomber far too rapidly.

By this time I had become somewhat cautious about putting up new ideas. Because of what I was currently trying to do I did not want to risk losing my credibility. A lot of wise men told me that I should get *Wilde Sau* working properly before I dug a pit for myself, which was something I didn't intend to do. So what I knew I must do was to try out any new ideas I might have very cautiously. Before long the Me 262 was chasing Mosquitos in the sky over Berlin at night, as if to the manner born.

But by now it was time for me to up sticks in Berlin and head west.

Notes

1 Avus: a stretch of Autobahn on the outskirts of Berlin, specially built to test and race motor cars.
2 Wilde Sau: translates into English as Wild Boar. In German it means crazy, unheeding and reckless.
3 Himmelbett: the Himmelbett (four-poster) system of close-controlled night fighting was based on a large number of circular control areas, each approximately fifty miles in radius and equipped with two Wuerzburg-Riese radars. One radar picked up the enemy bomber and the other picked up the defending fighter.

Chapter Eleven
Wilde Sau

Day and night attacks by the Western Allies. The Soviet offensive. Capitulation of the Germans and the Italians in North Africa. Mussolini is deposed. The Allies land in Sicily and on the Italian mainland.

It was a hot, close day in July in the year 1943. Here and there the humidity was bubbling up into dazzling white towers of cloud. I was in my Fieseler *Storch*, dressed in khaki shorts and a shirt of the same material that I had brought with me from North Africa, and I was flying from the Rhine up over the Sieg, quite low and throttled right back, looking for somewhere I could land. At a leisurely pace I overtook the local narrow-gauge bell-train making its way towards Waldbroehl. In front of me the engine was giving out heat like a baker's oven, so that my shins began to hurt. The sun was scorching me from above. In my flying greenhouse every piece of metal was red hot. I undid my collar and stuffed my tie into my breast pocket. To the right lay Hennef, and to the left *Schloss* Allner, the position of which Max Pill, the busy admin. officer and quartermaster of the *Geschwader*, had marked on my map. It was important that the staff should be mobile, and that meant we needed a landing ground for a *Storch*. What I could make out of the stretch of meadowland along the Sieg and below the *Schloss* was not very inviting. Pretty, green and flat, admittedly, without any treacherous drainage ditches crossing it, but rather narrow, and very short, which was worse. Man's hand had endowed it with a special hazard that one could not afford to overlook: a high-tension line of four tightly spanned cables, cutting the meadow into two and supported by twin legs, in the meadow.

I orbited slowly, scanning the surface and estimating the height of the cables from the shadow of the mast, intending to try to make my landing approach under them. Why should one go to the trouble of climbing over an obstacle when one can crawl under it? That sort of exercise had been part of our infantry training. Flaps down, approach slowly, heading for the obstacle, which by now was looking like a huge gate of iron and wire. I landed, taxied past the masts, and came to a standstill.

Here I was, then, at the place from which in the next few weeks I would hop over in my *Storch* to Bonn-Hangelar, ten kilometres away, and climb into my Me 109 to take off on fateful nocturnal enterprises. I had chosen the grass-covered airfield at Bonn-Hangelar after careful consideration, in the hope that I would be able to deploy north or south equally rapidly in order to reach the places where the British bombers were unloading their cargoes of terror.

Within a few days everything that was necessary had been set up in the *Schloss* and its outbuildings and grounds. *Oberleutnant* Holler, our Signals Officer, had installed bundles of telephone and teleprinter cables and had set up a signals office. The blackout had been checked and found to be satisfactory, and all the vehicles and my *Storch* were well camouflaged. On the rare occasions that she appeared the lady of the *Schloss*, even though intellectually superior to a bunch of wild young officers, managed to disguise her concern behind formal friendliness. I was, however, rather mistrustful of the state of truce until one day the aristocratic lady with the lightly greying hair caught sight of a book that I had left open on a garden chair. The title, printed in gold lettering on its cover, was *Trost bei Goethe* (Comfort in Goethe) a comfort that I had brought with me from more peaceful times but which had occasionally provoked humorous comment on the part of the troops. I must be out of my mind, they said, to be seeking comfort from Goethe, of all people. (In German what they said makes a play on words, but it is impossible to reproduce in English.)

A lively conversation developed between the lady and myself that covered the entire spectrum of artistic creativity, including Johann Sebastian Bach, who — 'as, of course, you know' — was highly thought of by Goethe. At the centre of the spectrum the lady, exuding enthusiasm for the arts, placed Wilhelm Furtwaengler, the incarnation, she said, of the great artistes of the past. She added that she had his six *Brandenburgische Konzerte* (Brandenburg Concertos) on long-playing records — 'Marvellous! You must hear them!' When I assented, the fief of the Goethe Room of the *Schloss*, with its fine view over the *Siebengebirge*, was granted to me so that I could use it as my office. Only one condition was imposed: the telephone cable should not lead in through the *Schloss* itself, but should be brought in from above through the window. We needed no further encouragement to accept that condition, nor to be on our best behaviour, when we learned, with a feeling of great respect, that our hostess was the niece of *Graf* Zeppelin. Given this spiritual relationship with things aeronautical, it was only natural that the daughter of the house should, with all her inherited strength of character, go behind my back and ask for a ride in our *Storch*, and that she should be successful.

One evening, after I had come to the end of the fourth record, one per day off, and was thus suitably ennobled with the music of Bach, and the occupants of the *Schloss* had retired to bed, the indefatigable and resourceful Max Pill opened the door with an elaborate gesture and made his way through it, carrying a tea-tray in front of him. On a gleaming porcelain plate was cowering a hedgehog. 'Instead of the boar I promised you — another wild, bristly beast.' We wanted to live up to the 'Wild Boar' reputation of our *Geschwader*, so I had let it be known that I would like someone to get hold of a boar's head, still fresh and dripping blood, recently shot in the wild, or a stuffed and prepared one, perhaps, swapped with a butcher, an innkeeper, or a forester for a bottle of Hennesey — but that would take some time.

I allowed the little visitor to sit by me on the sofa. He erected his defensive spines and defied this unknown, hostile world, ourselves included. Alas! — very soon a good dozen flea-like creatures had emerged from the animal's protective quills and were hopping happily across the table in the lamplight. In the Goethe Room, of all places! What if the noble lady had seen them!

Our preparations went on apace. I reached an excellent understanding with *General* Burkhardt of the 7th *Flakdivision* in Cologne. *General* Hintz invited me to a discussion in Essen, to which town he had recently been moved with his Staff. I touched down in my *Storch* on the Essen-Muelheim racecourse and hurried to the conference, where I found the Commanders and Battery Chiefs high-booted and belted, whereas I was wearing my khaki shorts and shirt, sandals and white socks. I had not been told in advance of the high-level nature of the conference, at which the participants were eager to learn more about *Wilde Sau*.

On 24 July 1943 the radio announced a British night raid on Hamburg. Only radar-controlled night fighters were sent up against it. We, the *Wilde Sau* of *Jagdgeschwader 300*, were still in the process of forming up.

My training programme was stretched. There was no way I could go any faster. I still had four to five weeks to go, and I needed them urgently. Other branches of the *Luftwaffe* trained their pilots for months in Operational Training *Gruppen* before they went into front-line service. Throughout the period of waiting and training I half-expected that I would be called upon if things got hot. This springing into the breach was par for the course in the *Luftwaffe*, which was no wonder when the situation was as tense as it was.

As I feared, Staff *Oberst* von Brauchitsch rang me up from Karinhall the morning after the attack on Hamburg. The question he asked was inevitable: 'How near to being operational are you?' Then Goering came to the phone. He asked the same question. I answered, 'Mid-September, at the earliest.' The *Reichsmarschall* said, in a comparatively quiet, but nevertheless insistent, voice that I was to be ready for action that night with as strong a force as was possible. What had happened was very bad, earth-shattering. I would learn the rest by teleprinter. The teleprinted message arrived. The controlled night fighters had been rendered ineffective by means of jamming, by the dropping of vast amounts of silver-foil strips.[1] Scarcely any of the bombers had been shot down. There had been considerable damage. A further attack on Hamburg was to be expected. The number of times that I was called to the telephone that day confirmed to me that a catastrophe had struck Hamburg, and that there was still more to come.

At about 2300 hrs the following night, when the first aircraft of the British bomber stream had crossed over the middle of the North Sea, twenty-five of our aircraft took off from Bonn and set course for Bremen, expecting that city, or Hanover, Hamburg, Luebeck or Kiel, to be the target. It was the first time that single-engined fighters would fight at long range rather than on their own door-steps. The night was very dark, and our navigational searchlights were not fully operational. In the blackness, a number of the pilots lost their nerves. About a third of the aircraft turned back. But the majority, pilots from Bonn-Hangelar, Rheine and Oldenburg, headed for the battlefield. In the distance, Hamburg was still burning.

It was Hamburg once again. The terror above which we twisted and turned and shot down approximately twenty bombers became well known. When we had finished I landed at Lueneburg and went into the flying-control building just as an enemy intruder sent a burst of fire through it. When I took off the following morning for Bonn together with a number of my single-seaters, a broad banner of thick, black smoke stretched across the sky from the direction of Hamburg. Again the ground-controlled night fighters had had hardly any success. When the drama of Hamburg had passed Goering called a number of conferences. I found it very embarrassing when he harshly rebuked the Commanding General of the *XII. Korps*, the night-fighters, in my presence: even more embarrassing was the fact that he greatly exaggerated my own performance.

Before one of the ensuing conferences Goering discovered that as long ago as Autumn the previous year I had proposed a system by which night fighters should cooperate with the searchlights over the cities, and that I had carried out trials without any support — indeed, in the face of obvious disapproval on the part of the *General* — and that the *General* had not taken any action after my encounter with the Mosquito over Berlin, and, more importantly, after our success over Cologne. All these plans and the successes we had achieved had been widely discussed by the Staffs and had penetrated as far as units of the Fighter Korps, some of which had attempted individually to wage their own mobile war.

I was asked to either confirm or correct these facts. I confirmed them. The *Reichsmarschall* then said in a sharp voice, 'I am giving you command of *XII. Jagdkorps.*' He said that I would have to give *General* Kammhuber the necessary orders and tell him that I had overall responsibility for everything from then on, and that I was to act at once. He turned to von Brauchitsch and told him to see that teleprinted messages to that effect were sent. Then he left me alone with von Brauchitsch.

Seldom in the history of the war can a soldier have received an order such as that: a *Major* was to give orders to the General in Command. I asked myself what I had let myself in for with my plans. They had been so easy to work out when sitting at my desk, knowing that there were superiors who would countersign and approve them and carry the responsibility. Now, suddenly, I was standing there defenceless, under orders to overcome the yawning danger that faced us, to take on, at a moment's notice, an enemy bitterly resolved to destroy us. 'Am I crazy, or was he joking?' I asked von Brauchitsch. He told me that I should read the book Ghenghis Khan, then I would be better informed. I hadn't read the book, so I was in the dark.

I could not bring myself to work in such a way, but I promised to do everything within my power to achieve the desired result. I said that I would like to fly at once to *XII. Korps* at Deelen, Holland, and sit down with the officers of the Staff. Staff *Oberst* Hoffmann, Heiner Wittmer, Mueller-Trimbusch and Dyrchs, and explain mobile night fighting that would not be affected by British jamming, in all its aeronautical, tactical and navigational details. I suggested that the Staff could then incorporate it into the necessary orders, over Kammhuber's signature, and bring it to the attention of unit commanders. Brauchitsch said that he would put this to the Chief the following morning, but I was to set off at once.

The *Reichsmarschall* had so unequivocally placed the burden of command on my shoulders, that I felt very strongly that I ought to insist upon a clear statement of my position in the command structure. That is, that I should completely refuse to give orders to the Commanding *General*: it would be better if he were relieved of his post and I were put in his place. I knew that I was the man of the hour. Everyone said I was. Goering would surely be compelled to give his agreement. I spent the next few days turning the whole thing over in my mind. I couldn't bring myself to take the step. If the *Reichsmarschall* didn't agree, I didn't want to have to put pressure on him by saying that, without formal authority, legal competence, disciplinary powers and the ability to decorate soldiers or propose them for medals, I did not feel myself able to build up a system of air defence from a position of defeat and to lead men in perilous operations. Subsequently I regretted many times, when foreseeable difficulties arose, that I did not speak out along these lines.

First of all I flew to Deelen. I worked there a day, a night, and the following day in close collaboration with *General* Kammhuber's Staff. Nobody knew when the storm would break again, or where it would erupt. When Kammhuber summoned his *Kommandeure* shortly afterwards for instruction in the procedure, Goering insisted that I should fly in from Bonn to take part in the briefing. He said that I was to speak out clearly, and that I should give orders if necessary. Even if he himself was not yet speaking clearly, at least I knew what I had to do, and how I was to do it.

I flew in the *Storch* from Bonn and found that tables had been set out in the shape of a large 'U' on the lawn of a fine estate. Nothing in the world, I thought, could bring me to sit at the head of those tables and spout big words. I sought Staff *Oberst* Hoffmann immediately and assured myself that we were now of equal rank — I had a quick look in the written orders — and I told him that I would take a place at one end of the 'U'. I asked him to tell this to the *General*, so that there wouldn't be any awkwardness in front of the *Kommandeure* when we came to sit down. He did so, and I reported my presence to the *General*, smartly and in proper military style.

In the meanwhile, the Commanders had gathered, and I was happy to see among them my old friend Karl Huelshoff, *Kommodore* of the long-range night fighters, and many other friends and comrades.

The *General* began his address by giving a clear picture of the current air situation and asking that all efforts should be directed to going over completely to the *Wilde Sau* system. In doing this, he said some very kind words about the part I had played. Then he handed over to Staff *Oberst* Hoffmann, who gave an exemplary explanation of how such an operation was to be conducted. During this official occasion, I did not speak at all. When it was over I flew back immediately to Bonn-Hangelar, sat down in my Goethe Room and asked myself whether or not in the last week I hadn't done a year's work.

Following the attacks on Hamburg, and with the nights lengthening, we had to reckon with attacks deeper into Reich territory, particularly on Berlin. *Reichsmarschall* Goering had impressed upon me that I was to pay particular attention to Berlin. That boiled down to tying ourselves down, to standing sentry, just the opposite of mobile warfare, but I obeyed because I was virtually convinced that Berlin would be attacked. But the British had calculated that we would be thinking along those lines — so they did something different. On the night of 17 August 1943 they sent a few Mosquitos to Berlin, but the main force, coming in over Schleswig-Holstein and the Baltic, did not turn south towards Berlin at the mouth of the Oder but attacked the V-weapon experimental station at Peenemuende, not far from Garz, where those remote-controlled bombs were tested.

I felt a personal responsibility for guarding Berlin, so I tore into the sea of searchlights and anti-aircraft fire as the Mosquitos were dropping their pathfinder markers, usually a sign for the heavy bombers to open their bomb doors. When I saw that there were no bombs bursting below and that the Mosquitos had flown swiftly through, I looked around and saw that the bell had tolled in the north. It was there that the main bomber stream was causing its havoc. For us above Berlin it was too late to engage them. But even the spoof attack and the huge amounts of silver foil dropped did not help the British as they had done over Hamburg.

Single-engined and twin-engined fighters following up got among the bombers over the Baltic and shot down twenty of them. The night fighters had arrived from far away for the first time, young crews who until then had had to yield priority in the '*Himmelbett*' boxes to the experienced specialists. Now it was a case of free movement and freelance fighting. A revolution in night fighting, as one young pilot who had taken off from St. Trond in Belgium described it.

The diversionary attack on Berlin had had one good effect: *Feldmarschall* Milch, who was very angry at the waste of flak ammunition used against his own targets, spoke with me and then intervened very strongly with *Generaloberst* Weise in favour of the fighters, with the result that the Fighter and Flak Arms reached a noticeably better degree of understanding. What the 1st *Flakdivision* had practised with me in our exercises was now declared sensible and legal.

We were therefore better prepared to meet an attack on Berlin, and the night fighters as a whole had their first wide-ranging defensive battle behind them. We set up additional navigational aids posthaste, with *Leutnant* Holler pulling strings day and night. Without the cooperation of the anti-aircraft artillery and their controllers, the *Luftgaue*, we couldn't have coped. Avenues of searchlights were set up across the flak zones so that after the bombers had gone we could find our way home safely. At the end of each of the lanes, which were about 100 kilometres long, was an airfield, additionally identified by a flashing beacon. Three days after the attack on Peenemuende I breathed more easily. We had been able to capitalise on our experience and to achieve a great deal. I could sit down again in the Goethe Room and enjoy a glass of Mosel provided by the lady of the house, at the same time letting myself be transported to higher spheres by Johann Sebastian Bach.

Once again things began to happen. Our monitoring service had picked up indications that an attack was being prepared. The weather forecast for central Germany was that conditions were favourable for an attack. Further, because it was towards the end of August, the length of the nights was such that darkness would cover both the inward and outward flights of the bombers. Their radar jamming, which had posed new and difficult problems for us since Hamburg, would provide them with an extra safety factor. We would not have to take off too early or too late. We would need every drop of petrol, even though we would be carrying overload tanks. Should the attack be in the north, we in Bonn would have to start earlier than those units based in Westphalia. If the attack was in the south, the opposite would apply. It followed that all of us, including our twin-engined colleagues, who had joined in *Wilde Sau* operations, would have to watch every litre of fuel and every minute's flying time.

After the shattering blow that Bomber Command had delivered to Hamburg at the end of July we were expecting the much-publicised offensive against Berlin which, in sixteen raids, was to 'reduce the city to ruins from one end to the other'. That was Air Marshal Harris's plan. To achieve this he was prepared to sacrifice 500 bombers but he would win the war, he said. That particular evening, with both tension and activity mounting, Johann Sebastian Bach had perforce to be silent.

In the operations room, I cast a final glance at the air-situation and meteorological charts. There was hustle and bustle all around: telephone handles were turned, teleprinter tapes spewed out, men scribbled, and maps were plotted.

A blue-blooded gentleman gazed down benevolently from a heavy golden frame, a minor prince, his head covered in silver locks befitting his rank: he could surely not have had the faintest idea why his countrymen from a later age were working so frantically.

We were to be at immediate readiness in our aircraft at Bonn-Hangelar in thirty minutes. The Adjutant, *Hauptmann* Kroska, callsign *'Wilde Sau 2'*, and *Wilde Sau* 3, Karl Friedrich Mueller, nicknamed 'Nasenmueller' — if he had been Welsh it would have been 'Mueller the Nose' — were already there. He whose job it was to lead and set a good example, *Wilde Sau* 1, would be last to arrive in his *Storch*, and change aircraft. I telephoned the *Luftflotte* in Berlin. At the other end was Aircrew 1a Ops, *Oberstleutnant* Boehm-Tettelbach, together with Flak 1a Ops, *Oberstleutnant* Ruhsert. They were struggling desperately to clarify the air situation, what was spoof, what was real, where the main thrust of the attack was to be, which were the diversionary raids, and where the beginning and end of the enemy bomber stream were. Should the fighters take off in ten minutes, twenty minutes, or in half an hour? Any decision they took could be the wrong one. Would it be Hamburg all over again?

I glanced at the clock. We synchronised our watches. Scramble was due for 2305 hrs, in twenty minutes. I picked up my shaving kit, which was my entire luggage, stuck it in my jacket pocket, raised my hand, went out into the darkness down the steps and along the path to the River Sieg. A rickety suspension bridge led to the landing field. The people in the small village had long been in bed. Perhaps one of them heard me, trembling on the narrow footbridge, as Goethe had written. What a strange wayfarer I was, setting out with the absolute minimum of gear to range hundreds of kilometres above the Fatherland!

My *Storch* was ready for take-off. The two men from the technical wing positioned themselves with red lamps in accordance with the drill, one at each of the high-tension masts, thus marking the 'goalposts' through which I had to pass. It was not possible to pull up over the electric cables. The distance was too short. I sat in the cockpit, strapped myself in, switched on and began to taxi. The red lamps flew past. Airborne, I glanced quickly at the instruments. The *Storch* purred low over the unlit countryside.

After a few minutes I flashed my landing light, and the airfield lights at Bonn-Hangelar were switched on. Throttle back. I taxied in, turned and stopped abruptly near to my dispersal. All was dark once more. There was a deep calm over the airfield. The mechanic passed me my flying overalls and gave me a hand to pull them up over my shoulders. I felt downwards, left and right — the Very pistol and the knife were in place, fastened to the cord with snap-hooks. To my right I could hear *'Wilde Sau* 2's' East Prussian accent; to my left, *'Wilde Sau* 3' speaking pure Mannheim. That was how I could distinguish unmistakably between them in the air. Nobody could recognise me from my German unless I was very angry, when the going was rough and the heat was on. I didn't allow myself to be provoked into shouting, but I made a virtue of necessity by letting sharply-phrased High German hiss through my teeth. There are times and places when everybody has to let off steam.

The first *Gruppe* of *Jagdeschwader 300 'Wilde Sau'*, led by *Hauptmann* Gerd Stamp, started its engines. They were under orders to head in the direction of Bremen, ready like those from Westphalia to alter course as instructed should new targets be identified. Both the airfield lighting and the runway lights were switched on, and the long chain of aircraft navigation lights, green and red, began to move. The first engines bellowed as they started their take-off run towards the west. I stood on the wing of my Me 109 and watched attentively. Then the last man of the *Gruppe* was airborne. He switched off his navigation lights. The noise of the aeroplanes' engines rolled darkly into the distance, swung round to the north and then lost itself towards the north-east.

The three of us got ready. Mueller, who couldn't give them up, drew on his cigarette until it glowed white, then threw it to the ground so that sparks flew. I heard the sole of his shoe scuffing. The Adjutant, a physical fitness fanatic, bent forward with a groan, and I heard something rustling. I knew that he was putting a dextroenergen tablet into his mouth. We three members of the *Geschwader* Staff were supposed to head for Brunswick. Someone passed the telephone receiver up to me; the *Luftflotte* was on the line. There was no new information. They knew exactly now what they had known before: North German Plain. That was a big place.

The bombers crossed northern Holland and neared the borders of the Reich. Our night fighters in Holland and Belgium, near Metz and Wiesbaden, were already in the air and heading for Muenster and Hanover. We took a calculated risk and held back. I said I would report at once whether I could make out the main target or whether I thought I had found a diversionary raid. In a low voice I said to my trusted comrades, 'Get on board,' and added, 'Press thumbs in good time.' In German 'Press thumbs' means 'fingers crossed,' but I meant 'Press your thumbs on your firing buttons in good time.'

I climbed into my aircraft and strapped myself in. My oxygen mask was there, ready. It was very quiet and very dark. I felt the controls and the instrument panel: we had practised blindfold in daytime so that we knew our way around in the dark. When we did it wrong our punishment was to be laughed at by the others. Where is the oil-temperature dial: where is the pressure indicator? Where is the jack for the R/T headset? Where is the altimeter? To be able to locate them in the dark would pay off when things were for earnest. We would know without a second's thought where to look, where to reach for. You became an integral part of your 'flying saucer', the brain in a metal body.

I switched on the electrics and allowed the ultraviolet light to shine on the instruments, then I turned it down. To sit in an Me 109 ready to leap into the air, a thousand horsepower at my command, was a pleasing sensation. The aircraft was an Me 109T. We had got some from the *Marine* and collected them from Pillau in East Prussia. The Mark T had been intended for the aircraft carrier *Graf Zeppelin*, which did not go into service. The 'T' had a braking-hook under its tail, which was an unnecessary embellishment for us; a greater wing area than the Mark G, which was good, and spoiler flaps to shorten the landing run, which was not essential for our airfield. Operating by day, the 'T' had an inferior performance to the 'G', and therefore was not wanted; but we accepted them gladly for our night operations.

The time had come for us to be on our way. I flashed my navigation lights. The three of us started up. We didn't test our engines at full power: the first mechanics would have done that and then topped the aircraft up with fuel. I never checked my machine when the mechanic had done it already. He had to be conscious of his responsibility and the trust I placed in him. I switched on my navigation lights. That meant 'Chocks away!' The mechanic's torch shone green — the chocks were away. I flashed my landing light. The perimeter lights and the runway shone out from the darkness.

I taxied slowly to take-off, followed by my Number One and Number Two. Without stopping at the first green lamp I gave full throttle — tail down, nose up. To my left, the green lights streaked past. I brought the aircraft into a horizontal position. I could see the end of the runway ahead of me. I accelerated, took off, levelled out and held the aircraft near to the ground. I pressed the undercarriage button and brought the flaps smartly into cruising position. I stayed low down on the deck. The perimeter lights flashed past below me. My ASI read 300 kph. Ahead of me it was pitch dark. Those wonderful visual aids, horizons of lights far ahead, avenues of lights stretched towards them, have not yet spread all over the territory of the Reich. This is a quasi-underdeveloped area.

The transition from the visible area of the illuminated airfield to the blackness of night was like descending into the underworld. Many succumbed to fear, which gave rise to wildly deceptive impressions. I switched on my instrument-panel lighting to full and paid no attention to the black shadows below and ahead of me. Reject the illusory perceptions. The artificial horizon in my aircraft, a small, round instrument less than 10 cm in diameter, was my helper. In the same way, the altimeter, clock, turn-and-bank indicator and the compass all posed their questions and gave me their answers. It was as bright as day in the cockpit and my eyes followed the rising pointers and the changing numbers calmly and peacefully as they danced in front of my control column.

I turned down the lights and made a starboard turn, saw the airfield lights go out on my beam. All three of us were airborne. I let my navigation lamps burn a minute or so longer. There was no danger just at that moment. There had not been any reports of enemy intruders so far. Then I switched off my navigation lamps. It was a mild night, a covering of summer haze reaching high and keeping the earth warm. I turned on to a north-easterly heading. My compass was steady. I did not climb too steeply but held my boost and engine revolutions at cruising settings to save fuel. From time to time I illuminated the phosphorous numbers and figures, pointers and marks on the dashboard with ultraviolet light. From them I could read, as if from an open book, how my aircraft was sitting in their air. Nobody could tell me that that aircraft wasn't suitable for blind-flying. She flew beautifully, responding to the most tentative pressure on the control column or the gentlest of pushes with the foot on the rudder bar, reacting as a thoroughbred does to friendly pressure from the thighs. As it delights a horse to feel an expert rider on his back, so my Me 109 carried me willingly, as if she could feel the warmth of my body and the beat of my heart. The steel motor purred with satisfaction, no rumbling or hesitating spoiled its powerful bass. I was suspended up there alone and I imagined myself motionless in space. I pulled up and let down a little so that I could feel in the pit of my stomach the thrill of acceleration and of flying. Once upon a time man must have been a Pegasus before he was banished to the surface of the earth, first on all fours and then on two legs.

I climbed a little faster. The Messerschmitt lifted her head and gained height a hundred metres at a time. How easily I was being borne aloft! Compared to that the twin-engined aircraft I had flown, the He 111, Do 217, and the Ju 88, were all cold-blooded creatures. This, I thought as I looked ahead through the bullet-proof windscreen and along the slender neck, a bluish mane flaming out from the exhaust outlets — this is breeding.

The layer of haze sank below me; I was through it and above it. In the northern sky the sun had not left any lighter streaks behind, but the horizon could be seen encircling the haze-veiled earth. I felt uplifted. 'The star-studded heaven above me' — was it that phrase from the Koenigsberg philosopher,[2] which we had had to learn by heart at school, that made me marvel, or was it the wonder of that moment that made me remember it? Under that star-studded heaven, common to all, men had assembled to kill each other, each according to his own moral law.

At 4000 metres' altitude I took the control column between my knees and put on my oxygen mask. Where will I fly to? Where will I fight? Where will I land? So far I hadn't looked at the map, a small piece of paper mounted on linen, folded in the middle, and drawn to a scale of 1:2,000,000. I didn't carry my bigger map which had woods, rivers and towns marked on it. It was of no use. We in *Wilde Sau* had undergone hard training. We had learned our geography by heart. Many times we had marked in German cities to dictation on a sheet of paper and written in the direction and distance from one point to another, had drawn in rivers in blue and mountains in brown. At first they were all childish, amusing and amazing efforts which, fifty years later, could have been categorised as highly creative, existentialist works, but gradually we were able to produce drawings which, highly stylised though they might have been, were true to life. The R/T crackled, 'This is Teuto. Leading bomber approaching the Weser, heading east,' came the voice in my earphones, a voice from a bomb-proof bunker at the Muenster Air District Headquarters into which all reports of air-activity were channelled.

I looked to the left, towards the north. Everything was dark. No aircraft going down, no burning bombers lightening the darkness as they once did as soon as the bomber streams had reached the coast and headed inland. Since Hamburg about four weeks earlier the British had taken to hiding themselves behind clouds of silver-foil strips, dropping them continuously from their aircraft so that they could creep undetected through our fighter boxes. Once our close-controlled twin-engined night fighters had marked the direction of the enemy's advance and their target with their kills — huge, flaming torches of burning bombers. Now it was a matter of stalking them, of sensing them, of cunning and of feel.

Was that a shadow against the haze, the lower clouds, the high veil of cirrus, or against the Milky Way? Were those stars or exhaust flames? Was the rocking of my aircraft caused by turbulence from the airscrews of a four-engined machine? Was that faint streak a contrail, the warm trail of a bomber? Those fat, red parachute flares, dropped by the artful Pathfinders — were they route indicators for the main force, markers for a terror attack or simply decoys? The searchlights probing over there — did they indicate friend or foe? If the British had fooled us with their techniques, all we could do was rely on our sixth sense: to sniff around, to listen, to keep our eyes open, just as way back in history our ancient forefathers lay in wait for the heavily armed Roman attackers.

All remained quiet. To the north I saw the flashes that marked two aircraft shot down by flak. Seconds later two flare-shells lit the sky, one above the other, then died out after ten seconds. That was the Bremen recognition signal, the occulting light of a vast lighthouse, its structure unseen. A minute later I saw two flare-shells next to each other, directly ahead and in the distance. That was Brunswick. I was pretty well on track. To the starboard and astern I saw three flares one above another. That was Kassel, a marker for night fighters approaching from the south-west. More or less straight ahead but a very long way off I saw single flares: Magdeburg. All these, one felt, confirmed ones self-orientation in the unknown: there was a sense of being looked after and controlled by human beings on the ground below.

The ground station transmitted: 'Target provisionally 1 - 3'. That meant that the bombers were expected to advance as far as 13 degrees East, roughly along the line Leipzig, Berlin, Stettin. Our Air Fleet Command had obviously been able to read the enemy radio traffic: the British broadcast the forecast weather to the crews for their times of return and from that we could calculate how far east the bombers would penetrate. Was it Berlin? Was the Battle of Berlin about to begin? With the thousand bombers, of which Air Marshal Harris was prepared to sacrifice so many?

Ahead, far below, a pundit was flashing. Over North Germany the sky was becoming clearer. A searchlight reached out towards me. Surely the blokes below must know that we are coming. They must be able to distinguish between the noise of a single-engined machine and that of an armada of four-engined ones! I cursed explosively behind my oxygen mask. Or had the first of the bombers perhaps arrived already, and were we three single-engined fighters flying unsuspecting among them? The searchlight came closer towards me, so that it almost had me in its beam. I hesitated to fire recognition signals. The British were very good at imitation and deception. As we had discovered on earlier occasions, they carried a large quantity of our recognition signals with them. Nor was I prepared to flash my navigation lights. The searchlight would certainly pick me up then and hold me long enough for a young gunner with binoculars to recognise me as a Me 109 — and long enough, too, for one of the Mosquitos protecting the bombers to shoot me down. I made a gentle curve and continued on my way.

Again there is a crackling in the R/T. 'Enemy bomber stream, leading aircraft to the north of Hanover', came over in plain language. I was flying south of Hanover, over the Weser, near to Hannoversch Muenden. Ahead, quite faintly, I saw more searchlights. They were casting about the sky. Down near the ground I could make out the beam, milky in the haze. As I gained altitude I lost it almost completely. Higher up, I would only be certain that it was there at all if it came into contact with an object — an aeroplane, which would light up in the darkness like a snow-white pinpoint.

The flak started to open up: I resisted the temptation to turn towards it. I climbed, keeping a good look-out. When green, red or yellow target markers started to go down, then perhaps it would be a different matter: would it prove to be the main raid or a diversion? There was always the worrying feeling that one might do something wrong: one could be late, could let destruction take place, all for the sake of a town one imagined was threatened, but where nothing happened.

A further message came over the R/T: 'Enemy bomber stream north-east of Brunswick'. I was south-west of Brunswick, still some way behind. Too much caution could cause flying times to overlap, resulting in our night fighters being stretched beyond their limits. We couldn't allow the rearguard of the bombers to get through to the town and drop their loads unhindered after our fighters had used up all of their fuel and have had to land. I decided to catch up a little: there would be others to fill the gap if the forecast depth of penetration materialised.

Up to that point the ground station had not issued any orders; they had only broadcast a commentary. The leaders of the units in the air had all maintained R/T silence. We above were somewhat less well informed than those below. It was quite clear to all of us that we had to keep heading in the direction of Magdeburg. For the listening service that stretched over the entire country, the situation would be getting difficult because the pack of night fighters was moving gradually towards the bomber stream from north, via west, to south. Some were even coming from the east, having barely taken off.

We couldn't hear any of the noise in the air, but the brave man of the listening service on his high tower in the woods, doing his duty just above the treetops, could turn and listen in any direction that he wanted to. All he would be able to hear, until his eardrums burst, would be the thunderous surge of thousands of whirling propellers and the noise of millions of ignition strokes. It would be impossible for him to give any further details about the aircraft of either friend or foe: their number, their height, or their direction. All that he could report would be the beginning and the end. In the air we only trusted the broadcast commentary on the air situation until our eyes informed us better. But the Pathfinder aircraft, which flew ahead with their radar sets and were responsible for finding the target and identifying the city by dropping markers, transmitted their signals to our direction-finding stations at the same time. In that way they were accurately fixed.

The Berlin flares were going up — two flares at a height of 7000 metres, one above the other. Their location was near to one of the flak positions on the southern edge of the city. We changed the flak position from time to time to confuse the British. Approximately twenty kilometres ahead I saw a British bomber going down in a huge ball of flame, painting an ever-steepening parabola.

I heard the word '*Horrido*' on our frequency, so loud that it hurt my ears. Could that be my Nasenmueller? He spoke again: 'This is *Wilde Sau* 2. Enemy bombers. Four engines. Heading east.' Mueller's instinct was good. He had worked his way through the darkness into the bomber stream, 100 kilometres away from Berlin. He had bided his time, matched his speed to that of the bombers, and had ascertained their heading from his compass. He had taught himself to see in the dark during the course of innumerable barge trips up and down the Rhine. His report rang true, and was extremely important. I repeated it to the ground station and they retransmitted it on all frequencies, to all the fighter units.

Time passed. I began to get fidgety. A sudden alteration of course to the south by the enemy and the target could be Halle/Leipzig, Merseburg or Leuna; if they turned north-east, Stettin; or, if the leaders turned through 180 degrees, it could be Magdeburg. That was also possible. It was one thing to have to fly to a detailed plan and carry out someone else's orders in the air, and quite another to cook up a scheme with elegant speeches, to do the rounds of the established night-fighter units, teaching Grandma to suck eggs. Now I was facing the moment of truth: ahead of me could lie a lot of criticism and mockery: I was conscious of a trembling in my knees.

The curtain was due to go up at any minute; if not, we would have missed the action. The Berlin flare-shells went up again. I headed left of them, towards the centre of Berlin. I was at over 6000 metres. The flak would not be expected to fire up to that height, where we should be able to hunt freelance, unimpeded. Lower down we would have to compete with the flak for our prey. But it was a contest not without danger, as we knew from experience.

The Mark Brandenburg was in darkness. In the distance I saw a flare, but apart from that nothing else. A further worry manifested itself: after it's all over, where are we to land? Enemy night fighters took the opportunity to lay siege to the few airfields suitable for us to divert to. The bombers, too, could cause problems. A crater in the middle of an airfield could make us homeless and hopeless at the same time. But the thought of being left helpless up there didn't worry us.

The *Luftflotte* had decided on a bold measure: all airfields, far and wide, around the scene of the battle were to be lit up towards the end of the attack both perimeter and runway lights. In addition, green Very lights would be fired. Should the target be Berlin, therefore, the entire North German plain would be lit up as far as individual night fighters could follow the bombers. Then the Mosquitos' efforts would dissipate, leaving them to clutch at straws, and many an airfield commander would find himself suddenly promoted from the back of beyond up to the front line. Even if, without him having accepted a single, brave night fighter, a heavy bomb landed on his airfield, he was under orders to hold out, to keep the lights on fully. Blacking-out was forbidden: that had to be understood by all and sundry. Orders were orders. Even more was asked of the 'Commanders' of the dummy airfields: it was their task to attract the enemy and shut the door in the faces of our own fighters, switching off the lights so that they didn't come to grief in a swamp or a gravel-pit.

If Berlin was to be the Brits' target, the sparks should start flying at any moment. My watch showed 0020 hrs. It was 24 August 1943. Still nothing — nothing — darkness — darkness. What had the enemy got up his sleeve, what crafty scheme? Another target to neutralise our defences? I experienced a nervous feeling, a type of tension in the region of my stomach. The agony of uncertainty made me feel in need of help. My tongue was dry; I couldn't think. Was anyone waiting for an order from me, in my lofty but wretched position? I simply wouldn't have known what to say.

From my position, south of Genthin, I saw a light cascade to earth. Suddenly I was alert. Was it a decoy like the one we fell for the previous week when Bomber Command launched an attack on our guided missile research centre at Peenemuende and cascades such as that were dropped on Berlin? Further marker flares fell to earth. An area of several kilometres square was marked out on the ground.

The searchlights reached up into the sky and formed cones. Already one or two aircraft were glittering where they intersected. Damn! Two, three, four British bombers were heading from Potsdam in the direction of the city. The Flak unleashed its fury on the ground and hurled it aloft — 1000 guns gave their all. The air was filled with hot metal. Where were the fighters? Without thinking, I applied full throttle. Suddenly, and without my having seen a fighter, I saw a bomber burst into flame; then a second, and a third. But others were streaming in behind them. Berlin was in flames, a witch's cauldron 100 kilometres across. The curtain had gone up. The bloody drama had begun: triumph for one would bring death or suffering to another. Heavy bombs crashing onto fear-filled air-raid shelters. Above, the fighters' cannons hurled wild vengeance at the bombers. I jettisoned my overload tank and headed towards the south of the city.

The flak searchlights were splendid. When they caught a bomber they didn't let it go but offered it up for sacrifice. And they were coming down: a good dozen already.

Our young men had come from everywhere, from far away, from Holland, Belgium, France, Denmark, from every part of the Reich — the baker's apprentice taught to pilot an aeroplane, the schoolboy, the sixth-former, the father of a family, the unshaven youth, prince, *Graf*, gamekeeper, farmer, or popular song-writer: alone and unfettered in the darkness of the night they came, fearing no man, to do their duty, to stand guard.

As I neared the city I saw a massive bomb strike in the square marked out on the ground, which was almost completely spread with rows of incendiary bombs. I saw burning and combustible material erupt, leaving a black crater behind. But at that moment there was nowhere else I would rather have been. I was where I wanted to be, with my countrymen, above a Berlin violated, above my people, friends and comrades. I was filled with a solemn, bold endeavour, as if I had heard a thousand, bright, Bach trumpets sounding from on high. I pulled my seat-belt tighter and reported over the R/T: 'Wilde Sau 1 over Berlin'. To hell with radio silence! Now it is a confrontation, eyeball to eyeball.

To the starboard, half-a-dozen bombers had been captured by a similar number of searchlights; they were all prisoners. If they managed to escape from the outstretched arms they were picked up mercilessly by others. This was where the bomber had to forego its protection of darkness. I dived into the path of the bombers and turned left, in behind one of the 'couriers', as we called them. I was higher than he was, and I descended towards him. The incendiary bombs that were scattered in the target area ahead of me showed through the searchlights, dazzling me. But I kept my eyes fixed on the bomber. I would not let myself be distracted by the scenes to the right and left of me; by the silent, ghosting searchlights; the ceaseless storm of flak; the night fighters' tracer gleaming high and low; or by the burning bombers, even though in my anger I rejoiced when I saw them, huge torches falling to earth.

I closed in on the bomber, throttled back and positioned myself well below him. Now! Power off and nose up to reduce my speed. I was within 800 metres of him. Flak burst close around the bomber. I was just short of the cluster of flak bursts. I heard a muted explosion. A heavy flak salvo! Look out! I fired a Very light, my instruction to the flak to leave me alone and the bomber to me. But the flak didn't stop: they had picked out their victim and were not going to let it go. The shells burst dark-red, close around the bomber. It swerved to the right to avoid the flak. I cut the corner and closed in on it. The flak had become less intense; it was to my starboard now, along the bomber's former course. It took some time for it to readjust. Now was the moment for me to get into an attacking position unhindered. But the searchlights had become less intense as well. The bomber curved to the right, in the direction of the target area. The cone of searchlights began to break up. I could see the bomber, but faintly. I was afraid that it would disappear into the darkness at any moment. This was my last chance. I fired from a range of 300 metres at the turning four-engined machine. I couldn't afford to miss. I gave another burst. He didn't catch fire, but vanished into the dark. I groaned with anger behind my oxygen mask and steered into the darkness between countless lights, flashes, and burning objects. At full throttle I made a steep, climbing turn towards the direction from which the bombers were coming. High above me, they were flying towards their target. I couldn't reach them; I had to let them pass and leave them to other fighters.

The R/T was full of noise. Curses were being flung about, against each other, against the *Flak* that was peppering the fighters with gunfire or dazzling the pilots with searchlights, against the enemy that wouldn't go down but got away: curses at their own stupidity and bad luck. The curses of the anti-aircraft crews erupted on other frequencies and so were unheard by our ears. Everything looked red. Suddenly there was a triumphant cry amidst the tumult: '*Pauke. Pauke. — Horrido!*'[3] An aircraft fell to earth like a comet and impacted. *Wilde Sau* was on the rampage!

I pulled my aircraft up to height, using full throttle — that'll do nicely! A bomber was coming towards me, coned in the lights. I had to curve in quickly so as not to have too much to catch up. I'd got him, 100 metres dead ahead. He was lit up beautifully. I closed in with a touch of throttle, just under the turbulence from the propellers, closed my left eye, saw the bomber in the shimmering circle of the gun-sight and pressed the button. Another second — but what's that? The bomber was in flames and another burst of fire streaked into the flames from behind, not ten metres above my head. Then I saw a twin-engined fighter gently banking away above me, to the right, to avoid the wreckage of the bomber. Blast! I hauled my Me 109 to the other side, climbing again, dissatisfaction mixed with despair because someone else had clobbered the bomber, literally above my head, certainly without seeing me. It seemed as though I was going to look a fool over Berlin again, only a week after having stood sentry in the air there, fooled by a Mosquito diversion raid, while the main heavy-bomber force struck Peenemuende on the Baltic coast. On that occasion I saw the fury of the air battle in the north, too late to take part, obeying orders from the top.

In desperation I pulled my Messerschmitt round in a steep curve on to the bomber's attack heading, the G-force pulling my cheeks and jaws downward. Burning bombers were falling to the hands of my comrades. On the single-engine frequency I heard the '*Horrido!*' of many a *Wilde Sau*, among them those of Mueller the Nose several times. Was I going to miss out? I was determined to do anything, no matter how desperate. I breathed deeply, turned the oxygen valve and felt wide awake. I cast a glance below, where innumerable dark-red fires were eating their way from building to building. Would this be another Hamburg?

I moved in on the next plump visitor. He had been picked up by one of the big searchlights on the edge of the Flak Zone and handed on to the smaller ones. It was a proud Lancaster. I'll make short work of this one! Nobody else is going to shoot this prize away from under my nose. It was no use trying to cooperate with the flak. They were firing up above 6000 metres, into the zone that was reserved for the fighters. I crept in closer. The bomber was flying straight ahead, unharmed, through the millions of watts of the shining cage that was raked with flak shells bursting red. Their detonation clouds either swam past into the darkness, seeming like clumps of cotton wool, or I flew through them and could smell them in the outside air that was mixed with my oxygen.

The bomber maintained its course. The pilot had got nerves, that was for sure. Or maybe he was a new boy, afraid that he'd cock things up if he put his machine into a dive. Undeterred, he flew towards the target area marked out below. I stalked him into the flak barrage. Things were warming up. The senior Flak man, *General* Weise, had warned me that there was a lot of iron in the air there. Don't worry, I had said. The London flak hadn't made much of an impression on us bomber-men. It had been kind of that great anti-aircraft artillery man to pardon this piece of impertinence on the part of an undiplomatic *Major* who was trying to be clever.

After my experience earlier that night, I decided not to fire another Very light before I attacked. Everybody was hyped up on this occasion, the first of the threatened major attacks on the capital of the Reich. I waited for the British pilot to turn to evade the flak. Then I'd close up. He didn't. And so I positioned my Messerschmitt at a suitable distance and pressed the firing button: my night-tracer reached out towards the bomber. Before I could fire a second burst, the Lancaster made a steep turn to port and dived into the depths, followed by a dozen, bright, greedy arms. I went after him. Down we went, then up again: a steep turn to port, a steep turn to starboard.

I glanced quickly at my instrument panel — the instruments and the pointers were all in a wild dance. The rate-of-climb pointer somersaulted a couple of times. Given the chaos in the cockpit, the vast span of the bomber's wings was all I could concentrate on; it was my artificial horizon. I followed it, not knowing at any given moment where heaven and earth were. Sometimes searchlights flashed through the cabin roof. It was only from the almost impossible pressure on my control column that I could guess when the bomber pulled up sharply or turned steeply. The man in front of me must have been a stunt pilot. Whatever he did, I did. A dark compulsion drove me after him, the hunter's lust. If he crashed to the earth he'd take me with him; but surely he knew what he was doing with his machine; and he had a whole crew to help him and protect him.

The flak had been shaken off long since, but the searchlights hadn't let him go. I hadn't any idea where I was. Suddenly, the rushing, whistling noise of my Messerschmitt ceased, and it felt and sounded as though I was flying normally. It looked as though he was flying straight and level too.

Then I saw his bombs drop out of the glare of the searchlights, into the darkness, into the depths, into the conflagration. The hideous picture of Hamburg stared me in the face — man-eating lava. Bastard! Swine! I trembled, pleading fervently that my cannon-shells would strike home. Could I do better? I must fire: he must be destroyed. The tracer would help. I fired; my cannon hammered. I pulled up slightly. Another burst. My heart jumped — I'd hit him!

The bomber veered into a steep, diving turn to port. It wasn't burning. I followed it as it continued to dance wildly, until the pilot thought that he had shaken me off. He was flying straight ahead but losing height and travelling fast. He wanted to get out of the reach of the searchlights; but I was determined that I would bring him down before he did so. I closed in, saw streaks of dirt on the aircraft's fuselage, and in the vivid light I saw the rear gunner behind his four guns. I was flying in the darkness. He must, he's got to, go down. I thrust forward into the cold light of the searchlight's beam, and I could physically feel the four guns pointing at me. I aimed and fired into the starboard wing. Again, I heard the dull hammering of my cannon, and my aircraft vibrated, giving me a warm, cleansing feeling of self-fulfilment.

Suddenly, I heard the rattle of bullets against my aircraft. Then emptiness. Silence. My engine had packed in. Strangely, I had no sensation of fear. Ah! I thought, now it's your turn. My Messerschmitt was losing height. Dispassionately, I watched the Lancaster go down, flames consuming it. Shock had conquered triumph. Smoke began to fill my cockpit. Acrid fumes were coming from somewhere. The words 'You've got to get out!' flashed through my mind. Was I afraid to jump? I didn't know. What I knew I was afraid of was that the kite would explode and burn me and my parachute with it. One fear chased another. Oxygen mask, off! Headset, off! Pull it out of its socket! Release seat-belt!

I pressed the canopy release — and again, harder. Was it pressure or suction that was taking hold of me? I was going down steeply, but I pulled back on the control column so that my aircraft went into a steep climb, gaining 200, 300 metres while I pulled my feet out of the rudder-bar stirrups. I reached 5000 metres and crouched, ready to jump. Before the aircraft lost its motorless forward momentum I shoved the control column forward with all my strength. Weightless, I floated away from my faithful Messerschmitt, having ruthlessly pushed and kicked her to the depths below, towards which she was heading, a thin veil of smoke behind her, crying out in torment.

I had passed the peak of my self-inflicted catapult trajectory and was twisting and turning about every axis. Dream-like but earthly things — lights, fires, turmoil — circled round me. For a while I didn't deploy my parachute because I didn't want to spend too long drifting down through the busy, metal-rich airspace. I heard engines roaring, flak detonating. I descended faster and faster. The sleeves and the legs of my thin summer overalls started to flap violently. After the heat of the combat aloft and the violent acrobatics the air felt cool as it brushed my cheeks.

It was time to stop this bloody twisting and turning! I didn't want to find myself on my back, with nothing but ever-changing beams of light in my eyes. Must turn over on to my stomach, must be able to see what I think is the ground and where my steep descent is taking me. I turned onto my stomach, but undefinable forces turned me slowly, like a grilled chicken on a skewer, around my axis. Involuntarily I stretched out my arms, as though to support myself, then I thought how stupid that was. I felt the wind under my hand, soft as a kiss; it seemed to help. I turned slowly towards the horizontal. In that way I learned swiftly how to control myself — left arm; right arm; spread the fingers; close them; close my legs; spread my feet. No doubt an expert parachutist would laugh at my efforts: but whatever wisdom I had was the product of my first experiments.

I stared downwards, and estimated my height from the base of the searchlight beams and from individual fires outside the main target area. I saw nothing, either three-dimensional or two-dimensional, between the areas of light; only blackness and infinity. I still hesitated to pull the ripcord. Who knows where the wind will take me if I have to drift a long time? Then warmer air kissed my face. I took a last look around. Falling in a horizontal position, face down, I raised my head to peer into the far darkness, then lowered it to look along my body to my feet. Ahead I could see a broad area of red flames. Suddenly the air felt like a warm breeze, and I realised that I was close to the ground.

It's time! I grasped the handle and quickly, anxiously, asked myself whether or not the parachute would open. Nothing I could do, no power of will, no effort, no skill, could ensure that. Hope and farewell, a feeling of finality and dispassionate readiness to accept what fate has in store for me, mingle one with the other.

I pulled the ripcord. There was a swishing noise. Then a jerk. My head was pulled downwards and my chin struck my chest, so that my neck tendons protested. I looked up. I was drifting, swinging through the air beneath the silken canopy. My God! What a miracle, to emerge from nothingness into life. I hung in the sky, a spectator in the arena where the battle was raging. I heard the many-toned whistles of innumerable splinters of shrapnel, the roar of aircraft engines above me, the rolling fire of the anti-aircraft artillery, and the dull explosions of heavy bombs, and I felt the pressure waves. Here and there I heard the bark of night fighters' cannons. Here and there fire was consuming men and aircraft alike in the firmament. I heard and saw all that above me while I descended.

Suddenly I found myself suspended in a searchlight's beam. I was blinded; my eyes hurt. I looked up at my snow-white parachute. The crews of the flak searchlights made a practice of following shot-down British pilots down to the ground so that they couldn't evade capture but would be delivered to the ARP. I drew my flare-pistol from my trouser-leg pocket, cocked it and fired. The searchlight moved away to look for better prey. As I watched my red and white flares go down they suddenly doubled in number, and, to my horror, I realised that they were being reflected in a seemingly boundless stretch of water. Swim? In these clothes? Drown? The flares had extinguished. I looked down and felt as though the whole globe was coming up at me, a vast monster. As I approached the surface, waiting to arrive, time passed slowly. Now? Not yet. Not yet. Into water? Admittedly water wasn't a sweet-smelling, soft haystack, the type of landing place a nocturnal parachutist dreamed of, but it was better than the point of a church spire, high-tension cables or a sewage plant — such places flashed through the mind of, and frightened, the lonely traveller between heaven and earth. I peered downward, straining my eyes. What looked like a wide, dark, broad-brimmed hat encircled me, came towards me, its middle filled with water. At the last moment it occurred to me that I could swim better without my boots on. I let my Very pistol drop, so that it hung on its line two metres below my feet. Boots off! I pulled up my right leg and fumbled with the blasted solid brown Africa boot. They were said to give excellent protection against those desert pests which had a penchant for boring beneath one's toe-nails. I pulled the crossed laces out of the hooks. Boot away! As it plopped into the water I splashed in after it. All around me was blackness. I thrashed wildly with arms and legs. I had to get to the surface; I couldn't breathe. My head shot above the water and I filled my lungs with the night air, taking the deepest breaths I had ever taken.

At the end I had been taken by surprise. There wasn't time to breathe, to see, to think. Panting, and keeping myself afloat with my arms, I undid my parachute harness. Gradually my pulse became more regular. I was no longer enveloped in my parachute, no longer captured and bound by its lines. I must have hit the water at the extremity of a swing, so that the parachute came down to one side. It had not occurred to me to do what people who had had similar bad experiences had recommended — release the parachute while you're still in the air and free-fall the last five to ten metres so that the parachute drifts away with the wind. I had been lucky. At night one could easily misjudge height and break one's neck.

I was still treading water, and my parachute was nowhere to be seen. The water had found its way into my overalls; it was cold at first, then more friendly. I looked around me, hoping to see the safety of a bank. At one point I saw some woods, silhouetted against the red glow of a fire. It could well be the bomber, my quarry. Was that the nearest bank? There was nothing much to see in the other direction, so I swam, one-booted and in my overalls, towards the red glow.

After five minutes I was out of breath. I was treading water with tired movements of my arms. I set off again, but after a few minutes I stopped, exhausted. I thought that the bank would be nearer. Just the opposite! It looked to be miles away. Was I losing my reason? Half-consciously I sensed some type of resistance: something was rubbing against my leg. I felt with my hand and touched a line; I pulled it up, through my hands. On the end of it was my Very pistol. I had forgotten all about it. But the pistol and its cord were not alone: a confused mass of parachute lines was entangled with them. I was attached to a huge anchor, possibly already caught on the bed of the lake. I hadn't made a metre's progress! I could have wept. I took my knife from the left leg of my overalls and cut the lines all around me. I dropped the pistol into the depths, and finally the knife as well. My efforts had exhausted me, and I had swallowed a large amount of water. But my arms were free to paddle again, and I began to tread water and gather my strength.

For some strange reason I didn't think of shouting for help now that I needed it. I didn't want to disturb anyone. Or perhaps it was the desire, innate or indoctrinated, to help myself in all things. With moderate exertion, as if set for a long journey, I struggled towards the silhouette, using every swimming style I could think of. I crept forward: on my stomach, on my back, on one side. My arms felt heavy when I did the crawl. I paused for breath. The silhouette was a little higher. I breathed in deeply, then breathed out. On again. Further. My heart was beating its fastest. I swallowed more water. I was at breaking point. The sky was streaked with blue. My mind seemed to be playing games with me. I saw a Bavarian Gasthof. I heard Bavarian voices. I thrashed my arms continuously. Suddenly I hit reeds!

I regained control of my thoughts and looked up to see a thick, high wall of reeds. I embraced and held on to a large clump of them. I needed air. Air and rest, until the wild beating of my heart slowed down. I wanted to rest. I wanted to sleep for a long time; there in the water, on the reeds. The bomber — my bomber — the capital of the Reich, they all meant nothing to me any more. My world consisted of a clump of reeds, chafing and scratching my cheek.

Gradually I became colder. I didn't try to touch the bed of the lake with my feet; I was afraid of getting stuck in the mud. So I worked my way deeper into the wall of reeds, pulling myself from clump to clump, drifting through the water until I touched land with my hands. I stopped, hung on, then pulled up, first with my left arm, then with my right, until my body was on the land. I pulled up my legs after me and crept a few metres on all fours up a gentle slope, water streaming from my overalls. I was in woodland.

It was quiet. The bombers had flown west, the flak had ceased, and the searchlights had been extinguished. Peace covered the land. Suddenly a night-bird aired its voice and crickets chirped. I stood up, undid the zip-fasteners on my breast, legs and sleeves, and struggled out of my overalls. Then I pulled myself out of my uniform jacket: the lining in the arms seemed to be stuck to my shirt. I rolled them all up together, wrung the water from them, and set off at random along one of the narrow paths that ran beside the lake. I trod carefully through the darkness, catching my bare foot painfully now and then. As my warmth and strength returned slowly, so did my confidence. I was, after all, in friendly Brandenburg countryside, and there would be friendly folk to welcome me.

There they were! I could hear voices. I stood still, and could hear their words. I shouted 'Hallo!' and heard the frightened cry of female voices. A man's voice broke in: '*Deutsch oder englisch?*' There was a pause. 'Are you British or German?'

'German pilot. Shot down,' I called out. The man was not convinced. 'Where did you come from, and with what kind of aircraft?' 'From Bonn, with a Messerschmitt 109.' A long pause followed. 'There's something wrong here. Come closer, but slowly. I'm going to shine a light on you.' A hand-operated, dynamo pocket lamp gleamed, then its full beam dazzled me. 'Stand still! Halt!' I heard him say, above the noise of the dynamo. The beam moved slowly down the length of my body to my feet, where it paused for a moment. I pushed my wet hair back from my forehead and waited.

'Man,' he said, out of the darkness, then he was silent. The female whisperings had stopped. I told them that I had fired recognition lights, red and white, over the lake some time ago. 'Come with me, then, young man.' The voice seemed more friendly. He let the torch-beam pass over five or six young girls, workers by the look of them. Then he shone it on himself and I saw the grey of a *Luftwaffe* shirt. The group turned round and marched towards me. The man, a sound-detector operator in a raid-reporting regiment and a reservist, was the first to recognise from my signal that a German pilot was about to take a dip, and he had alerted the camp situated on the bank of the lake. At once the young girls had broken camp in flocks in their enthusiasm to rescue 'their' airman and bring him to land. Instead, however, a Sergeant Smith had fallen into their hands: he had baled out from the burning bomber and on landing had expressed his fear of the wood nymphs in his mother tongue and taken to his heels.

The sound-detector man handed me over to the matron of the camp. After a rapid, frightened look at me, the lady took me by the wrist and pulled me over the threshold. 'Now then, *Herr Oberleutnant*! Come on into the cookhouse and get dry.' Several dozen young maids had prepared a triumphant reception for me in a big barrack block equipped with several stoves. They were shooed away by the matron, 'Off to your beds!' By then it was four in the morning. 'Now, *Herr Oberleutnant*! Give me your wet things. Good lord, they're so heavy! Get undressed — here's a blanket. Sit down by the stove. Give me a shout when you're ready.' I was out of my clothes very quickly, and I put the wet things in a heap on a chair, wrapped the blanket round myself, and was ready to receive visitors.

As I let the heat from the stove warm my back, several girls from the early shift, on the orders of the matron, took my clothes and draped them over the stoves. Then the fires were made up. Pans were pushed here and there, oven lids rattled, and I looked with concern at my dripping underclothes. I told myself not to show embarrassment in front of so many beauties, but to remain triumphant. And so, seated on my throne and wrapped in my toga, I adopted an imperial pose, causing one of the girls to ask if I wanted to be painted like that. 'Not by me,' the pert little thing added. 'By her over there. She's an artist.' 'Her over there', smooth-limbed and with brown curls, blushed sweetly, more sweetly than a poet could have described. I didn't feel beautiful enough to be painted just at that moment. What was more, they would have no sense of time. The sitting would have taken a long time, that was certain. The matron was very proud of the artist. All at once I felt very good, having been elevated to an object of art: but I also felt awkward before the artist's eyes.

Out of the corner of my eyes I looked at the tanned faces, innocent and free from make-up, from which young eyes were watching me, inquisitive or shining. While the pans were being moved backwards and forwards and much else was going on around me, I heard amused whispering, and I was able to enjoy comments such as ' 'E ain't no *Oberleutnant*! Look at the badges on his tunic . . . 'is 'air's going grey . . . 'is shavin' soap's all mushy.' With the joy of discovery a little *Berlinerin* shouted out, 'Look 'ow big 'is feet is!' Everybody laughed. I was on the point of being mildly offended when another little miss said, 'Well 'e's a sight bigger than what we are.'

I was given an enamel mug of ersatz coffee, proffered with a curtsey, and my naked arm emerged from my toga; then a slice of black bread with syrup but without margarine. It tasted very good.

As dawn broke a car arrived from the nearest airfield: the matron had ordered it. The driver, a *Luftwaffe* lance-corporal, reported smartly and put two capacious army boots in front of me. On loan, he said, and I had to sign a receipt for them. I had to force myself to begin the process of getting dressed: it was too pleasant in that idyllic place. 'Out you go! Or do you want to see a naked man?' The girls vanished in a trice.

I had to report to my base, where I was long overdue, by telephone from the nearest airfield. The commander of the airfield and the aircraft depot told me that he had taken half-a-dozen British airmen into custody. One of them was in the sick quarters. I asked to see him. I was inquisitive. Air battles between pilots and flak, almost like the rules of duelling, imposed a distance between the combatants. I had never met my enemy, a fellow inhabitant of the earth, on solid land and been able to see the whites of his eyes. The doctor took me into a small, light ward, gave the British airman a friendly nod, and then withdrew.

The Englishman, in a snow-white covered bed, looked at me earnestly, somewhat fixedly, but didn't say a word. His hands lay calmly on the bedspread. I wondered what I wanted with him. I tried to say a few words, to ask about his experience, but I was unsuccessful. Suddenly I found myself feeling apprehensive. What could we have to say to each other now, when only a short while ago we had been shooting at each other, trying to kill one another? Would empty words be substituted now for bullets? We had gone into action against each other, each according to his orders, each for his own country, Mueller against Miller, Wilhelm against William. It was our fate to have to do that, to be willing to do that. In the very centre of Europe, in the flaming dome of the sky above Berlin, we had fought, as had the warriors of the same blood in the bursting banqueting hall of Attila, King of the Huns. For a short time we looked at each other, with neither amity or enmity. After violent combat we no longer knew how it had all happened, what it was all about. Together we had leapt over the highest precipice, but despite that our common fate could not bring about a reconciliation. There was silence and a growing embarrassment on both sides. The enmity of our two countries stood between us. Was their way really better than ours? Or were their ambitions less honourable than ours, born of jealousy or a lust for revenge or gold? I closed the door slowly. For him: the doctor, being looked after and no more fighting. For me: fresh orders.

The *Luftflotte* had been asking urgently for my report. Staff *Oberstleutnant* Boehm-Tettelbach came to the telephone. I learned that the suburb of Lankwitz had suffered severe damage, but that it was scattered and not to be compared with Hamburg. He said something about 70 to 80 bombers having been shot down. He asked me where I had been for so long and ordered me to drive to Karinhall immediately. The airfield *Kommandant* gave me a car and a driver, and

I set off into the Schorfheide. I arrived at Karinhall in my army boots, unpressed trousers and shapeless tunic. Unshaven, I stood in front of *Oberst im Generalstab* von Brauchitsch, the Adjutant-in-Chief, who was wearing trousers and polished knee-boots. He looked me up and down and smiled winningly. 'You look like a real *Frontschwein*. We don't get many of them here. A proper *Wilde Sau*! You're to see the boss.'

While I was waiting to be summoned into the big office[4] I sat down in the breakfast room. Being a 'front swine', I got *Wurst*, ham and a cup of real coffee. Brauchitsch returned. 'Do you know what the boss has just asked me? Whether your pilots are all proficient swimmers! If not, I've got to take the necessary action!' Soon afterwards I was summoned into the big office.

When I went out through the high door some time later I had a weighty object in my hand. There was a lot of gold and platinum on it, and it glittered with diamonds. 'Now off to Berlin-Staaken, quickly!' urged von Brauchitsch. 'There's a new aeroplane waiting there for you. Press on back to your *Geschwader*.'

I set off from Staaken. The sunshine augured well. I felt rather drowsy, and I hummed tunes, never reaching the end of any of them. I was constantly aware that my Muse was suddenly anchored in the geography beneath me, as I dreamed my way through the air. Near Hoexter on the River Weser, a place I used to visit on class excursions twelve years previously, I found myself singing a few bars of a wistful song, 'Looking down into the broad valley, myself and the world forgotten!' The twelve years seemed a lifetime ago. I had travelled a long way since those days. At Hangelar, my Messerschmitt bumped over the turf and came to a halt. My mechanic approached me sadly, his hands buried in his black overalls. His ancient, old-fashioned No. 1 was no more. In its place there was a mirror-smooth, new one, soulless. But surely an aeroplane is only an inanimate object. No! Objects cease to be objects when feelings come into play.

I changed over into my *Storch*, cruised upstream at tree-top height, throttled back, touched down and taxied through my iron gate. I switched the power off, left everything lying as it was, and ambled, overalls over my shoulders, across the rickety bridge. Twelve hours, more or less, had passed since I'd started my mission.

That afternoon I was sitting in the Goethe Room again, waiting to receive radio signals from the other side of the Channel and for the resumption of the methodical destruction; nothing. Nothing happened for days.

It came about that 'Mueller the Nose', who in the meanwhile had been endowed with a new soubriquet 'Felix the Lucky', and who continued to expel de-tarred smoke through his mighty nostrils, finally shot our boar: the Adjutant cultivated his health and his night vision even more assiduously, continuously crunching radishes between his teeth. The Signals Officer, Holler, spread out his networks, some sparkling with rotating beacons, some with wires and some without, which Max Pill used, like an alert spider, to call for supplies and iron rations for men and aircraft alike. While all of this was going on I, a man of culture haunting his surroundings, whistled and sang three catchy bars of Bach, always *da capo*, even when I was thinking or dozing.

A fortnight more or less passed by. Then a charming, framed oil-painting arrived through the official mail. There was a card with it that said simply, 'Your Lake'.

'My' lake in warm sunshine, wind-wrinkled and reflecting clouds, surrounded by woodland. It lay there, dreamy, quiet and small. And there was 'my' clump of reeds, the one I had embraced, and in it, as if in a picture puzzle, I found two initials apparently growing from the water.

My thoughts went back. I saw myself falling in the night sky. A small, friendly light gleamed through the blackness.

But war had no time for such things. I was there, and I was ready for action. My feet were in half-length boots. They were easier to kick off if you had to go for a swim!

Notes

1 The strips of silver foil first dropped by the RAF during the Battle of Hamburg were code-named 'Window'. They were cut to half the wavelength of the German radars, against which they were deployed.
2 The Koenigsberg Philosopher: Immanuel Kant (1724-1804).
3 Pauke! Pauke! and Horrido! both meant 'Target destroyed!'
4 'The big office': Goering's.

Chapter Twelve
The Winter Battle for Berlin, October 1943–March 1944

American offensive in the Far East. Battles in Italy. Monte Cassino. The Teheran Conference.

According to the loudly proclaimed British 'Master Plan', Berlin, the capital city and the industrial and organizational centre of the Reich, was to be laid waste. And so, immediately after the devastating blow against Hamburg part of the population was evacuated into the Mark Brandenburg and to places more distant. The horror of the recent past was plain for all to see. The successes of the defences during the night of 23/24 August 1943 gave some grounds for us to breathe more easily, but nevertheless, it was suspected that serious mistakes had been made. That such was the case was confirmed by the news that *Generaloberst* Jeschonnek had committed suicide, following a dispute with Goering between the attack on Peenemuende and that on Berlin.

In the period immediately afterwards I was summoned by the *Reichsmarschall* on several occasions and required to report on discussions with the Chief of the General Staff and to explain how I thought the battle should be conducted in the future. We sometimes sat together late into the night after the Adjutant-in-Chief, von Brauchitsch, had gone home to his family. Sometimes *Generaloberst* Loerzer was present, but he made hardly any contribution to the practical discussions. I formed the clear impression that Goering wanted to get away from the confident, unquestioning ways in which the battles had been fought up to that time, and that he wanted to understand my expositions and proposals, both in general terms and in detail.

It seemed that many criticisms of my concepts, and of myself, had found their way to him. During the First World War he had been an intelligent and successful pilot, which enabled him to ask me some shrewd questions that helped me in my explanations. He told me how, in 1918, he had sometimes found himself in difficult situations but had overcome them by taking chances. 'You remember, don't you Bruno?' he would say to his Head of Personnel.

Being a qualified blind-flier myself, the aerobatics he described to me made my hair stand on end, but I couldn't help admiring the instinct and the daring that he had shown in those hazardous episodes. I asked myself why this mentally alert man, who grasped new ideas so rapidly, had not intervened more promptly in our present difficulties, or formed a more clear picture and set priorities. I noticed how he listened carefully to what I had to say, and I was at pains not to express myself didactically but in broad terms and as a front-line officer. I was speaking to my Commander-in-Chief, whose prestige had suffered as a result of the

Hamburg failure and other shortcomings, and who had lost his influence with his Supreme Commander.

I was at pains not to dwell on operational planning, air warfare and strategy: I simply maintained that previously the close-controlled night fighters had waged positional war, lying in wait in a type of Maginot Line. What I wanted was for us to be more like a fire brigade, deploying rapidly here and there as required. That, I said, was essential, in view of the numerical inferiority of our fighters when compared with the bombers. When I spoke in that manner, he would become very alert. His eyes would sparkle and he would exclaim, 'Did you hear that, Bruno?'

During our first conversations his attention and his sympathy were attracted almost exclusively by the fact that pilots of single-engined aircraft had taken to the skies at night at all, and had dared to ride through the anti-aircraft fire. He jokingly christened me 'Young Siegfried'. He had watched the attack on Berlin from Karinhall. Gradually, however, he warmed to the logic of the operational concept, occasionally cursing the General Staff violently, apparently comparing them to the late-lamented Jeschonnek. The General Staff should have issued appropriate operational guidelines, he said. I chimed in cautiously, in such a way that he would not get the idea that I thought that he should share the blame. In that way I was able to speak somewhat more specifically about the failures of the leadership and to outline in general terms what I had put down on paper and passed on to those responsible during my previous year on the Staff.

I told him that I considered the fact that the Officer Commanding Night Fighters and the Inspector of Night Fighters were one and the same person was unfortunate. It was too inflexible a position, I said, and it was not for nothing that *General* Kammhuber was called the 'Pope of Night Fighting': someone incapable of making a mistake. In my view, I ventured, it would be better if the job of the Inspector of Night Fighters were incorporated into that of the Inspector of Fighters. Goering always showed himself very receptive to new ideas, and I also spoke with him on the subject of personnel. That he didn't have to call on 'Bruno' for an opinion on this subject, and that the latter joined in the conversation, saying '*So. So,*' was explained by the fact that Bruno Loerzer was Head of Personnel.

In 1942 *General* Kammhuber had reacted somewhat coolly to my suggestions, drawing attention to his earlier lack of success with searchlight-assisted night-fighting, which had seemed to be a good idea initially but which had become outmoded by then. Nevertheless, when suggesting a division of responsibilities, I was in no way attempting to satisfy any personal feelings that I might have had: all I wanted was for the matter to be properly handled and a decision to be reached following mature considerations and discussions.

At one particular meeting I formed the impression that I hadn't been summoned to discuss the issues of the day. Goering wanted simply to talk with me and to see how things could be done in future. I was not happy at that type of meeting unless there was some special reason for it, because I had enough to occupy me with the *Geschwader*, the Divisional Commanders of the Flak, and the Heads of the Air Districts.

Sometimes, however, he had been thinking things over, and he would put some unexpected questions. Where did I tell my men to drop their overload tanks — over the town, or here in Karinhall, for example? I said that I had given orders that the tanks, which constituted a fire hazard, were to be dropped before flying into the flak zone, but had discovered that my pilots weren't doing so, preferring to prolong their time in the air. I told him that latterly I myself had done the same. He said that the day fighters should carry tanks as well, and then they too could move about here and there and act as a fire brigade. If the worst came to the worst they could jettison the things before going into combat.

Goering had become very animated. We had given the British something to think about, he said, and so far they had not done anything more about Berlin. Now we would have to deal with the Americans just as energetically. He pursued his line of thinking with considerable imagination. He was determined to do something. His manner of speech became bombastic and somewhat theatrical: he would win back the control of the skies, he said, and hoist the victory as his banner. He asked what my views were.

In the beginning, I said, even the twin-engined night fighters had found it difficult to cope with a wide-ranging war of movement. The *Herr Reichsmarschall* had heard, from the mouth of *General* Kammhuber, that his night fighters were not able to fly from the Rhine/Main area to Berlin. To be able to do that they needed further training. I added that it could also pose a navigational problem for the day fighters. From the flying point of view carrying overload tanks was no problem. They could, indeed must, be jettisonned before aerial combat. I expressed my opinion that the single-seaters would be more in danger by day than by night. The pilots would be sitting on powder kegs. Goering said that he would like to talk the matter over with *General* Galland, and he told Brauchitsch to send for him.

When I was flying from Staaken to Bonn my thoughts turned to the prize essay I had written when I was a *Leutnant* and the question that was set: 'What is the most effective way of fighting a war?' My answer was typed on page eighty-two of my *opus*: concentration of forces, an inner line, sorties from the centre to the perimeter, all strictly according to Clausewitz. I asked myself how it was that even before the war wrong decisions and incorrect assessments had been made, and why, during the war, basic principles had been ignored. Simple things, it seemed, were difficult. Clausewitz had been vindicated on that point as well.

I received a visit from *General* 'Beppo' Schmid, who had commanded the Hermann Goering Division in North Africa. When the Army capitulated there he had been flown out because he possessed secret information of which the Allies could have made use. Before the campaign he had been Head of 1c, studying enemy dispositions on the *Luftwaffe* Command Staff. I had met him in 1942. Some malicious tongues had said that we should have let the Americans have him, because he would have told them as big a pack of lies as he had previously told to his own leaders. The latter assertion I would have taken with a pinch of salt. Even in the business of waging war there were those who talked big — even in Department 1c.

Schmid was inexperienced in both flying and tactics, and I explained the concept of mobile air warfare to him with a degree of self-confidence. I found him to be interested, ready to learn and of a practical turn of mind. I had no reservations concerning his future roles. He wore the Blood Order of the Party, which had come his way in 1923, not by having been involved politically but because he had marched with them as a cadet. He paid me compliments in an unobtrusive way, which I felt to be friendly and sincere.

In the middle of 1943 he was appointed Commander of the Night Fighter Corps, which surprised me; although it was apparently no surprise to others. He replaced *General* Kammhuber. I was not subordinated to him but remained *reichsunmittelbar* — independent and responsible directly to the *Luftwaffe* Commander of the Central Area, *General* Stumpff, who had been recently appointed, and whom I knew very well from my time in Norway.

Shortly afterwards Goering issued an order to the effect that I was to form two more *Geschwader* and call the new Fighter Division the 30th *Jagddivision*. I was very pleased that the Inspector's responsibility for my single-seat aircraft Division was not given to *General* Kammhuber, who would not have been happy with it, but that it was given to *General* Galland, who had proposed the expansion of my command.

And so I had to leave my beautiful *Schloss* Allner and its dear occupants, forsake Johann Sebastian Bach, and walk across the rickety bridge to my *Storch* for the last time. *Wilde Sau* 2 and 3 went with me to the *Division*, as did Signals Officer Holler and Max Pill, the great organiser of things material. Further happy memories and recollections of carefree experiences at the front were awakened by the arrival of my incorrigible old subordinate, Weinreich, who joined the *Division* and took command of a *Gruppe* of single-seat fighters. Later, on being promoted to *Major*, he took over a *Geschwader*. *Major* Kettner, formerly the leader of the Rheine *Gruppe*, assumed command of *JG 300* at Bonn.

From being a comparatively junior officer, I became a *Kommandeur* of a Division, with a Staff which was situated near to the Olympic Stadium in Berlin. Soon afterwards I took over *General* Kammhuber's responsibilities as Inspector. I organised the latter in conjunction with Staff *Major* Mueller-Trimbusch, who had been on the *General's* staff. It was to be a temporary appointment with a view to the planned unification of the entire air defence organisation under *General der Jagdflieger* Galland. He and I flew together to East Prussia and visited the Command Chief of Staff, *General* Koller. In less than an hour the proposal had been considered in detail and committed to paper. Galland became *General* i/c Fighters, and under him were *Oberst* Trautloft (Inspector of Day Fighters), and Herrmann (Inspector of Night Fighters).

In my opinion it was a rational division of the leadership of the fighting men in a way that catered for the possibility that the Allies could go over completely to either night attacks or daylight raids. In addition training, planning and arms procurement against so dangerous an eventuality were vested in one officer.

I was highly satisfied with the entire set-up. I had retained my dual role: that of Inspector of Night Fighters and *Kommandeur* of the single-seater *Division*. The latter function was envisaged for the transitional period only, until the territorial Divisions took over the command responsibility for my three *Geschwader*. It looked as though I was going to put down my roots in Air Defence.

Although following the catastrophe of Hamburg the number of enemy aircraft destroyed had in individual cases been doubled, they remained on average at their previous level. It was therefore necessary to see if radar-controlled interception could operate in conjunction with *Wilde Sau* operations without being jammed. A breathless race began to accelerate the development of existing equipment and techniques, a task to which Staff *Oberst* Lossberg, who was on *Feldmarschall* Milch's Staff, applied himself devotedly. Up to that time he had been unable, like myself, to get anywhere with the 'Pope'.

We also had to respond swiftly and positively to the sophisticated deception tactics that the British had introduced following the attack on Peenemuende. Spoof attacks with displays of marker flares, violent alterations to course by bombers, attacks on widely separated targets, misleading German instructions — all these were blows that we had to parry. Correct decisions could be taken minute by minute only, otherwise defence was like striking aimlessly in the air. Sometimes it seemed like a guessing game: trying to decide what the British thought were our intentions and strategies, so that in turn we could forecast what they would do. This involved an assessment of the air situation using nebulous and hypothetical premises which had to be revised, in an instant, when we obtained factual information. It was necessary to have a pilot's highly-developed instinct, a great store of experience, and the ability to understand the weather and how it might alter during the period of an operation.

To a pilot the weather could be friend or foe, insensitive to the beating of the pilot's wings, yet sometimes furious. The knowledge that one could easily make an incorrect assessment of the forces of nature, and that one was working on the brink of a mass catastrophe, put demands on clear thinking, as did the fear that one might miss the enemy completely, thus delivering a town to unopposed annihilation. By night the lines between the *Luftflotte*, the *Fliegerkorps* and the Divisions were hot with discussions conducted over distances of hundreds of kilometres. Accusations, abuse and oaths alternated with friendliness, appreciation and words of praise.

Previously the British had not shunned moonlit operations, preferring to operate in clear skies; then they made it a rule, following their heavy losses over both Peenemuende and Berlin, to fly in when the sky was cloud-covered. By doing so they hoped to avoid the dangerous cooperation between our searchlights and fighters. At the same time their aircraft were being equipped with the new airborne radar that we called 'Rotterdam'[1] after the place where we had found and recovered a sample. This equipment enabled them to display prominent geographical features on a screen in the aircraft. To form an opinion of the accuracy of the equipment I flew over Berlin one day in a Ju 86 which had been equipped with a set recovered from a crashed bomber. The East-West Axis, *Unter den Linden*, Tempelhof airfield, the lakes around Berlin, all could be easily recognised. I was shattered. The enemy had something like this, while our bomber crews had to rely on their eyesight. At night our fighter pilots operated in darkness, while their bomber crews could see almost as clearly as by daylight. I realised what we were up against.

Following our first operation over Cologne/Muelheim I foresaw that enemy attacks would be carried out in cloudy weather, particularly if our successes should increase. We planned that in overcast conditions all the searchlights available would shine vertically so that the haze would scatter their light, and that we should also burn magnesium flares on the ground so that the upper surface of the cloud would resemble a dull grey, milky lake, against which the bombers would stand out. We code-named this procedure '*Leichentuch*' — 'Shroud'.

If the layer of cloud was so thick that the lights could not penetrate it to the upper surface, a *Gruppe* of Ju 88s was at readiness to transform the cloud into a '*Leichentuch*' by dropping flares from above it, thus creating a background against which the fighters could see their targets. Like the fighters, the illuminators were sent off in the direction of the predicted target. Then, following the RAF's usual alterations of course and deceptive manoeuvres, the illuminators would fly to the area that the Pathfinders had picked out with their sky markers. In such weather conditions they had ceased to use the glowing, coloured 'Christmas Trees', visible from a long way off, which fell to earth and continued to burn, so marking the corners of the target area into which the four-engined bombers poured their bombs.

Above the clouds the Pathfinders were restricted to using parachute flares that drifted with the wind and had to be replaced in the correct location by fresh ones. This made the attack more difficult to carry out. Our illuminators made it harder still by dropping vivid parachute flares into the area selected.

Anyone with any imagination could understand why the heavy, cumbersome bombers were unwilling to venture into a brightly lit Hell in the heavens. I didn't waste my time marvelling at the decreasing numbers of those who ventured over the '*Leichentuch*', but I did note the fact that many of the 'heavies' were creeping along its edges. The police reports of where bombs had fallen confirmed this. If, for example, the bombers' target area was marked out in the sky as a four-kilometre square, as it was over Berlin on 4 January 1944, the bomb-hits were spread out over an area 40 kilometres square, from Oranienburg to Potsdam and from west Berlin to Koepenick, so that — fortune from misfortune — fires were prevented from spreading. That indicated that the 'shrouds' deterred the bombers more than the searchlights did. Searchlights could only pick out and hold on to a small number, while the remaining bombers were able to weave their way between the searchlight cones.

The man on the other side who led Bomber Command, who brought together the crews and the machines and got them into the air, was Air Marshal Arthur Harris. But it was not he, but D. C. Bennet, whom I saw as the main imaginative genius and about whom I tried to gather information when I was with Department 1c of the General Staff. I considered the Air Vice Marshal to be my personal enemy, and I refused to concede his superiority.

Earlier, pyrotechnic flares designed to resemble enemy markers had been fired from the ground on the approaches to the towns in order to combat the machinations of the Pathfinders, but they were not convincing. I made it my business to get hold of better imitations, and I had them fired experimentally, obtaining good results. I also suggested that they should not be stored on the ground by the hundredweight, but should be carried and dropped by Ju 88s, my illuminators.

It was pointed out to me a few days later that my display of lights and fireworks had trespassed into an area of activity outside that of night fighting. The man I had offended was the Inspector responsible for dummy installations throughout the Greater German Reich. He approached me in a friendly but condescending way. Hiding both my astonishment and my displeasure, I stood to attention and expressed my regret, but to myself I thought, 'You poor little man with your piddling little command, what have you got to worry about? Who gives a bugger who does what, as long as it's in the common cause?'

There was a further aspect of the business of combating the bombers. Until recently the night fighters had not been involved with the deception and diversion tactics, but had gone into action almost invariably ahead of, and a long way away from, the scenes of blood and fire. To take on Bennet and spoil his *son et lumière* became a personal obsession. From my own experience of bombers

I knew how difficult the enemy had made it for us to find and hit our targets.

At a conference chaired by the Director General of Air Supplies on 31 August 1943 I said, 'We plan the operation so that our markers are dropped from a Ju 88 which carries a man with a special monitoring receiver tuned to British R/T traffic. This man uses his judgement to drop the markers in open country, either at the same time as, or shortly before, the British drop theirs.' I requested that more of these flares should be made available to me. In his concise way *Feldmarschall* Milch said, 'You can have as many as you want, no matter who we have to steal them from.'

To form a better idea of Pathfinder Chief Bennet's tactics I paid a visit to the transit camp for prisoners of war at Oberursel. Our uninvited guests spent a few days there in one-man cells before they were transferred and joined their comrades in permanent camps. They were put through an interrogation process, so I joined in myself. The majority of them curtly gave me their service number and name, nothing more. They would not confirm their squadron, even when I named it and the Commanding Officer. One man did weaken under the torture of having to go without cigarettes for a couple of days, inhaled greedily the secondary smoke from my cigarette and began to talk hesitantly. I borrowed this man from the Camp Commandant for two days and flew him in my *Storch*, on a beautiful September day, to *Schloss* Allner, where he was able to smoke to his heart's content and wine and dine under chandeliers. A good *Mosel* helped to loosen his tongue. To this day I can hear him saying how wonderful the countryside was, that he knew Germany from his night visits only, and that he had always believed it to be a den of thieves. Despite the fact that all statements made by prisoners of war were passed to the Command Staff, thus being available to me, I paid a further visit to Oberursel. The jigsaw puzzle fell gradually into place.

Autumn was passing. The British chose not only cloudy weather situations, but also those in which it was difficult for us to take off and land, while they, with the clag below them, could fly in clear, starlit skies and return to their bases and land as comfortably as they had set out. It was a difficult situation for us. After a respectable pause — there had been one weak attack in September and several visits by Mosquitos — the British resumed their offensive against Berlin in the middle of November. Throughout Central Europe, as far as the Channel Coast, the weather was so bad that nothing could take off. The British came. I left my Battle Headquarters in the Olympic Stadium, which I shared with the *Luftflotte*, and drove to the *Zoo* bunker in the *Tiergarten*, where I was to meet Minister Speer.

Following my talk with him, and while the attack was under way, I went up to the roof of the tower where there was a radar operated by young soldiers. I looked around. Incendiary bombs were lodged high in the trees and burning on the pavements. There was a shrill organ concert of thousands of flak splinters whistling down and striking sparks from the concrete as they landed, punctuated by the cracking of bombs and the pressure waves of aerial mines. All around me was a light-grey to white, luminous sea of fog. In the centre of this chaos the young men on their exposed tower carried out their duty. I was appalled. This was what the terror looked like to the eyes of a defenceless victim. I was not wearing a steel helmet, and I withdrew below to the protection of the thick concrete walls.

It had been the previous year in Berlin that I had begun to consider the problem of defence, working from theories and figures on paper. There too I had experienced heavy raids, the most recent of them in March 1943, when I had been able to see 'Rigoletto' as far as the second act. From the steps I had watched the rest of the drama unfold in the sky. It had seemed to me to be a bad thing that night fighters had their command post in Holland. Now and then, at the very least, a leader should be in the middle of the action. Rear echelons, frequently but not always justly reviled, were of course usually behind the lines. Here, they were right up front. The Flak was always in the thick of things while others took cover in bunkers and cellars, in the middle of the rain of flak and bomb splinters. I had visited their senior commanders and had been able to form an idea of the sufferings of the armed forces and of the civilian population. I had also discussed ways in which there could be cooperation, especially with the *Luftwaffe*, a subject that until then had not been addressed. Following that March 1943 attack I cursed everything and everyone above me in rank and position, that went under the name of leadership. What Speer had said to me shortly before we watched the attack about further increases in production, coupled with his friendly exhortation to hold out, made me feel very bitter. It seemed to me that before any action could be taken aerial mines had to strike home on the very walls of the bunkers, by which time it would be too late.

I drove westward through the city's burning streets. I felt completely overwhelmed. I asked myself whether I should admit defeat. Who would want to go on? Who *could* go on? To my 1a in the *Division*, I said that, if the bombers came back the next day we must get into the air.

Towards late afternoon there were signs of activity on the other side of the Channel. Harris and Bennet had seen their opportunity to destroy Berlin in a rapid series of raids. The weather was in their favour, and it looked like keeping us on the ground. I got into my BMW and drove out to one of my *Gruppen* of single-seat aircraft. The British were heading our way and were already over Holland.

I went with the *Kommandeur* of the *Gruppe* to the tower and had the perimeter and runway lights switched on. A moderate wind was driving orographic cloud very low over the ground just above our heads. The Met man switched on the vertical searchlight. The cloud base measured from 50 metres down to 30. The far boundary of the airfield could only be seen intermittently. The illuminated approach and take-off funnels outside the airfield could not be seen at all. That meant that the visibility was between 700 and 1000 metres. The top of the layer of stratus was at 800 metres. The only landing ground in Germany that it would be possible to operate from was Muenster in Westphalia. There it was hazy, with a beacon visibility of four kilometres.

I felt myself unable to give the order to take off. I asked the *Kommandeur* to tell the pilots to come to me. I described the weather situation to the men, and I also described what I had seen in Berlin the previous day. I asked if anybody would volunteer to fly. I said that I would not hold it against anybody if they did not wish to do so. Of the 25 to 30 men, seven raised their arms. I was pleasantly surprised. From the remainder, I called one forward and said that he looked as if he could make it. He laughed, and the others laughed with him.

As the pilots climbed into their aircraft to go on to immediate readiness I went up the tower again with the *Kommandeur*. The visibility had not improved. It was cold and damp, and I found myself shivering again: but it wasn't only because of the weather. I was asking myself where the war was taking us, and wondering whether we were asking too much of our airmen and of our civilian population.

We returned to the general situation map and the *Kommandeur* telephoned the divisional command post. Staff *Oberst* Kern informed him 'Weather in the east, unchanged. Leading bombers in the Brunswick area, heading east.' The *Kommandeur* remained on the telephone. I went up into the open air again and stood there alone — alone and responsible for the defence of the capital city of the Reich. Tensely I watched the drizzling mist thicken and lower, then thin slightly and lift. The perimeter lights on the far side of the airfield gleamed, then they were obscured. There was not one star to be seen; the landscape was pitch black. I pulled myself together. Take-off must be now or never. The *Kommandeur* at the map didn't have to make a decision, nor do the men in the aeroplanes. If I didn't say something now, if I stood here for another five minutes of this dreadful night, the film would run out.

I stood watching the shimmering perimeter lights.

The first engine burst into life. The bass chorus swelled to *forte*. Red in colour, port navigation lights started to move. The first red light raced past. Shortly afterwards the noise of an aircraft's engines howled over us. The light shot past and was gone. The second . . . the third . . . all swept away below me. The noise grew to *fortissimo*. Then the aircraft had gone. A dull bass came to my ears from the east, became weaker, softer, softer and faded.

I stared eastward. Would something dreadful happen — a burning wreck on the ground? But what I had seen had encouraged me. My crews had taken off flat, and had retracted the undercarriages and flaps flying fast and low, as we had practised, as had been drilled into them three times, ten times, on the clearest of nights or during air tests in bright sunlight.

I could not see or hear anything. All that was left was the inhospitable, pitiless night. I cursed myself for having sent them off without me leading them, for having watched them go like a stupid idiot. I walked unsteadily into the radio centre where I found the *Kommandeur*. Over the loudspeaker I heard, 'Splendid weather up here. Fantastic!' Unnecessary chatter could clutter the frequencies, but the pilot's relief could be detected in his voice. I felt a surge of pleasure. I hoped that the other crews felt the same. I couldn't bear to drive back to Berlin and be without news for the next hour. I had all the other crews called up. They all checked in. Up there the weather was great. I gave thanks to God.

The command posts began their various measures to mislead the British.

Approximately ten four-engined bombers were shot down, and the eight fighters from my *Jagddivision* landed at either Rheine or Handorf near Muenster. A taxying mishap had been the only misfortune.

When I drove up to our villa near the Olympic Stadium, I found it ablaze. Equipment, papers, desks and chairs were all collected together in the garden under the watchful eyes of staff members. *Oberst* Kern had his shirt-sleeves rolled up and was going into the office on the ground floor, from which the furniture had already been cleared, to take two large portraits off the wall, one of the *Fuehrer* and one of the *Reichsmarschall*. I shouted, 'Stop! the ceiling's coming down!'

The Staff personnel, their work done, were sitting on chairs and desks waiting to see what would happen. Kern looked towards me, laughed, strode inside with fragments raining down about him, took the pictures down and came out triumphantly, holding them over his head like a shield. 'Couldn't leave them there to be the only items that were burned,' he said, and everybody laughed.

There was one unpleasant after-effect of the operation. Goering bawled out the officers responsible for the other night-fighter units. If Herrmann's men could do it, why couldn't they with their two-man crews and better radar equipment? The next time that the 30th Fighter Division took off they would do so also, he had said. Being their Inspector, I had to represent the entire night fighter force. I pointed out to the *Reichsmarschall* that the crews had never flown before in such weather, and that they weren't trained to do so. That would be remedied. But he remained unbending. During a subsequent enemy raid I remained in close contact by telephone with the Divisional Commanders involved, with *General* Ibel in the Hamburg area and *General* Huth in Munich. The *Luftflotte* and the *Fliegerkorps* both waited to see what the Divisional Commanders would decide to do. There was much discussion. Quite clearly, nobody wanted to be the one to order the aircraft off. I cannot say that I wanted to be the one to do it. Everybody waited for me to give an unequivocal 'No'; but I disappointed them. Why shouldn't I order aircraft off, if I thought that it was possible? Just so that those people who hung back wouldn't be shown up? I told them that they each had to make a decision for their own area. As their Inspector I could only advise them to base their decisions on abilities of their crews. I didn't want to give a direct order: I would have liked to call for volunteers.

I didn't feel that I would be justified in making my decision solely on the basis of the wishes of the night-fighter pilots or the risk involved. Millions of people were sitting in their shelters. The Divisional Commanders didn't want to take the responsibility because of the threat of the *Reichsmarschall's* wrath. Nobody — and that included me — wanted to take the first step. I had not received any orders to the effect that the fighters had to fly. The *Luftflotte* hadn't dared to give such an order. But one more attack and the British would have turned Berlin into a practice bombing range, laying waste to one district after another —Wedding, Moabit, Steglitz, Friedenau, Berlin W 1 to W 35. The night-fighter force was on the ground. Should they try to get airborne? I was afraid that if I gave the general order to take off they would do so and rush into the air all together and create a very dangerous situation.

That was what happened on the next attack on Berlin in November. Admittedly the number of enemy aircraft shot down increased, but a number of our fighters were written off on take-off. Having to land in adverse weather conditions also led to further losses. Aircrews had to bale out of their aircraft, and several aircraft crashed, some of them single-engined. I was accused of having set brutal operational weather conditions. I defended myself by saying that as defenders of the Reich we could not afford to be a fleet-in-being like the British lurking in Scapa Flow. I thought that it was unacceptable to consider our losses alone, or to compare enemy bomber losses with those of our fighters. Why were we there? To take the burden off the civilian population and industry in every possible way, direct and indirect. We could only do that, I said, by being in the air.

Further accusations were made against me, and they reached Goering. In *Wilde Sau* operations the fighters shot down bombers when they were over towns or cities, instead of before they reached them. I had welcomed the bombing, it was said, because the fires it caused illuminated the clouds from below and made the bombers visible to the fighters! With Goering I did not hide my anger at these accusations. When the previous defence system was in operation the bombers broke through the night-fighter boxes, reached their target and got home again with a loss of about five percent, and even that was not before they reached their target, but to a large degree on the way back as well. I was not obsessed with the idea of fighting above the town or city that was being attacked: on the contrary, it had been my intention to use uncommitted reserves in searchlight-assisted defence while other aircraft operated freelance in the darkness.

Unfortunately, since Hamburg, we had been unable to do that because we had been short of radars that were immune to jamming. Despite that we tried to get into the bomber stream as early as was possible. The more of us that could do that, the sooner we could get a bomber in our sights, not only in moonlight. The main thing was that the ground-control stations reported the positions of the bombers accurately.

As far as the fires were concerned, I went on, it was an insult to say that I consciously looked upon them as part of my technique. There had been fires before, but then the night fighters had been forbidden to fly into the flak zone and turn the light of the fires shining on the clouds to good effect. I, however, had worked closely together with the *Flak* and the searchlights. I had had flares dropped from the air and set out on the ground to make the bombers visible. If fires occurred it would be wrong not to make use of their illuminating effects, as had been the case previously.

I added that it went without saying that as Inspector I was in touch with every organization that was involved in the development of night-fighter equipment. Nobody could argue with that. Until such equipment was available we would continue to fight as we had done since Hamburg, striking blows against the bombers, mainly above the cities but also in the surrounding areas. That, I said, would be effective in the long term. It was my opinion that we could attain a ten percent rate of kills during every raid. We could have reached that figure before the British began their jamming operations. I explained my theories to the population in a radio broadcast.

I had the feeling that I was going to be unable to convince Goering completely, or else he didn't want to let me see that he was convinced. Perhaps he didn't say everything he was thinking. Somebody maliciously informed my staff that I was desperately trying to come up to the expectations that had been put in me: that I was ambitious. I knew that I had no ulterior motives. I was a bomber man and nothing had been expected of me in the field of air defence. I had wanted to do nothing more than to put forward my idea and to prove it in the face of rejection and opposition.

In the autumn and winter months we had fended off the worst: my name had been mentioned in the newspapers and on the radio; the 'Song of the Wild Boar' had become popular at Sunday concerts; and gifts such as chocolate, shirts, wrist watches and so on had been sent to the pilots. And now my zeal and dedication were turning sour. The words *General* Galland spoke to me in the face of these rotten accusations were comforting and encouraging: it was his opinion that I had been right to send the fighters up — there had not been any alternative.

In one of my discussions with Goering I proposed that we should operate our night fighters over northern Italy during a full-moon period, a period when the British did not usually send their heavies against us. Already the British had flown over France and Switzerland on a number of occasions, in clear weather and brilliant moonlight, to attack Turin, Milan and similar targets. I said that we could prepare a real Cannae for them there. Brauchitsch supported my idea by saying that where we attacked the enemy was not important. What was important was to cause them losses.

I stated that for the operation I wanted the single-seaters to be based at Woerishofen, and landing grounds to be prepared in Italy, camouflaged as forward bomber airfields. If necessary the twin-engined fighters could fly back to Germany and land there.

Goering heard me out in silence. Then he said no. He did not see why we should come to the aid of the Italians when they had deposed Mussolini and gone over to the Allies, royal family and all: and he did not propose to expose German cities for the sake of the Italians. I said that I had been thinking first and foremost of ourselves and of the next dark period. If my plan could be executed, the British would have fewer bombers to send against us. But it was to no avail. Nor did I have any success when I suggested a smaller operation using single-engined and twin-engined fighters. Even a smaller force, I said, would do considerable damage. I received an outright 'No!'

Bloody official channels! I could have had my pilots take off from Woerishofen. I would have flown with them, even though I was officially forbidden to fly operationally: we called it '*Denkmalschutz*', the protection of ancient monuments. We could have landed where my former *Geschwader, III./KG 30*, the *Adlergeschwader*, was based: since I had left them they had been transferred from Norway and Finland to Northern Italy.

The *Reichsmarschall* having issued his categorical veto, I did not dare to press my suggestion any further. It was too late for a cavalry charge! From something that Brauchitsch said I gathered that Goering was afraid that if anything further went wrong in Germany he would be in trouble with Hitler. It seemed to be wrong that a Commander in Chief should be so inhibited. Without taking some risks, nothing gets done. I was not going to take the risk of being called to account for disobedience. Later I was to curse my attitude.

At the beginning of January 1944, the monitoring services reported that a heavy attack was on its way to the capital of the Reich, and the code-words that had been decyphered suggested that the target would be the government quarter. The weather was heavily overcast as usual. Horizontal visibility at ground level was from two to four kilometres and the cloud base 500 metres. That was suitable for even less experienced crews to take off, but the cloud tops were at 3500 metres and there was a risk of icing. Because it would scarcely be possible for the clouds to be illuminated from the ground, the illuminator aircraft would have to create the 'shroud' from above.

After the experienced crews had taken off, and Staff *Oberst* Kern had taken control, I drove out to Staaken with the famous 'Mueller the Nose' and Adjutant Naroska, and we climbed into our Fw 190s and scrambled at 2330 hrs. Our plan was to stay under the cloud at full throttle until we had reached our maximum speed, then we would climb steeply, passing through the icing zone as rapidly as was possible: icing was the main danger on this occasion.

When we had broken through the cloud it was comforting to pick up the Flak crews' friendly Berlin flares. We climbed to 7000 metres. Economical cruising speed until they arrive. It wouldn't be long: we had timed our take-off very precisely. Flying above Berlin, we saw no sign of any flak below. I wondered if the illuminators had arrived yet. Through my earphones I heard: 'Leading bombers, Brandenburg.' Things would be happening at any moment. I saw markers falling to earth, red and green against the mantle of the sky. Could anyone see them, the Pathfinders, the harbingers of disaster? Back-up markers followed. Where were the illuminators?

From below the storm erupted up to 6000 metres. Then I saw our first illuminating flare . . . the second . . . the third . . . and more. Splendid! In we go! I could see a heavy approaching from the south. I swept in astern of it, throttled back, dived, and fired into its wings and its cockpit, a burst of several seconds. My aim was good. I pulled up over him, and a large object flew past my aircraft. 0257 hrs: I reported a probable kill. I turned into the bright, colour-filled arena. Just below me and between 500 and 1000 metres away I saw another bomber silhouetted against the 'shroud'. For a few seconds our flares dazzled me, then I opened up. The bomber caught fire. I gave a further burst. The bomber was blazing furiously: it was 0305 hrs, and I reported one bomber destroyed.

There was a loud banging, crashing noise all around me. I felt something hit my leg. There was a sudden loss of pressure in the cabin. Shooting past me and ahead and fading, I saw the tracer of an enemy night fighter. I had become a victim of my own shroud: the blazing bomber had made it even brighter. I lost all the feeling in my leg. I looked down cautiously. It was there — a ridiculous discovery, when I thought of it afterwards, but frighteningly real at the time.

I called up the ground station. Silence! My R/T had been shot up. Ice-cold air blew on my face and neck. There could be no question of my trying to land during the attack and without radio. My engine was running normally, and the weather was supposed to be better in the west. I steered with the left pedal by putting my foot in the stirrup and pulling on it. All I could feel with my right foot on the pedal was a dull pain. You've been lucky to get away with it again, I thought. Then I began to feel faint. I gave myself a burst of oxygen, but it didn't help. I took hold of the leg-pocket of my overalls, and felt it and my trousers beneath it. Damp — and my leg hurt. I had to get out before I lost too much blood or passed out completely. I saw the stars shimmering but so very dimly. I shouted to myself, 'Hold on!'

I thought that I would try to come down in the area north of Dortmund. Every three minutes a flare had gone up, true and reliable. They would be my signpost. I reduced the power and held the compass reading and the turn indicator as steady as was possible, using my left foot. Outside the cabin there were small flakes of snow. I was down at 200 to 250 metres above the ground, and still I could see nothing, no searchlights, no avenue of light. I applied full throttle and climbed. I vowed that from then on there would be no more experiments.

My Daimler Benz 801 took me out of the clag and into the sky. I could see the stars. My forehead was wet and I felt weak. I couldn't see the upper limit of the Rhine/Ruhr searchlight avenue. I felt wretched above that sea of clouds. There would have been some small comfort if I had known where I was: on the ground they might have been calling me up and saying, 'This way'; but if they were the transmitters at Kassel, Cologne and Venlo were calling out to deaf ears.

I felt ill. My weakness made me disheartened, hopeless. I went through the drill: pulled my right leg up against my body, jettisoned the canopy, pulled up and then shoved the nose down sharply. I was free. I pulled the ripcord quickly. My motion and the force of gravity took control of me. My head went forward, the parachute harness cut into me, and I was swinging from one horizon to another. Below me I heard the scream of the engine, then a dull thud when the aircraft impacted. Weak and half-conscious, I fell into the clouds. It was cold and damp. Soon wet snow was falling before my eyes. All around me it was as quiet as the grave. Without knowing why I became aware that it was getting wetter as I descended.

A thump and pain. I had landed. The dampness and the cold helped me to recover from the impact. I pulled the parachute towards me and made myself a nest. Get into it and wait for daylight, I thought. I felt towards my right boot, and put my hand inside it. It was wet with blood. I had to find someone. I crawled, more on all-threes than on all-fours, downhill, where I was likely to find some people. After a short time I saw a door less than 50 metres in front of me, the light from it shining on a front garden. It was approximately 0600 hrs, and somebody was going to work. The door was still there, but the light had gone. I called out. A woman came to me.

I was taken to the Reserve Hospital in Hagen for treatment. I had a message sent to my command post. Within a short time *Oberst* von Below, an adjutant from the *Fuehrerhauptquartier*, telephoned. I was wheeled along a corridor to the doctor's office. Below told me that the Fuehrer sent his personal congratulations on my escape and that at the next possible opportunity, when both my legs were in working order, I was to report to him. Below hinted that there would be a decoration for me.

My old Wild Boars from Bonn didn't allow me to stay in Hagen. They transported me to the hospital in Bonn-Enderich, which was run by a friend of the *Geschwader*, Dr. Weiss. I was put into a room that had been occupied for a short time by Robert Schumann. It was a great joy to my stressed, worn-out soul to have dear, friendly people coming to visit me. There there was no war. In my mind's eye I saw far-off, peaceful times, small things, fine things, brotherly love.

When I returned to Berlin a few days later the wrath of the Gods awaited me. Goering sent a message via von Brauchitsch asking me if I had considered that it had been necessary to draw attention to myself by playing such tricks. He asked if I had forgotten that he had expressedly forbidden me to fly operationally and had ordered me to concentrate on leadership on the ground, training and planning. I was to report to him by teleprinter how I had come to be flying.

This is the teleprinter message I sent at 0330 hrs on 8 January 1944:

> *To the Herr Reichsmarschall of the Greater German Reich:*
> *Asien — Secret*
> *With reference to my operational flight of the morning of 3.1.1944, I beg respectfully to report as follows:*
> *A) Reason for the flight:*
>   1. *At 0145 hrs assessment of the air situation indicated strong enemy forces.*
>   2. *Shortly afterwards, I received a report from the monitoring service that the enemy raid had been allocated the code-word 'Adolf Hitler'. I considered that it was of great importance to take defensive action against this attack, and I wanted to let my crews know by R/T that I too was in the air.*

3. *I ordered those fighters that were airborne to be directed to Berlin. I then considered myself free to fly. Landing instructions had already been given.*

4. *Previous operations had been conducted in very adverse weather conditions. The same applied to the operation in question. By taking part myself in such flights, I hope to strengthen the crews' confidence in the viability of operations of this nature.*

B) *Originator: (Signed) Herrmann, Oberst.*

Goering was genuinely angry that I did not understand the reason for the flying ban. In all modesty, I have to say that he needed me, for a few weeks at least, until everything settled down and the newly developed techniques and tactics began to take effect. I had scant regard for the Commander-in-Chief's concern because I honestly did not think that anything serious could happen to me. As an individual fighter I was confident that I was the equal of the enemy and the weather. He was more angry with my comment about future operational participation. He had, he said, taken note. If I had intended it as a request, the answer was an emphatic no.

For a period of weeks Goering did not speak to me, even when I was at the Fuehrer's Headquarters at the end of the month to present a personal report and to receive my decoration, which I had been awarded without his recommendation and on which he did not congratulate me. It was an unpleasant and awkward situation for both of us. Things changed for the better after the successes of the defences over Berlin on the 25th of March 1944, which was at the same time the final major British raid against the capital of the Reich.

And so the air war dragged on through the autumn and winter months with its painful, nerve-wracking problems and its reflex annoyances, with the night fighters playing hide-and-seek in the worst cases and sometimes, when things were more favourable, ambushing the enemy and demonstrating their marksmanship. All the control organisations strove to work together. The observer corps, once belittled by the night fighters; the men above the tree-tops; the anti-aircraft gunners with their listening posts and radars and their searchlights of various calibres; the ground illumination people; the *Luftgaue* with their early-warning service and their dummy airfields; 'Beppo' Schmid, by now settled down well as commanding officer and supported by a staff tailor-made for him, well disposed but rough-and-ready; the day fighters with the aircraft that they lent to us: one and all they contributed what they could to the common purpose of overcoming the terror, getting the fighters airborne and into contact with the bombers. This was reflected by Minister Speer in a telegram at the end of January that read as follows:

. . . in the name of German war production I wish to express my thanks for the enormous relief that you have brought about . . .

With the exception of the disagreement of which I have spoken, and in particular before it occurred, my conversations with Goering were out of the ordinary and very unmilitary in style. On many occasions he would telephone me or send for me, almost always circumventing not only the *Luftflotte* Command

Staff, but also the *Luftwaffe* Command Staff. For that reason I very rarely took advantage of my right of direct access to him. Our meetings were very informal. After supper, Goering would put on a jacket of an artistic style that one would not expect a soldier to wear, pull up an armchair, put his legs up on it, and pour champagne. *Generaloberst* Loerzer enjoyed the wine with obvious relish, but I was too preoccupied with answering Goering's questions to enjoy the champagne and the good cigars that were on offer.

Standing on the carpet by the side of the arm of Goering's chair was a huge, Bavarian clay pipe. When it went out he would call his servant Robert, who would appear as if from nowhere, take out a huge match approximately twenty centimetres in length, strike it and thrust it into the depths of the bowl of the pipe, while Goering, his eyes rolling and his cheeks sucked in, would generate the necessary low pressure.

From time to time he showed films. Sometimes they would be American, and we would sit side-by-side in armchairs quite carried away by the humour of the Anglo-Saxons and forgetting that we were at war with them. After I had said goodnight and had taken my leave from Goering, Robert would offer me, with a wink, two or three cigars. It goes without saying that I accepted them with due caution so that my 1a and I could enjoy them later, relaxed and at peace with the world.

Meetings and discussions took place at Karinhall; at the hunting lodge in Rominten, East Prussia; on the Obersalzberg, near Berchtesgaden; and, several times, on Goering's train 'Asia', which he had shunted into a tunnel overnight, particularly in the West. There were also meetings when he paid official visits to *Luftwaffe* units.

By reason of her beauty alone, Emmy Goering-Sonnemann must have made an outstanding impression on the stage. She mixed with front-line officers with a sure and skilful touch. When I, unlike those who tended to fawn on her, would not concede that her macaroons were superior to those which my mother made, she took not the slightest offence. Together with Frau Bouhler, the wife of the author of the book on Napoleon, she used to sew parachutes; she liked to make herself useful. She told me I should be careful: I didn't have a horny hide.[2]

In the Goering household I had two specific conversations, one of which could have played a small part in the political history of the time. Ten of us sat down to dinner at Karinhall; I sat next to *Herr* Bouhler, whose book 'Napoleon' I had read. The topic of conversation turned to a comparison between Napoleon's and Hitler's campaigns in Russia, and a forecast of future developments. Being insufficiently informed concerning the conditions on the Eastern Front and those of other sectors and areas, because I was too burdened with my own responsibilities, I was unable either to contradict Bouhler or to support him. As I recall, the discussion was based on either the foreword, or the epilogue of the book. Goering had only been half-listening, and wanted to know what we had been discussing. To a man, we said that we hoped that everything would turn out well.

The second discussion, at his house on the Berghof, was of a more serious nature. In a circle of people in which a Deputy President of the Reichsbank was present, I had ventured the rather bold question as to whether it might not be that the Russian campaign was in fact a war of conquest. I also asked if it was not natural and acceptable then, as it had been in the past, to take something away from somebody else. At school I had to some extent developed an interest in history, and one only needed to look at the British and the French to see that those who owned things, no matter how they had come by them, were the fortunate ones: the most recent example was the Treaty of Versailles, which had been to our cost.

Later I was most taken aback when I received a bawling-out on the telephone from *Generaloberst* Loerzer. I tried to remember what I had actually said. The *Generaloberst* tried to convert me, in a paternal, pastoral way, to the belief that the war we were waging against the enemy in the East was altruistic, defensive, and so on. In addition he made it clear to me that I had done considerable damage in the presence of civilians because I was no ordinary soldier, I was a Divisional Commander and an Inspector who enjoyed the confidence of the *Reichsmarschall*. By speaking as I had done I could cause great difficulties both for Goering and for the Government of the Reich. The reprimand seemed to me to show that I had become suddenly more important than I had thought I was, and I tried to come to terms with the idea.

Goering himself had a go at me, telling me that I had been talking absolute nonsense. The statement was followed by a dissertation on the state of the nation that could not have been put any better had it been delivered in front of the *Reichstag*. He said that we wanted nothing more than that which had been taken away from us: the Polish Corridor. Had we declared war on England and France? Had we not made the most generous of offers? From the very beginning, they had wanted to annihilate us, to subject us to another, much worse, Versailles. And the Russians had been on the point of attacking us. I should hear what the 1c-East had to say on the subject.

When he got into his stride on this subject we were in his house on the Berghof. He was speaking loudly and dogmatically, so that when Emmy brought Edda in for a goodnight kiss, she went to close the door again. But he told little Edda to come in, and Emmy waited at the door, looking at me apprehensively. The incident seemed to have calmed Goering down. He was wearing a loose silk shirt that had wide sleeves, a sleeveless green waistcoat over it, and a sort of baggy knickerbockers. He told Edda to shake hands with 'Uncle'. I offered my hand in some embarrassment. Then the subject turned to the day's agenda.

As I flew back to Berlin through a clear, starry night, all sorts of thoughts were going through my mind. I asked myself whether he mistrusted me, whether he wanted to put me on the proper lines or whether he simply liked to hear himself talk. I could have read it in the newspapers that the war was caused by the enemy; he didn't have to tell me that. I wondered if anybody really wanted to find out who was right and who was wrong. Who knew, either before or during a war, what the other side wanted? Which side was virtuous; which one at fault? No matter what anybody said, I believed that the German people were the godfearing ones, the less evil: the enemy were more evil and less godfearing. If I hadn't thought that, I could not have worked, flown and fought.

I called the *Division* in Doeberitz, on the R/T. I heard the announcement, 'Bombers approaching'. From August 1943, when the German night-fighting force had abandoned the automatism of a war of position, with its predictable results for friend and foe, a war of mobility had developed over Central Europe, facing both sides with risks that could no longer be calculated, dangers that could only be circumvented at great cost, and opportunities that could only be exploited with hot, relentless determination.

At the end of February 1944 the three *Geschwader (JG 300, JG 301* and *JG 302)* were subordinated to the geographical Divisions of the First *Jagdkorps*. From the organizational aspect it was the best solution. By then the '*Wilde Sau*' system was well enough established within the various Divisional areas: fighters could be controlled in the air, information could be disseminated, and twin-engined fighters were also participating. I continued my role as Inspector of Night Fighters, available to advise across the board.

The previous six months had inevitably left their mark on me. My Staff had noticed that I often fell asleep in my chair. I would gather strength to take part in operations. But now that I was no longer unduly subjected to operational pressures, a discussion of leave fell on fertile ground. Rest and sleep — wonderful! Brauchitsch and his wife both brought up the subject. I went with them to Zuers on the Arlberg. In wonderful sunshine, fur coats unbuttoned, we climbed cautiously upward, bones and sinews healing. Brauchitsch prescribed, for himself and for me, a complete abstinence from newspapers, the radio, and telephone calls: for the first two days I found it quite unbearable. But the healing comfort of the hotel had its effect, a hotel in which five years before Mr. Churchill and his daughter had been guests. The countryside, the weather, the food and the people all seemed to be too good to be true.

Almost predictably, a top-priority message from Berchtesgaden arrived when we had been there for five days. Goering wished to speak to me immediately. Brauchitsch issued a top-priority message to the Traffic Minister, Dorpmueller, who ordered the express from Bregenz to Innsbruck to wait for half-an-hour. It stood, letting off steam, at the quaint little station of Langen bei Zuers, until the passenger it was waiting for waddled up on skis out of the moonlight, knocked the snow off them and climbed on board. The guard called me '*Herr Minister*'. This unexpected episode had caused the *Reichsbahn* considerable confusion. When the man saw me in the light, hatless, red-cheeked and immature-looking, he stammered, 'Forgive me, er, forgive me . . . *Herr Minister*.' The circumstances were such that he had to find an appropriate title. Not to have used one would of course have been unthinkable. I asked the driver to return the skis the next day to the local mountain huntsmen from whom I had borrowed them. Later, I slept in the car to Berchtesgaden, where I learned in the early hours of the morning that arguments and incriminations between the fighter and the flak divisions had arisen during the course of an attack on Augsburg.

The dream was over. My leave was finished. My last leave had been after Sicily in Summer 1941.

Notes

1 Rotterdam: an undamaged H2S set was recovered from an aircraft that had been shot down over Rotterdam. H2S was a radar device which, by means of a rotating aerial beneath the aircraft's fuselage, produced a rough map of the terrain below the aircraft.
2 '. . . I didn't have a horny hide': a reference to Goering's jocular description of Herrmann as 'Young Siegfried'. Siegfried, hero of the first part of Wagner's '*Nibelungenlied*', killed the dragon and then bathed in its blood, rendering his skin impenetrable except at one spot between his shoulder blades where a leaf had stuck to his skin.

Chapter Thirteen
Air Defence Around the Clock, March-September 1944

Invasion. Withdrawal from France. 20 July 1944. Uprising in Warsaw. Romania signs an armistice with the Soviet Union.

In the middle of March 1944 Goering informed me that I was to take over *1. Jagddivision* — the First Fighter Division. It was a short step only from Elsgrund, the last location of the *30. Jagddivision*, to Doeberitz, where I took over from *Oberst* Franz Luetzow, an excellent and very successful pilot. Because *1. Jagddivision* undertook both day and night operations I had no time to carry on with the job of Inspector of Night Fighters. *Oberst* Streib replaced me in that function, an appointment that was welcomed by everyone concerned.

Now that I was subordinate to the First Fighter Corps — *1. Jagdkorps* — I lost my independence of action. My task was to protect the area between the Mecklenburg and Pomeranian Baltic Coast in the north and the Thuringian Forest and the Harz Mountains in the south, twenty-four hours a day. Not only did I have to control the operations of single-engined and twin-engined night fighters in accordance with the instructions given to me by the *Jagdkorps*, but I also had under me the day fighters and the communications and control and reporting organizations surbordinate to the *Division*. There were in all about 25,000 officers and men, plus a further 8,000 to 10,000 female personnel in the form of *Luftwaffenhelferinnen* (Female Air Force Auxiliaries), *Blitzmaedchen* (Signals Girls) and other workers.

As he had done previously, Goering warned me to keep a special eye on the capital of the Reich. He was not worried by day raids, but I myself was. I brought with me to the job bitter experience as a bomber pilot and a lot of theory, together with second-hand knowledge that I had gleaned in conversations with the *Reichsmarschall* and the *General der Jagdflieger*, Galland. I was very happy that the latter was nearby at Hottengrund, on the Havel, and I drove the short distance to see him many times. It was the 23 March 1944 when I took over with some reluctance the responsibilities of *Oberst* Luetzow, the very day on which the *Kommodore* of *Jagdgeschwader 'Udet' No. 3, Oberst* Wilcke, who was known as *'Der Fuerst'* (the Prince), was killed in an aerial combat with Mustangs. My arrival was not welcomed by the Staff, made up as it was of old Kammhuber men and fighter pilots. I felt as though I ought to apologise for being alive.

The Chief of Staff (1a) was *Oberstleutnant* Schaller-Kalide, a quick-thinking, quick-talking tactician, who had considerable experience in both leadership and organization. Eager for action, mocking, exceedingly dynamic, he was sometimes called a *'Selbstkocher'* ('self-boiler') because of his dynamism. Several years older than I was, and the son of a General to boot, he was a man of considerable self-confidence. On arrival in the huge Staff building, which had been constructed by Kammhuber, I knocked at Schaller's door, entered when he called '*Herein*', and said I would like to introduce myself. He was to tell me much later, following many days and nights of battle together, that the immediate impression he had formed of me was not one of being a cowboy, a tearaway, or a born '*Wilde Sau*': in short, I was not what he had expected me to be.

I set about learning my new job conscientiously, and I marvelled at the organization that had been conceived and built up by Kammhuber and at the state of training of the personnel. But the very basic questions that I put as an outsider, once a night-fighter pilot and now to be in command of day fighters, sometimes gave the experts food for thought. I had been at my new job for two days when the British mounted a major attack on Berlin on 25 March. I was in my element again. The sky was overcast. A strong north wind was driving a low layer of stratus over the city and the surrounding countryside, but there was reasonable visibility below the cloud. The anti-aircraft command had sent their liaison officer, *Pour-le-Mérite*-holder *Oberst* Werner, to the *Division* command post and were waiting for the order '*Leichentuch*', the signal to switch on the searchlights at diffused beam and to ignite thousands of phosphorous flares. Up to the last moment the decision was in question, because there were a number of scattered gaps in the cloud that would let the bright light through and dazzle the fighter crews up above. I stood on the roof of the building together with Schaller-Kalide and the meteorologist. The decision was taken and the Flak Liaison Officer informed.

Suddenly it was as bright as day on the ground. Black-out orders had become irrelevant. The light not only penetrated into the stratus, but was also bounced back to the ground and then back up again. The amount of electricity that was used in the ensuing half-hour, and the number of tons of phosphorous that were burned, were incalculable. The scene was intoxicating. If only the sky would remain covered. From everywhere the flak stations were reporting ten-tenths cloud cover. Anything from isolated gaps to five-tenths would have spelt failure; if that had been the situation the flak searchlights could not have picked out the enemy bombers for our fighters. It would not have been enough for them to be lit up for a few seconds.

Fighters were brought in from everywhere. The battle was on: blow after blow. Seventy kills were reported, the majority of them over Berlin and its suburbs. The British, attacking from the north, used a tail wind of approximately 200 kph to help them, which saved them from an even greater catastrophe: with this extra thrust those who had not dropped their bombs early or to one side were able to overfly the danger zone, the 'shroud', very quickly. Had it been different, the fighters would have been able to make more attacks. As it was, they had to make their painstaking way back home in the teeth of the gale. On 31 March 1944 we in North Germany and Berlin were not the victims. On a night of half-moon Harris despatched his Bomber Command aircraft to Southern Germany. Fighter aircraft from north Germany were deployed to the Rhine/Main area and put at the disposal of the *Jagddivision* there. More than 100 enemy bombers were destroyed. We succeeded in picking out the enemy's radar-equipped aircraft with our recently improved homing devices, and we marked the bombers' track, by means of illuminator aircraft. On 1 April 1944 the wreckage of those bombers destroyed in the attack was counted. Air Marshal Harris had promised the British Government that he would have bombed the Germans into capitulation by that date.

Now we had some breathing space. Even I, in *1. Jagddivision*, did not need to worry over-much about heavy four-engined bomber raids. What we did have to be on our toes against, however, were the nightly nuisance-raiders, the Mosquito bombers that flew in at heights of between 9000 and 10,000 metres carrying large-calibre bombs, which represented a very real danger. That danger lay in the fact that when the civilian population heard the words 'Light bomber formations approaching' reported over the radio they were unwilling to go down into their air raid shelters. Consequently the few bombs dropped by the Mosquitos often cost more in human lives than the hundred-times greater loads dropped by the heavy bomber force did. When the enemy bombers approached the civilians always went into the shelters in a very disciplined manner.

The single-engined fighters that remained in *1. Jagddivision* were earmarked to operate against these pests, using a system worked out between the searchlights and the gun-batteries that became increasingly effective. It was the high note of the Song of the Wild Boar. From the Victory Column, situated in the centre of the city, a huge searchlight shone, confident of victory, steady, erect and unearthly. Around it our brave Messerschmitts circled at altitudes of between 10,000 and 12,000 metres, like dapple-grey circus horses trotting on a long line, patient, obedient, until, in the west and outside of the city, a further three lights sprang up into position at Potsdam, Spandau and near Oranienburg. Then the fighters went off to hunt where, as had been calculated to the minute, the Mosquitos would arrive, a few of the fighters remaining in reserve over the Victory Column.

The Mosquitos arrived at the three points. The flak guns remained silent, but suddenly, as if from nowhere, the close-knit light phalanx of searchlights shot up into the sky, pointing in the direction from which the fast bombers were coming. They all reached out for them, silent but deadly. High above, single-seat fighters were already on to them. They dived after the Mosquitos, which were hoping to cross the zone of lurking danger at high speed and full throttle. The fastest of them would survive. A Mosquito that didn't drop its load within three or four minutes would be reduced to matchwood.

The high-speed hunt came lower. Then the flak barred the paths of the Mosquitos. I stood on the roof of the control room at the range-finder, while the wiry Schaller-Kalider, his eyes rolling and his chest thrust out, conducted the orchestra of telephonists, radar operators, navigation assistants and meteorologists. *Oberleutnant* Holler, busy with his circular slide rule, continuously forecast the times of the arrivals of the Mosquitos at points 1, 2 and 3 and at the possible points 4, 5 and 6.

Above the sky was clear and starlit. The first Mosquitos had passed Spandau. Another one was approaching. The searchlights coned it as it flew directly towards me. The pilot held his course, straight ahead. 10, 15, 20 seconds passed: nothing happened. I was on the point of cursing: our fighters must be asleep! Suddenly the Mosquito pulled up into a steep curve on to a reciprocal heading. One of our aircraft must have been on him, and I hadn't seen it or its tracer. Being a bomber pilot I didn't need anybody to tell me that the Mosquito's bomb would have been released in the direction of Berlin. It would land somewhere near to where I stood. It would take approximately forty seconds to reach the ground, travelling faster than sound. I wouldn't hear it until it had landed. Nor would I hear it if it landed on me! Then it would be curtains for me. From the ballistic point of view that was incontrovertible.

A stupid thought occurred to me: it'll all be over before I've even had time to be really frightened. I wouldn't have wanted that. In my final few seconds before I died, I would like to think about it, to feel something, for the last time.

A vivid flash of light, a heavy blow to my chest, a deafening noise. When I opened my eyes I saw the wooden building whirling, fragmented, in the air; pine-trees beginning to burn, and the shattered windows of the *Richthofen Geschwader* barracks glinting as they were blown in. The wounded were rescued, the buried dug out. Nobody could say that we were a rear echelon there.

Previously, we had established that, even over a long period of time, the Mosquitos had suffered hardly any losses: one couldn't have spoken of their losses in percentages, but would have had to calculate them on the basis of so many per thousand. Now they were regularly losing one or two aircraft per raid, sometimes three or four, all accounted for by the excellent Me 109s. From zero to a measurable number was a comparatively huge statistical increase, if you find comfort in figures. In addition, however, it proved that what was needed to overcome the danger was not simply a massive injection of forces, or the new super-fighter, the He 219, but dedication and fighting spirit plus a healthy optimism from all concerned on the ground and in the air.

In the autumn and winter months of 1944/45 our Me 262 jet-fighters, led by the dashing *Oberleutnant* Welter,[1] the most successful '*Wilde Sau*' pilot with more than sixty kills to his credit up to the end of the hostilities, carried the war to the Mosquitos.

At the beginning of 1944, after the American Flying Fortresses had already attacked strategic targets deep within the Reich, penetrating as far as Berlin, there was good reason to fear that worse and more effective attacks would follow. In comparison with the enemy escort fighters alone we were numerically far too weak. They would have to be destroyed, or at least tied down, before any attack on the bombers could succeed. Against this great advantage in numbers we could expect only modest successes, and to achieve them we would have to improve our techniques. It had been shown that it was not enough for our fighters to be controlled to a point within visual range of the bomber formations so that they could then position themselves individually for an attack. When we had carried out that time-wasting technique, the escort fighters from the head, tail and flanks of the bomber stream had formed up together and engaged our fighters in wild aerial combat, something we had to avoid in order to concentrate on our priority target, the bombers.

So we went over — *Oberstleutnant* Schaller-Kalide was an experienced fighter controller himself — to a precise form of close control, in which it was not individual fighters that we vectored into an attacking position, but the formation leader with his *Geschwader*. Before our fighters could see the enemy they were controlled on to the projected course of the bombers, heading towards them at the same height, so that the attack could be carried out in as close a formation as was possible against the hostile aircraft, stacked up as they were at various altitudes, thus providing an opportunity for our fighters to fire one after another at the enemy bombers approaching them. Then our fighters, maintaining a tight formation, would break down and away. They were not allowed to carry out further attacks on the bombers unless expressedly ordered to do so by the controller on the ground. Fighters that arrived on the scene individually or in small formations were almost invariably shot down or severely damaged by the heavily armed bombers.

I can only compare the bitterness of these battles with that of those carried out by our bombers against the enemy fleets and convoys and their fighter escorts.

This method of attack was also appropriate when the enemy escort fighters were at the head of the bomber stream or flying some distance in advance of it. The Mustangs, flying considerably higher than the bombers, found difficulty in picking out our fighters lower down against the multiple colours and shapes of the terrain; if and when they did, it was often too late. Then they had to follow them, which was not a pleasant job when it took them through a Jacob's Ladder of their own bomber formations.

It was of course inevitable that in this war of rapid movement there were sometimes individual dog-fights between our fighters and the Mustangs. If that happened, the *Kommodore* would have to bring his powers of leadership to bear, bringing his pilots together and under his control again. To have persisted with rearguard actions would have been disastrous.

In order to counter these surprise attacks from far ahead, the enemy began to send large numbers of their fighters in strong formations perhaps 100 or 200 kilometres ahead of their bombers with the task of finding possible opponents. They also sent their flank cover on ahead. Then we at control centre had to calculate, as accurately as it was possible, the battle order of the entire enemy air fleet and its track, using the Kammhuber radar stations. We also had to evaluate the reports of the *Flugmeldedienst*, the equivalent of the Observer Corps in Britain, including the reports from the advanced *2. Division*, enabling us to direct our fighter formations, including those sent in from other Divisions, into the gaps in the bomber stream to carry out their attack. We had to do all this with our nerves stretched to breaking point. It goes without saying that our formation leaders were faced with difficult navigational problems, particularly when there was partial cloud coverage of the ground and they had to pay close attention both to their turning circle and to the wind displacement.

It was the function of the control centre to obviate as far as possible this kind of difficulty and to relieve the formation leaders of the task of navigation. I was always very conscious of the restricted space in a single-seat aircraft and of the necessity of the formation leader to hold his aircraft smoothly and steadily when either flying horizontally or climbing, so that his inexperienced pilots could maintain formation. Whereas by night the difficulty was in finding the bombers, by day the task was to attack the bombers, once they had been found, in the way likely to achieve maximum surprise. Battles carried out during the day had to be waged with a great strength of purpose and relaxed, but unquestioning, discipline.

Despite all this the fighter pilots were criticised. Goering accused them of being 'yellow'. There could have been some justification for such an accusation in individual cases, but to abuse all the pilots in this way was outrageous. It hurt more to hear it from the mouth of the Commander-in-Chief. I considered these accusations against our fighting men to be completely unfair, because our lack of success went right back to faulty planning and lack of foresight on the part of our leaders. Accusations like this were designed to cover that up.

I showed to my 1a the concept I had committed to paper in 1942. I said that the imbalance had now become apparent. The fresh supplies we needed were not arriving: every day, that fact had to be paid for with blood. The admittedly considerable material that Speer was producing had come too late for us to catch up, let alone for us to overhaul the enemy and so offer our fighting men acceptable combat conditions.

Schaller-Kalide and I almost gave in to our depression, but we did our very best. The war was becoming increasingly bitter, but our fighter production was going not only into the defence of the Reich, but to our extended battle fronts as well. Invasion was threatening. How could we deploy fighters to England's front door when we couldn't achieve success in the heart of the Reich? At the Channel Front, the enemy's air superiority would be ten to one, and our effectiveness would be precisely nil.

It would have been too easy, in my opinion, and in any case quite pointless, to attribute the difficult position in which our front-line fighters found themselves to the Commander-in-Chief alone, to counter his accusations by pointing to the failures of the leadership, and, simply, to bemoan the situation. High-ups have made mistakes in every war and on all sides. Leaders, at whatever level, should not have to fight to clear their names: fighting should be done to protect people, nothing else. All that could be done was to make good, as far as was possible, the gaps created by the failures of the leadership, and not to take the accusations at their face value but to see them as the devices of a poor, naked man who had nothing better to offer.

At the height of periods of operational activity, I had been on the receiving end of criticism and reprimands of the most severe kind, delivered in the loudest of voices, from my Commanding *General*, 'Beppo' Schmid, so much so that *Oberstleutnant* Schaller-Kalide, astounded, had asked me, 'Why don't you shout back at the man in the same way? You know that what he's saying isn't true!' I felt sure that Schaller-Kalide thought that 'Beppo' wanted to finish me, that he had chosen me for his Divisional Commander only to keep me on a lead and, in doing so, shine himself. I didn't believe that it was like that. It was my opinion that the Commander was being pressurised by shortages and the High Command's requirements, and that he was using, in the common cause, the method of leadership that came naturally to him. Treating me as a whipping boy, rightly or wrongly, was another matter.

It seemed almost as if the Americans didn't need to defeat our Fighter Arm in the air: they aimed for our Achilles' heel, the hydrogenation works. Poelitz and Leuna were both situated within my area of responsibility. The enemy could starve us out — or, dry us out, rather. Nobody could foresee to what extent this drying-out process would succeed. If we were not to skate, be it open-eyed or blindly, past the danger of oil shortage, we had to take action. We were being forced, increasingly, into a corner. The plan I conceived to combat this sitation will be discussed later.

To defend the Leuna Works a unit equipped with Me 163s, the '*Kraftei*' ('Powered Egg') was stationed at Brandis, near Leipzig, and put at my disposal. The unit had some outstanding pilots, some of whom had been the subjects of disciplinary action and reduced in rank. I visited them, and instead of medals and rank-badges I presented them with Swiss watches that a benefactor had donated. From the aerodynamic aspect the Me 163 was outstanding, but it suffered from lack of range and was therefore of limited operational use. As things stood, a strong force of them would have to be stationed at each and every strategic target.

How, then, could we mount a successful defence against an invasion in such circumstances?

The codeword 'Dr. Gustav West' was allocated to the expected invasion. It was based on the initial letters of the words '*Dringende Gefahr West*' ('Extreme Danger in the West'). As and when the codeword was invoked, we would be threatened with a catastrophe if the fighters were not brought forward until after the enemy had set foot on the French beaches at first light. On 21 April 1944, four weeks after taking over *1. Jagddivision*, I sent the following memo up through channels:

> *Should an invasion be attempted in the West (Dr. Gustav West) there are two ways in which our fighter forces (day and night) could be used operationally:*
> 1. *Reactively;*
> 2. *Pre-emptively.*

I ended my proposal, which covered two sides of a sheet of paper, as follows:

> *Summary:*
> *In the first of the two situations that might be expected the numerically superior enemy would have ample opportunity to deploy selectively: that is, enemy bomber and fighter formations (British and American) could make a combined attack on our day-fighter formations. The equivalent of a heavy enemy artillery barrage from the air would continue until the enemy troops stormed the landing sites more or less according to plan.*
> *In the second case we could deal a surprise blow against the enemy's plan, using an attack of short duration on the embarkation points with a comparatively strong force (day fighters, destroyers, night fighters, the 300. Geschwader, and our bomber units): this would involve the complete withdrawal of the air defences from the Reich area for the period in question.*

My idea was that we should remove all of the unnecessary equipment from the bombers, destroyers and night fighters. Then they would all be despatched, together with the day fighters from Holland, Belgium and northern France respectively, to attack the priority targets: the enemy's bomber and glider bases. Only if their range was inadequate would they attack the fighter airfields that were situated closer. They would attack with cannon or bombs, or both. The assault should be carried out either at dawn, or in suitable cloudy conditions; most certainly not on Party Day, as had been the case in 1940. I did not dare to mention sabotage troops, which I was to put into action later, for fear that my proposal could land in the waste-paper basket. It landed there, nevertheless. That was how initiative was encouraged in the German armed forces.

The time of the invasion could readily be calculated: if possible there had to be moonlight, as indeed there was; it had to be dawn, as indeed it was; and the tide had to be at its most favourable, as indeed it was. We were as capable of working that out as Eisenhower was. We could have been in position 24 or 48 hours before the ideal time. We had proved many times already in the course of the war that we too could plan and organise. In addition one had only to look at that great battle in France that began on 21 March 1918. Unnoticed by the enemy, a vast quantity of artillery was deployed during the night preceding the start of the offensive, every gun having its own carefully calculated position marked out both for the wheels and the gun carriage, thereby enabling it to contribute its maximum effort to the planned artillery barrage.

The deployment of the *Luftwaffe* to defend against the invasion was a complete failure. Our leadership had failed to recognise the difficulties that faced us, our numerical strength and our state of training. Alternatively they had failed to appreciate what was our only chance; or they had lost the will and the nerve to take a risk. Inaction sprang from apathy. It was the beginning of the downward path to annihilation.

My Commanding General insisted that I should follow service procedures. He mentioned my suggestion, but he didn't discuss it with me. It seemed clear to me that he did not have sufficient nerve to dispense with a few shootings-down over the homeland. What difference would it have made if we were to have let the bombers fly unmolested over the Reich a few times, particularly when, if we had opposed them, we would also have suffered casualties? It was not easy to estimate what success a pre-emptive attack, executed with both conviction and determination, would have had, but the results would certainly not have been insignificant, even over and above the disruption of the enemy advance, which was of course the first and most important aim. Within the Reich they could make an exception and rely on the Flak alone, which had in fact been the case on those occasions when weather conditions were very bad.

Perhaps our leaders had been hoping for a miraculous tempest, such as had once driven the Spanish Armada asunder. I had been through one catastrophe already, that in Oslo-Fornebu in 1940. Normandy was the brink of disaster. What happened to the *Luftwaffe* in the West in June 1944 drove from my memory everything that I had ever before experienced or even thought possible in the field of bad planning.

We continued to fight between the Baltic, the Thueringer Wald and the Harz Mountains in order to bridge the time until the appearance of a reserve of 2000 fighters, hundreds of jet fighters and remote-controlled missiles. Following the attack on Peenemuende I had been able to learn something about those other miracles, the V-weapons, but I had to beg that information in order to know where the enemy might send its bombers. As late as Summer 1944 my Division was unaware that in Posen, which was in my area, aircraft were being constructed. Schaller-Kalide was puzzled, just as I was, why the Americans showed an interest in the area. Perhaps they were heading for Russia? No! They slammed the aircraft factory and then returned to their bases in England. But *Oberstleutnant* Boehm-Tettelbach's destroyer *Geschwader*, taking off from Königsberg-Neumarkt, did a good job on them with their 5 cm cannon.

During this period there was sometimes entertainment within the four vast walls of the control centre. Something quite droll happened, which one could with justification describe as fiddling while Rome burned. Two emissaries suddenly appeared in front of my desk and sat down. The first was Professor Martin, an official Reich sculptor, who wanted to do a sculpture of my head. The second was an official Reich writer, *Herr* Neher, who was concerned more with divining my inner characteristics. He wanted to see my Divisional Orders, my flying log-book, my school reports, the essays I had written when I was at school, and photographs of me wearing my sailor suit. He also wanted a sample of my handwriting for his graphological assistant. No! Not something I had written carefully which would show my better side: that scribbling pad, there!

There was no question of my being able to sit still for the plaster bust. Instead the sculptor watched me carefully. Meanwhile the writer went to other people and asked them about me. Then he returned triumphantly with an assessment of my writing. This only included the favourable points. I said that I presumed that the graphologist had been afraid I would lock him up. But one quality was mentioned twice in the text as being my main characteristic, as it were: I was incapable of acting dishonourably. To claim to have been able to read that from my scribble was as irresponsible as reading the future from coffee grounds. I found the entire passage laughable, because it was so obvious. I would never steal silver spoons: to make a point of confirming that to me was almost insulting. Later, in improbable situations, situations that could not have been foreseen, I had occasion to consider more closely what he had said.

Eventually, the plaster head was finished. After the plaster had been turned into bronze I more or less came to terms with my cosmetic metamorphosis, to the extent that I accepted one of the two models and shipped it to my relatives. They put it high up on a bookcase so that they could well and truly look up at me.

The numerous notes that *Herr* Neher wrote presumably did not survive in printed form. After his book on Dr. Roentgen, which he gave to me to read, I would have agreed in the interests of both of us that his piece about me should be produced. It was for similar reasons that I myself ultimately decided to write a book. Serving a sentence brings with it not only hardships, but sometimes surprising insights also. Later I was to learn that, quite literally, Neher was of the same opinion. He told me that he had pursued the subject of the *'Wilde Sau'* eagerly for weeks, but it was not until he sat down to write about it that he began to feel he was really on its track.

The Divisional Control Centre before the gates of Berlin also attracted other visitors, diplomats from allied countries and gentlemen from the ministries. Before sitting down to conferences the Japanese Ambassador, Mr Oshima, the Finnish Attaché and a Hungarian, would all pause reverently in front of the glass showcase in the Officers' Mess in which was displayed the uniform of Manfred von Richthofen. Young people from the surrounding countryside appeared with baskets full of asparagus or strawberries; or apprentices appeared with their masters to see what was going on. One pitch-black night the Countess Stauffenberg, aircraft captain and test pilot at Rechlin, landed in a Ju 88 on the small fighter airfield at Doeberitz to explain her new night-landing technique to me.

Above all I was beset by development people, because I had become familiar with their ideas in the initial stages and had encouraged them to develop them further. Among them were people from Zeiss Jena, who asked me to give an opinion, at long last, on their sight for catapult bombing. I obtained an appropriately equipped Ju 88 from somewhere or other and loaded it with cement bombs. I took off, climbed to height and dived down at full throttle to tree-top height, then pulled up hard and released the bombs on the Fahner Heights near Gotha, my practice range of earlier days. Using this method, the bombs were hurled forward a considerable distance, so that one could avoid flying into zones of rapid-firing flak.

Dr. Karl Holzamer came to gather information about our air defence. He posed well-informed questions and proved to be an attentive listener. Then a gentleman in civilian clothes (if I remember correctly, he was called Haertle) addressed us and gave a general description of the political and military situations, in the course of which he spoke about the bombing raids. He said that following the catastrophe of Hamburg 'we' had managed to get back on to our feet at night — I betrayed no emotion when Schaller-Kalide dug me in the ribs — and 'we' would do the same thing against the Americans by day. Something was bound to happen. If nothing happened, there would be no point in carrying on. Therefore, something would happen. 'Have courage! Have trust!' It was a contrived, mass-produced speech, and it was delivered to us, of all people, the professionals whose job it was to make that 'something' happen.

One man who was particularly keen and insistent was the senior research officer from the *Reichspost*. Following the Hamburg disaster he had promoted the cause for infrared detection equipment to be installed in our single-seat night-fighter aircraft. That kind of person never showed any signs of tiredness, even at night.

As an experiment I drove with Professor Heymann at midnight through the streets of blacked-out Berlin in a car which had its lights switched off. On the corner of the street we saw a man standing. He was an air-raid warden. We stopped, and I said, '*Guten Abend*'.

'You're not right in your head, mate. Blackout — fair enough, but at least you ought to show a slit or two!'

One day, the *Reich* Post Office Minister, Ohnesorge, invited a few officers to his shooting lodge outside Berlin, and I experienced the first television broadcast of my life when the actor Rudolf Platte appeared as large as life on the screen and addressed us in a friendly manner: 'As guests of the Minister, I greet *General* Galland, *Major* Baumbach, *Professor* Heymann . . .' We were speechless. I had a conversation with the Minister afterwards. It was his intention to set up an aerial mail service, with its own aircraft, after the war: small aeroplanes would carry important mail, documents, and so on with the speed of the wind to all corners of Europe, perhaps even further, faster than the pre-war Heinkel 70, which was called the 'Blitz' ('Lightning'). The Minister continued by saying that, as he had heard that I had made myself independent of both the time of day and the weather to a great extent, who else but the *Wilde Sau* should take on the job? I'd be glad to do it, I said, glad to be a flying postman, or a foreman postman, but let's win the war first. The Minister was being serious. Later his senior officer from the *Reichspost*, Professor Heymann, sounded me out about it.

I had also visitors from Nordhausen in the Harz Mountains, my peace-time base. Two carefully dressed men, whom I knew from skittles evenings in the Officers' Mess, appeared before me wearing doleful expressions. They told me a sad story: the chairman of the board of their agricultural company, a member of the Party, had been put in a concentration camp for an offence against the wartime economic laws. Some syrup he had made from sugar beet had not flowed where it should have flowed, and the sugar had not trickled where it should have trickled. The reputation of their firm was ruined, and they needed a 'personality'. I wouldn't have to do anything except to sign the occasional paper, for which I would receive a salary of 1000 Reichsmarks in addition to my service salary. The gentlemen needed a brass plate they could put up, it seemed, a name. They put their case with some embarrassment. I assured them of my sympathy for their loss and promised to put their request to a higher authority. I said that I couldn't make a decision on the spot, and that they would hear from me. As I didn't want to put the *Reichsmarschall* in an embarrassing position again, I informed his Chief Adjutant of the matter and asked him to ascertain the Chief's views, but not to forget to mention that I was sorry for the men and that Nordhausen meant a lot to me. Shortly afterwards, *Oberst* von Brauchitsch spoke to me. He said that if I wanted to be a purveyor of jam I had better put on an apron and hang my medals on it!

I would have genuinely liked to be a director of a company. I had never been in a position to be able to say, 'Money doesn't stink'. Needless to say, it was quite clear to me that it should not stick either.

Developments in both the day and the night air battles had meant that middle-level leaders, in particular Divisional Commanders, could not lead large formations in the air. They were tied down to the vast intelligence and signals apparatus that covered huge areas, and at the same time dependent on the succinct reports from units in the air and on being able to reach any one of them, using one of the numerous frequencies, at any given time. I was able to appreciate that readily, having considerable front-line experience in both attack and defence. In that respect I had an advantage, as did Galland and Peltz, over those who had not done much flying during the war, or at least in the last three years. It worried me, however, that my knowledge of day fighters, from both the theoretical and the operational points of view, had been gathered only indirectly. I wanted to participate, to fly with an experienced fighter leader as either his wing-man or his number two, but first of all I wanted to gain experience against enemy reconnaissance aircraft. An Me 109G, without an underwing cannon, was available at Doeberitz airfield. The continuing lack of success against reconnaissance aircraft had contributed greatly to the ill-feeling among the leadership. The enemy were bombing and then photographing factories around the clock until they saw that production had resumed. Then the next mass raid was due.

It had been proved that the fast-flying Mosquito could be combated more successfully by night than by day. That was not only because the bomb-carrying, night version of the Mosquito cruised rather more slowly than did the reconnaissance version — in any case the bomber used its maximum speed through the flak area — but also, and primarily, because of the way in which our defence was managed. At night, interceptions were controlled so as to give a turn-in which was calculated to the second, whereas during the day the fighters were taken in to visual contact on a curve of pursuit. Theoretically, if both fighter and bomber were flying at the same speed, the fighter could never catch up. If it was flying approximately 20 kph faster, it would need thirty minutes to make up a distance of ten kilometres astern. That meant, assuming a Mosquito to be flying at 660 kph, that the pursuit would cover a ground distance of approximately 300 kilometres. In addition the Mosquito could fly very high and was equipped with a pressurised cabin.

In discussion with Schaller-Kalide I based my arguments on the most unfavourable case, that of an equal or slightly superior speed for our fighter. One option was the same procedure as that we used when attacking bomber formations with our fighter formations — attack from dead ahead. From this, we went on to consider an attack on a collision course from the beam. For that purpose our fighter must have a height advantage and be able to have his target at the one o'clock position, for instance, holding it at the same angle until the last phase of the attack, with the decreasing distance between the two aircraft being broadcast to him continously. Once he had visual contact with the reconnaissance aircraft, he would proceed as in the '*Wilde Sau*' system against Mosquito bombers.

I remember that we achieved a number of successes using that method, but I was unsuccessful in one operation because the Lightnings turned tail over Hanover. I was at almost 12,000 metres over Stendal. I wouldn't have caught them up on the German side of the English coast. Quite wrongly, defence against reconnaissance aircraft was placed second to defence against bombers. One example will indicate graphically the disaster that can result from neglecting reconnaissance. We Germans were unable to make any reconnaissance flights over South-East England to see if there were invasion forces located in that area. It was that lack of knowledge on our side that made the invasion of Normandy possible.

But things had not yet got to that point. Sitting in an aeroplane or a car is as sedentary as sitting at a desk. Between operations, Schaller-Kalide let off steam on our tennis court, an activity that remained barred to me because nobody wanted to come down to my level of play. Instead I played football on a nearby sports field in front of our operations room; a call from the window would ensure that I was in the middle of the action within seconds. Our Staff football team was outstandingly good. Its reputation had reached the State Opera and stimulated the ambition of the *Oase* team, formed from the artistes, to take us on. My main job as centre-forward was to mark the nationally fêted singer, Domgraf-Fassbender. The artistes had to concede defeat, but at the party afterwards they insisted that we had only won because of our uncivilised, aggressive and dirty play. They said that they almost felt sorry for the British.

6 June 1944. The invasion had begun. The codeword 'Dr. Gustav West' had been given, and everybody knew what he had to do. Up to the last moment the Americans had visited us, and we had been unable to achieve any perceptible success. The battle in the West would have to be fought in much harder conditions, conditions imposed on us by the enemy. I felt very sad. The rotten fruits of bad planning were dropping from the trees, over-estimation, under-estimation. I felt no sense of self-satisfaction, only a dreadful bitterness, when I thought back to my revolutionary suggestion of Autumn 1942: multi-purpose aircraft for interception and bombing, both by day and at night, with the invasion specifically in mind. The blanket had been too short: only one had been able to fit under it, and the rest had had to try to make it bigger, but in vain.

But leaving that to one side, why were we hanging back? Why not attack? Never before had I led crews against the enemy or sent them into action with such a sense of impending disaster. I stood there with my Staff and the remnants of many units, and I thought of those who had died. My friend Hanke, in the North Sea; my old *Kommandeur*, in the Mediterranean; with him, the ever-smiling Adjutant Sommer; my unfailingly cheerful, cheeky, Weinreich, during a night-time mission over Mannheim; the ocean-obsessed *Oberleutnant zur See* Friedrich as a U-boat captain in the Atlantic; others in the deserts of Tunisia and

Algiers, or in the vast wastes of Russia. Why did Peter Holm have to go: Peter Holm who had given us the 'Song of the Wild Boars' and who had come to us with so much enthusiasm? How many of our warrior fighter-pilots had died in the murderous battles over the Reich? When I looked in the mirror and saw the unnatural grey of my cheeks I felt very old. I felt fatigue and hopelessness.

Sometimes I made music during the midday break. In the house of the *Kommandeur* of the 'Richthofen Men', set in the middle of a pine wood, some five minutes away from the operations room, was a magnificent piano, and I had my violin, provided by Army Welfare and on the inventory of my former bomber *Gruppe*. At the *Gruppe* I had not found much interest in the violin, but here I practised many a small piece together with an artistically-minded Corporal from the Staff. I remember him sitting on the piano stool one day, leafing through the music, and I remember that I had had enough of the music, so I poured him a glass of wine and we drank.

Hot summer days in the Reich, and our fighters continued to throw themselves with rare courage, courage born of a sense of duty, against the American bomber formations between the Baltic and the *Mittelgebirge*, and now and then a fat bomber was shot down. Towards evening it became calm. The land, the old troop exercise area at Doeberitz, the airfield I had driven to through the tunnel under the main road from Berlin to Hamburg, the familiar Brandenburg Heath, the Brandenburg sand — all were there, all was peace as I gazed, together with Schaller-Kalide, out of my office window.

Suddenly we heard doors slam, women weeping out loud. A young officer shouted something to us. Schaller and I stared at each other. What did the man say? An attempt on Hitler's life: Hitler dead? We rushed outside. 'Is he dead?' 'What are they saying on the radio?' We telephoned, but couldn't get a clear answer.

Then the news began to trickle through. There had been a bomb in Hitler's Headquarters. Army officers were involved. A state of emergency was declared by the *Korps*. But against what, and whom?

I was summoned to the telephone. *Reichsmarschall* Goering spoke: 'Can you recognise my voice?'

'*Jawohl, Herr Reichsmarschall!*' 'You will not obey any orders that don't come by telephone from me personally. The conspirators are in custody in Bendlerstrasse.'

I could scarcely think. '*Jawohl!*' was all I could say. 'We must stand true to the *Fuehrer*. I demand your unquestioning obedience. Take protective measures against the Army at Doeberitz.' I took a deep breath, 'You've gone pale, Schaller.' He replied, 'You're stammering!' I telephoned the *Korps*. 'Beppo' Schmid had already been advised of the situation. He said, 'Blow the buildings apart, if the order comes through.'

'*Jawohl, Herr General!*' I might have had to blow my own home to pieces, No 11 Luetzow Ufer, a pleasant little ground-floor flat with a balcony looking out on to the *Landwehr* Canal, opposite a small bridge which led over the Tirpitz Ufer to Graf Spee Strasse. My poor, dear personal possessions!

Schaller and I took turns to telephone the Commanders of our units then on stand-down, as far away as Thuringia and Mecklenburg; and those at operational readiness, as far away as Königsberg-Neumark. All of the humour had left Schaller, the son of a General of Infantry. I thought, now we Germans must fight each other, blow each other to bits with bombs, and tomorrow the American four-engined machines will hurl thousands of tons of high explosive into the civil war being fought among their enemies . . . The very earth was shaking. Madness was about to break out. Who was the Brutus who had raised his hand against the Commander-in-Chief, our *Fuehrer* and Chancellor, destabilising the Reich, just as Rome had been destabilised, long ago?

I remembered, quite suddenly, something that had been said on one occasion, by an aristocratic lady who had been placed next to me at dinner, whose family had enjoyed the highest imperial favour. 'Dear Herrmann,' she had drawled into my ear, in a manner as friendly as to be appropriate when speaking to a bourgeois Captain. She continued by saying that there in the Tiergarten quarter were highly-placed officers — her eyes looked in the direction of a certain officer on the other side of the table — who were waiting for the next Stalingrad, when they would overthrow Hitler and the entire rule of National Socialism. She had added that I could have no idea what was going on. So it hadn't been idle gossip. It was in deadly earnest, and I had indeed had no idea at all.

I had expressed criticism of the highest of the High Command, including Hitler. I had recognised wrong decisions only too clearly, and they had subsequently been proved to have been wrong. When all was said and done, if those at the top were not man enough to voice their opposition, to risk their necks by speaking out against what they thought was wrong; or, if they did so, and their subordinates were prepared to take over from them and carry out their jobs compliantly in order to further their own ambitions instead of standing by their superiors; if they were ready to accept decorations from a *Fuehrer*, whom they regarded as incompetent, for the sake of the glory that went with them; then no conspirators' bomb would change things. I believed that Providence had seen to it that things had turned out in the only way possible. She had also caused the plotters to come to grief as a result of the very weaknesses for which they were blaming those in power. Both Hitler and Stauffenberg possessed a strength of purpose and a drive that was not matched by their followers. Therefore it was our common duty to follow the path that History, taking into her calculations the characters involved, had marked out for us. We had to do it conscientiously, with great wisdom, with obedience but with determination, carefully and boldly.

Those were my feelings that day, as they had been on the occasion when I had seen Hitler, spoken with him and stood before him, my pistol at my belt, loaded but with the safety catch on. What hopes of the struggle for the Fatherland possessed me. On one occasion, with Eichendorff's[2] pamphlet *Taugenichts* ('The Ne'er-do-well') in my hand, I had dreamed to Heaven, through the high tree-tops of a beech wood. I loved the works of Goethe and of Shakespeare, and my head swarmed with the winged words of Schiller. How did I see him, the mighty one, the honoured one, the uniter of all Germans, the scourge of others, the hated one? How did I, a soldier in a soldier's special, regulated environment of power, in a world filled with orders and obedience, see him? Should I have seen him differently from a Kaiser, perhaps, or a Reich President, whether he be called von Hindenburg, or Ebert, in whatever sort of state we happened to live?

Oberst von Below telephoned me from the *Fuehrer's* Headquarters. He told me to report to him, and that the *Fuehrer* wanted to speak to me alone.

For a split second, when I first saw into the room, Hitler seemed to me to be strange, remote in time and space, like an actor in an historical drama. I marched into his room and stood before him. When we were seated, I had no impression of greatness or of magic, but neither did I have the impression of evil: the only impressions I had were of simplicity and clarity. I was not overawed by him, and I spoke rapidly and copiously, afraid that I would be interrupted. I wanted to get everything off my chest that seemed important to me, and which I had told to other important men already. He listened quietly and attentively. I did not need to avoid using either technical words or jargon; I expressed my feelings as those of a front-line officer. I had always been unable to resist expressing myself picturesquely, which had often caused my comrades, superiors and subordinates to break into laughter. He, however, didn't laugh; but from time to time his eyes lit up in a friendly manner.

I noticed that he didn't look me up and down, and that he didn't look at my hands. On one of my fingers I wore a ring, in which there shone a large lapis-lazuli. It had been a present from my comrades at Nordhausen and the master watchmaker Gentzel. It had attracted the gaze of the *Reichsmarschall*, almost magnetically, and he had asked me about it. I did not feel as though Hitler was weighing me up from a distance and with reservation, as I had felt with many senior officers who had tried to impose their rank upon me. We talked business, business that affected us both, him probably more than me. At times it seemed to me that he was looking through me into the distance, seeing only the things I was speaking about. I felt almost as if I were being bypassed, being used as a medium through which he was confronting the issues. Then he would turn back to the man sitting in front of him, as if to ask his personal opinion.

I spoke of the adverse weather conditions over Germany, which didn't impede enemy operations, and also of my own intentions to fly even in the worst of conditions. It was over Germany that we had to fight them, I said, it was there that we had to overcome the spectre of danger. That was more important than shooting a few enemy aircraft down outside the battle area, far away from the homeland. To emphasise my point I told him of the police reports on the scattered bombing in the Berlin area. The problem for the night fighters was not one of taking off, but of trying to land in poor visibility. That had an adverse effect on commanders and often led to operations being cancelled.

At that point Hitler interrupted me. He suggested that the single-seat fighters should fly and, if landing conditions were impossible, areas of soft ground — agricultural areas, for example — should be marked with flares or something similar. Then the pilots could parachute down and not risk any personal injury. I didn't tell him that on the occasion of one bad-weather operation I had given similar instructions, but luckily we had not needed to carry them out. Subsequently, in fact, individual pilots did bail out in similar circumstances.

To me, who was directly preoccupied with these problems the whole time, and who had to give careful thought to each and every operation, this proposal from a layman was quite astounding. I replied, saying that night fighters were in short supply and I was concerned that we would not be able to make good the increase in aircraft losses that would ensue from such a course of action. I wisely refrained from drawing attention to the example of the British, who catapulted fighter aircraft from their merchant ships on the Atlantic route, with the pilots parachuting down after combat. Had I mentioned that, the result would probably have been a relevant *Fuehrerbefehl* — a *Fuehrer's* Order. Secretly, I had myself adopted the British attitude towards the balance of advantage: probable loss against probable gain.

Hitler returned to the subject of combating the bomber offensive directly above the cities. He spoke of the method of constructing blocks of flats in the Reich, and attributed the fire-proof design of attics in Vienna to the siege of the city by the Turks. The builders and the architects had been forced to take the necessary measures to counter the incendiary shells. Our conversation continued. At one point I interrupted him, thinking that he had got the wrong idea concerning a certain subject. He stopped and gave me a quick glance, so that I became aware that I had committed a *faux pas*, and that he wanted to continue. After he had spoken a few more sentences he turned to me and asked, 'What were you going to say?' This surprised me, as much as did the calm way in which he listened to my suggestions, which I knew he did not agree with, for instance producing more fighters and less bombers.

I told him that I needed more aircraft than I had at my disposal, and that I had to make do by borrowing single-seat aircraft from day-fighter units. He thought that that was not necessarily a bad thing. He explained with considerable fervour his watchword — 'Terror must be met with counter-terror'. I had spoken my mind. When I had agreed with him, it was not because I was afraid of disagreeing: it was the result of military training. In the past, senior officers had been yes-men without considering what the results of their acquiescence might be; or perhaps they hadn't looked far enough into the future.

Hitler put a number of specific and fundamental questions concerning the mobile war, British deception tactics and various other manoeuvres. Then he became romantic. He asked me who had coined and adopted the frightful name '*Wilde Sau*'. He had a great respect for the many night-fighter crews who flew above the cities, he said. He could sing a song about them, and he himself had experienced artillery barrages on the Western Front during the First World War. The Japanese had chosen a beautiful word for their fighter pilots: '*Kamikaze*' — the Wind of the Gods, he said. I ought to think up something similar, instead of '*Wilde Sau*'. I replied, '*Nein, mein Fuehrer*. That's impossible now. They want to be called 'Wild Boars' and to fight like wild boars.' He asked me how my health was following my recent parachute jump, and he asked after my pilots.

While he was talking, he would wet his thumb and rub the corners of his eyes, as thought he was wiping the sleep out of them. I assumed that not wearing spectacles caused him eye-strain. From time to time von Below made notes. In the corner, lay 'Blondy', his Alsatian bitch, well trained, raising her head, occasionally and seeming to show an interest in me, in the same way as she had done when I had entered the room. She had obviously caught the scent of my Berto-Ingo.

Hitler dismissed me, using the same words that he had used at the beginning of our meeting: 'You have accomplished a great deal.' It seemed to me to be the most simple formula with which to show recognition. It pleased me.

That, then, was that. I felt no personal aversion to him. Did I disapprove of his policies? Yes, to some extent. In a conversation with the Head of Air Supplies, *Feldmarschall* Milch I had said, half flippantly, half seriously, that if he carried on as he was doing, he was heading for disaster. The Field Marshal had not been surprised in any way by my act of disloyalty. He had laughed and made a joke of it, saying that there were too many hands on the tiller. Had the tiller been in his hand alone, I thought, he would have turned it in the right direction — fighters instead of bombers — and risked the consequences.

Around the middle of August I was summoned to Karinhall, after the *Reichs-marschall* had returned from the funeral of *Feldmarschall* von Kluge, who had committed suicide in France following the failure of his endeavours. The *Reichsmarschall* gave his views on the conspiracy and spoke appreciatively of the declaration of loyalty issued by the Field Marshals. Then he turned to operational matters.

The war continued. American bombers attacked Berlin in daylight. In addition to the Hitler salute we had to accept a *Nationalsozialistische Führungsoffizier*, an NSFO — a National Socialist Leadership Officer — whose job was to see that the troops had the proper attitude. The NSFO allocated to me aroused mistrust in Schaller-Kalide, who insisted that the gentleman should report to him before being allowed to speak to me, if indeed he was allowed to at all. In short, he insisted, in defiance of whomsoever it was had dreamed up that type of functionary, that the NSFO should not be co-equal with, but subordinate to, himself.

The NSFO was a gentleman from his monocle to the tips of his toes, a First-World-War officer and the Director of the Bayreuth Municipal Theatre in civilian life. If you didn't take him too seriously he forget all about his National Socialist job and reverted to a respectable comrade who behaved with a slight monarchical affectation. I was anxious not to cause him any conflicts of conscience because he was accountable to his superior, the NSFO at the *Korps*. I knew that he was hopelessly in love with the piano virtuoso Elly Ney, from meetings with whom he would sometimes return with highly coloured, exaggerated stories.

I didn't tell my NSFO that one day an *Obergefreiter* — a private First Class — a priest by profession, had officiated in that capacity at a wedding in a village in Saxony, and had preached such an offensive sermon that some of the wedding guests had reported him to the Air Reporting Company in which he was serving. Subsequently the *Obergefreiter* stood in front of me, on my desk the report of the offending sermon. I read it out loud, then said, 'If what is written there is true, it's a disgrace, and you ought to be made to pay dearly for it. I don't want to know whether you said it or not; but if you utter such a load of shit in public in the future, then you're on your own. After the war, and when you're out of uniform, you can say what you want.' While I had been speaking, I had raised my voice. Under the laws then in force what the priest had said from the pulpit, and had repeated later at the wedding breakfast, was quite simply subversion. The sermon which I delivered to him lasted less than five minutes, and then the PFC-priest went back to his unit on the train.

By this time the trial of the 20th July conspirators had been in progress for some time. The reports in the newspapers were unsettling. The fact that the plotters were officers seemed to indicate that their motivation had had its foundation in the criticisms of the military leadership. As far as I could see, it could not be denied that there had been failures by and weaknesses of the leadership. In common with other members of the Staff, I had a considerable interest in attending one of the court hearings. At the beginning of September 1944, two entrance tickets to the Supreme Court were made available to us. They probably came to us through NSFO channels. On the first day I attended a court session, and Schaller-Kalide did so on the second day.

I was seated at the front and to the right, so that I had a good view of the bench. The accused were to my left, their defence counsels before them, and next to them stood police officers in their ceremonial helmets. The light came through big windows on the right.

Freisler's questioning was penetrating, but concerned mostly events, discussions, meetings and statements, which seemed to me to be of little relevance. From statements made by Freisler, however, I gathered that the accused denied having been in touch with certain individuals and having said certain things. The day I was there, there were no soldiers in the dock: they were tried separately. One of the accused, a tall, dark, good-looking man, said clearly and firmly that he must take issue with the statement that so many crimes had been committed. Freisler interrupted him, shouted and became disagreeably sharp. He spoke of enemy propaganda and the war crimes committed by the other side.

Another of the accused said that there was no freedom in Germany. He too was interrupted. Freisler shouted at him, 'Do you call it freedom, when Christ on the cross can be drawn or painted with an erection . . .?' This comment stuck in my mind as being particularly obscene. I did not know if there was any truth in the statement.

Apart from those two incidents, I retain no clear memories of the proceedings. I asked myself why the men who had wanted change had not taken advantage of the forum, presented to them in the form of the crowded hall, to express themselves more forcefully, decisively. Schaller-Kalide told me the following day that he had asked himself the same question. I had gone into the courtroom fearing that I would see the authority of Adolf Hitler shaken. I left it telling myself, 'We must stand by him.' What else should we do — surrender unconditionally?

I could not overlook the fact that the conspirators' criticisms were aimed at the political system, and that they concurred with enemy broadcasts, extracts from which were at that time being passed to Divisional Commanders, under a 'Top Secret' classification. Occasionally I had listened to the broadcasts. The Allies were claiming that their aim was the overthrow of the German political system and the removal of Hitler. I found this explanation to be boring: a repeat of 1914/18 — 'Overthrow the monarchy, and remove the Kaiser!' When that eventually happened they took our colonies, our markets, our coal-mines and our wealth away from us. We were determined that that would not happen this time. We were not fighting for a *Fuehrer* and a system, but as German soldiers for Germany, no matter how much she fell, or was forced, into difficulties. What was National Socialist jargon to me? Nothing but a weak background noise. In all probability Marxism was nothing more to the Russians. Quite certainly their motherland meant more to them.

I was optimistic. More than twelve Fighter *Geschwader* were being formed in reserve and were expected to be ready to enter the battle within a few months: I had to make my contribution to the process. Coming up behind was a nucleus of fast jet-fighters, the vanguard of the future, which would leave all the Mustangs and Thunderbolts behind and get through to the bombers. Then there were our remote-controlled bombs. Their effectiveness was unbelievable. Using one of them my faithful observer, Schmetz, had sunk the Italian battleship *Roma* from a height of 7000 metres, which had to be either a fairy tale or something very revolutionary indeed. From that height the *Roma* had looked as small as a lancelet fish, but she displaced 35,000 tonnes of water.

I asked myself whether in fact the failures on the part of the leadership were as obvious at the time as they seemed to me to have been then, in the late summer of 1944. Even the question as to whether we ought to have built more bombers or more fighters could not be answered easily. You cannot hope to counter terror by defence alone, but also by means of counter-terror. Whether you achieve success depends simply on numbers. And thus it had been a theoretically viable concept to build up the strength of the bomber fleet, as *Oberst* Peltz had been instructed to do by Hitler as '*Angriffsfuehrer England*' — 'Leader of the Attack on England — and hammer the other side until the British gave up their attacks. The wrong decisions were not of a fundamental nature, but sprang from a faulty assessment of the increase in output potential for both sides. The challenge that faces a leader when he is planning ahead is to intervene at the correct point in time. He should not resort to criticism or oppose ideas until the mistakes are obvious: doing so robs the criticism of its credibility.

The majority of the *Geschwader*, both in reserve and reforming, were located in my Divisional area. 'Beppo' Schmid summoned all unit leaders and Divisional Commanders to Treuenbrietzen, where he had, in the meanwhile, transferred with his Staff, for a comprehensive discussion of future operational policy. Galland, General of Fighters, was present. The possibility emerged that I would be able to fly on daylight operations. My first attempt to do so, on a mission to Upper Silesia, where the Americans were making a number of raids from Foggia, Italy, was stopped by 'Beppo' Schmid. I was recalled when I was airborne.

When I had committed my worries to paper in 1942, I had thought that it would not be possible to achieve the increased output of fighter aircraft that Speer did in fact achieve and maintain bomber production levels at the same time. But hope was deceptive, because we had already offended against the maxim that one must be stronger than one's enemy earlier rather than later. For Germany 'too late' would be a better way of putting it. How would it have been a year before, in October 1943, if we had been able to meet the 400 bombers that had attacked Schweinfurt with 'only' 800 fighters? It would possibly have been seen as the decisive air battle of the war. Would we now have to send 2000 fighters against 3000 bombers with an escort of 1000 fighters? There was no point in crying over spilt milk.

For me it was a cause for satisfaction that there was a steadily growing reserve of fighters deployed on old and new airbases, as well as on temporary airfields, and that at last I would be able to take part in the 'Great Battle' that the General of Fighters was pursuing with great input of material and organization, and that I would be able to do so there in the key area of Central Germany, where Goering had placed me. There were many discussions, including some at Treuenbrietzen, and operating principles were worked out. Those carrying the responsibility returned to their bases and their staff headquarters with no little optimism.

Shortly afterwards, to my great surprise, I was summned by my Commanding General, 'Beppo' Schmid. He stood behind his desk and informed me that I had been removed as *Kommandeur* of the 1st Fighter Division. He explained my dismissal, in a brief statement, to the effect that I had paid insufficient attention to supervising the men I commanded, and that I was too young and too inexperienced to be a Divisional *Kommandeur*. He did not know what my new job would be, but he thanked me for the work I had done. I did not ask any questions. I turned and left the room. I had been sacked!

I heard later that 'Beppo' Schmid had informed his friend, Bodenschatz, *General der Luftwaffe* at the *Fuehrer's* Headquarters, that I had been in the habit of leaving Doeberitz in the evenings and going to Berlin to visit the Opera or the theatre. Was it, I asked myself, so terrible that in more than eighteen months I had, on a few occasions, treated myself to a visit to a show, including *Ein Bruderzwist im Hause Habsburg* by Grillparzer, *Das Leben ein Traum* by Calderon, and Shakespeare's *The Taming of the Shrew*, in which my former heart-throb, Marianne Hoppe, was playing the title role? My conscience was clear: I had not taken any leave and had worked a great deal of overtime. Confident of my innocence, I told my Commanding Officer that the noise of war had not deafened me to the Muses. I continued by saying that it was a good thing that we, unlike the harsh Romans, could speak, sing, dance, and so on. I had always been contactable during performances. The usher assigned to the seats reserved for officials had only to tap me on the shoulder and I could have been at my operational headquarters within fifteen minutes.

There were other reasons why I could not accept that my Commander's charges were justified. Looking after the troops' rations, alcohol consumption, clothing, lights-out and rest periods would have effectively taken up time and would have taken me out of the battle. The Fighter *Kommandeure* were capable and conscientious officers who knew what to do without me having to remind them to behave themselves and to see that their troops led a healthy, orderly life. They would justifiably have considered it to have been insulting if I had gone through their barrack-rooms behind their backs or smelt their cooking pots. It was my style, and indeed that of all front-line airmen, simply to express the hope during conferences that everything necessary was being done for the physical and spiritual well-being of the troops; that was sufficient. Had I done what 'Beppo' Schmid wanted me to do, I would have been an object for ridicule.

I could not believe what others told me: following *Oberst* Luetzow's departure I was the only Divisional Commander to leave his operational headquarters and fly on operations. In fact, 'Beppo' Schmid had recalled me when I was flying an Me 109 from Doeberitz to Upper Silesia on the occasion of an attack by Italian-based American bombers, even though my presence on the ground in Berlin was not indispensable. It could well be, some critical spirits said, that the Commanding General's concern for my person arose from his need to know that there weren't any Divisional Commanders fighting in the air during the 'Great Battle' when he was not. I found it hard to believe that any senior officer, in a position as difficult as ours was, in which expertise was indispensable, could act for anything other than objective reasons. I was rather inclined to the view that when I spoke at conferences of Unit and Divisional Commanders the Commanding General felt himself to be put on the defensive. That explanation was the only one which made sense to me, because he had not distinguished himself in the air. The *Luftwaffe* was suffering from the malaise that had inflicted it during the First World War and in the post-war period: the majority of the senior officers came from technical branches and were so far removed from modern technology, aviation matters, and vigorous youth that both they and we, who were younger, were poles apart from each other.

Relieved of my post as *Divisionskommandeur*, I had to continue to run its affairs until my successor, *Generalleutnant* Kleinrath, with whom I had had dealings in 1942 when I was in the 6th Department of the Staff of the Quarter

Master General, arrived. That included looking after the units, which were in the process of being built up, seeing that they were acquainted with the experience already accumulated within the Reich, and instructing them in operational procedures.

Generalleutnant Kleinrath was approximately fifteen years older than I was, and was an expert in matters concerning troop reinforcements and equipment supplies. He was an attentive listener and a kindly man, but he had not had any experience of commanding flying units. When I had explained the job to him, he said that he proposed to give the *Geschwader* greater operational freedom, which he thought would increase their effectiveness. When he had stated his views, I felt that I had to contradict him. I did so politely, but Schaller-Kalide, typically, was more blunt.

We said that nobody else could assess the overall air situation better than the personnel on the ground. Even if we could put 2000 fighters in the air, it would be a mistake to fight the battle by *Geschwader* or to allow individual members of the *Geschwader* to choose their own approach routes and points of attack. Concentration meant bringing all one's forces together at one point, To do that, the overall enemy situation had to be assessed from the ground. I spoke to him of such things as fighter concentration points, marked by smoke shells fired by the Flak; of pilot aircraft which would 'sky-mark'; and so on — but it was all said in vain. Even if the enemy fighters came to the concentration point — we had also to consider diversionary tactics — we had to make a stand in a confined area. It was there that the skills of individual formation leaders would prove themselves, particularly the prior training and education of the pilots. Then, in the name of God, fighter could take on fighter: 2000 German fighters against 400, 500, 1000 enemy fighters. Concentrate the formations for once, and leave the bombers alone. Which was exactly what the General wanted to do; but his approach was different.

When two people try to do the same thing, the end result isn't always the same. The success of proper thinking is dependent on the most simple of factors. My approach was to compensate for the navigational difficulties that the lead aircraft would experience by providing visual indicators in the sky. At Königgraetz, the Prussian General Staff had collaborated with the Royal Prussian Railways to ensure that soldiers travelling separately would arrive simultaneously, and operate united on the field of battle.

I feared that what was quite clearly, to me, the right way forward would become obfuscated. When I left I felt utterly discouraged. Shortly afterwards, far away, I learned that the General had been replaced by the experienced Staff *Oberst* Wittmer, formerly Chief of Staff of the Fighter *Korps*.

Notes

1 *Oberleutnant* Kurt Welter was credited with the destruction of six Mosquitos, by far the highest indvidual score against that type of aircraft at night. Welter shot down three Mosquitos piloting an Fw 190, and three when he piloted an Me 262 jet-fighter.

2 Joseph Freiherr von Eichendorff (1788-1857) was a traditional, humorous poet. He also wrote stories, one of his best-known being 'Aus dem Leben eines Taugenichts' ('From the Life of a Ne'er-do-well').

Chapter Fourteen
Hungary — in the Wilderness, October-November 1944

The Japanese retreat in the Far East. The defence of the West Wall. Fighting in Hungary.

It was with a heavy heart that I left my *Division*. I was out of a job as a result of events over which I had no control, transferred to the *Fuehrerreserve* (Fuehrer's Reserve), as my status was elegantly described. The office responsible for employing those officers who were out of a job was located at Königsberg/Neumark, where I reported to find out who could use me. I had no desire to visit the unit stationed there, *Zerstoerergeschwader 26*, which was equipped with Me 410s fitted with 5 cm cannon, and with which I had worked in difficult times. To listen to words of consolation was not my style.

The officer in charge of postings told me that I was to go to Hungary and make a list of all the retreating German soldiers entering Hungary from Rumania through the Carpathian forests, and I was to inform *Oberst* Fuetterer, who had been my commanding officer on the Reichsbahnstrecke at Berlin-Tempelhof, of my findings.

I reported to Fuetterer on the beautiful autumn heights of Buda, overlooking Pest on the other side of the Danube. He was greatly surprised to see me, believing that I was helping out in the emergency in the homeland. After the inevitable glass of *barack*, which brought tears to our eyes, we recalled nostalgically an evening party in the *Haus der Flieger* in 1936, when the Colonel gave his farewell dinner before going to Hungary as Air Attaché.

A Staff Officer who worked in the *Heldensammelbranche* (Heroes' Assembly Branch) showed me how to go about things. I started to meet the new arrivals and to enter on my list what each of them had or hadn't got, and to which unit they belonged. I had learned to count socks and army boots in the orderly room when I was a *Leutnant*, not to mention entering them onto lists and reporting discrepancies. Now it all came into its own. As far as I am aware I performed my job without causing any damage, though I did so with some reluctance. It was an effort for me not to pay too much attention to the air situation reports which were broadcast over the loudspeakers. Very often four-engined bombers would fly from the south to Vienna, Czechoslovakia and Upper Silesia. The industrial installations around Budapest were also attacked. When such raids occurred my colleagues and I didn't go down into the shelters but crawled to the top of the nearest vineyard and watched the spectacle from there, spitting out grape-pips as we watched our fighters, and those of our Hungarian allies, in their desperate struggle against the Mustangs.

I mentioned something about this to a Hungarian Field Marshal Lieutenant who had visited me in Doeberitz six months earlier. His astonishment on finding me there was not inconsiderable. Being responsible for certain branches of the air defence of Hungary, particularly administrative, he informed the Air Force *General* Dessloch of my presence. Shortly afterwards I visited the *General*, who was Chief of the 4th Air Fleet. As the roads through the *puszta*, although wide, were muddy, I caught a train somewhere or other: or, rather, I caught a solo locomotive on which, together with the soot-covered crew, I was the only passenger. At the end of the journey I arrived in Nyiregyhaza in pouring rain, half-trained as a stoker and a whistle-operator. There I was received, to my pleasure, by my first '*Wilde Sau*' ally, Staff *Oberst* Kern, who had been on the Staff there for some time.

During the days which followed I flew in a Fieseler *Storch* to visit our fighter units, some of which had come from the Eastern Front. They had had little experience in combating the American four-engined bombers, and they were not backed up by a ground organisation equipped with all of the western refinements. In addition I had in-depth stimulating and encouraging discussions with the brave — one might say dashing almost — Hungarian fighter pilots stationed at Veszprem near Lake Balaton. Theirs was a very difficult situation. The Soviets had already occupied a large part of their country. I also gave a talk to our night-fighter crews at Steinamanger. Among them I came across a bright young pilot, a nephew of *Reichsmarschall* Goering.

Wherever you are in the world, you have to contend with the weather. At that time of the year the weather in Hungary was similar to that in Germany. American bomber and fighter aircraft used to take off in fair weather from Southern Italy. They would cross the cloud-covered tracts of Croatia and Hungary at great height and appear over Vienna, Bohemia, Slovakia or Upper Silesia, where they would drop their bombs in conditions of better visibility.

The lack of a blind-flying ability by our fighter pilots could no longer be made good. The number of pilots being qualified did in fact match the vast production of aircraft, but their ability to cope with the weather conditions in Central Europe was not up to standard. The intrinsically simple redeployment flights from the Reich to the Eastern Front, to Sicily, and, latterly, to France to defend against the invasion, had highlighted this weakness. We had been able to narrow the gap in terms of quantity of equipment and numbers of men, but not in flying ability.

'The clouds are the pilot's terrain', a saying of *General* Wever, the first Chief of the General Staff of the *Luftwaffe*, used to adorn the walls of airmen's billets in peacetime. Bomber commanders took those words literally, forgot the idea of fighting under blue skies, and burdened each and every pilot with the labour of a Sisyphus, making them carry their tons' weights uphill, through the most filthy weather. They learned to do just that, reached the skies and outdid Sisyphus.

I was standing in the mud of the *puszta*, resigned to the fact that we could do nothing. Why, I asked myself for the hundredth time, didn't our peace-time princes in the fighter *Geschwader*, our old fighter pilots in the heavens of Flanders, Goering included, devote their thoughts to the cloud-terrain that was the element of the bombers, our own and the enemy's? Now, in 1944, there was no catching up. Our airmen were coming to the Front direct from training, while American pilots accumulated two to four times as many flying hours before they were let off the leash.

I sent a few simple notes on operating in bad weather to the *Geschwader* of *1 Jagddivision*. One *Kommodore* told me quite frankly that he hadn't passed the paper on to his pilots for their instruction, but had consigned it to the waste-paper basket. The *Kommodore* had been correct to do so, probably: the gap between the flying schools and the operational training units on one hand, and the demands of the front line on the other, was too great to be closed under the strain of operational flying.

Another wise saying was, 'The night is not the enemy of the pilot, but his friend'. That was also displayed frequently. In 1940 I made my first acquaintance with single-seat fighters. Some had followed us from England to Holland in an attempt to shoot us down while we were landing in weather that was not much better than that in which we took off from Jueterbog in Autumn 1943. If I am to believe the reports of 1c, the Russians used single-seaters at night over Moscow, also employing them in large numbers against ground targets.

We spent our evenings in front of a tiled stove or an open fire drinking Tokay, bitching, swearing, telling stories, exchanging views, in an attempt to discover if there was anything we could reasonably hope to do, even though the means at our disposal were insufficient. It was a complete nonsense to throw highly decorated, experienced, mature fighter leaders in with a bunch of brave beginners and send them all into the jaws of 1000 escort fighters ready to consume all and sundry, irrespective of rank or training. I could not speak with any degree of enthusiasm of the experiences of Galland and Trautloft during a daylight operation in *I. Division*'s area.

What was the solution? Would the 'Great Battle' succeed? Would we be able to hang on until the Me 262 was available in sufficient numbers? I was doubtful, and I was afraid. As early as late summer 1944, when I was in Berlin, I had started to think seriously, notwithstanding the increased fighter reserve numbers, of a major operation involving the use of 1500 rammer-aircraft flown by young pilots, to be recruited from the 20,000-plus then under training.

In the meanwhile the Soviets had advanced as far as the Theiss and had built a bridge, enabling them to begin their thrust against Budapest. The *Luftflotte* Staff proposed the use of night fighters to carry out a low-level, night attack against those troops which were concentrated on the approaches to the bridge. I said that I was prepared both to advise and to lead them in the attack. It was a difficult operation, but it succeeded. I was given the necessary combustible material, and I flew ahead of the others as a 'shining example'. Our ground forces were given some breathing space.

A visit to *Kommodore Oberst* Johannes Steinhoff, who had arrived from Sicily with his *Geschwader*, which was subordinate to *Luftflotte 4*, provided me with an opportunity to participate in an unusual cavalry attack, in the fifth year of that technically-orientated conflict. After breakfast, because the sky was overcast and the aircraft were unable to take off, Steinhoff and I had our horses saddled up, and the two of us rode through the countryside at a trot, intending to return to the airfield. At first we almost failed to hear, above the snortings of our horses, a suspicious engine-like noise. The noise became increasingly loud, until, from the clouds and the mist, a large aircraft appeared. It descended in a series of curves over the landscape, then it glided towards a stretch of open meadowland, where it touched down.

We had watched the performance from a bushy incline, and were surprised to recognise the aeroplane as being 'Old Aunty', a Ju 52, but with foreign markings. There was nobody else around. Watching from our vantage point, we suspected that we were seeing the arrival of an enemy commando. We stood up in our stirrups, as if electrified, when we saw huge men wearing heavy coats with what looked like towers of fur on their shoulders instead of heads, come out from the belly of the aircraft, look around conspiratorially, and engage in what appeared to be a council of war. 'What,' Frederick the Great had asked, 'should you do when you see a single enemy soldier?' 'Attack', was the answer. 'What should you do when you saw three, or even ten, enemy soldiers?' he continued. 'Attack. Always attack,' was the Warrior King's watchword.

We drew our pistols, spurred our horses on, and shouted, '*Haende hoch!*' The King had been correct: The five or six men put up their hands without hesitation. We rode towards them and were able to look at them more closely. They all burst out laughing and took the mops of fur from their heads. They were *Luftwaffe* airmen who had escaped from the Ivans, stealing everything they had needed — their clothes and the aeroplane. To the rolling of thunder, during the night of a dreadful storm, they had started the engines, had taxied out by the light of lightning flashes, and had taken off. They had flown through the turbulence, over the Carpathian mountains, rocked by wind and rain. That was their story, and they had been more than ready to acknowledge our German cry of '*Haende hoch!*'

The Hungarian Field Marshal Lieutenant, a polite and attentive colleague, always ready with a '*Bitt' schoen, Kamerad*', brought a message to me from the Regent, *Admiral* Horthy, that he would like to meet me. The meeting was to take place at the stud farm that Horthy's brother owned, north of Budapest. His brother welcomed me heartily, very sincerely, and gave me an extra-strong *barack*, which brought tears to my eyes. Through my tears I saw the skins of tigers, lions and zebra, elephants' feet and other trophies that served as wall-coverings or as pieces of furniture, which made the broad room of the bungalow seem narrower. The Admiral sent a message begging me to wait. Later, another message arrived in which he apologised and said that he had been prevented from coming. There had been disturbances in the town, the result of the Regent of the Royal Crown of Stephen having protested against his bigger ally, but he was sidetracked by Hungarian Party supporters. The political course remained unchanged.

With pride, Horthy's brother showed me around his stud, each horse more striking than the last, but there was one particular horse which made me exclaim with delight. Its nostrils seemed as if they had been sculpted. Its head and neck were majestical. Its eyes seemed to be calmly questioning.

Horthy's brother asked, 'Do you like the mare? Her name's "Friar Gin". I'd like you to have her.' He wouldn't take no for an answer. He said that the mare was a little something to mark my visit to Hungary. That's how it is, I thought. If you've done something, somewhere, some time, that attracts attention, all you have to do is to sit back and the gifts will come, unsolicited. Is the man a politician, perhaps? Does he want something of me? Others said, on seeing my beautiful horse, that Horthy's brother had given me something that would have otherwise fallen into the hands of the Russians. It was awful. The most innocent of self-deception is shattered as readily as the highest of hopes. But now, after my donkey and my dog had become prisoners of war with the British (I was comforted by the knowledge that they were animal lovers), I had a beautiful horse. Soon after, Steinhoff had her sent by rail with his kit to Germany, where he had been posted. 'Friar Gin' stayed with the cavalry in Krampnitz, near Potsdam, where she was well looked after and exercised.

The Russians advanced towards Budapest. Prisoners of war of varying nationalities worked or marched, in small groups, while German and Hungarian soldiers and armoured vehicles moved up to the front. Hungarian civilians and Jews, the Star of David sewn to their clothes, were all conscripted to dig trenches. The wounded streamed from the front in tram-cars. The front was situated at the tram terminus. From there, we could hear the rolling thunder of the artillery, while high-ranking officers, well-to-do burghers and members of the nobility all dined at de-luxe hotels, the Ritz and the Hungaria on the Danube, ready at any moment to leave their rented suites and head west. Among them there were many friendly people, friendly towards the Germans, and in their faces I could see the distress of those who had had to leave and lose their homes, their land and their fellow-countrymen.

In a peculiar way I could understand that they wanted to visit their Opera House for the last time, the noble ladies in their long gowns, wearing their precious jewellery; the men wearing tails and carrying walking sticks with silver knobs. With the noise of battle in our ears, we entered the foyer to see *Iphigenie in Aulis* by Willibald Glück. The play-acting continued during the interval: people greeted each other, chatted, behaved in a carefree way, maintained a fine composure. It was the final act before despair, the farewell performance of a culture. Somewhere, on the Danube there waited an old servant with the children; a coachman with horses, exhausted already from the long journey; a housekeeper, standing by a wagon laden with woollen blankets and a sack of oats, all would be ready to take to the road in the early hours of the morning. A great, terrible premonition of the imminent end of an era overcame me. Was this to be our end too, the end of the Germans? I could not believe it. I said, 'No!'

Chapter Fifteen
Westward via Berlin,
November 1944-January 1945

The Ardennes Offensive. The Yalta Conference. The Allies insist on unconditional surrender.

In my pocket I had my orders to proceed to Berlin. I got into my *Storch* and headed for Vienna, overtaking innumerable Hungarians, Germans, Jews as well, who, evacuated from Budapest, were streaming west on various roads, completely disorganised. Supposedly they were going to dig trenches on the approaches to Vienna. I found that surprising. There had been a rumour that those Jews who had not emigrated had been, or were to be, removed from the Reich and the Occupied Territories and sent to a special area allocated to them in the East. Why were those below me struggling up the Danube, away from Hungary? What a contradiction!

In 1939, when I was on attachment to the *Marine*, I had seen deep-sea steamers in the harbour at Hamburg, on the decks of which were piled crates containing the possessions of Jewish emigrants. At that time the Jews had been suspected of being the 'Fifth Column of International Zionism', as had the Communists, who clenched their fists and shouted '*Heil* Moscow!' thereby showing allegiance to a foreign power. Were the politicians' outbursts of hatred war propaganda only, or was their purpose to put pressure on others so as to intimidate those people they didn't like and employ them to do war work? A proliferation of abuse and threats made a balanced consideration impossible. The Russians were denounced as being subhuman, the Poles as being inferior, and the Jews as being exploiters. We were called Huns and Barbarians, and we were burned and suffocated in our homes with fire and sulphur. Who could hope to find out what lay behind it all?

As I looked down past the wing-strut of my Fieseler *Storch* at the wretched refugees, suddenly I thought of that evening when the noble lady had summed me up as being unsuspecting and incapable of resistance. At the close of a particular evening in 1943 my host, in his splendid house on the Graf Spee Strasse, *Baron* von Oppenheim, a Jew, had asked me to find a job for his son with the anti-aircraft artillery in Berlin. I had promised to see what I could do. In itself, the request didn't surprise me, but I could not help but to remember the statement, attributed to Goering: 'I decide who is Jewish!' Was I to allow the suffering of any, or anybody's particular group, to upset me, when I did not have the time to devote my full attention to my own tormented, harassed relatives and friends? Under the weight of the danger and the responsibility that I bore, I could not do so. Together with my comrades I was responsible for the Reich's air defence, for all its people, without distinction, including the prisoners. Any

242   EAGLE'S WINGS

thought or feeling for individuals disappeared as soon as they were out of my sight.

I reached the front of the long, thin column, made up of small groups. I did not waste my time wondering where they thought they were going: it is doubtful if they knew that themselves. The complexities of waging war and of conducting a security policy seemed to be the sense — or the nonsense — of this movement. I asked myself what direction, what escape-routes, I would have considered had my own fate been revealed to me. We were all part of a community of misery in old Europe, a misery created by both ourselves and others.

But I also had to keep a watch on the sky. The air situation report, given to me before I took off, included a warning that I should be prepared for attacks by low-flying aircraft. The attacks were being carried out ruthlessly against the population, small vehicles, farmers, and any air traveller who might have lost his way. My escort and I scanned the sky until our necks were sore, and we were ready to land in good time anywhere on the edge of a wood, should there be any sign of Mustangs, then continue the flight after dark. How low had we sunk!

It was *General* Dieter Peltz who had recalled me back home to the Reich. Goering had given him the task of setting up a meeting of unit commanders who had distinguished themselves during the war. The aim of the meeting was to assist in the total reform of the *Luftwaffe*. During the preliminary talks, Goering had asked Peltz where I was. He had professed amazement when Peltz had told him that I had been sent to the Carpathians some time ago. Goering did not reveal if the move had been made with his knowledge. Nevertheless I was to take part in a meeting at the War Academy in Gatow, at the headquarters of *Areopag*, whose name was so suggestive of aerodynamics.

Personnel and promotion items were listed on the agenda, as were numerous administration problems. But given the position that we were in at the beginning of November 1944 there was one point only of real importance that had to be solved, overcoming every difficulty and shortcoming to do so: we had to break the back of the enemy's superiority in the air, in particular that of the Americans. We did not seriously discuss anything over and above the current situation, the fighter reserve and our hopes for the jet fighters and the single-engined *Volksjaeger* (People's Fighter). My last radical proposal was lying in a drawer of the desk of the Inspector of Day Fighters. Until he addressed himself to the subject, I could not do anything more. So I listened to what was said.

The front-line commanders must have greatly welcomed the conference, In the absence of senior commanders, whom most of them considered to be, in many ways, inferior to themselves, they were able to speak uninhibitedly of the matters which were causing them concern and to offer their proposals for improvement.

The conference should have taken place earlier, not when the ship had already begun to founder. The front-line commanders were more than just dashing characters: they had a high degree of understanding; but only a few, including Peltz and Galland, had more comprehensive knowledge of the situation. My comrade from Military Academy, Rudi Kiel, had the idea of inspiring the men morally and operationally with classical music. Galland, sitting next to me, laughed aloud, and nudged me in my side. Cultural programmes had been running for years, and they hadn't had any effect.

If anything came out of the meeting, it was this: we would not accomplish anything by using only theories, slogans and long-term concepts.

At the end of November I was posted to *II. Fliegerkorps*, which was commanded by *General* Peltz, whose Staff was located at Flammersfeld in the Westerwald, and whose job it was to provide air support for the Ardennes Offensive, which began on 16 December 1944. I was not in a position to judge if a decisive battle in the west, aimed at breaking through to Antwerp and encircling 250,000 Allied troops, would have had a better chance of altering the situation, than an aerial battle between ourselves and the enemy air forces would have. I would have expected the greater success to come from the defensive action. On the other hand, air defence over the Rhine was not different basically to that over Thuringia or Lower Saxony.

Following very comprehensive discussions with Peltz and his Staff, I wrote a five-page paper in which I covered the experiences of air defence matters in my Divisional Area, which were confirmed by the General of Fighters, and I commented on those experiences. I said that 'our own, not inconsiderable, forces', should be concentrated in 'a geographically clearly defined battle area,' and I repeated my original basic statement, which had by now become something of a platitude, that concentration was a matter of navigation. My exact words were, 'If we do not succeed in locating it (the assembly area or the battle area), then any form of concentration will fail, and with it any hope of a successful or low-casualty battle.' I continued by detailing individual requirements: ground transmitters for homing on to, smoke generators, smoke shells, and ground control where possible.

I visited a large number of flying units, and spoke directly with the pilots: together with the unit commanders, I demanded of the young people, begged them, that they should not give way to panic. I told them that by staying close together in the battle area they would be strong enough to fight, and would come through with a fighting chance. When enemy fighters appeared they should not follow the precept, 'Every man for himself', dive out of a dogfight and try to escape at low level. If they did so they would be easy prey for their pursuers. In the event what happened was that although the fighters generally succeeded in forming up, they frequently failed to find the battle area, or arrived there too late. Then, when the minute and the hour were right, the force of fighters necessary to dominate the battle was lacking. A feeling of inferiority developed and young, inexperienced, less tenacious pilots took to their heels following a short period of intensive combat, leaving their more dedicated comrades alone.

Except when they were escorting their bombers, the enemy fighters never appeared in large formations. They often flew patrols in *Staffel* or *Gruppe* strength, and we could have taken them on from a position of superiority, as could be seen from the picture produced on the ground, and as I was able to confirm for myself from an Me 262 north of the Ruhr and in the Lower Rhine area. The air battles were ones of slow attrition: the efforts of a company of brave men foundered on the inexperience and panic of those coming up to take their places. Is there a will to win? If there is, what can it accomplish? Is there a law of Nature that brings about our demise? The ancient poet, Horace, spoke quite forcefully of death, in words that have often been denounced, but which experience has suggested to be correct: Death pursues the man who runs away, nor does he spare the knees, nor the backs of unwarlike youth.[1]

When the Army's offensive had come to a standstill and the enemy was ready to counter-attack, I suggested that we should use all of our available night-fighter units against the enemy's rear lines of communication in Belgium and northern France. *General* Peltz agreed.

Snow-covered, Westerwald, the Siebengebirge, the Eifel and the Ardennes lay like a fairy-tale landscape beneath the clear light of the moon. It was almost as bright as day. Because we were expecting heavy opposition from enemy night fighters when we had crossed the front line we flew in low below the radar, through the artillery girdle of both sides and through their thunder and lightning. Being '*Wilde Sau*' pilots, our men were familiar with firework displays of that type.

Our night fighters destroyed approximately 150 locomotives and a greater number of lorries, which were being driven in the enemy-occupied area with scarcely any attempt to black out. Such was the case with a tank transporter near Paris, and I didn't have any difficulty in getting it in my sights. In addition I brought back a souvenir from the flight — a quite large piece of metal plate from a locomotive, which had lodged itself in the belly of my Ju 88. My four cannon had caused its boiler to burst. The foreign body, a metre in length, was cut out on the airfield at Wahn. Such was my 1944 Christmas party.

Shortly after this Peltz and I were both summoned to Karinhall to see the *Reichsmarschall*. We were to report on the air operations in the West. We were surprised to find that 'Beppo' Schmid, the overall head of the *Luftwaffenkommando West*, had not been invited. The *Reichsmarschall* had nothing to offer us except complaints concerning the failure of the *Luftwaffe*, the Staffs, and the Inspectorate. The only hope that he expressed was that there would be a new broom that could sweep more cleanly. What I felt to be most depressing about this discussion was the knowledge that some of the inadequacies and delays were attributable to him. At that stage to express my indignation, to make accusations, to embark on opposition, was impossible. Pointless! Ridiculous! The ship must not sink.

Following our discussions we were invited to an idyllic wedding ceremony beneath a fine, great Christmas tree. Emmy Goering's friend, an actress who had worked with her in earlier days, was marrying a Corporal from the Flak Artillery, far from the chaos of war. When the small ceremony had ended, Emmy Goering called me to one side. She stood close to me, looked at me and asked, 'Tell me: we're past the worst, aren't we?' She was radiantly beautiful, but had become more serious. The shadows of confused worry surrounded the brightness of her eyes. It was hard to me to answer such a question from such a lady — to say that our country was incurably ill, and that its people were approaching their end. I wanted to tell neither the truth nor a lie. The questions which I put to myself at that moment, went to the heart of the matter: 'What do you still believe in? What do you hope for at the end of 1944?'

I said 'No. We are not in the clear yet. Things are bound to get worse. But we will come through.' As I said that, my belief and optimism returned.

A few hours later, sitting next to Peltz in our Ju 88, I looked down on the shattered Mittelland Canal aqueduct over the Elbe — the water had drained away, and barges lay in the empty canal. Peltz murmured, 'That's all we need!' But did we not have our Bomber *Geschwader*, whose pilots were experienced in blind-flying and operating by night, who were at that very time familiarising themselves with the Me 262, several hundred of which would soon appear in the heavens? It had to be so. Anything else, I couldn't bear to think of!

At this time a great battle between the combined fighter units in the west and the allied tactical flying units stationed on Belgian and French soil had long been planned. The enemy fighter and fighter-bomber units were causing a lot of trouble for our forward army columns. Therefore it was agreed between *General* Peltz and *Feldmarschall* Model that they should be hit on the ground in a low-level attack at dawn.

When *General* Peltz and his Chief of Staff, *Oberst* von Heinemann, advised me of the plan before the beginning of the offensive I expressed my reservations, which did not concern the difficulty of carrying out the attack, but concerned the target. It was my view that the four-engined bomber units in England would have been more profitable targets, because they could carry hundreds of times as many bombs to our country and could be put out of action on the ground more easily than in the air. Indeed, the heavy bombers, flying in both clear and cloud-covered skies, were able to cut our Army's main supply routes west of the Rhine, specifically at traffic bottlenecks in the hills, and block them with the debris from houses in towns and villages. Our night fighters and bombers were the only weapons that could reach the enemy's main force on the other side of the Channel. What would have been possible in the much more favourable circumstances of 1944 had to be abandoned now. I realised that a large-scale, pre-emptive attack was not possible, and that we would have to throw those forces we had against the enemy at our front door in order to help our Army, for a few days, in its attempts to break through.

For different reasons, a smaller, pre-emptive attack was the last and the best of the alternatives that remained open to us. As a tactical preventive attack, it was well prepared. Night fighters were allocated to the fighter units for use as pilot aircraft to fly ahead of them, as far as the front line. We had grounds to hope for the type of success which had so far eluded us in aerial combats. The fighters were not deployed in the front-line area as ground-attack aircraft, but as fighters to take on their opposite numbers, as the American low-level attackers had done when attacking airfields. Preparations were completed. All that we needed was favourable weather, then the codeword could be given and the action begun.

On the night of 31 December 1944 I was summoned by the *Reichsmarschall* to Kronberg in the Taunus. I went there from Flammersfeld in a cross-country Volkswagen. It was bitterly cold, and our driver was equipped with a snow shovel. Peltz was already there when I arrived.

In the early hours of 1 January 1945 the surprising news reached us that 'Beppo' Schmid, the Officer Commanding the *Luftwaffe* Command, had issued the codeword and that the attack was nearing its end. There were no further details.

Peltz and I met the *Reichsmarschall* and wished him a successful New Year. He thanked us and expressed the hope that we would help him to achieve that success. He gave each of us a signed photograph of himself. Then he asked me to accompany him on a drive in his car. It was an open vehicle. The *Reichsmarschall* sat in the front on the right next to the driver wearing a thick fur coat and a fur hat. I sat behind him, and beside me sat Dr. von Ondarza, his personal physician. After a short drive, we got out of the car. While I trudged beside Goering, wearing my leather *Luftwaffe* coat and my short boots, my feet ice-cold, the others walked fifty paces behind.

He embarked upon a long speech, starting with the build-up of the *Luftwaffe*, growing enthusiastic concerning the victories of his fighters — he did not mention the bombers of that period. He expressed his criticism of the fighter leadership, mentioning Galland as being one of them, as, indeed, he had done on other occasions. He said that he had misjudged the bomber men, who had planned better and knew how to fly on instruments, and so he had given them the green light. There was much that was erroneous in what the *Reichsmarschall* said, but also much that was accurate. I listened in silence. People leaving church and making their way home streamed past us on the hard covering of snow. They did not recognise Goering, except for one man who was dressed in his Sunday best and was about fifty years old. Suddenly, his eyes opened wide. He let go of his bewildered wife's arm, did an eyes-right and goose-stepped away. The *Reichsmarschall* returned his salute with due pomp, lowering his Field Marshal's baton, without being in any way amused or taken aback. He seemed to me to be detached and lost in his thoughts. I had to try hard to suppress my laughter at both of them.

Goering continued, 'Peltz will take over the defence of the Reich. You will replace *General* Galland.' He explained how he envisaged future cooperation, while I tried to grasp and assess the significance of what he had said. So much had collapsed in ruins, that sadness possessed me when I thought of what could have been planned, discussed and agreed long ago. Then I had been thrown out ingloriously, without a word of explanation, to be recalled at this time of great need, as though I could pull the chestnuts out of the fire as I had done in 1943. That, of course, was what von Brauchitsch had rather pointedly meant when he had said that I was a man who could get things done, but who could be employed only within certain limits in a traditional command structure. So that, I thought, is the sort of man I am.

It was quite clear to me that given the conditions prevailing in 1945, nothing would come from using the 1943-style of leadership and methods. If they had considered me to be a wild man with brutal methods then, from now on they would curse me and keep out of my way.

The *Reichsmarschall* ordered me to consider my thoughts and proposals and to let him have them. When we returned to the *Schloss*, he instructed von Brauchitsch to inform the flying units and the responsible offices of my appointment. Peltz had gone already, intending to cross the Rhine, in the direction of the Eifel, in his amphibious car, when I set off from *Schloss* Kronberg for Flammersfeld. Having arrived there I gathered together a few personal possessions, climbed into my Ju 88 and flew to Berlin to take over the job of Inspector as ordered by the *Reichsmarschall*. I telephoned *General* Galland and asked him if I could pay him a visit. He said that he was unable to receive me because he had a feverish cold.

Brauchitsch advised me to wait. The next day I telephoned Galland again and asked him to send me a copy of the teleprinter message concerning my appointment. He had not received the telex. The situation was intolerable.

From a different source I heard that a number of fighter pilots had had interviews with Goering. They had said that they would refuse to serve under me as their Inspector, and under Peltz too if he had any significant function in the fighter leadership. Being fighter pilots, they could not accept the fact that two bomber pilots should command the fighter force, which included Me 262 jet-fighters for which everyone was awaiting eagerly. I heard the result of this dispute by hearsay and *Oberst* Gollob became the Inspector. I did not hear of this appointment from the *Reichsmarschall*. The way I was being treated was bizarre. I wondered what sort of a predicament Goering must have been in to have countermanded the appointment that he had personally announced to me.

Despite my personal frustration I tried to understand the fighter men. The front-line units had been the *Reichsmarschall*'s whipping boys. Now, when the Messerschmitt miracle-aeroplane was due to appear in large numbers, both the aircraft and a decisive opportunity were to be taken away from them and two bomber men were to have the say. I considered myself to be a passionate air-defence man and had thought, made demands and acted as such. The opposite could not be said of me. As long as service men are regarded to be members of separate arms of their service, pride and ambition within individual branches will overcome personal whims and ill-feelings.

The *Reichsmarschall* had not thought clearly of the possibility that his forces would not be ready to accept his 'new broom'. Once the die was cast, however, an end had to be called to the heated arguments as to who had the best ability to control the jet fighters in the air. I had taken issue very strongly with the fighter men because of their regrettable, inadequate navigation and blind-flying capabilities, having done so with the American threat in mind. But men such as Karlfried Nordmann, an excellent and highly-decorated fighter pilot, did not lag far behind me when it came to arguing their points.

Notes
1 Horace: 'Mors et fugacem persequitur nec parcit . . .'

Chapter Sixteen
The Jet Fighters
and the Last Throes,
January-April 1945

The attack on Dresden. Königsberg in East Prussia falls. Budapest falls. Retreat and flight. The British and the Americans cross the Rhine.

Gordon Gollob was now Inspector of Fighters, being a brilliant fighter pilot and an officer of impeccable character. I was nominated *Kommandeur* of *9. Fliegerdivision*: within it, the Division comprised old, proven Bomber *Geschwader* which were at airfields located near Prague, Linz, Wels, Landau, Fürstenfeld-bruck, Ingolstadt, Neuburg on the Danube, Kitzingen am Main and Giebelstadt and included, in Pilsen, my dear old *III./KG 30*, the *Adlergeschwader*. My Staff were stationed on the airfield at Neubiburg near Munich, and later in Wasserburg on the River Inn.

Shortly before I had taken over the *Division*, the bomber pilots of *Kampfgeschwader 54*, led by *Oberstleutnant Freiherr* von Riedesel, had already had some success with the Me 262 jet fighter. The *Geschwader* had a few of these aircraft, and in their first operation, against overwhelming odds, they had broken through the fighter cover and had shot down several bombers with their 3-centimetre canon, much to the surprise of the Americans. Reidesel had been killed in this engagement. Nevertheless the revolution in air warfare was making itself heard with rolls of thunder. The number of aircraft did not matter any more: what mattered was the genius of the inventors and the constructors. A thousand American fighters were no match for ten jet fighters which dived straight for the bombers, leaving the Mustangs, Thunderbolts and Lightnings behind them, as a car driver outstrips a swarm of flies. It only needed a simple mathematical projection: if all our *Geschwader* were equipped with the Me 262, it would mean the end of the American bomber attacks on Germany, its cities, its oil installations, its communications, and the factories that made its tanks.

My recollection of the feeling I had experienced in 1943 when I first ascended into the sky in the aircraft inspired me, and I felt certain that the *Reichsmarschall* would prefer to have me leading his aircrews in the new aircraft and planning their operations, rather than on the Inspection Staff. I had to get down to the job of using what few aircraft we had to familiarise the pilots with flying them and firing their guns, while we waited for more to be produced.

Peltz took over the command of *1. Jagdkorps* in Treuenbriezen. He appointed *Oberst* Krafft von Dellmensingen as his Chief of Staff. The *Oberst* was one of the few officers of the General Staff who had front-line experience: as a bomber-pilot, he had seen hard fighting in Spain. He was also a knowledgeable leader. His style was to lead his men into battle, where he organized them meticulously, as his brave father had done before him. For a time I was to work for the *Korps* in the south, bringing the large reserve of Me 262s to operational standard.

Goering had decided that it would be a good idea to give the top fighter aces specially equipped jet fighters, no doubt with the idea of stimulating genuine competition with *Kampfgeschwader (J)* of *9. Fliegerdivision* — the Bomber *Geschwader* being employed as fighters. When Johannes Steinhoff had begun the task of training the pilots on the Me 262 in Brandenburg Briest, to where he had transferred from Hungary, together with my beloved 'Friar-Gin', *General* Galland took over the command of all of the holders of Diamonds, Swords, Oak Leaves and Knights' Crosses, a *primus inter pares* of heroes. Towards the end of March 1945 they arrived at Munich-Riem, near to where I was stationed, from where, despite their low numbers, they achieved brilliant results: no less had been expected of them, and indeed they did not have to prove themselves. Nevertheless, efforts were insufficient from the very beginning, even against the raids in North Germany, to break the back of the enemy fleet of heavy bombers and to put the fear of death into their crews.

To try to achieve this objective by tenacious, patient and unobtrusive efforts, was now a task for *Kampfgeschwader (J)*, now endowed with the small suffix 'J' — J for Jaeger. It would require a strength of approximately one hundred aircraft, not to tie down the enemy fighters or to shoot them out of the air, but to attack them in formation, scattering the concentrated fire-power of the enemy bombers as they had done formerly as bombers against convoys.

One precondition only had to be met, one which had persuaded the *Reichsmarschall* to give the jet fighters to the bomber men: independence from the weather. That could guarantee that sufficiently large formations would be able to climb through the clouds in good order and navigate accurately to intercept the enemy. Peltz showed me the equipment with which he had achieved this brilliantly on the very first Me 262 operation flown by *Kampfgeschwader 54 (J)*. It was a UKW transmitter with a continuous directional beam, not fixed, as was used at airfields for blind landing, but rotatable, enabling it to be directed towards the enemy formation and then track it.

From what I could see the operational concept was a developmental extension of my earlier work with *1. Jagddivision* in Berlin, taking in the main features of its operational innovations and incorporating subsequent discoveries. There was a considerable difference of opinion among the older fighter men: did the jet fighter necessitate a fundamental change in tactics, or did the former concepts still apply? The bomber pilots who were flying the fighters, *Kampfflieger (J)*, were less concerned, however, because they neither wanted nor intended to get involved in fighter-to-fighter combat. Over the Rhine I myself avoided getting involved with the swarm of fighters. *Kampfflieger (J)*'s task was to get the bombers within their sights.

Those fighter pilots who had learned their trade on propeller-driven aircraft were undoubtedly better at close combat than the bomber men. Hardly anybody could stay in touch with them in a dogfight lasting more than ten or fifteen minutes, using acceleration forces up to six times that of gravity. I would not have trusted myself, having a cracked vertebra that had become more sensitive from two parachute jumps on to hard ground, to have stuck it out. I knew that I was fit enough and capable enough to carry out a remorseless attack on heavy bombers, if I didn't have to concern myself with enemy fighters. So it was with the majority of the *Kampfflieger (J)* men. They were tough, steady, quiet men, used to flying into lead and flying directly at the enemy, rather than coming at him from behind. They were more like lancers in line-abreast than foil-fencers, like our great fighter aces. So I considered Goering's decision to be correct, and I helped to put it into action. The *Reichsmarschall*'s decision was vindicated by my '*Wilde Sau*' pilots who, in December 1944 and January 1945, flew over Berlin at night and shot down Mosquito bombers. Now we were competing with each other like rival brothers, bomber men and fighter men, for the new weapon. The nature of the problem, and the capabilities of the individuals involved, would decide the outcome.

My work was once again one of detail, and I found enough to stumble over, grab hold of and move to one side. The Division's 1a, Staff *Major* Wedderer, stood by my side. Like myself he was a former member of the Thuringian *Geschwader 'General Wever'*. He was attentive, modest, industrious and critical. He occasionally enriched me with political comments, and recommended that I should read Oswald Spengler's *Years of Decision*. Having done so, I began to understand the broader political synoptic situation.

An experienced fighter pilot, *Oberst Freiherr* von Maltzahn, was attached to me, and he taught *Kampfflieger (J)*'s pilots what they lacked by reason of their bomber-pilot backgrounds. I trusted von Maltzahn completely, and he oversaw administrative and disciplinary matters.

The small rewards from the work, the information that had been drilled into us, the blindfold actions on which I had cut my teeth when a young bomber pilot, and which had caused the blisters on my hands, all bred character and security.

Kampfgeschwawder 6 (J), stationed near Prague and commanded by *Oberstleutnant* Hogeback, had only two Me 262s available for conversion-training. Eighty pilots trained on them successfully, without a single crash. That was important, given the small numbers that were coming from the factories. In this respect, *Kampfflieger (J)* would not have to disappoint the *Reichsmarschall*, either. That had been his main reason for giving the bomber men priority.

I had been placed in a position similar to that of 1943, when, following the success of the experiment over Moenchengladbach, I had begun to prepare for operations at *Geschwader* strength. Would the enemy ruin the concept again and draw us, head over heels, into air battles? It went without saying that the enemy would do everything possible to thwart our last, desperate efforts. The enemy had got to know our jet fighters, both by day and at night, and were wary and far-sighted enough to recognise that they were facing a deadly danger: the loss of their mastery of the air, resulting in steady increase in our defensive-weapon production. Where would the American armies be without the Allies' control of the air? The Reich would become one great Monte Cassino.

The Americans began to besiege our jet-fighter airfields with low-flying aircraft, because, other than when they were taking off and landing, they hadn't got a chance of catching the Me 262s. There were only a small number of airfields, with runways suitable for the Me 262, for them to keep an eye on until such time as further aircraft, then under construction, were completed. Increased flak defences could have helped to offset this danger, but attacks by American four-engined bombers presaged disaster. Whenever one badly camouflaged jet aircraft was sighted, a hundred Flying Fortresses appeared promptly and smashed it to smithereens with a carpet of bombs. Hundreds of American aircraft flew to the airfield at Prague-Gbell and showered 45,000 splinter bombs onto the few Me 262 that *KG 6(J)* had on strength. Each bomb weighed nine kilograms and was fitted with a high-sensitivity fuse giving a shrapnel-type effect.

Enemy formations wrecked runways with heavy bombs at Zerbst and Kitzingen, for example. I made an intermediate landing at Kitzingen, coming from a visit to Peltz at Treuenbrietzen, so that I could see the damage at first hand, and I had great difficulty in landing my little 'Bucker', swerving gently between craters. After I had talked with the *Kommodore, Major* Baetcher, an older member of *KG 30*, a certain *Feldwebel* Fellbaum, who had been flight mechanic to my fallen comrade Weinreich, came up to me. He asked if he could work with me, and without more ado he was posted to the Staff of 9. *Fliegerdivision*. He gathered his kit together and climbed into the aircraft with me. If only he had stayed where he was!

Having checked the air situation, I took off from a straight strip of grass, passing countless craters and soldiers shovelling feverishly. I had been warned of low-flying aircraft north and south of the Danube, so my crew and I had to keep our eyes open: our aircraft was not carrying radio. When we took off, the sky was clear of four-engined bombers.

I headed along a southerly route, well-known to me from my training days, to Neuburg on the Danube where Baetcher's other *Gruppe* was located. I wanted to pay them a visit, also. I circled above the airfield, and was surprised to find that there wasn't anybody in sight: neither the *Kommandeur*, nor the Adjutant — nor could we see a car anywhere. The place seemed to be dead. Apparently the Americans were flying in at short notice over Italy and the Alps, and the entire personnel of the *Gruppe* had taken cover swiftly.

I landed and taxied off the field as rapidly as I could. I rolled as far as the edge of the airfield, continuing along a concrete path, past several Me 262s which were housed in well-camouflaged splinter boxes, and past a hole in the ground in which two flak gunners were crouching behind an automatic cannon. Neither of the steel helmets turned towards our direction, and the barrel of the gun remained pointing at the sky. I arrived at the end of the concrete path, at the so-called dumb-bell, switched off and opened the cockpit. As I did so I heard the steely bass of the propellers of hundreds of Flying Fortresses or Liberators. I looked up. The first rigid formation, flying at 6000 metres at least, was coming towards us. Poor little flak gunners with your pathetic little weapons! I didn't hear any heavy flak.

The leading bombers had reached their release point. They dropped their bombs ahead of the second and third waves following them through the haze. Fellbaum had jumped out of our aircraft, but I was standing on the wing, I grabbed my briefcase, which contained important papers and the booklet *Years of Decision*. Let's get away from the aeroplanes, now! From my little one as well!

Thirty or forty metres away from us was a square heap of farmyard manure, less than a metre in height and beaten level. The farmer clearly had an eye for beauty. We reached it. There were rushing and screaming noises in the air. We pressed ourselves close to the ground at the sides of the heap, bored our noses into the manure, squashed ourselves close to it, but drew the line at burrowing in.

The earth shook, and we shook. The roar of the explosions filled our ears. The quaking of the earth lifted us up and smashed us down on it. I was deaf from the waves of thunder rolling over us and away.

It was over. There was a short pause. Then the roar of engines approached again. Visibility was less than ten metres. Everywhere there was gunpowder smoke, the smell of burning, and dust. I could hardly smell the manure any more. I looked at Fellbaum. He was lying at my feet, rubbing the muck from his eyes. 'No point in running away,' I said. He squinted up at me and nodded.

Then the next steam-roller of fire arrived: shaking, roaring, tossing. I held my leather case tight against the back of my head and neck to protect them from splinters. One wave followed another for a full half-hour. The filth got thicker and thicker, the smell of burning, with rubber mixed in it, even worse.

When the second wave had passed, I tried to find a better hiding place; but the smoke was hanging close to the ground. From the shallow depression I was in, I couldn't see far. The thunder started again. Nose down, into the manure! Fellbaum jumped up, kicked me, and disappeared into the fog and the dust. Fool!

The third wave had passed. I looked along the ground and saw a dark shadow. I jumped up towards it. 'Fellbaum, get up! Quick!' I tugged him. He didn't move. His eyes stared fixedly. The rumbling, roaring noise was coming again, from the south-east towards me in my north-westerly corner. I was thrown into the air, again. My God! Will it never end?

Suddenly my leg received a blow, as if from a club. Then I felt pain. I'd had enough. I wanted to get out of there before I was riddled with thousands of splinters from thousands of fragmentation and high-explosive bombs. What's happened to my leg? I'll get out, no matter how! Limping, crawling, or rolling. How about getting to one of the aircraft splinter-shelters? The enemy aircrews could see as little of what was going on on the ground as I could. I clenched my teeth, I hopped and hobbled north-west, carrying my briefcase. When the next carpet of bombs dropped, I fell, head over heels, into a ditch, which was partly filled with water, landing where the soldiers had mounted their gun.

Two, three more waves, and my tribulation was over. Filthy, miserable and stinking, I climbed out of the ditch and lay on the grass. A long, needle-like splinter had pinned my trouser-leg to my calf. Again, it was my right leg.

The dirt and the dust settled. The fires were smouldering. I limped across to Fellbaum. I couldn't see anything wrong with him. I turned him over gently, and I saw blood beneath him. A vicious, little splinter must have made its way into his lower abdomen. I looked around. Here and there, I could see hares twitching or dead. How could anyone have survived? How could any aeroplane have survived intact? My aircraft was burned, my leather coat and my cap were in it; Fellbaum's belongings too. All that remained was a heap of glowing wreckage.

The *Kommandeur* returned, as did his men from nearby villages, fields and woods. He came towards me. When I had been jabbed and bandaged, and my uniform trousers and jacket had been consigned to oblivion, I was draped in a brand-new *Oberleutnant*'s dress uniform. It hurt me a little when the sentry demoted me to that rank. I didn't look old enough to him. 'I'm the Divisional Commander here, man. Can't you see?' The *Kommandeur* and his officers stood in the background, grinning. The balance-sheet of the attack showed that only two Me 262s had gone up in flames. Some small bombs had fallen into the blast shelters. A further ten aircraft looked, at first glance, to be quite respectable, but on closer inspection proved to be riddled with fragments. They were written off.

The total loss was eighty percent of our aircraft; twenty percent approximately could be repaired with some effort.

The Me 262 was our last hope, and mastery of the air was the key to our success. It must have been obvious to anyone who had eyes to see and a brain to think, who walked about on two legs and called himself man, that we were lagging behind again, and that the old propeller aircraft could not provide the cover beneath which the jets could multiply, one by one, in their tens, in their hundreds: that all the exhilarating numerical tables were being incinerated in the enemy's enterprise of fire; that they were wasting away in the mad rush to make good the inadequate training, and shrivelling up in the lack of fuel. Whoever could see and comprehend all this and not hope, or try, for a last-minute reprieve from the death sentence, would do well to creep into the forest, or behind a stove.

I asked that the ineffective elements of the fighter force and their propeller aircraft be disbanded; and that 1500 of these aircraft should be manned by young pilots who, on a specific day, would ram the enemy bombers. This would strike such fear into the hearts of the Americans that they would not dare to venture out again for a number of weeks or months, as had happened following their Schweinfurt defeat. Then we would have some respite. Then we could gather our strength and move forward.

I had been obliged to surrender my Berlin units for use on the invasion front, while the new reserve was being built up gradually. I considered it to be a matter of self-deception to add up the bill without asking the landlord. The enemy could easily mount a surprise attack as they had done at Arnhem in September 1944. The *Wehrmacht*'s High Command had its own plans, as was shown by the Ardennes Offensive. Given the way things had gone from Summer 1944 onwards, I had lost my belief that we would win: I could hope only that we would come through without too much damage, and that bar-room strategy would put things right. Nevertheless, I did not intend to stand back and wait to see how the situation turned out: I wanted to use force to create the cover behind which we could produce our jet fighters.

In default of earlier planning, the question had arisen urgently in September 1944: how was the cover to be set up? Since then a proposal to use ramming aircraft to solve the problem had reposed in Goering's pending tray. It was a proposal that could have cost the lives of between one and two thousand young men, or their health. It would have been a bloody affair, but no more so than bleeding slowly to death in the hopelessness of half measures.

The draft of the proposal, which was supported by General Peltz, the Commanding Officer of *1. Jagdkorps*, ran as follows:

The time until Me 262 operations can be expanded must be bridged: the time is also approaching by which the conventional fighter force, which, as is known, has only a slight prospect of success, will be completely exhausted and grounded. We need to achieve success of such numerical significance that the enemy will change both the frequency of his attacks and his methods. We need the consequences that only success can bring. The enemy's reserves of personnel and equipment are known. The enemy has fought for months and has sustained few casualties. Therefore, the enemy is reluctant to take risks, and would be hard hit by a heavy loss of blood. Our Luftwaffe men possess

high operational motivation. No change may be expected or hoped for in the
coming weeks using other means and methods.

One serious problem had to be solved: the production of aviation fuel was drying up as a result of the precise bombing raids by the Americans. At the beginning of 1944 fuel production totalled 170,000 tonnes. That total had declined to 26,000 tonnes by December 1944, and was zero by March 1945. For some time, our Me 262s had been towed by teams of oxen to their take-off positions, being switched on only when they got there. The small quantity of fuel that we had stored at the airfields and in our aircraft was our last: our last powder, our last shot. At whom were we to fire? How were we to fire?

The experienced pilots had to be held back in reserve. So young pilots were brought into the action. They were barely capable of getting an aircraft off the ground. They were to climb to high altitudes, carrying the minimum amount of armament, ammunition and armour-plating.

They were to fly high above the enemy fighters, then descend and fly towards the enemy bombers.

Ramming took place often, intentionally and unintentionally. Two '*Wilde Sau*' pilots rammed their aircraft into enemy bombers on one particular night, when their aircraft had been damaged badly by enemy action. One of the pilots bailed out, but the other pilot's engine broke away from his aircraft's fuselage, leaving him trapped in the cockpit. The aircraft fell to the ground like an Autumn leaf, and yet he survived, uninjured. Following discussions with the Research Unit in Rechlin, I evaluated the precedents. The most effective, and at the same time, the safest method was to ram from above and astern against the trailing edge of the enemy aircraft's wings, with airscrew rotating fully, acting as a circular saw. The impact would cause the wing to break off, and the enemy bomber to go down. This was subsequently proved to be the result.

The *Reichsmarschall* wanted to know if men would volunteer. I told him that I was quite sure that they would, if he, *Reichsmarschall* of the Greater German Reich, would sign the appeal that I had drafted and have it sent to all the relevant Staffs and units. Goering hesitated. I reminded him that he had appointed me to an important post and that he had expected great things of me. On that New Year's Day 1945 he had told me that I should do as I had done in 1943, after Hamburg. Today, I said, I had no other ideas — only this. 'Let me see it!' He read the appeal, which covered half a page, considered it for a short time, then dismissed me, adding that I would hear from him.

In my draft I had written the words 'The war is lost, if you do not . . .' By signing the draft, Goering would have acknowledged his responsibility for our catastrophic position. Faced with having to demand the ultimate, the most bitter sacrifice, from his young pilots, he must have been overpowered by feelings of guilt and remorse.

He signed.

A few days later I held his teleprinter message in my hand in the Operational Headquarters of my Division at Neubiberg near Munich. I compared it with my draft: verbatim, with one exception. The exception, or should I say, omission, was one short sentence, which read, 'I will speak to you personally before your arduous mission.' I had wanted that to be put in for his sake as well as for that of the pilots; but it seemed that that was too much for him, the second man in the

State, the *Reichsmarschall*, who had only been accustomed to appearing in a position of power and right. He had baulked at those words because he could not, with a clear conscience, bring himself to be the *demandeur*, the one who was asking for and, even worse, taking away their lives. Young German men, who were quick to show their enthusiasm, brought home to him how much one had to want to overcome the emergency. Goering, a soft man deep inside, artistic and romantic, would not have been able to play the part of a *Reichsmarschall*, baton in hand, in front of the young men.

I had set my requirement as between one and two thousand aircraft: which begged the questions, could, and to what extent would, they be manned? In my draft, I had intentionally set the risk higher than my researches had suggested it would be. I did not want to minimise the danger, under any circumstances. The self-examination involved would have to be as uncompromising as was possible.

I had chosen the airbase at Stendal to be the Reporting Centre. The leader of the '*Lehrgang Elbe*' ('Elbe Training Course'), which was the codename of the operation, was *Major* Koehnke, an experienced officer who had been severely wounded in action and who had always supported me ably when I was on the Staff in Berlin. The result of the appeal was rapidly apparent. On average, ninety percent of those who were asked to do so volunteered for this deadly operation. Each of them was given time to decide, and they were not pressed to do so. Having volunteered, a man could withdraw. I granted such a request in the only case that came before me. It was usual for the local Commander to decide such cases.

The *Reichsmarschall*'s telex had been sent to an active night-fighter *Gruppe* in error. From the *Kommandeur* to the most lowly pilot, they all volunteered. I had to refuse their requests, and I had also to stop the wider dissemination of the appeal because more than two thousand men had already volunteered. I had never doubted that there would be a good response, but this genuinely astounded me. It showed what the German soldier was capable of, and highlighted his determination when danger showed him the truth, and the way to the target was pointed out to him. One had to think of only a few examples: the Narvik expedition in 1940, the airborne landing on Crete, and the stubborn heroism of our Eastern-front warriors in the snow and the mud of Russia. The hopelessness of the war of attrition in the air had forced this determined, bitter reaction in an effort to find a solution.

Next it was a matter of aircraft. The Command Staff of the *Luftwaffe*, for whom the *Reichmarschall*'s appeal was an order, had to pull out all the stops. For a long hour I sat down in Wildpark-Werder, not far from my old accommodation, together with the Chief of the General Staff, *General* Koller, and Walter Panitzki, his capable and serious aide, and we began to calculate and to juggle with figures. Koller feared that if he went to the *Fuehrer* Hitler would ask him how many aircraft were available for army support. I told Koller that the Army in the east would be best served if the Americans were unable to disrupt the production of tanks and bazookas and sabotage the communications lines to the Front. I added that if I were given too few aircraft for the ramming operation the operation would be pointless. The Chief of the General Staff temporized: he said that I should start off with a smaller number of men. When he saw that the scheme was working, then more aircraft could be made available.

I repeated — at least a thousand: that was the *Reichsmarschall*'s wish. *General*

Koller said the *Fuehrer* was a better judge. The *Fuehrer* was privy to the production figures for guns, ammunition and aircraft, down to the smallest detail, down to the last item: he was purely and simply a genius. I would have to make do with 350 aeroplanes in the first place.

The *General* had known me to be a stubborn man since the time I had disobeyed orders and flown over the Irish Sea to Liverpool. His blast from the Palais de Luxembourg had not frightened me then. A more recent bawling-out had been more difficult to stomach. Two weeks previously the *General* had shocked me out of a deep sleep in the middle of the night. *Major* Koehnke had called his Command Staff colleagues useless bastards, and he had told them that they should have been at the Front and read my earlier proposals more carefully, because they spelt out how the job was to be done. I apologised in every way I could for this incredible, unmilitary outburst. I said that one person could not be held to answer for everything. Koehnke had come from the Engineers, I supposed, and it was internationally known that they were congenitally impolite, and, in addition, he came from Friesland. The result was that the *General* and I lit a reconciliatory cigar and smoked them peaceably. Just wait, I said to myself.

The young pilots began to arrive at Stendal. *Major* Koehnke trained them, organised ancillary helpers, then distributed the pilots to other airfields in Saxony and Czechoslovakia, while I busied myself with obtaining the aircraft. At the same time I was trying to organize an operation against US bomber fleets on their airfields in Italy, which had been planned for some time. The pre-emptive strike that I had proposed to counter the invasion on the Channel front was planned to take place, in a modified form, from the Graz/Klagenfurt area or from the Po Plain, if possible using small aircraft. The two-men crews, flying in over the Adriatic, would land on the bomber airfields at twilight, approach the bombers carrying machine-pistols, attach 1-kilogram charges to the aircraft's wings, and then beat a retreat. The charges would detonate after ten seconds.

I had conducted an experiment for my Staff at Neubiberg using an He 111 that had been written off. The explosive charge, attached in the undercarriage cavity, had completely destroyed the aeroplane. The crews were under instructions to fight their way into the open and to surrender as soon as they could after they had dealt with the enemy aircraft. The raid was also intended to take the pressure off us, particularly off the Me 262 airfields I was using in Southern Germany and Austria, which were mainly bombed from Italy.

There were more than enough volunteers for the operation. They came from the surplus applicants for '*Kommando Elbe*', and from the assembly stations from where aircrew under training were being posted to ground units. They preferred to come to my '*Kommando Bienenstock*' ('Beehive Commando'), which I had also placed under the command of Major Koehnke. It was quite natural that men could be recruited comparatively easily for this operation. In training circles the conviction was gradually taking root that long-term training plans would be overtaken by developments if something didn't happen soon. A handsome little armada came together, many a pilot arriving with an aeroplane that had come from God knows where. We were approaching the type of military practice of earlier days, when warriors brought their horses and their weapons with them.

At this time my old comrade from the War Academy, Rudi Kiel, *Kommodore* of *KG 27*, made me very angry by firing several well-aimed shots at a picture of Hitler that hung in the Officers' Mess at Linz. The Mess Sergeant had filed a report, and the written charge, together with the evidence, was lying on a round table at which von Maltzahn, the Court-Martial Judge Advocate, and I were sitting in a state of considerable concern. The Judge Advocate said that he would have to proceed with the trial. I didn't have any time to spare, and von Maltzahn was on the point of leaving for one of our airfields. The matter was postponed a number of times.

Eventually the trial took place. I went directly to the *Kommodore*. 'Did you take leave of your senses, or were you drunk?'

'Neither.'

'Say you were drunk, or you'll be properly in the shit.'

'That wouldn't wash. All the shots were right on target.'

'You've got to do something. Neither von Maltzahn nor I can help you.' Kiel shrugged his shoulders. 'Tell me what this whole nonsense means.'

'I don't want to cause you any embarrassment.' 'I see. You wear a gong round your neck; but when things are going badly, you don't want to know.[1] If things were going well, you'd be one hundred percent onside. That makes me sick. You'll have to carry the can.' I got into my *Storch* and flew off, but with the firm intention of pursuing further delaying tactics, even if it meant the Judge Advocate kicking up a stink against von Maltzahn and myself.

While the 'Bees' were gathering together in the Alps, Koehnke completed the training of the rammers in North Germany. I flew there to control the operation from the *Korp*'s Operations Room. Two hundred aircraft stood ready, but hundreds of pilots would have to remain idle. *General* Koller had promised me that I would have strong reinforcements for the second, decisive, operation, but everything depended on the first, small, vanguard. How would the men fight, would their bravery compensate for their small numbers? As I watched the general situation map and saw the bombers coming closer, I had to force myself to stay calm and to think of the operation cold-bloodedly.

The fuel necessary for flying was running out visibly. What do you do when you've filled your aircraft for the last time? Do you leave it standing and run away when the enemy is flying in? Or do you strap yourself in and say, 'All, or nothing!' The enemy is advancing, taking your country and your freedom. Do you not fire a loaded weapon? Everywhere, German soldiers are defending German soil, their people and their Fatherland, with a valour born of desperation. Will you, flying soldier, hang back? Nobody gives in when things are going badly, neither the champion of the right of virtue nor the arch-villain.[2]

I prayed that there would be a sign to convince the General Staff, to teach them constancy of purpose; that the thousandth example of history would occur, the example of the redeeming power of human courage. Might there not be for us, too, a Clausewitzian saviour, '*General* Fortune', in the hour, the last second, of our tribulation? I gave the order to take off. Into their microphones the female radio-operators recited the direction from which the enemy formations were approaching. They added, 'Think of Dresden!' The battle raged over the Teutoburger Wald and Lower Saxony. Then all was silent.

Next day the Army Bulletin reported that sixty four-engined bombers had been brought down by ramming. I spoke with at least a dozen successful rammers, who had escaped by parachute. Most of them had been injured.

I telephoned the Chief of the General Staff and requested — insisted — that the larger number should be deployed in the last, desperate blow. I was told I must wait . . . I stood in the centre of a state of equivocation, unworthy of the courage that thousands had brought to bear.

The young men had scarcely any idea of what they had achieved. On the long, German road out of the darkness of history they had erected a monument and a signpost to the future that would mark a nation, men of flesh and blood, which superior might could batter down but could not bow. Mine was a secondary role. Some called me stupid, or mad; some said that I was unprincipled and ambitious. Others said that I had acted with propriety. I let them get on with it.

Koehnke ordered all those rammer pilots who had not been detailed for action, and all those who had bailed out after ramming, to head south, where *Luftflotte 4*, commanded by Dessloch, was under instructions to set up his *Festung Alpen* ('Alpine Fortress'). '*Kommando Bienenstock*' was also subordinated to Dessloch.

Meanwhile our old fighter aces were fighting their last battle from Munich-Riem. After one whirl of aerial battle, Johannes Steinhoff landed at my base, Neubiberg, in his Me 262. When the sky was clear again he went to take off from the small grass field. I waved him along until he was ready to take off, his aircraft's tail against the fence. I pressed both my thumbs for him. He turned to me one last time. I never saw that face again. The take-off was successful. A few days later I visited Steinhoff in hospital. His youthful freshness was burnt away. He was breathing with difficulty, behind a white shroud of bandages. I couldn't utter a word.

In the Munich area we gradually ran out of fuel. In this connection, I visited *General* 'Beppo' Schmid, who was based with his Staff in a forest in Lower Bavaria. He sat down with his officers at a table in front of his tent. I sat down with them. Our business was quickly finished. I could not avoid staying for a drink with 'Beppo' Schmid afterwards. He said that the times were difficult, and we must stick together. '*Prost, Hajo!*' he said, suddenly. I replied, 'I do not wish to be on first-name terms with the *Herr General*.' He gave me another glass, and made his overture of friendship again. I emptied my glass and took my leave. My memory was too good. Sometimes it was very impractical.

While the Americans were approaching Munich, I went with my Staff from Neubiberg to Wasserburg, on the River Inn, to take up quarters in the psychiatric hospital, which we christened 'The Lunatic Asylum'. The 1a, *Major* Wedderer, was put into the best padded cell, and the others, according to their more lowly status and spheres of responsibility, into the narrower ones. As a precautionary measure the doors remained open. If one of them slammed shut by accident, the occupant could bang long and loud before the way to the outside world opened up again.

How would it be if all our doors were to shut and after a period of hectic frenzy we were to sink into a long sleep, and then one day some kind person should open the door, chocolate in one hand and a palm-leaf in the other, while birdsong gladdened us and the sound of church bells told us we were at peace?

That dream was too good to be true. Reality stood in its way. Reality was me, the Director of the Lunatic Asylum, walking free through the corridors and seeing that the doors to the cells stayed open so that we could move in and out. So that the war could continue.

Notes

1 The 'gong' Herrmann referred to was the Knight's Cross (Ritterkreuz), known colloquially as the 'Doedel'.
2 'Champion of the right of virtue'? Lohengrin, Richard Wagner, Erzaehlung vom heiligem Gral (The Story of the Holy Grail).

Chapter Seventeen
Alpine Fortress

Roosevelt dies. Hitler shoots himself. Mussolini is shot by his own countrymen. Unconditional surrender.

From about the 24th or 25th of April I had the impression that as far as the *Luftwaffe* was concerned only my 'Beehive' units were swarming. In the meanwhile, the *Reichsmarschall* had moved to Berchtesgaden. I flew to Salzburg in my *Storch* to speak with him. I wanted to obtain some information on '*Festung Alpen*' and to find out if I should carry out the final blow against the bombers with our last forces. The thought of the meeting was rather painful, given that during our New Year's walk together the *Reichsmarschall* had associated the importance of my job with 20th April, a significant date, both in historical terms and promotion terms.[1]

I landed in Salzburg accompanied by one of the '*Kommando Elbe*' pilots who had used his circular saw, with a power of 1000 horses, to bring down a bomber and had come away with no more than a cut on his forehead. I made him my permanent messenger-pilot. When we landed at Salzburg a friendly SS officer came up and asked us what our business was. His friendliness did not prevent him from drawing his pistol and stopping us getting into a car. Madness seemed to have broken out again. I was not allowed either to fly or drive, even though I explained to the gentleman that I was on service business. The piece of theatre from the lunatic asylum would have reached its climax had I not also drawn my pistol. I always carried it loaded and with the safety catch on. I asked for an explanation. I was told that Hitler had expelled Goering from the Party and relieved him of all his posts. In reply to this devastating news I assured the SS-officer that I would withdraw my application to see the *Reichsmarschall* and that I would discuss my business with the Chief of the General Staff, Koller.

I sat, a young front-line officer, prematurely grey-haired, opposite the old Chief of the General Staff, who was burdened with worry. I believe that it was in the same place and at the same table where two years ago I had answered *Generaloberst* Jeschonnek's questions and explained my ideas to him. How many hopes and opportunities had vanished since then? Koller, who had escaped the encirclement of Berlin by the skin of his teeth from Wildpark-Werder, outlined the situation at Headquarters to me in a deep voice, clearly and accurately. He said that the *Fuehrer* wished to remain there and die in battle. If that should not be granted to him he would shoot himself. Hitler had expressed the wish that *Generalfeldmarschall* Keitel and other personnel should leave, but they had refused to do so. He had said that Goering was to conduct affairs from '*Festung*

Alpen' in the south. Koller did not know why Goering had been dismissed since then.

The first man in the State against the second. The world was bursting asunder. If that was history and the Last Judgement, then damn everything to Hell! I felt alone and crushed, God-forsaken and hopeless. Yet, as I sat opposite Koller, spooning up noodle soup, we gathered a final strength and warmth from the feeling of a shared doom, to which we did not propose to yield but, albeit in desperation, against which we would fight, we two, a Bavarian and a man from Holstein.

The telephone rang shrilly. Berlin. The *Fuehrerbunker*. The Chief of the General Staff was summoned to Berlin. His secretary panicked. The soup remained unfinished. Koller sent for his car to take him to some airfield or other. I asked what was going on. Koller didn't answer. All that he said was, 'Thank you for everything,' then he left. I watched him drive away with his secretary to his flight into hopelessness.

Together with my rammer pilot, I drove to the *Reichsmarschall*'s residence at Berchtesgaden. When I arrived *Generaloberst* Loerzer came towards me. He was wearing civilian clothing. I concealed my surprise. I learned that the SS had surrounded Goering's house on the Obersalzburg: Goering had not only been dismissed, but had also been arrested and sentenced to death. There had been shooting, it was said. Edda, Emmy . . . it was terrible! One more piece of news like that and I, as a frightened child caught between grown-ups fighting with each other, would begin to howl.

The *Generaloberst* spoke of '*Festung Alpen*', of the Allied armies that would meet in North Germany and would soon be fighting each other. We should hold a bastion, here in the mountains. It was time for political action. He did not have any great hopes for my strike against the aerodromes. I thought: 'You've thought of everything.' I felt terrible. Why not take my uniform off and hide myself in the woods? No! Return to the lunatic asylum! The Staff would continue its work. The struggle would continue.

The Americans continued to advance. We left Wasserburg and moved further east — a flight from one misery to another. My strike against Foggia seemed to hold the promise of liberation, relief and final peace. If only I could be at the controls of an aircraft flying low over the Adriatic, wearing mountain boots and an Army greatcoat, with the necessary equipment in a rucksack. I would leap out of the aircraft with the explosive charge, and then — nothing. The rest of the world, and everyone in it, could go to hell. Telephone; issue your orders; redeploy; fight; retreat as long as you want. I would be out of it all — happy.

Luftflotte 4, which had moved by this time to one of the lakes in the Salzkammergut, in a flower-covered, green landscape beneath the snow-covered mountains, gave orders that the attack on the four-engined bombers' bases in Italy was to be cancelled and that we were to use our explosive charges to destroy Soviet supply lines. I said, '*Jawohl, Herr General*!'

While our busy 'Bees' were humming around the northern slopes of the Alps, I made a stop-over landing on the small airfield at Prien, on the Chiemsee. I found the Braun family to be in very low spirits. The *pater familias*, a *Luftwaffe* officer, had put his pistol to his head and shot himself. He had not been able to bear the thought of defeat. After a meagre supper I listened to the news with *Frau* Braun and her daughter, who was a competent gliding instructor. Over the radio *Admiral* Doenitz announced: 'The *Fuehrer* has fallen in Berlin'. The women wept; I did not weep. This conclusion seemed to me to be inevitable, necessary. I was in a strange state of mind, somewhere between dull and exhausted. In my mind I saw dresses shimmering through soft May green. What would the Reich be without him? . . . It was the Reich! We were here. So, carry on!

The sun was low when I prepared to take off for Salzburg. *Frau* Braun asked me to look into the cellar. She said that a few days previously *Generaloberst* Loerzer, a friend of the family, had had a large sealed packing-case placed there. She feared that there were weapons in it and that she would be in great danger if the Americans searched the house. I followed her down into the cellar and attempted to lift the packing-case so that I could try to guess what it might contain. My strained vertebrae prevented me from lifting, so I broke open the lid.

I was speechless, as was *Frau* Braun. Tins, tins, and more tins. Sardines, corned beef, stew! That was Bruno Loerzer's '*Festung Alpen*', which he had come in civilian clothes to defend. I said that it was good of Bruno Loerzer to provide so generously for his friends in their hour of need. *Frau* Braun looked at me incredulously. 'Go on! Help yourself!' I encouraged her. 'I'm serious. But leave him a tin in case he comes to visit you!'

I flew away into the dusk, beneath a broken heaven, above the ruins of one-time faith. As I flew along the dark pine-slopes to my right, Nature seemed to me to be scarred and colourless. The beauty of the landscape was suffering from the wretchedness of the people who lived there. Beauty, austerity, fruitfulness and the stretch of the countryside had always all cried out to me to be worthy of them.

As I neared Salzburg the clouds opened up. Above the darkness below me the Watzmann towered, as if conjured up in the Alpine glow by the hand of Goya. The world hadn't changed, I thought. We can cope with all the rottenness as long as men work and fight truly or, like our rammers, offer up their lives against Fate.

I was happy to be back with them. The air smelled fresh. Koehnke had moved, together with the majority of the 'Bees', to fields in Kaerten and the Steiermark, and had already reported the first raids to the *Luftflotte*. In early May I landed on an improvised airfield near Klagenfurt.

This is what my 'Bees', my knights errant, had done under orders: far behind the Russian line of advance they had landed secretly near the main railway lines. Armed with canisters they had crawled like Red Indians to lay their charges on the rails. They had not primed them until it was too late for the locomotives to brake. Then they took off before the Russians could recover from the railway disaster. Others had crept by night into a railway marshalling yard and had fixed an explosive charge beneath each wagon of singing, humming or chatting soldiers. They had heard the dissonant transformation to lamentation, cries of woe, and wild firing. The notorious cruelties practised by the Russians meant that our fliers felt no remorse.

One evening a man appeared at the farm which, equipped with a radio transmitter, I was using as my headquarters. He was a Party member, and he said that he had come to collect the farmer's Party dues for 1945. The farmer asked if it was necessary to pay. 'Of course! That's the rules!' Ineffable simplicity! Other Party members, petty local officials and the *Buergermeister* all came to me for *Luftwaffe* uniforms. I issued the uniforms. OK, I said — but then make for the mountains or the woods. I refused to issue military paybooks in false names.

I also received a visit from the Foreign Office. Two most respectable civilian gentlemen from Berlin, dressed in Central European fashion, asked to speak with me, suggesting that our discussion should take place in a *Schloss* nearby that had originally been earmarked for the *Duce* following Italy's secession from the Alliance. Of course Mussolini did not live there, the gentlemen told me, but the Grand Mufti of Jerusalem did: he had made himself popular in Berlin with his anti-British attitudes and would not wish to fall into the hands of the Allies. That evening, seated at the fireside sipping non-alcoholic drinks, the Grand Mufti expressed to me his desire to be flown to the Middle East, where he would be out of reach of the British. The gentlemen from the Foreign Office supported his request and asked me to take the necessary action. The Reich, they said, was very much in the Mufti's debt.

I organised a light, twin-engined aircraft, a Siebel Si 204 D, and detailed an officer who had the Ritterkruez and was something of a linguist to fly it. The following day the highly decorated officer took off for Switzerland together with two Arabian escorts. We received a report by radio that he had landed 'as ordered' — which meant that he had landed in open countryside. When the radio message finished I looked at my farewell gift from the Mufti, a tastefully designed, gold-chased pistol with an Arabic engraving which, so I was assured, read, 'In eternal friendship to the German people'.

Berlin had fallen. The Americans were approaching from the south; Tito's men from the south-east; and the Russians from the east, in the direction of Graz. The 'Bees' continued to fly as busily as ever.

Was that a *Wiedersehen* after three years! I saw Theo Blaich wearing a camouflage suit and carrying a machine-pistol, sitting in an open Volkswagen cross-country car at the head of a caravan of alarmingly rickety vehicles decoratively camouflaged with green paint. 'Theo Africanus! What are you doing here?'

'A bit of Andreas Hofer,[2] so to speak!'

'Against whom?'

'Against everybody for the moment!'

Theo had been decidedly pro-West. In Africa his experiences of the British administration had not been unpleasant, and those of the people had been of the best. Now, he was older and more worldly-wise than I was. He knew more about Communism and Capitalism, and he boiled over with rage when he came to speak of the British Prime Minister and the American President — madmen, bunglers, idiots, who didn't know what they were doing. Go over to them? Perhaps: that would depend on their readiness to see sense and to repent. I was unable to join their caravan; but I made a note of where they were aiming for. Perhaps I would follow them when the war ended.

I telephoned the *Luftflotte*, which had become the *Luftwaffe* Eastern Command, before the lines were cut, and asked what the situation was concerning the partial armistice with the Americans. Would they allow us to fly against the Russians, or would they prevent us from doing so? Would they fight us? *General* Dessloch said that he would try to clarify matters. When I said that we could be overrun within a matter of hours, he repeated his statement.

My fervent hope, that of all of us, which had been encouraged by the old Reich government and was being encouraged by the present one, was that if we did not continue to fight against the Western Allies, they would support us against the Russians. Wasn't it possible that Roosevelt's death three weeks earlier might have led to an American change of heart? I told the *General* that I couldn't make any sense of what was happening. I would send my Staff and my pilots, fully supplied, into the mountains and, as far as the aircraft allowed it, onward to the homeland. He said that I was not to do so, but that we should continue to operate against the Russians as long as it was possible. End of conversation.

If one listened to the enemy broadcasts, one had to accept that all hopes would founder on the united front of West and East. The fascist beast — which meant us — must be beaten to death in his lair and eradicated from the world, so that human beings could live in peace and quiet, free from hunger and threat, finally and for all time. If they meant what they said, and were not saying it for effect only — then to hell with them!

Apparently the *Luftwaffe* High Command was in contact with Doenitz. I telephoned Staff *Oberst* Kern, my experienced '*Wilde Sau*' man, at the *Luftflotte*, and ascertained the latest situation as far as he knew it, and I received target instructions. 'OK!' I said. 'But what if the Americans are on the airfields with their tanks?'

'Then surrender! Join them against the Russians!'

'Are you mad? Do you really think they'll fight the Russians? And if they do, are we to fight with them? Are we to be their lackeys? They beat us into the ground and we have to trot along with them against the Russians?' Kern said that he could not disobey the *Luftwaffe* High Command and the Government, like it or not.

I could not contain my fury and my desperation. I told him that anybody who wanted to hire me out to the Morgenthau people could take a running jump. I'd sooner clear off, take to the hills with my rucksack, which I had packed already, and the mountain boots for which I had swapped my half-boots. Then I could look down and see how the precious Allies made out with each other, or, better still, how they didn't make out with each other. Kern said that he would not remove his red-striped General Staff trousers and put on mountain boots. Kern stayed where he was. So did I, because I was a serving officer.

Wishful thinking took root in my Staff and among the pilots. I became very angry: why should we help the Americans? It was my opinion that the Americans were well able to kick the Russians out by themselves, and very quickly at that. The Russians did not have anything to use against the bomber fleet. I hoped that the Americans would be stuck in the Russian mud for three years, as we had been. Our chance didn't lie in their being victorious: it lay in their getting bogged down in the East. Then we would be needed, and we could demand something appropriate in return. Of course, I would have preferred the Western Powers to push the Soviets out and occupy Germany; but they could, and should, do that by themselves. Surely that was what they wanted to do? But we didn't have to help them! That would be a load of crap. Whether one side or the other, in their own different ways, would exterminate more of us, we had no way of knowing. The bloodthirstiness of Dresden incensed me as much as the bestialities in East Prussia, Silesia, and elsewhere had.

Quite suddenly I had overstepped the borderline between the military and the political, a dangerous boundary but one which had shown up quite clearly and concretely: military action against the enemy in the East, accompanied by a dubious offer to the enemy in the West, which the latter had unmistakably rejected. And a provisional cease-fire to go with it? 'Let's march with the Americans!' I couldn't listen any more. I rebelled against the word 'with'. Anyone who kicks me into the cesspit and asks for my help next day, insults me. If I offer him my help, I dishonour myself. It was more degrading to have made an offer, as the new Government had done, and to have had it scornfully rejected. Our officers and leaders had been captured in masses, and *Feldmarschall* Keitel, the top man of the High Command, had had to give himself up. Someone said that we should put on Russian uniforms and fire at the Americans, or put American uniforms on and shoot at the Russians. Then the fat would be in the fire, and the Russians would flee. They had never experienced anything like the American Air Force.

On the 8th or 9th of May, the official news filtered through that the *Wehrmacht* had capitulated; I received confirmation from the Chief of the *Luftwaffen-kommando Ost, Oberst* von Maltzahn. As depressed as I was he said the only good thing was that the Party clique were finished and done with. He spoke of the acts of harassment which his family had experienced. I hadn't heard such reports from my family or from those of my wide circle of acquaintances. Admittedly occasionally I had heard joking, sometimes hurtful, comments. At that moment, I wasn't interested. The questions went round in our heads: to the Americans? To the British: to the Middle East? To Switzerland, Canada, South America? No-one thought of Russia, except me. Fight? For this side or that side? If not for ourselves, then for no-one! Look, listen, advise, misadvise — do only that which could create a chance for us to get out of the chaos that prevailed. To the Russians? 'That's stupid', I heard somebody say. 'They'll put you up against a wall because of your sabotage troops.'

'I don't know,' I said. 'Perhaps they'll think I can help them. They're hopelessly outclassed, and they'll end up on the other side of the Urals if the Americans attack them.'

'Rubbish! They know who you are. They've even eliminated their own officers.'

Alright! I'll hang about, until our dear enemies make their minds up. Then they'll squeeze our advice and our knowledge out of us, cost-free. I was convinced, as seemed to be guaranteed by the declared intentions of the Western Allies and possibly strengthened by German propaganda, that we did not have a future at all; that we would become Russians, Poles, Czechs, Slovaks, Slovenes, French; that we would be decimated; that the remaining tenth, living off the potato fields, would be Americanised; that we would not be one iota better off if the Americans, after overthrowing the Russians, had a free hand.

I had finished Spengler's book *The Years of Decision* and returned it to *Major* Wedderer. The question was: America, or Russia? Were we no longer anything? Ants under a foreign jack-boot? My faithful reservist Fiedler, an Upper Silesian and a gardener by trade, his face lined with deep wrinkles, packed his rucksack, putting in it the diamonds I had received from Goering, together with my most important decorations and a message to my parents to the effect what I was hiding out in the Alps. 'It's all been a waste of time,' Fiedler said to me, in a choked voice. He seemed to sympathise with me. He said that he would be OK. It upset me that I was upsetting him. I was a miserable creature.

I allowed the men to share out everything that would fetch a price — clothing, footwear, typewriters, motor-bikes, cars — and I gave those who wanted them aircraft to fly home or anywhere abroad, whichever they chose. Somehow or other, the items could be turned into money.

American tanks rolled along the main road leading north. In the villages, the villagers were hiding literature and emblems from the Third Reich. I couldn't stand by and watch one woman throwing books onto a heap of manure. There were three or four of them, beautifully bound. I looked at them. One of them was Hitler's *Mein Kampf*, and on the front inside cover it was noted, in beautiful handwriting, that the book was to be a companion for a bridal pair, from their wedding day onward. The book seemed new, and it had hardly been read. I asked if I could have it. I hoped that one day I would find time to read it.

My Staff had gathered together. I looked at their familiar faces. There were women among them, and my messenger, the rammer-pilot. He looked at me, friendly, expectant and trusting — me, one of his leaders on the road to ruin. So much bravery had been called for, so much blood and suffering demanded, that those making the demands would have to expiate the crime of failure in hell. I started to speak of the great battles we had fought together, and to tell them that the time had come for us to go our separate ways. In mid-sentence, I faltered. I turned away to hide my tears, ran deep into the woods and threw myself down on the ground.

It seemed to me that this day was not the work of Man, but blind Chance, Fate, Injustice, crying out to be heard. Or was it — a small, painful sensation of self-satisfaction touched me — punishment for our weaknesses and lack of insight; punishment because we hadn't been able to hit the British with a blow the same as they had used against Hamburg and Dresden; because we had been too clumsy and too stupid to generate strife and treason, espionage and assassination. Help me, O Heaven, to understand that which I abhor!

We had fought for victory in Poland, out of conviction and against injustice. Then we had fought against danger, out of necessity and under compulsion, and finally against defeat, against hate and the desire for our destruction. Such feelings were alien to me, and to my comrades. I could never believe that if we had won, we would have sent foreign statesmen to the gallows, as Lloyd George had demanded in the First World War — 'Hang the Kaiser!' It was impossible for me to imagine that we could have been so despicable as to rob another nation of its honour, as had happened to us at Versailles and as was threatening again. In my eyes, all Germans were good and respectable. The overwhelming power within the world that had joined up against us did not convince me that we were the evil ones. On the contrary, it showed me that we were strong, capable, hardworking and inventive; that we could match any one of our enemies and claim our share of the world's goods, that we could bring our achievements to bear in all areas of the community of nations. If others felt the same way, responding to some impenetrable law of Creation, then it was just and proper to fight and hold our ground and to accept God's judgement: the joy of victory on the one hand, or want and horror on the other. Want and horror were our lot. To curse what had happened, from the beginnings to the bitter end, was pointless: it would be no more than helpless mouthings against history, an unworthy rejection of our one-time enthusiasm, our belief in our right, and it would be an insult to our fallen comrades. We were conquered, but we were not broken. Our will remained. I pondered what to do.

I was alone in the Alps for two days, sleeping in the open air on a bed of fir twigs. On 11 May 1945, *Hauptmann* Schmidt returned from Budapest, the seat of the Soviet Army High Command, where I had sent him to take soundings — tentative ones, as I had believed. If the discord between East and West were to break out soon, I had thought, then it would be advantageous for German people to be on both sides, so that they could see and do what seemed to be most favourable at any given time. But we would never give in!

'Where are the other two from the crew, Koenigs and Goetz?' I asked. The Russians were holding them. The Russians wanted me to go over to them within two days. 'What do they mean? Within two days? What if I don't go?'

'Then it'll go badly for the other two. They're behind bars. One day of the time is past already.' The chains of a foreign power were pulling me. It was a painful sensation, to see freedom but not to be free. Why hadn't I flown with *Hauptmann* Paulsen to Schleswig, dumped the aircraft on his field near the Schlei, and become a day-worker there.[3] Why hadn't I flown to the Orient with the Mufti, to the mountains of gold he had promised me? Why hadn't I clambered up the hill, to his hut, with Theo Blaich? I had flown into flak fire, into enemy bomber streams, into storm-clouds, and into nights of darkness; but I had done all of that of my own free will. Now I was being compelled to fly somewhere.

Schmidt and I flew to Budapest in my *Storch*. Somewhere on the way a Russian shot a hole in our wing. We landed at Budapest and a Russian officer took us to a solitary building outside the airfield. Through the open door, across the shoulder of the Russian, I caught sight of the white, hopeless, frightened faces of my comrades. Then they recognised me. I shall never forget the way in which their eyes lit up, their cries of joy, and I felt ashamed of myself for having hesitated between flying to them, whose duty had kept them in Budapest, or to some less troubled, quieter country. I was ashamed of my disloyal thoughts. They said that they knew I would come. I breathed more easily, knowing I would not have to live with my disgrace.

The joy of meeting soon paled. Things went from bad to worse, until, at last, steel prison gates clanged behind me. The handcuffs cut into my wrists, Tartars pressed me against the floor and squeezed my throat so that they could shave me bald. I had become a criminal for nothing.

Ahead of me were ten years, during which Heaven and Earth, dull and grey, cut through with bars and barbed wire, hurt my eyes. Unheeded had been my prayer to be a saviour of the nation for a second and last time, to be allowed to fly at the head of a thousand brave rammers, to show defiance against the overwhelming power of the purveyors of disaster. We had been too trusting and too dilatory, too powerless and too bereft of ideas, to avoid distress. Hunger and cold, slavery and derision were our reward.

Self-doubting, I scarcely cared what happened to me. I no longer knew what I was to do. That was my debt to those who had given their lives.

Notes

1 20 April was Hitler's birthday, and was the promotion date in the Armed Forces.
2 Watzmann: the highest peak in the Berchtesgaden Alps.
3 Schlei: a bay on the Schleswig-Holstein Baltic coast, northeast of Schleswig.

Index

Note: In general, ranks etc. attributed are those first given in the book. In the case of widely-known individuals — for example Goering and Harris — the ranks given are those by which they are now commonly known.